The Party of Reform
Democrats in the Progressive Era

Twentieth-Century America Series
Dewey W. Grantham, General Editor

The Party of Reform
Democrats in the Progressive Era

David Sarasohn

UNIVERSITY PRESS OF MISSISSIPPI
Jackson & London

In memory of my mother

Library of Congress Cataloging-in-Publication Data
Sarasohn, David.
  The party of reform: Democrats in the progressive era/David
Sarasohn.
  p. cm. — (Twentieth-century America series)
  Bibliography: p.
  Includes index.
  ISBN 0-87805-367-0 (alk. paper)
  1. Democratic Party (U.S.) — History. 2. Progressivism (United
States politics) 3. United States — Politics and
government — 1901–1909. 4. United States — Politics and
government — 1909–1913. 5. United States — Politics and
government — 1913–1921. I. Title. II. Series.
JK2316.S27 1988
324.2736'09'041—dc 19
                                                                88-31614
                                                                CIP

British Library Cataloguing-in-Publication data is available.

The paper in this book meets the guidelines for permanence
and durability of the Committee on Production Guidelines
for Book Longevity of the Council on Library Resources.

Contents

Acknowledgments

Understandably, an author of a book with this long a gestation period has a number of people to thank.

The list begins with Professor Frank Otto Gatell of UCLA, who helped me select the topic, and more importantly, taught me how to think and write about it. In a range of different ways, every page bears his imprint.

The late Professor Fawn M. Brodie of UCLA provided an important reminder to think about the people as well as the number.

Historians who provided advice and encouragement at various points included Lewis L. Gould, Howard Allen, and particularly John Milton Cooper, Jr.

Articles related to the research for this book appeared in the *Western Historical Quarterly*, *Social Science History*, and *Journalism Quarterly*. Papers related to it were delivered at the Social Science History Association convention in 1979 in Columbus, Ohio, and the Western Historical Association convention in San Antonio in 1981.

Financial support was generously provided by the UCLA History Department, the taxpayers of the state of California, and by Reed College.

Indispensable assistance was provided by the staffs of the UCLA Graduate Research Library, especially the ingenious and untiring inter-library loan staff; the Library of Congress; the National Archives; the libraries of Princeton University; Yale University; Columbia University, including the Oral History Research Office; Occidental University; Oregon State University; Portland State University; the New Jersey State Library; the New York Public Library; the New York Historical Society; the Historical Society of Pennsylvania; the Oregon Historical Society; AFL-CIO national headquarters; and the Huntington Library.

Throughout the process, essential support and derision came from Dr. Vernon A. Fagin.

And most important to its completion was Lisa T. Sarasohn, who was there at the beginning and at the end, and who now knows more about the Democratic party in the Progressive Era than any other European intellectual historian.

Introduction

In the last two decades, the study of progressive politics has gone through a kind of methodological bushwhacking: the closer scholars get to answers, the less interest there is in the questions. The entire idea of a progressive movement and a progressive era has taken a considerable battering during the period, with many scholars coming to doubt that there was such a thing and others arguing that, if there were, it was either a fraud or a failure. Any efforts to take progressive reforms seriously enough to track down their roots and their supporters have seemed to be as irrelevant as the progressives themselves.[1]

Beginning in the 1960s, attacks on progressive politics for what it did not do — fundamentally redistribute wealth and power — have come to overshadow interest in what it attempted to do — cope with vast waves of corporate growth, immigration, and industrialization while preserving the values of democracy and opportunity. The progressive politicians, it is agreed, should have been bolder, smarter, more innovative — more like *us*, although Americans' present political patterns are not likely to embarrass previous generations. Yet that reality, far from causing historians to be kinder to earlier reformers, has instead made us harder on them. Progressives have been made to bear not only their failures but also our own.

The idea and image of progressivism, as Daniel T. Rodgers points out, began to get into serious trouble during the 1970s, and its decline has continued. "By the 1980s," David P. Thelan observes about recent writing in the field, "when the objective possibility of restructuring power seemed more remote than at any time in a half-century, the more basic question appeared to be how the rulers preserved their power rather than how the ruled tried to create democratic futures."[2]

In a sense, it is certainly true, as one of the most influential recent works about progressivism charges, that "Most of the time . . . progres-

1. Daniel Levine, review of "The Reconstruction of American Political Ideology," by Frank Tariello Jr., in *American Historical Review* 88 (April 1983): 492.
2. Daniel T. Rodgers, "In Search of Progressivism," *Reviews in American History* 10 (December 1982): 113–32; David P. Thelen, "Where Did Progressivism Go? A Search Around the South," *Georgia Historical Quarterly* 68 (Spring 1984): 61.

sivism left later generations with examples of ineffective legislation and superficial analysis." A large element in this judgment, however, is closely tied to what Richard L. McCormick calls "a widespread sense, both within and without academe, that liberalism historically has been characterized by both insincerity and failure."[3]

An additional reason for progressivism's decline may be the massive burden it has been expected to carry. The specific conclusions of Richard Hofstadter's *The Age of Reform* may have suffered from the examination of subsequent historians, but its portrait of the Progressive Era as a clash of ideologies and identities has persisted, depicting a war of world views that inevitably dwarfs the achievement of a worker-safety law. By casting the progressive protagonists as native stock middle class—Americans more likely to suffer from an identity crisis than a twelve-hour work day—the book firmly couched the progressive struggle in psychological terms.[4]

Even as historians have introduced numerous other progressive actors and explanations, some fascination with the old-stock elements endured. In *Ministers of Reform*, Robert Crunden again views progressivism as the product of predominantly middle western Protestant activists and concludes that many of those who did not fall within these lines were not progressives at all, but "precursors of the social democracy of the New Deal." Not coincidentally, from this perspective, progressivism dissolves as a movement and melts into "a climate of activity within which writers, artists, politicians and thinkers functioned."[5]

Given that progressivism was a many-leveled nationwide response to the re-creation of American society, it is impossible to reject any definition of it as too broad. But within its full range of social, cultural, economic, and intellectual activity, there was a specifically political progressivism, which was largely what contemporaries meant when they used the phrase. Progressivism as a political movement was an effort to limit the power of wealth in America and to provide some protection to those who lacked it. The most effective reform politicians of the era never expected to replace the emerging corporate system with either a New Jerusalem or an older America, but simply to reduce the power wealth exercised over government and the benefits business received from the arrangement.

3. Robert M. Crunden, *Ministers of Reform* (New York: Basic Books, 1982), p. xi; Richard L. McCormick, "Progressivism: A Contemporary Reassessment," in *The Party Period and Public Policy* (New York: Oxford University Press, 1986), p. 264.
4. Richard Hofstadter, *The Age of Reform* (New York: Harper's, 1955).
5. Crunden, *Ministers of Reform*, pp. ix, 15, 275–78.

Even squeezing progressivism into these relatively narrow political terms, however, does not produce unanimity. Many who proclaimed their wish to limit the power of business were equally reluctant to encourage the rise of competing power centers, especially any composed of immigrants or workers. The native stock middle-class reformers who still capture the imagination of some students of the period often seemed to feel as threatened by the weakest elements in society as by the strongest. Twenty-five years ago, as the concept of a progressive movement was first beginning to dissolve under scrutiny, Robert Wiebe suggested, "The way to reopen the question of the progressives is to start with content rather than with people." It has taken a while for this prescription to be swallowed, but the approach has provided one reason why, as progressivism itself has been losing ground historiographically, there has been a shinier image for one group of political progressives: the early twentieth-century Democrats.[6]

Traditionally seen as a formless, atomized mass waiting off the coast of history for the Republicans to shatter in 1912, the Democrats have come to be regarded as a more effective, clearly motivated element in Progressive Era politics. Scholars have even begun to think that Woodrow Wilson's election as president had something to do with the reform identity of the Democrats as well as the identity crisis of the Republicans.

Reconsideration began with new studies of the political roles of southerners, urban machines, and William Jennings Bryan: Democrats whom historians had traditionally considered not leaders of reform but objects of it. Like Frankenstein's monster, the Progressive Era Democrats have been resurrected limb by limb. Beginning with Anne Firor Scott's redefinition of many southern Democratic congressmen as "unsuspected progressives" and culminating in Dewey Grantham's massive survey of southern progressivism, the South has risen again in its reputation as a breeding ground for reformists. At the same time legal and institutionalized racism was firmly entrenching itself in the South and the nation, southern Democrats in both Congress and state legislatures supported political, economic and regulatory reforms that fit the progressive model.[7]

Led by the reformers' dramatic worst example, Tammany Hall, the

---

6. Robert Wiebe, *Businessmen and Reform: A Study of the Progressive Movement* (Cambridge: Harvard University Press, 1962), p. 211.

7. Anne Firor Scott, "A Progressive Wind from the South," *Journal of Southern History* 29 (February 1963): 52–70; Dewey Grantham, *Southern Progressivism: The Reconciliation of Progress and Tradition* (Knoxville: University of Tennessee Press, 1983).

Democratic urban machines have shouldered themselves into reform respectability. The work of J. Joseph Huthmacher and the subsequent research of John D. Buenker depict machines that helped their voters not only with Christmas turkeys but also with advanced reform legislation. Nancy Weiss' biography of Charles Francis Murphy and the recent, more systematic study of New York Democrats by Robert F. Wesser reveal a Tammany Hall unrecognizable to the middle-class reformers of its time. This new view helps to explain why not only at the national level, but also in most of the industrial states, progressivism hit its legislative peaks when Democrats were in power.

Unless *Inherit the Wind* is on the Late Show, it is almost hard to recall the time when William Jennings Bryan was largely a one-dimensional figure of fun. Lawrence Levine's study of Bryan's later years, Louis Koenig's political biography of the Commoner, and Paolo Coletta's three-volume biography dramatically spurred a reconsideration of the man who largely created the modern Democratic Party.[9]

Bryan turns out to be the overlooked answer to many of the questions about the Democrats' progressive identity. The party could not be an effective reform force, it has been attested, because "the historic American commitment, on the one hand, to weak government, local autonomy, and the preservation of individual liberties — reflected in the doctrines of the Democratic Party — presented a strong barrier to any significant expansion of government." Yet this party, presumably paralyzed at the prospect of power, three times nominated someone who proposed to invoke the power of the federal government massively in support of his objectives. As their actions in power later demonstrated, Democrats revealed their true attitudes when they voted for Bryan, not when they quoted Thomas Jefferson.[10]

By the late 1970s, Lewis L. Gould's study of Progressive Era politics revealed a markedly different view of the Democratic role and identity than earlier works. In 1983, John Milton Cooper, Jr., perceived that

8. J. Joseph Huthmacher, "Charles Evans Hughes and Charles Francis Murphy: The Metamorphosis of Urban Progressivism," *New York History* 46 (January 1965): 25–40; Nancy Joan Weiss, *Charles Francis Murphy, 1858–1924* (Northampton: Smith College, 1968); John D. Buenker, *Urban Liberalism and Progressive Reform* (New York: Charles Scribner's Sons, 1973); Robert F. Wesser, *A Response to Progressivism* (New York: New York University Press, 1986).

9. Lawrence W. Levine, *Defender of the Faith, William Jennings Bryan: The Last Decade, 1915–1925* (New York: Columbia University Press, 1966); Louis Koenig, *Bryan* (New York: Putnam's, 1971); Paolo Coletta, *William Jennings Bryan* (Lincoln: University of Nebraska Press, 1964–1969, 3 vols.).

10. Richard L. McCormick, "The Discovery that Business Corrupts Politics: A Reappraisal of the Origins of Progressivism," *American Historical Review* 86 (April 1981): 258.

party identity was a major difference in the careers of Wilson and Theodore Roosevelt: "Roosevelt inherited from William McKinley a proto-capitalist Republican party, which he tried unsuccessfully to redirect toward a more nationalistic, less materialistic brand of conservatism. . . . Wilson inherited from William Jennings Bryan a reformist Democratic party, which he refined and solidified as a coalition of less advantaged groups seeking to advance their interests through the welfare state."[11]

Slowly, historians are moving from the traditional bipartisan view of reformism to a view that Wilson offered seventy-five years ago. "The chief difference between the Democratic and Republican parties," he explained, "is that in the Republican party the reactionaries are in the majority, whereas in the Democratic party they are in the minority."[12] Still, given the simultaneous shift in attitudes toward Progressive Era reform in general, the early twentieth-century Democrats may end up with nothing more than a historiographical booby prize: recognition as a much more important element in a much less important movement.

Under the leadership of Bryan and Wilson, they were more than that. If the Progressive Era Democrats had only limited ideas of redistribution, and if they failed to achieve a permanent public mastery over private wealth, they could still claim significant reform achievements. When Samuel Gompers led the American Federation of Labor into politics in 1906 to reward its friends and punish its enemies, most of the former turned out to be Democrats and most of the latter, Republicans. Protecting the right of labor to organize and strike and establishing an eight-hour work day for federal employees to serve as a model for private employers were high priorities in Democratic platforms and congressional strategies throughout the period. Democratic capture of state governments was an equally good omen for legislation on union wish lists, bills to improve working conditions and encourage organization. The Democrats' close alliance with organized labor not only produced substantial pro-labor legislation, but it also advanced a political empowerment of workers that most progressive Republicans found unnerving.

Popular government issues, the measures most widely identified as

11. Lewis L. Gould, *Regulation and Reform: American Politics 1900–1916* (New York: 1978); John Milton Cooper, Jr., *The Warrior and the Priest* (Cambridge: Belknap Press of Harvard University, 1983), p. xii.

12. Josephus Daniels, *The Wilson Era, Years of Peace, 1910–1917* (Chapel Hill: University of North Carolina Press, 1946), p. 11.

progressive, were also stressed by Democrats, whose strategy included a healthy dose of self-interest. Their eagerness for full disclosure of campaign contributions reflected the party's unvarying scarcity of funds. Urban Democrats living under malapportioned Republican legislatures understandably favored direct election of senators, but many other Democrats supported the reform for broader reasons. "Until we can get a United States Senate elected by the people," wrote Bryan early in 1908, "it is impossible to get anything in the way of national reform." By the time the Seventeenth Amendment went into effect in 1913, the Democratic states of the South all had binding Senate primaries.[13]

Historians have also slighted the significance to reform of the most traditional Democratic issue, the tariff. Not only Democrats derided a protective tariff as a corporate subsidy; the Populists also complained about it, and Republican insurgency was first revealed in a rebellion against excessive protectionism. Tariff revision, wrote Senator Robert M. La Follette of Wisconsin, the symbol of Republican rebellion, offered "one direct, simple way to reduce the high cost of living and curtail the power of monopoly."[14] The party had opposed high tariffs long before the coming of the trusts, but early on, Democrats from all wings of the party made La Follette's connection between the two. Grover Cleveland's tariff message of 1887 warned that protectionism contributed to the emergence of trusts, and Bryan's first speech in Congress was on the issue. Even the most conservative Democratic newspapers proclaimed the connection, as did independent muckrakers such as Ida Tarbell.[15]

Democrats during the Progressive Era had an additional complaint about the tariff. "Indirect taxation by means of a tariff is always an oppressive tax," wrote Democratic tariff authority Franklin Pierce, "because it is not imposed upon property, but falls upon the food or necessaries of the people." The *New York World*, the Democrats' journalistic flagship, translated this reasoning into succinct terms, trumpeting, "Tax Wealth, Not Poverty." The party had a definite idea of how this

13. William Jennings Bryan to Walter Clark (March 13, 1908), in A. L. Brooks and H. T. Lefler, eds., *The Letters of Walter Clark*, 2 vols. (Chapel Hill: University of North Carolina Press, 1950), II:96; Arthur Link, "The Progressive Movement in the South, 1870–1914," *North Carolina Historical Review* 23 (April 1946): 192.

14. John D. Hicks, *The Populist Revolt* (Minneapolis: University of Minnesota Press, 1931), pp. 80–81; Robert M. La Follette, *La Follette's Autobiography* (Madison: La Follette Co., 1913), p. 708.

15. Ida M. Tarbell, *The Tariff in Our Times* (New York: Macmillan, 1911), pp. 151–352; Coletta, *William Jennings Bryan, Political Evangelist*, p. 53.

could be done: since 1894, it had stood almost as a body for a federal income tax.[16]

In that year, the last Democrat-controlled Congress had actually passed an income tax, only to see it thrown out by the Supreme Court. Since then, the party had worked for an act of Congress or a constitutional amendment that would reinstate the levy. Democrats had introduced such legislation into every successive Congress. Bryan had stressed the issue since 1896, and the *New York World* since 1883. The unexpected capture of numerous state legislatures by the Democrats in 1910 and 1912 paved the actual path into the Constitution for the Sixteenth Amendment.[17]

On the overall trust issue, the Democrats' seemingly anachronistic emphasis on trying to dissolve the trusts into smaller, honestly competing businesses is often scornfully compared to the Bull Moose plan of recognizing that the world had changed and of scientifically regulating trusts. But, if the Bull Moosers knew many things about economics, the Democrats, especially Louis Brandeis, knew one big thing: that economic power had a way of overcoming political power, however scientifically the rules were drawn. "They are unable to understand," the *New York World* warned of Roosevelt's followers in 1912, "that the thousands of millions of capital which they propose to regulate will as certainly seize the government as the slave-holding oligarchy seized the government."

The Democratic party's united commitment to an income tax, to tariff reduction, to labor legislation, and to stronger forms of corporate regulation formed a wall that kept most businessmen and conservatives out of the party. "Republicanism permeated the business community," in the words of Robert Wiebe. "Its press and a vast majority of its articulate members spoke as if party loyalty did not require discussion." Whatever feelings of righteousness the Democrats derived from the arrangement, they also keenly felt their financial disadvantage. "For years past," Democratic Senator Francis Newlands of Nevada complained in 1912, "it has been the case that whenever a Democrat made fifty thousand dollars, he became a Republican."[19]

16. Franklin Pierce, *The Tariff and the Trusts* (New York: Macmillan, 1907) p. 44; *New York World* (March 25, 1909).

17. John D. Buenker, "Urban Liberalism and the Federal Income Tax Amendment," *Pennsylvania History* 36 (April 1969): 194.

18. *New York World* (October 30, 1912).

19. Wiebe, *Businessmen and Reform*, p. 117; Francis G. Newlands to William G. McAdoo (October 10, 1912), Newlands Papers, Yale University.

Hostility between Democrats and business was sharpened by the career of the man who shaped the modern Democratic party: William Jennings Bryan. In terms of personal effect on party alignments, Bryan was the most important Democrat between Andrew Jackson and Franklin D. Roosevelt. From 1896 to 1912, Bryan dominated his party, keeping it on a course of reform and blighting the prospects of other potential leaders.

When Bryan, a defeated Congressman from Nebraska, broke with President Grover Cleveland and seized the 1896 Democratic presidential nomination on the issue of expanding and inflating the currency by the free coinage of silver, numerous party members fled to the Gold Democrats, or directly to the corporate Republicanism of William McKinley. But those who remained in the party, even if they despised Bryan and did little or nothing for any of his campaigns, were hardly conservatives, and certainly not in the Republican sense of the term. As J. Rogers Hollingsworth has pointed out, the division between Clevelandites and Bryanites was a split between different kinds of reformers.[20]

Bryan's second nomination, in 1900, demonstrated again the party's commitment to reform, transcending the now-tarnished silver issue. Clevelandites made no real effort to reclaim the party, and on a platform of opposition to McKinley's pro-business administration and of anti-imperialism, Bryan even won some unexpected eastern support. Although he lost worse in 1900 than he had in 1896, the party's identity—and the identity of its opponents—was reaffirmed.

In 1904, the Democrats discovered the immutability of their destiny in the same way most people do. They tried to escape it, with disastrous results. Against a Republican president who loudly proclaimed himself the enemy of trusts and exploiters, the Democrats spurned Bryan and nominated Alton Parker, a respectable New York jurist and staunch friend of the gold standard. In their new guise as conservatives, they sat back and waited for the support—and money—of business.

It never came. Even as Roosevelt boasted of his radicalism, his managers "collected large sums of money from financiers who preferred any Republican to any Democrat." Roosevelt easily outcollected the Democrats, spending well over $2 million, 73.5 percent of it coming directly from corporations. J. P. Morgan, who gave the Rough Rider $150,000, later told a Senate committee, "Nobody ever questioned that we gave

20. J. Rogers Hollingsworth, *The Whirligig of Democracy* (Chicago: University of Chicago Press, 1963).

our support to the Republican nomination." Meanwhile, Samuel Gompers of the American Federation of Labor again voted Democratic.[21]

In their new guise as a "safe and sane" party, the Democrats absorbed their worst beating since the Civil War. Their presidential candidate won only the South — losing even Missouri — and the party was reduced to one-third of the House of Representatives. The Democrats had learned a valuable, if expensive, lesson. "The Republicans may appeal with success to the conservatism of the country," admitted the anti-Bryan *Louisville Courier-Journal*; "not so the Democrats."[22]

The result stripped the Clevelandites of their favorite argument, that Bryan could never carry the country. It made the Commoner once again the dominant figure in the party and its likely candidate in 1908. "I do not expect the democratic party to advocate all that I have advocated," Bryan wrote a close friend a week after Parker's humiliation, "but I do believe that it is going to turn its face to the future and take up the problems we have to deal with."[23] Beginning with the next Congress, in which Roosevelt tried for the first time to pass progressive national legislation, the Democrats stressed their position as the party of reform. Beginning with the next election, they began to grow stronger.

The importance of parties in the Progressive Era has been a declining stock in the historiographical market recently, with stress on reduced voter turnout and depiction of diminished interest in politics and an end of the party period. For much of this period, party involvement did indeed seem to be declining, with less participatory campaign styles and the opening of many more political avenues outside the parties.[24]

Yet, if Progressive Era elections, compared with campaigns of the early 1890s and later 1920s, lacked some of the passion of ethnic confrontation, they offered voters a wider choice between visions of government. Predictions of the imminent collapse and reorganization of the party system, widely heard during William Howard Taft's administration, virtually disappeared by the end of the period. The two parties'

21. John Morton Blum, *The Republican Roosevelt* (Cambridge: Harvard University Press, 1954), p. 63; *Testimony before a Subcommittee of the Committee on Privileges and Elections* (Washington: 1912) pp. 416, 438, 446; Samuel Gompers, *Seventy Years of Life and Labor*, 2 vols. (New York: E. P. Dutton, 1925), II:76.

22. *Louisville Courier-Journal* (March 17, 1906).

23. William Jennings Bryan to Louis F. Post (November 12, 1904), Post Papers, Library of Congress.

24. Richard L. McCormick, *The Party Period and Public Policy* (New York: Oxford University Press, 1986); Michael E. McGerr, *The Decline of Popular Politics* (New York: Oxford University Press, 1986).

joint monopoly on elective office was, if anything, stronger after the Progressive Era than before it. Both in 1912 and twenty years later, political change, nationally and locally, arrived on a partisan ticket.

The political history of the Progressive Era is the story of a Democratic surge in both votes and imagination. "There is no way," John D. Buenker writes, "that a political party could enjoy the kind of electoral success the Democrats did . . . unless the electorate perceived that party as progressive."[25]

Contrary to established historical belief, it was this deep-rooted Democratic progressivism, not Theodore Roosevelt's bolt from the Republican party, that won the White House for the Democrats in 1912. The Democrats had been gaining strength steadily since 1904 and had dramatically improved their national image in the previous two sessions of Congress, developments rarely considered in accounts of the election. The Democrats fought the election of 1912 on the same issues that had fueled their party's eight-year surge. Their candidate, Woodrow Wilson, would have defeated either Roosevelt or William Howard Taft in a straight two-party race.

By running separately, the two Republicans managed to maximize the Republican vote and outpoll Wilson. But they each won votes that the other would have lost to the Democrat in a two-candidate contest. Many of Roosevelt's supporters could not have been lured back to Taft against an attractive Democrat reform candidate. Many of the conservative Taft supporters, by principle and past history, could not have supported a candidate running on Roosevelt's 1912 platform, and would have preferred losing the election to losing their party. The speculative merging of Taft's and Roosevelt's individual votes into one mythical Republican figure could be done only on paper, not in the political world of 1912.

But, if Wilson has historiographically suffered from one myth, he has gained from another: that the outpouring of reform legislation of his first term derived mostly from the force of his personality. In reality, many of those legislative accomplishments had long been on the Democratic agenda, and many of the best-known bills were spearheaded, often against Wilson's opposition or lack of interest, by Democratic congressmen who had been progressives far longer than he had. "Much that is good in the work of Congress had been achieved not because of the President's insistence, but on the initiative of Congress itself," judged the *New Republic* in September 1916. "In almost every case the

25. Buenker, *Urban Liberalism and Progressive Reform*, p. 223.

bills originally introduced were substantially improved during transit through the House and Senate."[26]

It was on this record of domestic reform, even more than on the claim, "He Kept Us Out of War," that the Democrats went to the country in 1916. Repeatedly reciting its list of legislation, the party added to its normal strength western Progressives, more laborers, Jews, and reformist intellectuals, in a proto-New Deal coalition. Instead of saving the Democrats in 1916, the war issue nearly defeated them by stripping Wilson of hundreds of thousands of German and Irish votes. It returned two and four years later to shatter the new Democratic coalition and to defer realignment for nearly two decades.

The Progressive Era Democrats may not have compiled a legislative or electoral record comparable to their New Deal descendants. But they did accomplish something that, according to the political scientists, parties are supposed to do and rarely manage: they set out a program, ran on it, won office on it, and then enacted it. Doing so, they shaped the partisan identities that have lasted throughout this century.

26. *New Republic* (September 2, 1916).

The Party of Reform
Democrats in the Progressive Era

CHAPTER I

Democrats
and the Big Stick

T hroughout his career as a reformer in the White House, congressional Democrats protected Theodore Roosevelt from his own party. After winning election in his own right in 1904, Roosevelt declared his determination to seek major reform legislation from a heavily Republican Congress. For the next four years, only the constant and enthusiastic support of the minority Democrats obliged the Republicans who controlled the Congress to take his proposals seriously. "It is not Republican control of Congress," observed the Democratic *New York World* as the new Congress met, "but President Roosevelt's control of the Republican party that remains in question.".[1]

From 1905 to 1908, the nation grew accustomed to the spectacle of congressional Democrats providing the strongest support for a Republican president. The Democrats even fought the congressional campaign of 1906 on the issue of their greater loyalty to the president's program. Only the bitterly partisan Roosevelt himself seemed oblivious to the situation, never acknowledging the support that had furnished his achievements, and his historical reputation. "Born in an era when to be a gentleman in the North was to be a Republican," explains George Mowry, "Roosevelt all his life viewed the Democrats with a feeling akin to contempt.'"[2]

But as the 59th Congress gathered, Roosevelt's first legislative priority, federal regulation of railroad rates, was clearly most popular with the decimated Democrats. The last three Democratic platforms had called for regulation, and party leaders and newspapers quickly endorsed Roosevelt's efforts. "If he means business on the rate-making program," promised South Carolina Senator Benjamin Tillman, Dem-

---

1. *New York World* (December 4, 1905).
2. George Mowry, *Theodore Roosevelt and the Progressive Movement* (Madison: 1946), p. 15.

ocrats would "help him use the big stick on recalcitrant Republican heads."[3]

The Hepburn bill passed the House of Representatives easily in February 1905. It empowered the Interstate Commerce Commission, upon complaint by a shipper, to investigate a railroad's freight rate schedule and substitute another one if the ICC deemed the schedule unreasonable. Although Democrats supported the bill, they complained of weaknesses in the appeals procedure. (The railroads, realizing the difficulties of defeating the bill outright, shifted their efforts to securing the broadest possible court review of ICC rulings.) Foreshadowing the Senate debate, House Democrats demanded "narrow review" provisions, ensuring that the court of appeals would not duplicate the entire rate review process but rule only on the constitutionality and legality of the ICC rate. Second, Democrats urged that "the rate was not to be set aside except by a final decision" of the court. Otherwise, they pointed out, a railroad could get a preliminary injunction maintaining the old rate and then prolong litigation for years. These two questions on review dominated the debate in both houses.[4]

Although the House proceedings revealed the issues, they obscured the opposing forces. Reactionary Republican Speaker Joseph Cannon had sent the bill to the floor only as part of a deal; in exchange, Roosevelt had pledged not to touch the tariff. Republicans voted for the bill in the confidence that the Senate would kill or maim the president's measure. Two Republican leaders who voted favorably attacked the bill on the floor, and the few who declared their opposition to it received heavy applause. One of them later estimated that on a secret ballot, fewer than twenty Republicans would have voted yea. "There is only one reason why you swallow this bill, and that is because your President wants it," jeered one Democrat. "You are afraid when he shows his teeth, and you squirm and cower when he cracks his whip."[5]

Neither Roosevelt's teeth nor his whip had much effect upon Re-

3. Kirk H. Porter and Donald Bruce Johnson, eds., *National Party Platforms, 1840–1960* (Urbana: University of Illinois Press, 1961), p. 132; Sam Hanna Acheson, *Joe Bailey, The Last Democrat* (New York: Macmillan, 1932), p. 186; *St. Louis Republic* (November 30, 1905); William Jennings Bryan to Charles W. Bryan (undated), Bryan Papers, Occidental College, Los Angeles; Benjamin Tillman to William E. Chandler (October 19, 1905), in Nathaniel W. Stephenson, *Nelson W. Aldrich* (New York: Charles Scribner's Sons, 1930), p. 279.

4. Robert Wiebe, *Businessmen and Reform* (Cambridge: Harvard University Press, 1962), p. 55; *Congressional Record*, Vol. 40, Part 1, p. 354; Part 3, p. 2251; Part 4, p. 3778; John Sharp Williams, "The Democratic Party and the Railroad Question," *Independent* (March 1, 1905).

5. William Rea Gwinn, *Uncle Joe Cannon, Archfoe of Insurgency* (New York: Bookman Associates, 1957), p. 101; Evans C. Johnson, *Oscar W. Underwood*, (Baton Rouge: Louisi-

publican senators, who did not have to face the voters that fall or any other time. Five of the seven GOP members of the Interstate Commerce Committee, led by Majority Leader Nelson W. Aldrich, saw no reason to rush the bill to the Senate floor. Jonathan P. Dolliver of Iowa, Roosevelt's spokesman, had planned for this; he and another Roosevelt supporter joined with all four Democrats present to report out the bill, 6 to 5. But Aldrich had also come prepared, and now caused Tillman, the ranking Democrat, to be named floor manager instead of Dolliver. "The bill is now where it ought to be," explained conservative Republican Joseph Foraker of Ohio, "in the hands of its friends, the Democrats."[6]

Benjamin R. ("Pitchfork Ben") Tillman, probably the best-known Democratic senator of the time, had gained his nickname when he threatened to jab Grover Cleveland in the ribs. Ten years after reaching the Senate, he retained his volatile streak, cultivating it to avoid any appearance of selling out. "Deliberately," wrote one observer, "he paints himself as a savage wearing a breechclout and brandishing a club." He had stopped speaking to Roosevelt several years earlier, when the president withdrew a White House invitation after Tillman had physically attacked his South Carolina colleague on the Senate floor.[7]

But Senate watchers recognized Tillman as more than a bully and much more than his self-description as a "cornfield lawyer." Lacking intellectual brilliance, he had become one of the hardest workers in the Senate, with a bipartisan reputation for integrity. Tillman now needed all his virtues in piloting the favorite bill of a man he despised. In a report accompanying the bill, Tillman found himself in an "anomalous position . . . without precedent in legislative history" but doggedly declared his intention to play out his role. The question, he told the Senate, came down to two premises: "The people want the railroads regulated. The Constitution gives the right to regulate the railroads to Congress." Representing a minority party, in tenuous alliance with Theodore Roosevelt, Ben Tillman would try to put the two together to produce a law.[8]

ana State University Press, 1980), p. 75; *Congressional Record*, Vol. 4, Part 3, pp. 2088, 2270, 2101, 2165; *New York Times* (February 24, 1906).

6. Thomas Richard Ross, *Jonathan Prentiss Dolliver* (Iowa City: State Historical Society of Iowa, 1958), pp. 202–205; *New York Times* (February 24, 1906).

7. Charles Willis Thompson, *Party Leaders of the Time* (New York: Dillingham, 1906), p. 132.

8. Gilson Gardner, "The Real Senator Tillman," *Independent* (July 12, 1906); Zach McGee, "Tillman, Smasher of Traditions," *World's Work* (September 1906); *Congressional Record*, Vol. 40, Part 4, p. 3835.

He could expect little help from the Democrats' ostensible Senate leader, Arthur Gorman of Maryland. Two years earlier, Gorman, a Gilded Age spoilsman, had regained his Senate seat, and the Democrats named him leader for lack of a better idea. Gorman's policy of opposing Roosevelt on every issue had succeeded only in making the party's situation worse, and ill health and political reversals at home had virtually neutralized him as a factor in the senatorial power structure.[9]

Insofar as Gorman's fall left any vacuum, "a big, handsome, proud, rather arrogant Texan" came closest to filling it. People either adored Joseph Weldon Bailey or despised him, a polarization that for twenty years kept the Texas Democrats in a state of civil war. While one publication labeled him "the most brilliant and forceful intellect in Congress," another counted him among great men "too beclouded by their own greatness." Although he often flashed a temper at least as explosive as Tillman's, his oratory made listeners "find little thrills running up and down their spines, and feel a desire to bite pieces out of the furniture." Although neither Tillman nor Bailey qualified as an ideal party leader, together they formed a potent team for Roosevelt's bill — despite the slight complication that neither of them was on speaking terms with Roosevelt.[10]

Throughout March 1906, this problem appeared irrelevant, as Democrats fought for the bill without encouragement from the White House. Like their House colleagues, Democratic senators worried about the extent of judicial review and the power of suspending injunctions. Bailey introduced an amendment forbidding the court of appeals to alter the ICC rate except by a final decision, and other Democrats introduced weaker amendments to limit the injunction power. Seeking to tighten the bill, Bailey and Tillman clashed not only with conservative Republicans but with the administration forces, who followed Roosevelt's lead in opposing any amendment to the House bill. They also faced a few defections in their own ranks, the octogenarian John T. Morgan of Alabama decrying any "attempt to follow the President in his insincere and unworthy course."[11]

9. John R. Lambert, *Arthur Pue Gorman* (Baton Rouge: Louisiana State University Press, 1953), pp. 297–308, 343, 360, 362; Thompson, *Party Leaders*, pp. 109–14.

10. Mark Sullivan, *Our Times*, 6 vols. (New York: Charles Scribner's Sons, 1926–1938), III:269; Lewis L. Gould, *Progressives and Prohibitionists: Texas Democrats in the Wilson Era* (Austin: University of Texas Press, 1973), p. 16; *St. Louis Republic* (February 11, 1906); "Men We Are Watching," *Independent* (January 24, 1907); John Braeman, *Albert J. Beveridge* (Chicago: University of Chicago Press, 1971), p. 58; Thompson, *Party Leaders*, pp. 125–27.

11. *Congressional Record*, Vol. 40, Part 4, pp. 3956, 3959, 3953; Part 5, p. 4556; John T. Morgan to Francis G. Newlands (March 18, 1906), Newlands Papers, Yale University.

A month after the bill had come into the Senate, it seemed to Aldrich that "even an attempt at an agreement is decidedly premature at this point." But both Democratic and Republican proponents of the bill feared that the Republican leadership was preparing a new review amendment that would gut the bill, that would, in Dolliver's phrase, "solemnly transplant the entire controversy to be redetermined, rejudged, and redecided by a circuit court of the United States."[12]

The Democratic duumvirate had additional problems. A skilled stump speaker and Chautauqua circuit orator, Tillman could not match legal logic with the formidable corporation attorneys across the aisle. Under one barrage of precedents, he was reduced to blurting, "There you come with your decisions. I am getting back to the common sense of it now." Bailey, the party's intellectual champion, had other limitations. Gifted with a unique talent for antagonizing opponents, he snapped at one Republican, "I am acquainted with that case. I know enough of it to know that it does not apply to this question at this time."[13]

It took a full month for Roosevelt to abandon the hope of accommodation with Aldrich. "The Republican leaders," he wrote darkly to his son about the bill, "have tried to betray me and it," presumably in that order. But to ally himself with the Democrats, as John Morton Blum points out, "Roosevelt had to move cautiously but clearly to the left of his original position."[14]

Fortunately, Roosevelt rarely had objections to moving in any direction. On March 31, he unveiled a new "narrow review" amendment before five friendly Republican senators, including Dolliver and Chester Long of Kansas, who agreed to sponsor the change. He also declared his willingness to support a Democratic injunction limitation amendment. That night, he called to the White House ex-Senator William E. Chandler of New Hampshire, an antirailroad Republican and friend of Tillman, and through him made the same offer to the Democrat. Roosevelt later claimed that Chandler had asked to see him, at Tillman's request, and denied most of Chandler's version of the conversation.[15]

12. *Congressional Record*, Vol. 40, Part 4, pp. 3102–20; Part 5, pp. 4335, 4377, 4115, 4100, 4329, 4078.

13. Ibid., Part 5, p. 4561; Part 4, p. 3947.

14. Theodore Roosevelt to Kermit Roosevelt (April 1, 1906), in Elting E. Morison, ed., *Letters of Theodore Roosevelt*, 8 vols. (Cambridge: Harvard University Press, 1951–1954), V:204; John Morton Blum, "Theodore Roosevelt and the Hepburn Act: Toward a System of Orderly Control," in ibid., VI:1568.

15. *Cleveland Plain Dealer* (April 1, 1906); *Congressional Record*, Vol. 40, Part 5, p. 4638; Leon Burr Richardson, *William E. Chandler, Republican* (New York: Dodd, Mead & Co., 1940), pp. 661–62; Owen Wister, *Roosevelt, The Story of a Friendship* (New York: Macmillan, 1930), pp. 240-44.

Democrats retained doubts about Roosevelt's amendment and complained that they had not participated in drafting it, but they signed on. Throughout April, Roosevelt consulted with Democratic senators, as well as with Chandler, representing the uninvited (and probably unwilling) Tillman and Bailey. By the terms of the emerging agreement, the Democrats would provide twenty-six votes for the Long and Bailey amendments, and Roosevelt would supply twenty Republicans.[16]

The Democratic leaders now intensified their efforts to line up votes. On April 10, Bailey, the temporary and unlikely administration leader, spoke for his amendment. Defending its constitutionality, for four hours he dazzled the Senate with quotations, citations, and precedents. The *New York World* called Bailey's effort "one of the great speeches the Senate has heard since the Civil War." He and Tillman used its momentum to call a party caucus. According to most estimates, they found they could rely on twenty-five Democratic votes for the arrangement.[17]

Roosevelt could not claim similar success at his end: only one Republican had endorsed the Bailey amendment. Newly elected Robert M. La Follette of Wisconsin, snubbed by Republican senators and denied patronage by the administration, thought that it "will enhance the value of this legislation beyond all computation." A slightly weaker Democratic amendment had to be substituted.[18]

Still, prospects appeared bright — when Roosevelt suddenly capitulated. Consulting with neither his Democratic allies nor his attorney general, he accepted from Aldrich a judicial review amendment with no limitations on jurisdiction or injunction. Two months of maneuver had resulted, as Gabriel Kolko puts it, in "a clear victory for Nelson Aldrich and the Senators he represented."[19]

The retreat seemed utterly unnecessary. Twenty-five Democrats stood with the president; he needed fewer than twenty of the fifty-five Senate Republicans. "The Aldrich group were beaten and they knew it," according to the *New York Times*. "They could not muster more than forty votes to save their lives."[20]

16. Richardson, ibid., p. 663; *Louisville Courier-Journal* (April 6, 1906); Acheson, *Bailey*, p. 199.

17. *Congressional Record*, Vol. 40, Part 5, pp. 4978–90; *New York World* (April 11, 1906); *Cleveland Plain Dealer* (April 19, 1906); Stephenson, *Aldrich*, p. 308.

18. *New York Times* (April 24, 1906); *Congressional Record*; Robert M. La Follette, *La Follette's Autobiography* (Madison: La Follette Co., 1913), p. 411; Denver *Rocky Mountain News* (March 13, 1906); *Congressional Record* Vol. 40, Part 6, p. 5688.

19. Gabriel Kolko, *Railroads and Regulation, 1877–1916* (Princeton: Princeton University Press, 1965), p. 143.

20. Blum, "Theodore Roosevelt and the Hepburn Act," p. 1569; Stephenson, *Aldrich*, p. 308; Sullivan, *Our Times*, III:256; *New York Times* (May 5, 1906).

Roosevelt adjusted his position for reasons less pressing if no less pragmatic. He did not attach as much significance to judicial review limitations as Democrats did, and the idea of dividing credit with the Democrats repelled him. Most important, despite his admiration for the God-given fighting virtues, Roosevelt never really felt that the Almighty had created them for use against Republicans. However thunderously he demanded radical reform legislation, he would always, in the end, accept whatever Aldrich and Cannon would give him. Democrats had noticed this tendency before and had speculated about a possible "inglorious backdown" on the Hepburn Act. Nevertheless, though forewarned by experience and political inclination, they managed to be surprised again.[21]

As much embarrassed as angered, Democrats attacked Roosevelt's action but continued to fight for their kind of bill. They joined with western Republicans and forced the inclusion of some limitations on injunctions. Despite unusual party unity, a series of Democratic amendments to limit the courts' power lost badly, often with only La Follette joining the Democrats. Four La Follette amendments, including one for physical evaluation of railroad property by the ICC, suffered the same fate.[22]

By the time the bill passed, with only one Republican and two Democrats voting no, Tillman and Bailey had brawled with Roosevelt over veracity, and Bailey had insulted two Republicans on the Senate floor. This highly publicized epilogue effectively obscured the Democratic achievement. Though comprising little more than a third of the Senate, they had forced the bill out of committee, helped attach some strengthening amendments, and could claim some credit for its final passage. On a long series of roll calls, they had consistently favored tougher regulation than Roosevelt or the Republicans and maintained unaccustomed and heartening unity. Except on one vote, the Democrats never had more than five defectors, and they frequently voted unanimously. On the first major congressional fight of the Progressive Era, the Democrats began to find the effectiveness and purpose they had been missing for twelve years.[23]

21. John Morton Blum, *The Republican Roosevelt* (Cambridge: Harvard University Press, 1954), p. 104; William Henry Harbaugh, *Power and Responsibility, The Life and Times of Theodore Roosevelt* (New York: Oxford University Press, 1962), p. 260; *Commoner* (February 2, 1906).

22. *St. Louis Republic* (May 10, 1906); *Congressional Record*, Vol. 40, Part 7, pp. 6455, 6676, 6672, 6673, 6678, 6695, 6571, 6809, 6821, 6774.

23. Democrats had, however, no illusions about the value of the bill. House Minority

Despite these limited achievements, the Democrats had not resolved their curious relationship with Theodore Roosevelt. At the same time Tillman was calling Roosevelt a liar, he admitted to the Senate that only Roosevelt could have passed any bill at all. For his part, Roosevelt badly needed Democratic support in his progressive moods. "At this moment," wrote a Tammany congressman, watching the rate fight wind down, "the only support in either House of Congress which Mr. Roosevelt can depend upon with certainty is the democratic vote."[24]

In his fight to regulate the railroads, Roosevelt enjoyed the backing not only of Democratic lawmakers but of most of the party press. Democratic newspapers had been calling for curbs on railroads and trusts for years and had played a key role in producing general Democratic support for such measures. On those and many other questions, Democratic defeats since 1894 had only increased the influence exercised by the party's newspapers and their proprietors. Surveying the wreckage after the election of 1904, the Democratic party might have listed its negotiable assets as the South, Bryan, and the *New York World*. The golden dome of the World Building, in lower Manhattan, symbolized the considerable power that its tenant and several other Democratic newspapers exerted in party affairs.

Several circumstances had created this influence. Since 1896, Democrats north of the Mason-Dixon line could look to no major elected leader. In the long corridor, stretching from Connecticut to Illinois, where Gilded Age elections were decided, Democrats failed to elect a governor or a senator from 1893 to 1905. Several nationally read party newspapers partially filled this leadership vacuum and provided eastern Democrats with their only alternative to Bryan.

Bryan, and the low ebb of Democratic fortunes, had further increased the importance of individual party organs by decreasing their number. Since 1896, many previously Democratic journals had either rejected the party or become irregular in their support. If the *New York Herald* refused to endorse a Republican ticket, the GOP could still look to the *Tribune*, the *Press*, or the *Sun*. If the *New York World* bolted

---

Leader John Sharp Williams wrote a constituent that although the bill was "an enormous stride in advance," he was not satisfied. Thomas Patterson of Colorado, perhaps the most radical Democrat in the Senate, abstained from the final vote and later wrote that government ownership was now inevitable. Williams to R. L. East (undated, 1907), Williams Papers, Library of Congress; A. L. Brooks and H. T. Leffler, eds., *The Papers of Walter Clark*, 2 vols. (Chapel Hill: University of North Carolina Press, 1950), II:87.

24. *Congressional Record*, Vol. 40, Part 8, p. 7087; W. Bourke Cockran to Montague White (May 17, 1906), Cockran Papers, New York Public Library.

the Democratic party, its ticket might find itself unrepresented in the nation's largest and politically most important city.

The most influential Democratic publisher in America spent most of his time on a yacht across the Atlantic, imprisoned by blindness and hypertension. Joseph Pulitzer ran the *New York World* (and the *St. Louis Post-Dispatch*) by means of an endless stream of transatlantic cables, unleashed each day after a long-suffering secretary read him his newspapers. The *World* could afford its cable bill; it occupied an unquestioned position as the country's foremost Democratic newspaper, a position conceded even by those who resented it. Ten years earlier, Ben Tillman had complained of southern businessmen "who say 'Me Too' whenever the *New York World* speaks."[25]

Since coming to New York in 1883, the Jewish-Hungarian immigrant had pioneered in what would later be called yellow journalism, combining sensationalism with muckraking. Pulitzer frequently reprinted his own 10-point platform, including demands for an income tax, an inheritance tax, a low tariff, civil service reform, and an anti-corrupt practices act. In pursuit of these ends, the *World* accumulated a somewhat larger number of dislikes, a list that by 1906 included militarism, imperialism, free silver, Tammany Hall, and Theodore Roosevelt.[26]

Despite its position in the party, the *World* reserved the right to criticize or flatly oppose the party. It attacked Cleveland, and refused to support Bryan in 1896, although it endorsed him in 1900 on the imperialism issue. Although the *World* praised Bryan when they agreed, it steadily fought his control of the party, which it charged had led only to disaster. "Be Democratic," Pulitzer instructed an editor during one conversation, "but even more independent."[27]

The *World* followed the same independent policy with Theodore Roosevelt, who responded by unsuccessfully trying to prosecute Pulitzer for criminal libel. Its cartoonists invariably drew him stomping about in a cavalry uniform, and its editorials repeatedly demanded an accounting of his 1904 campaign funds and asked why none of the people Roosevelt called "malefactors of great wealth" had yet gone to jail. Yet it often lauded Roosevelt, both as governor and president, when

25. Joseph Pulitzer memo to Frank Cobb (October 5, 1908), Pulitzer Papers, Library of Congress; Francis B. Simkins, *Pitchfork Ben Tillman: South Carolinian* (Baton Rouge: Louisiana State University Press, 1944), p. 317.
26. W. A. Swanberg, *Pulitzer* (New York: Charles Scribner's Sons, 1967), p. 76.
27. Ibid., pp. 99, 151, 172, 212–14, 274; *New York World* (February 4, 5, 1908); Cobb, memo of conversations with Pulitzer (March 22, 1909), Pulitzer Papers.

he followed a progressive course. In the railroad rate fight, the *World* supported the bill but felt that strict controls on campaign contributions would be needed to prevent the roads from controlling the entire process.[28]

Just below Pulitzer in the hierarchy of Democratic journalists stood Henry Watterson, a one-eyed, mustachioed ex-Confederate. Watterson edited the *Louisville Courier-Journal* and was often called the last of the great personal editors, the Horace Greeley breed whose names and persons were synonymous with their newspapers. Watterson enhanced his cult status with an editorial prose style Henry James might have found a bit prolix. "Its sentences," explained the *Baltimore Sun*, taking a deep breath, "proceed with the seductive sinuosity of a stream of molasses; it glows and glitters with recondite and exotic metonymies, synecdoches, prosopoeias and antonomasias; it is in both prose and verse, and has strophes, tropes, apreggios, and a cadenza."[29]

Whether due to the tropes or the cadenza, Watterson's style brought him a national readership and an important if quarrelsome position in the Democratic party. Temporary chairman and keynote speaker of the 1876 national convention, he searched for the next 40 years for a leader as inspiring as Samuel Tilden. Neither Cleveland nor Bryan had qualified, and Watterson's support of the Gold Democrats in 1896 gave Kentucky to McKinley. It also almost killed his newspaper, which scuttled back to party regularity in 1900.[30]

Watterson avowed himself a follower of "the Star-eyed Goddess of Reform," and he steadily maintained that her eyes shone most brightly for a lower tariff. By 1906, he had extended his advocacy to government controls on tariff-protected big business. "The Republican party," he fulminated, "is the slave of Mammon." This position led him to a strong fight for the Hepburn bill, and an attack on Roosevelt when he surrendered.[31]

The third, and most prominent, of the Democratic press lords had little in common with the blinded immigrant or the wordy rebel. Whereas both Pulitzer and Watterson belonged to the generation that fought the Civil War, William Randolph Hearst had been two years

28. James E. Pollard, *The Presidents and the Press* (New York: Macmillan, 1947), p. 588; *New York World* (March 1, 1906); John T. Hetterick, *Reminiscences*, Oral History Research Office, Columbia University; *New York World* (May 6, 1906; March 22, 1906).

29. *Baltimore Sun* (June 24, 1908).

30. Joseph F. Wall, *Henry Watterson* (New York: Oxford University Press, 1956), pp. 205, 226, 244–45.

31. Wall, ibid., p. 248; *Louisville Courier-Journal* (March 24, 1906; May 14, 1906).

old when Lee surrendered at Appomattox. Starting with one newspaper — and a great deal of money — inherited from his father, by 1906 Hearst published newspapers in New York, Boston, Chicago, San Francisco, and Los Angeles, selling almost 2 million copies a day. Although no single Hearst paper had the prestige or the influence of the *World* or the *Courier-Journal*, when all spoke in unison — as they generally did — the sound was loud enough for Democratic leaders to hear, if not always to heed.[32]

Loudness was not a problem for Hearst's newspapers. Their proprietor took Pulitzer's formula one step further, with bigger headlines, more daring illustrations, and less attention to accuracy. Readers also found wilder attacks on trusts and conservative politicians; the viciousness of Hearst newspaper blasts at William McKinley caused a persistent feeling that Hearst had incited the president's assassination. On the other side, Hearst was one of the few large publishers openly sympathetic to organized labor, which often responded with warm support.[33]

But Hearst papers showed the most enthusiasm over their proprietor's political ambitions. Entering politics as a prominent Bryan support in 1896, Hearst rapidly utilized his journalistic clout to acquire the presidency of the National Association of Democratic Clubs and a congressional seat from New York City. In 1904, the freshman representative struck directly for his party's presidential nomination and won 263 votes on the national convention's only ballot. His newspapers not only reported "Mr. Hearst's lifelong championship of the cause of the people," but also limited their coverage of possible challengers, as well as measures (such as the Hepburn bill) in which their publisher showed little personal interest.[34]

With his newspapers, his labor support, and a surprisingly effective campaign style, in 1905 Hearst ran an impressive independent campaign for mayor of New York, splitting the city sharply along class lines, losing to the Tammany incumbent by six-tenths of a percentage point. It was generally assumed that Tammany had simply counted Hearst out, and his showing sent shock waves through a party chroni-

32. *Collier's* (September 29, 1906).
33. Grace Heilman Stimson, *Rise of the Labor Movement in Los Angeles* (Berkeley: University of California Press, 1955), p. 272.
34. W. A. Swanberg, *Citizen Hearst* (New York: Charles Scribner's Sons, 1961), p. 181; John W. Winkler, *William Randolph Hearst, An American Phenomenon* (New York: Simon and Schuster, 1928), p. 172; Nancy J. Weiss, *Charles Francis Murphy, 1858–1924* (Northampton: Smith College, 1968), p. 41; *Los Angeles Examiner* (February 26, 1906); *The Public* (October 6, 1906); *Denver Post* (March 13, 1906); *Los Angeles Examiner* (May 4, 5, 1906).

cally short of leadership. One Democratic senator immediately labeled Hearst the front-runner for the 1908 nomination.[35]

Aside from the *World*, the *Courier-Journal*, and the Hearst papers, no Democratic journal could claim truly national influence. The *Baltimore Sun*, perhaps the party's leading regional newspaper, wielded considerable power in Maryland politics and was often read in the neighboring District of Columbia. The *Sun* disliked Maryland's Gorman machine, Bryan, blacks, and the protective tariff. Although it had supported the Commoner once, in 1900, it strongly opposed his power in the party. While joining with the *World* and *Courier-Journal* on that issue, the *Sun* rejected their relatively enlightened racial policy. It always found space on the front page for stories about black men attacking white women, especially if the females were underage and the blacks could be described as hulking. The *Sun* felt equally strongly about the protective tariff, which it considered "a plot to fill the fat wallets and add to the idle luxury of those whose money happens to be invested in tariff-protected industries."[36]

The *Sun*'s warm support of the Hepburn bill reflected a new interest in reform for the newspaper. It was soon calling for regulation of public utilities, pure food laws, and a corrupt practices act and by 1909 had clearly become a reform (if not quite muckraking) journal. These tendencies intensified a year later, when Charles H. Grasty, the former crusading publisher of the *Baltimore News*, bought the *Sun*.[37]

In the significant state of Ohio, Democratic journalism reflected both the new and the old in the party. The *Cleveland Plain Dealer*, the dominant Democratic newspaper of northern Ohio since 1842, allied itself closely with Tom L. Johnson, Cleveland's Democratic reform mayor. Johnson, a wealthy single-taxer, had consulted with *Plain Dealer* editor Charles Kennedy before running for mayor and enjoyed its support in all his campaigns, as well as in his struggles with local streetcar companies. The paper's progressivism did not stop at the borders of the Western Reserve; it had endorsed Bryan in 1896, and it supported the

---

35. Weiss, ibid., p. 41; *New York Times* (November 9, 1905); John L. Heaton to Joseph Pulitzer (August 5, 1906), Pulitzer Papers, Columbia University; Richard L. McCormick, *From Realignment to Reform* (Ithaca: Cornell University Press, 1979), pp. 206–208; Francis G. Newlands to E. L. Bingham (December 27, 1905), Newlands Papers.

36. Gerald W. Johnson, Frank R. Kent, H. L. Mencken, and Hamilton Owens, *The Sunpapers of Baltimore* (New York: Alfred A. Knopf, 1937), pp. 100, 164, 191, 204; Lambert, *Gorman*, p. 218; James B. Crooks, *Politics and Progress, The Rise of Urban Progressivism in Baltimore* (Baton Rouge: Louisiana State University Press, 1968), pp. 68–71; *Baltimore Sun* (November 2, 1910).

37. Crooks, ibid, pp. 70–71.

Hepburn Act and gave friendly coverage to the American Federation of Labor.[38]

Across the state, John R. McLean, owner of the *Cincinnati Enquirer*, represented all that progressives disliked about Democratic politics. Boss of the city's Democratic minority, McLean actually resided in Washington, where he had made a fortune in public utilities and had recently acquired the *Washington Post*. Johnson and the Cleveland reformers, aided by the *Plain Dealer*, had recently ended McLean's control of the Ohio state party, but McLean still played a prominent party role by means of the *Enquirer*, unpublicized subsidies to county weeklies, and an unabashed willingness to spend money at election time.[39]

The Boston Irish, probably the most loyal Democrats in the North, found journalistic sustenance in the *Boston Post*. Originally a stolid, mugwumpish Democratic journal, it had altered radically when acquired by Edwin A. Grozier in 1891. Grozier, a former city editor on Pulitzer's *World*, rapidly applied the lessons of New York to Boston. By 1914, the *Post* enjoyed the largest morning circulation in America, 450,000.[40]

Grozier achieved this pleasant standing by making the *Post* "one of the most sensational papers of the country," easily able to match yellow hues with its Hearst competitor. But Grozier also imported the *World*'s tradition of municipal crusading and took a reformist position in national Democratic politics—unless he felt New England interests to be endangered. (This caveat caused the *Post* to oppose Bryan in 1896 and to retreat from its early backing of the Hepburn bill.) George Fred Williams, the Bryan leader in Massachusetts, praised the *Post* as "the most nearly and truly Democratic" newspaper in Boston, and its massive circulation made it easily the leading party journal in New England.[41]

38. Archer H. Shaw, *The Plain Dealer* (New York: Alfred A. Knopf, 1942), pp. 20, 231, 282, 297–98, 313; Hoyt L. Warner, *Progressivism in Ohio, 1897–1917* (Columbus: Ohio State University Press, 1964), p. 79 n; *Cleveland Plain Dealer* (April 30, 1906; March 25, 1906; March 3, 1906).

39. Warner, ibid., pp. 6, 69, 119–21, 149, 157.

40. William Shannon, *The American Irish*, rev. ed. (London: Macmillan, 1966), p. 190; Frank Luther Mott, *American Journalism* (New York: Macmillan, 1950), p. 560.

41. Mott, ibid, p. 560; Louis M. Lyons, *Newspaper Story, One Hundred Years of the Boston Globe* (Cambridge: Belknap Press of Harvard University Press, 1971), p. 137; Richard M. Abrams, *Conservatism in a Progressive Era* (Cambridge: Harvard University Press, 1964), pp. 62, 67; J. Rogers Hollingsworth, *The Whirligig of Politics* (Chicago: University of Chicago Press, 1962), p. 70; *Boston Post* (April 4, 1905; May 25, 1905; April 7, 1906); Lyons, *Newspaper Story*, p. 137; William G. McAdoo to Woodrow Wilson (September 17, 1913), McAdoo Papers, Library of Congress.

"Democrats often complain of the lack of representation among the dailies of the large cities," mourned Bryan's *Commoner* in 1907, by which it meant the lack of Bryanite representation. Although all of these newspapers had supported Bryan in his most recent outing, none considered him the ideal Democratic leader. Even the Hearst papers, who had twice supported Bryan enthusiastically, had someone else in mind. Outside the South, Bryanites could not find a congenial major journal east of the Mississippi.[42]

A good deal west of the river, the Denver *Rocky Mountain News* qualified. The *News* had left the party not in 1896 but in 1892 to support the Populist James B. Weaver. Its owner, U.S. Senator Thomas Patterson, guided the journal on a militantly Bryanite and prolabor course. A recent analysis of Patterson's Senate career has classified him as more radical than progressive, and he often refused to vote on reform bills he considered too weak. He followed this course on the Hepburn bill, although his newspaper had supported it.[43]

No southern Democratic paper had real national influence, and in the region's one-party system, Democratic newspapers represented all shades of opinion. But if the South was "the most thoroughly Bryanized area of the country," many of its newspapers could claim some credit. Among others, Josephus Daniels's *Raleigh* (N.C.) *News and Observer* and the *Atlanta Journal*, once owned by the politically prominent Hoke Smith, consistently advocated economic change on both the state and national levels. But the virulence of their racism meant that such newspapers could win only limited respect outside the South.[44]

In the thin ranks of conservative Democratic newspapers, the *New York Times* held first place. Adolph Ochs, its publisher, had a history strikingly similar to that of Joseph Pulitzer. Both Jews, they had each achieved success with their own newspapers in the Upper South—Pulitzer in St. Louis, Ochs in Chattanooga, Tennessee—and had migrated to New York to seek wider audiences. But they differed sharply in the kind of newspaper each published.[45]

42. *Commoner* (March 8, 1907).

43. Robert L. Perkins, *The First Hundred Years* (Garden City: Doubleday and Co., 1959), pp. 34, 382–88; Robert Earl Smith, "Colorado's Progressive Senators and Representatives," *Colorado Magazine* 45 (Winter 1968): 27–41, 32, 40; Denver *Rocky Mountain News* (March 21, 1906; March 23, 1906; December 5, 1905; May 6, 1906).

44. C. Vann Woodward, *Origins of the New South* (Baton Rouge: Louisiana State University Press, 1951), p. 469; Dewey Grantham, *The Democratic South* (New York: W. W. Norton, 1965), p. 52; *The Public* (August 24, 1907).

45. Gerald W. Johnson, *An Honorable Titan* (New York and London: Harper and Bros., 1941), pp. 13–169.

Ochs produced a newspaper conservative in both politics and style, aimed at the middle and upper classes of the city. Only its advocacy of a lower tariff testified to its nominal Democracy. Ochs felt for Bryan "a distaste that almost amounted to a phobia," and the Commoner reciprocated in kind. In the Hepburn fight, the *Times'* sympathies lay completely with Nelson Aldrich.[46]

In the wilderness that was the national Democratic party in 1905, the party press provided most of the signposts. Despite differing styles (and differing objectives), Pulitzer, Watterson, and Hearst ranked with the best-known and most influential Democrats of their day. Along with their sometime enemy, sometime ally, Bryan, they guided the Democratic party onto a platform of lower tariffs, controls on business, and friendliness toward labor. With a candidate who could appeal to both the Bryanites and the *World*, the party could hope to be both progressive and successful.

"It was the prevailing Progressive theory," recalled Bull Mooser Donald Richberg four decades later, "that the Democratic Party could not be permanently progressive because of what we regarded as the ultra conservatism of the South." This view of the Democrats' stronghold region as a reactionary weight on the party lasted far longer than did the Progressives. The reality was almost the exact opposite: because of its strong Populist legacy, extensive Bryanism, and limited corporate presence, the South provided not only votes but a persistent reform pressure for the national party.[47]

But, for the Progressive Era Democrats, the South was still a poisoned legacy. Its racism, recently hardened and embedded into law, scarred the entire party's credibility among many northern reformers, hampered efforts by northern Democrats to attract the emerging urban black vote, and provided a ready stick with which both regular and insurgent Republicans could beat their partisan opponents. Early on, observers noticed one particularly embarrassing aspect about southern Democratic reformism: "It is a curious and regrettable thing," noted the Democratic reform magazine *The Public* in 1907, "that the politicians of the South who are progressive on economic issues are reactionary on the race question."[48]

Racism and reformism in the South not only involved the same people but shared some common roots. Just as the Populist insurrection

46. Ibid., p. 189; *New York Times* (April 28, 1906).
47. Donald Richberg, *My Hero* (New York: Putnam's, 1954), p. 81.
48. *The Public* (August 24, 1907).

of the late nineteenth century had spurred southern Democrats to entrench themselves by violently expelling blacks from politics, Populist ideas had infused the Democratic party in many southern states, even as outside observers still recited the ancient image of the traditionalist, antigovernment South. "Southern Democrats in the early years of the twentieth century increasingly accepted the Populist concept of the positive state," Dewey Grantham points out. "The persistence of agrarian radicalism . . . helped nourish antitrust sentiment and the regulatory impulse."[49]

Even more than the Midwest, the South was a raw-materials exporter heavily dependent upon capital and corporations from outside. This situation made it not only the most strongly Populist region but also sent it ardently into battle behind Bryan in his crusades against the money power. Besides shaping the South's presidential choices, the region's Bryanism also produced senators and representatives who supported the party platform's call for business regulation and labor protection and backed Roosevelt's limited steps in those directions.[50]

It also produced, in the first decade of the twentieth century, a wave of economic reform legislation in southern state legislatures, and southern Democratic machines as well as insurgencies could claim progressive achievements. The American Federation of Labor, although able to claim only limited membership in most of the southern states, still carried influence in the region's legislatures and found considerable support for its positions among southern congressmen and senators in Washington.[51]

Southern legislatures played vital roles in ratifying the constitutional amendments providing for an income tax and direct election of senators: eight of the first nine states to approve the income tax amendment were southern and border states, followed shortly by four more. Direct election of senators was accepted equally easily, since all southern states already had binding Senate primaries of their own in effect.

In supporting the Seventeenth Amendment, of course, southern Democrats were seeking to open up the process to white voters at the same time they were closing it to black voters, with poll taxes, literacy

49. Dewey Grantham, *Southern Progressivism* (Knoxville: University of Tennessee Press, 1983), p. 13.

50. Jack T. Kirby, *Darkness at the Dawning, Race and Reform in the Progressive South* (Philadelphia: Lippincott, 1972), p. 54. For an example of Populist infusion into one southern Democratic party, see Worth Robert Miller, "Building a Progressive Coalition in Texas: The Populist-Reform Democrat Rapprochement, 1900-1907," *Journal of Southern History* 52 (May 1986): 163–82.

51. Kirby, ibid., pp. 43–44; Grantham, *Southern Progressivism*, pp. 291–97.

tests, and grandfather clauses. The separate and unequal varieties of electoral reform in the South demonstrate the unbreakable limitations on southern progressivism.

When race and reform came into conflict, the outcome was inevitable. When House Democrats in 1906 supported a measure requiring public disclosure of campaign contributions, Republican leaders added to it an amendment providing for federal supervision of congressional elections and watched southern Democratic support for the bill disappear. With the same tactic, Republicans managed to delay for an entire Congress a constitutional amendment for direct election of U.S. senators.[52]

The racism of the southern reformers limited their scope, marred their national and historic images, and made it impossible for any southern Democrat to make a serious bid for the presidency—unless he'd had the foresight to move north when young.

It did not, however, mar their relations with the party's national leader. William Jennings Bryan's own racial policies, whether from conviction or convenience, were everything southern Democrats might wish. He defended Jim Crow laws and black disenfranchisement and, in 1908, when a black bolt from the GOP raised hopes of Democrats drawing some northern black voters, would not even go so far as to oppose lynchings. The state constitution of Oklahoma, drawn up under heavy Bryanite influence, included its own poll tax and literacy test requirements.[53]

Northern Democratic organizations, however, had more interest in the emerging urban black vote. Tammany Hall had been courting New York black voters since shortly after the Civil War, and during the Gilded Age, black voters had some balance-of-power influence in Ohio, Illinois, and Indiana. Tom Taggart, Indiana Democratic boss and manager of the party's 1904 presidential campaign, had drawn considerable black support during his earlier campaigns for mayor of Indianapolis.[54]

Some northern Democratic progressive figures had reform horizons wide enough to include black issues. Cleveland reform Mayor Johnson made a special effort to reach out to black voters, a policy continued

52. *Baltimore Sun* (May 23, 1908, March 1, 1911); *Congressional Record*, Vol. 47, Part 2, pp. 1485, 1923–24; Vol. 47, Part 3, pp. 2433–37, 2544; Vol. 48, Part 7, pp. 6348–67.

53. William H. Smith, "William Jennings Bryan and Racism," *Journal of Negro History* 54 (April 1969): 137–38; Louis R. Harlan, *Booker T. Washington, the Wizard of Tuskegee* (New York: Oxford University Press, 1983), p. 337; Kirby, *Darkness at the Dawning*, p. 16.

54. Lawrence Grossman, *The Democratic Party and the Negro, 1865–1892* (Urbana: University of Illinois Press, 1976).

by his successor, Newton Baker, later Wilson's Secretary of War. The *New York World* editorials attacked lynchings, especially in the North, in a position that prefigured its dramatic campaign against the Ku Klux Klan during the 1920s.[55]

The reform spirit of the northern Democratic Party was part of what drew black activist W. E. B. Du Bois to launch his bolt in 1908. That year, he discovered, as Johnson did, that the black ties to the GOP were just too strong to be broken.[56] But there remained among the northern Democrats some degree of openness to blacks, which would surface again when Woodrow Wilson brought southern racial attitudes into the operation of the federal government. In a primary fight with administration-supported reformers, Tammany appealed to black voters by contrasting its policies toward them with Wilson's. Robert J. Bulkely, a congressman from Cleveland (and later a New Deal senator from Ohio), attempted to block the imposition of Jim Crow seating on Washington streetcar lines, and Massachusetts Democrats complained publicly to Wilson about his segregation policies — conveniently, just before the 1914 election.[57]

Northern Democrats would not, of course, ever go so far as to break with southern Democrats on their racial policies. They preferred to stress common ties, which were substantial. The Democratic party of the Progressive Era was fundamentally a coalition of outsiders, an identity held strongly by the immigrants, workers, and farmers of the North who voted Democratic. Southern Democrats, although in control of their immediate political environment, similarly felt themselves isolated within the nation, especially in economic terms.

"The advantage that the Democratic party has at this point," wrote Clarence Poe, a prominent southern agrarian reformer (and antiblack activist) in 1912, "is that it has a great body of its representatives in the South, where these special interests — with a few notable exceptions — certainly do not exist in the degree that they exist in the North. Moreover, in the North the Democratic party represents more largely

55. David A. Gerber, *Black Ohio and the Color Line*, (Urbana: University of Illinois Press, 1976), pp. 340–41; John K. Hutchens and George Oppenheimer, eds., *The Best in The World* (New York: Viking Press, 1973), pp. 5–9.

56. Francis L. Broderick, *W. E. B. Du Bois* (Stanford: Stanford University Press, 1959), pp. 83–85.

57. Tammany pamphlet (1913), in Woodrow Wilson Papers, Library of Congress; William D. Jenkins, "Robert Bulkley: Progressive Profile," *Ohio History* 88 (Winter 1979): 57–72, 62; David I. Walsh to Woodrow Wilson (October 26, 1914), and James A. Gallivan to Wilson (November 11, 1914), in Arthur Link, ed., *The Papers of Woodrow Wilson* (Princeton, 1966–), Vol. 31, pp. 237–38, 297.

the farming and labor element whose interest is not that of the big corporations, but the reverse. It is for those reasons that the Democratic party is the freer and so much more likely agent of reform."[58]

Eventually, the southern Democrats' hostility to blacks would cause major divisions and conflicts in their party. But during the Progressive Era, their hostility to northern corporate capitalism was more politically significant and contributed substantially to the Democrats' identity as reformists.

Barely a year after the party's 1904 debacle, surviving Democrats saw some signs of hope. "Several members of Congress are anxious to become Chairman of the Congressional Campaign Committee," noted one of them, Henry D. Flood of Virginia, in February 1906. "The outlook for Democratic success has encouraged them to wish to accept this position." With Roosevelt watching from the White House rather than heading the ticket, Democrats hoped that their own claims to reformism might be recognized.[59]

The state and local elections of 1905 had fired party hopes with signal triumphs in major Republican states. Democrats in Ohio, running on a strong progressive program, elected a governor for the first time since 1889. The man responsible for the platform, Tom Johnson, also won his third term as mayor of Cleveland. Pennsylvania, where a Republican machine controlled the cities as well as the countryside, provided a less spectacular but still encouraging victory, as Democrats combined with Republican reformers to elect the state treasurer. The year before, Roosevelt had won the two states by a total of 750,000 votes.

The party's theme on the stump in 1906 would be the same as in Congress: Roosevelt and reform. "The President is at odds with his party on practically every important measure before Congress," claimed James Griggs of Georgia, chairman of the Democratic Congressional Campaign Committee. Voters wanting to support Roosevelt, urged Griggs, should elect Democrats.[60]

The Democrats also looked to another ally. American Federation of Labor president Samuel Gompers, under pressure from the Socialists in the labor movement, had decided to abandon his cherished policy of AFL neutrality in politics. He submitted a Bill of Grievances to

58. Clarence Poe to J. H. Patten (March 12, 1912), Woodrow Wilson Papers, New Jersey State Library, Trenton.

59. Henry Flood to Joseph Button (February 14, 1906), Flood Papers, Library of Congress.

60. *Louisville Courier-Journal* (March 3, 1906).

Roosevelt and Republican congressional leaders, threatening retribution at the polls if the GOP ignored labor's demands. Roosevelt seemed largely unsympathetic, but he could have done little anyway: Cannon had systematically stocked the House Labor Committee with business-minded Republicans. Gompers now had no choice but to raise his standard of revolt, calling upon labor voters to reward their Democratic friends and punish their Republican enemies.[61]

Although Gompers denied any partisanship, promising to support prolabor candidates of both parties, his efforts amounted to a bonus for the Democrats. The party had supported labor's major demand, limitations of strike-breaking court injunctions, since 1896, and allied with Populists, Democrats had once even passed such a bill through the Senate. Even in 1904, when the eastern Clevelandites had named the party's presidential candidate, Alton Parker, the platform had contained a strong labor plank. In the 59th Congress, the only AFL-supported bill to escape the House Labor Committee did so because of a temporary excess of Democrats over Republicans. When the AFL asked congressmen to reply to its Bill of Grievances, most Democrats responded favorably, while Republicans responded heavily in the negative. Indeed, Democratic support for labor, as Robert Wiebe has pointed out, "explained in part the Republicanism of the business community."[62]

Given these circumstances, Democrats considered Gompers's new policy the best thing to happen to them in fifteen years and bestirred themselves to welcome the AFL to politics. Democratic politicians now boasted of their labor record and solicited labor's support. The party's 1906 Campaign Book contained a lengthy section, "Democrats First to Recognize Organized Labor." Gompers responded with warm endorsements for friendly candidates, mostly Democrats.[63]

The party also hoped to gain from an apparent change of attitude

61. Marc Karson, *American Labor Unions and Politics, 1900–1918* (Carbondale: Southern Illinois University Press, 1958), pp. 32–43; *Cleveland Plain Dealer* (March 23, 24, 1906); Janice A. Petterchak, "Conflict of Ideals: Samuel Gompers v. 'Uncle Joe' Cannon," *Journal of the Illinois State Historical Society* (Spring 1981): 31–32. Samuel Gompers to A. J. Weber (September 22, 1916), American Federation of Labor Letterbooks, Library of Congress.

62. John W. Davis, *Reminiscences*, Oral History Research Office, Columbia University, p. 80; Porter and Johnson, *Platforms*, p. 132; *Congressional Record*, Vol. 40, Part 2, p. 1608; *St. Louis Republic* (May 30, 1906); *American Federationist* 13 (September 1906): 643–88; Wiebe, *Businessmen and Reform*, p. 173.

63. Henry Flood to B. M. Fontaine (September 26, 1906), Flood Papers; Francis G. Newlands to Samuel Gompers (October 18, 1906), Newlands Papers; *Democratic Campaign Book* (Washington and Chicago: 1906). See, for example, Gompers to Warren S. Stone (October 10, 1906), AFL Letterbooks.

toward its idol, William Jennings Bryan. Ten years after the mention of his name had caused apoplexy in certain eastern circles, the Nebraskan's candidacy looked like an idea whose time had come. With the recent posturing of Roosevelt and Hearst, Bryan no longer appeared "the most terrifying bogy of politics." Muckraking exposures of the insurance industry had revealed that massive corporate contributions had poured in to defeat him in 1896. His popularity soared, even among old-line Cleveland Democrats, many of whom now endorsed him for 1908. "Mr. Bryan," commented one magazine, "seems now just come to the day of his real public strength."[64]

The object of this affection had been on a lengthy world tour during much of 1905 and 1906, and the process had benefited from his absence. Awaiting his return, nervous Democrats staffed the welcome wagon. They feared that Bryan, who cherished his place in the reform vanguard, would say something to reestablish his cutting edge credentials, especially since his newspaper, the *Commoner*, had started to discuss the idea of government ownership of railroads. No issue would more effectively shatter Bryan's new respectability and revive his reputation as a wild-eyed populist. Senator Bailey, House Minority Leader John Sharp Williams, and other Democrats went to London to head off Bryan and try to talk him into behaving sensibly. But the Commoner had made up his mind, and on such occasions opposition only reinforced his convictions.[65]

Landing in New York, Bryan went from the pier to a welcome home rally at Madison Square Garden, where he unveiled a complicated proposal for state and federal ownership of railroads. Although he desperately tried to explain afterward that he only favored such a program when and if regulation proved inadequate, the political landscape shifted, endangering Bryan's chances in 1908 and the Democrats' chances in 1906. "Within six hours after he had landed at the Battery he had split his party wide open again," commented the *World* acidly. "That was indeed peerless leadership."[66]

Democrats soon had other things to think about when William Randolph Hearst seized the party nomination for governor of New York. Although no one ever really seized anything from Charles Francis Mur-

64. *Collier's* (June 23, 1906); *New York World* (April 9, 1906); *World's Work* (August 1906).

65. *Commoner* (April 6, 1906); Arthur Wallace Dunn, *From Harrison to Harding*, 2 vols. (New York: Putnam's 1922), II:18; Bryan to Charles Bryan (August 28, 1906), Bryan Papers, Occidental College.

66. *Commoner* (September 21, 1906); *New York World* (September 7, 1906).

phy, the quiet, bespectacled boss of Tammany Hall, Hearst wrested the nomination by threatening to run as an independent. As Democratic candidate for governor of New York, the flamboyant publisher presented a fearsome threat to conservatives. Roosevelt, rarely one to maintain perspective in such a situation, assured Hearst's opponent, Charles Evans Hughes, that he was fighting "the battle of civilization," and few Manhattan businessmen disagreed. Hearst strongly supported unions and municipal ownership of utilities and suggested that the proper beginning for trust regulation would be "one law-defying millionaire in jail."[67]

Residence in New York's executive mansion, which had been occupied by five of the last ten Democratic presidential nominees, would give Hearst the clear post position for 1908. Looking ahead, the publisher — not known for underplaying his position — attempted to ensure selection of friendly convention delegations from three other states where he published newspapers. In California and Massachusetts, Hearst's agents organized conventions of his Independence League (IL) and nominated candidates for governor, offering Democrats a choice between ratifying the IL selections or division and defeat. California Democrats defied the erstwhile native son and named their own radical candidate, but the Massachusetts party compliantly nominated the IL (and Prohibitionist) standard bearer. With no state election in Illinois, Hearst could field an IL county ticket only in Chicago. The forty-three-year-old congressman was attempting his own hostile takeover of the national Democratic party.[68]

Bryan, who had his own ideas about party control, also took an active role, campaigning for progressive Democrats in the Midwest and Rocky Mountains. Although he did not appear for Hearst — and there is no evidence that he was asked to — Bryan endorsed his would-be challenger warmly in the *Commoner*.[69] The once and future candidate led his party's effort to grab the coattails of an opposition president. "The best way to stand by the President," Bryan said early in September 1906, "is to elect Democrats to Congress and the Senate, for the Democrats

67. William A. Prendergast, *Reminiscences*, Oral History Research Office, Columbia University, p. 234; Roosevelt to Charles Evans Hughes (October 5, 1906), in *Letters of Theodore Roosevelt*, V:443; *New York World* (September 29, October 21, 1906).

68. George Mowry, *The California Progressives* (Berkeley and Los Angeles: University of California Press, 1951), p. 61; Abrams, *Conservatism in a Progressive Era*, pp. 151, 156; *The Public* (October 13, 1906).

69. William Jennings Bryan to Henry T. Rainey (September 8, 1906), Rainey Papers, Library of Congress; Louis Post to Bryan (August 4, 1906), Post Papers, Library of Congress; *Commoner* (October 26, 1906).

have stood by him far better than the Republicans." Party candidates down the line proclaimed their fidelity to Roosevelt, one congressional hopeful standing "with [Secretary of War William Howard] Taft on the tariff, and with Roosevelt on his square deal policy and reform measures."[70]

Aside from producing "a lifeless campaign," the strategy left Democrats open to counterattack. In response to a request from Speaker of the House Joseph Cannon, Roosevelt made a blanket endorsement of all Republican candidates for Congress. Answering the AFL attack on the speaker, Roosevelt made the extraordinary statement, "It is a simple absurdity to portray him as an enemy of labor." He dealt with Hearst by sending Secretary of State Elihu Root into New York, carrying Roosevelt's curse and reminding voters of McKinley's assassination. Once again, Democrats found themselves in the totally exposed position of supporting a man who spurned their aid.[71]

Others besides Roosevelt took a special interest in the Hearst campaign. All over the country Hearst's effort regularly made the front pages, even of newspapers outside the Hearst chain. The *Cleveland Plain Dealer* compared the widespread anxiety to that of a presidential election. National magazines attacked Hearst frantically, parodying his newspapers and calling him a puppet of his highly paid staff. In early October, Joseph Pulitzer's ocean-going yacht nosed into New York harbor, bringing the *World* publisher home to take personal charge of his newspaper's campaign against its competitor. For the next month, New York's most influential newspaper featured only one lead story — the attack on Hearst.[72]

But Hearst's loss, by 60,000 votes out of 1.5 million cast, resulted less from establishment rage than from Tammany's cutting him off the ticket. He ran so well in upstate cities, however, that he helped elect the rest of the state ticket and presented Governor-elect Hughes with a Democratic lieutenant governor, attorney general, and state controller. Hearst had the same mixed results in his national efforts. His can-

70. *New York World* (September 11, 1906); Agnes Wilson (Secretary of W. B. Wilson) to J. S. Chambers (October 31, 1906), William B. Wilson Papers, Historical Society of Pennsylvania. Secretary of War William Howard Taft was generally thought to favor a lower tariff than most Republican leaders.

71. *New York World* (November 7, 1906); James E. Watson, *As I Knew Them* (Indianapolis: 1936), p. 73; Roosevelt to E. E. Clark (September 5, 1906), in *Letters of Theodore Roosevelt*, V:397; *New York World* (November 2, 1906).

72. *Cleveland Plain Dealer* (November 6, 1906); *Collier's* (October 13, 1906); "Q. P.," "The Hearst Myth," *World's Work* (October 1906); Don C. Seitz, *Joseph Pulitzer, His Life and Letters* (New York: Simon and Schuster, 1926), p. 287.

didate for governor also lost in Massachusetts, but he did succeed in defeating the Democratic nominee in California.[73]

The New York results symbolized the outcome for Democrats across the nation: less than they had hoped for, much more than they had had. The party did not win control of the House but gained more than 30 seats, mostly in the East and Midwest, in the crucial large states that the party would need for a national victory. As the Republican House majority dropped from 112 to 55, Democrats could hope to play a more significant role.

State elections confirmed the pattern of undramatic improvement. Democrats won the New Jersey Assembly, and added governors in North Dakota and Rhode Island, but in most cases their candidates could only point to narrower losses, and voters chose no additional Democratic legislatures to select Democratic U.S. senators. Many party members, however, rejoiced that the Democrats had begun the road back, and Republicans concerned for their own careers did not misread their victory.

Philip R. Vandermeer, in his recent study of Indiana voters, concludes that the 1906 election began a clear shift in that state, challenging the concept of an 1896 realignment that endured until the Depression. Eighty years earlier, Indiana Republican Senator Albert Beveridge had reached a similar conclusion: he examined the 1906 returns and became a tariff reformer.[74]

The Democrats had guessed right on Roosevelt's vote-pulling power but wrong in thinking that they could get a share of it. Observers saw the election as a personal victory for Roosevelt, a perception that limited Democratic discouragement. "No one man, not even Roosevelt," commented the *World* grimly, "can keep a whole party afloat indefinitely." Bryan's speech had clearly hurt the party, and it had suffered through its usual money troubles. Had the Democratic Congressional Campaign Committee collected any substantial money, wrote its secretary, "our candidates would not have asked in vain for assistance."[75]

The party's new ally, the AFL, hardly filled the vacuum, raising only $8225.94 in its crusade to transform the House of Representatives. When Gompers failed to deliver a labor bloc vote, he indignantly de-

73. *New York World* (November 8, 1906); McCormick, *From Realignment to Reform*, pp. 220–27; Abrams, *Conservatism in a Progressive Era*, pp. 151, 159; *Los Angeles Examiner* (November 7, 1906).

74. *New York World* (November 8, 1906); Philip R. Vandermeer, *The Hoosier Voter* (Urbana: University of Illinois Press, 1985), pp. 15–17; Braeman, *Beveridge*, p. 125.

75. *New York World* (November 8, 1906).

nied that he had ever tried to do so. But the AFL and the Democrats decided to maintain the alliance; with the Republicans so closely tied to the business community, they had little choice. Although the AFL, unlike the British labor movement, never formed its own party, or even formally affiliated with one, its fortunes and those of the Democrats would be closely linked after 1906.[76]

"Unquestionably this was a great Democratic year everywhere from New Hampshire to Indian Territory," wired Pulitzer to the *World*. More accurately, it was a great Democratic beginning. Samuel Hays notes that the Democratic wave that elected Woodrow Wilson began gathering in 1906. In that election, and the three immediately following it, the party went in four rising steps from the shambles of 1904 to the national triumph of 1912.[77]

Richard L. McCormick has depicted a sea-change in progressive politics in the 1905–1906 period, when, in response to a wave of muckraking, middle-class voters began to see business as a corrupting force rather than a benign and efficient one. It should not be surprising that such a conceptual shift paralleled a political shift toward the Democrats — who, as Daniel T. Rodgers points out, had already been using the language of oppression for a decade.[78] (Figures 1.1 through 1.3 illustrate the shift on a congressional level.)

The party took a significant step itself in 1905–1906. By supporting Roosevelt's progressive policies, Democrats permanently turned away from the conservative strategy of 1904. By aligning with the AF of L they abandoned attempts to outbid the Republicans for business support. Throughout the country, Democratic state conventions hailed Bryan as their choice for 1908. After a dozen years of fratricide, the Democratic party was united — at least for Democrats — in a progressive, prolabor identity.

Even with their heightened numbers and purpose, the Democrats returning to Washington in December 1907 could expect little opportunity to influence legislation. Nobody expected the 60th Congress, meeting just before the presidential election of 1908, to do anything. The Republican leaders avoided action not only out of conservatism and

---

76. Karson, *American Labor Unions*, p. 45.

77. Joseph Pulitzer to *World* (December 5, 1906), Pulitzer Papers, Library of Congress; Samuel P. Hays, "The Social Analysis of American Political History," *Political Science Quarterly* 80 (September 1965): 368.

78. Richard L. McCormick, "The Discovery that Business Corrupts Politics: A Reappraisal of the Origins of Progressivism," *American Historical Review* 86 (April 1981): 247–74; Daniel T. Rodgers, "In Search of Progressivism," *Reviews in American History* 10 (December 1982): 123.

Figure 1.1 Democrats Elected to the House
of Representatives.

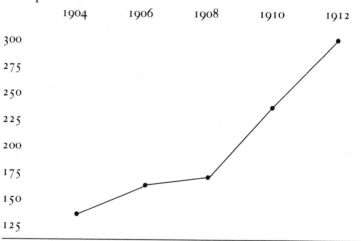

Source: Based on statistics from *Historical Statistics of the United States* (Washington, D.C.: Government Printing Office, 1960), p. 691.
Note: With 1912 election, House increases from 387 members to 435.

Figure 1.2. Democratic Percentage of National Two-Party Vote for Congressional Representatives.

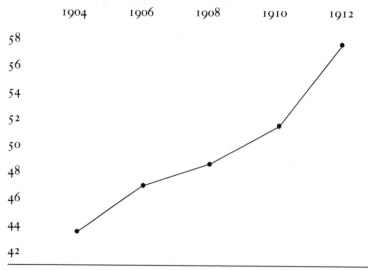

Source: Based on statistics from *Historical Statistics of the United States* (Washington, D.C.: Government Printing Office, 1960), p. 692.

Figure 1.3. Democratic Representatives Elected from New York, New Jersey, Pennsylvania, Ohio, Indiana, and Illinois.

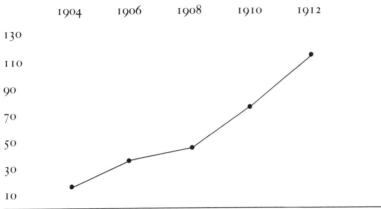

Source: Based on statistics from *Congressional Directory* (Washington, D.C.: Government Printing Office, 1906, 1908, 1909, 1911, 1913).

caution, but also in the comforting knowledge that Theodore Roosevelt had become a self-made lame duck, able to exact no further concessions on their part. Regarding Roosevelt's new reform proposals, his friend, Senator Henry Cabot Lodge, assured a Boston businessman, "Congress will not take any action in those directions, so that nobody need be disturbed."[79]

This attitude, which Cannon and Aldrich did not trouble to conceal, did not prevent Roosevelt from proposing a new reform package, in one message at the opening of Congress and another in late January. The reading of both these communications produced the extraordinary result that was now ordinary: members of the administration party sat on their hands, while opposition congressmen cheered and applauded. But no bill Roosevelt requested reached the floor of the House, and not even Roosevelt could have expected much when he loosed his third salvo at Congress on March 25, after three and a half months of inaction.[80]

This time, however, Minority Leader John Sharp Williams of Mississippi decided to alter the equation. He announced that if the president would provide 29 Republican votes (of 233 in the House), the Demo-

79. Henry Cabot Lodge to H. L. Higginson (November 22, 1907), in Abrams, *Conservatism in a Progressive Era*, p. 167.

80. *Louisville Courier-Journal* (February 2, 1908); Horatio W. Seymour to Joseph Pulitzer (January 25, 1908), Pulitzer Papers, Columbia University.

crats would immediately pass a number of bills he wanted: a railroad employers' liability act, an employers' liability act for federal employees, limitations on labor injunctions, removal of the tariff duties on wood pulp and paper, publication of campaign contributions, and prohibition of child labor in the District of Columbia and territories. Furthermore, he announced, the Democrats regarded these six proposals by Roosevelt as so important that they would attempt to obstruct all House business until the Republican leaders put them up for a vote.[81]

George Mowry calls Williams "the essence of cotton-planting traditionalism." Personally, Williams did resemble something from the 1850s. Short and slight, with a drooping fire-eater mustache and the southern statesman's black frock coat, Williams came unmistakably from planter aristocracy. "He would not be a rich man in New York," wrote a contemporary, "but he is a rich man for Mississippi." To prepare for public service he had studied at the Universities of Virginia and Heidelburg, and his sharp intelligence surmounted even what one party functionary diplomatically called "a weakness for the flowing bowl."[82]

Williams's politics, however, owed little to the past. Besides the traditional southern policy of low tariffs, he called for the dissolution of all trusts, had introduced an income tax bill in every session since 1894, and favored "drastic federal regulations" over interstate corporations.[83]

But despite Williams's classical education and progressive views, he had acquired an impossible job. "Chaos is the best word of description" for the House Democracy since 1896, noted a contemporary journalist. Williams's four immediate predecessors had relinquished the post after one or two sessions, and he himself would soon escape to the Senate, having won the primary the previous summer. Under Mississippi's unique election procedure, the Senate term he had won in 1907 would not begin until 1911, but Williams had already opted to return to Mississippi and rest at the end of his current term. Having survived three sessions as minority leader, Williams had no desire to push his luck.[84]

For one of his problems, he had to look no further than the other Democrat on the Rules Committee, David De Armond of Missouri.

81. *Louisville Courier-Journal* (March 27, 1908).

82. George Mowry, *The Era of Theodore Roosevelt* (New York: Harper Press, 1958), p. 119; Thompson, *Party Leaders*, p. 190; Robert Woolley, "Politics Is Hell," unpublished autobiography, Chapter 13, Woolley Papers, Library of Congress.

83. George C. Osborn, *John Sharp Williams, Planter-Statesman of the Old South* (Gloucester, Mass.: Peter Smith, 1964), pp. 111–12, 214; John Sharp Williams to R. L. East (undated, 1907), Williams Papers, Library of Congress.

84. Thompson, *Party Leaders*, p. 184; *New York World* (December 17, 1907).

The capital's master of "bitter, stinging, savage irony," De Armond hated Republicans, and he hated Williams. The choleric former judge felt that he had a better claim to the minority leadership, and he had forced Williams to campaign for reelection at the start of Congress. Soon afterward, their mutual dislike had erupted into a short but spirited fist fight on the House floor.[85]

Considering his difficulties, Williams had achieved some degree of success as leader, especially when compared to his predecessors. A skilled speaker and debater, he was called by one magazine "about the only man of whom Joe Cannon is afraid." Although sometimes cold, he usually tried to persuade his colleagues rather than browbeat them. Becoming House leader at the same time Gorman stepped up to Senate leadership, Williams took exactly the opposite tack, supporting Roosevelt whenever the president adopted Democratic policies.[86]

Extending his strategy one step further, Williams soon opened a filibuster. On April 2, 1908, Democrats began refusing unanimous consent, demanding roll calls on issues such as accepting the previous day's journal. That day, Williams managed to force eleven roll calls and three teller votes, keeping the House in session until 10:00 P.M., setting a tone for weeks to come.[87]

The minority leader blithely denied that he was conducting a filibuster, a declaration that generally provoked Republican laughter. "A filibusterer in the parlimentary sense," he explained with southern charm and Heidelberg sophistry, "is a man that is engaged in the business of preventing legislation. We have been engaged in the business of trying to force legislation at the hands of the majority."[88]

The House GOP leaders were unpersuaded. The majority, not the minority, would decide which bills to pass, coldly announced Majority Leader Sereno Payne; he advised Democrats not to ask unanimous consent to print anything in the *Congressional Record*. The Committee on Rules now began producing new regulations to gag the filibuster; a "legislative day" could now stretch for weeks, thus limiting procedural motions. In one vote on one new rule, to facilitate closing debate on a bill, Democrats received their only Republican assistance of the

85. Thompson, ibid., p. 214; Watson, *As I Knew Them*, p. 258; W. Bourke Cockran to Williams (November 22, 1907), Cockran Papers, New York Public Library; *St. Louis Republic* (December 20, 1907).

86. *Independent* (December 27, 1908); De Alva S. Alexander, *History and Procedure of the House of Representatives* (Boston: Houghton Mifflin, 1916), p. 208; Thompson, ibid., p. 186.

87. *Congressional Record*, Vol. 42, Part 5, pp. 4324–37.

88. Ibid., p. 4354.

campaign: the votes of two congressmen from Wisconsin, supporters of Senator Robert La Follette, and two other midwestern insurgents.[89]

Williams did not enjoy support from Democratic leaders and some Democratic newspapers, who pointedly urged the country to observe who supported Roosevelt and who did not. Bryan came to Washington to consult, and party journals saluted Williams's "courage and brilliancy," although admitting that he could claim little legislative accomplishment. The filibuster had little to do with the session's passage of either a limited child labor bill or a railroad employers' liability act, and even after Roosevelt unburdened himself of a fourth special message, no other labor bill escaped from either the labor or the judiciary committees. Insurgent Republicans did succeed in bringing injunction limitations up in party caucus, but conservatives voted them down.[90]

Inability to pass a bill providing for publication of campaign contributions particularly frustrated Democrats. "It is not superior political purity" motivating them, commented one magazine. "It is simply that the Republicans have more money."[91]

Conservationists, tariff reformers, and newspaper owners combined to exert heavy pressure to abolish the duties on paper and wood pulp. With an estimated eighty Republicans in favor, a floor vote would pass the bill, so Cannon set up a special committee, from which it was not intended to emerge. Williams, never fearful of histrionics, set up a table in front of the speaker's chair, on which he put a pen, an ink bottle, a blotter, and a discharge petition, signed by every Democrat. No Republican signed the petition.[92]

Despite his lack of legislative achievement, Williams would not abandon the enterprise, even in the face of Republican countermeasures. Speaking on a bill to prevent tea sweepings and tea dust from being used as food, he deplored the attempt to cut off debate on "a bill which in the opinion of the Speaker of the House of Representatives, is the most important that can possibly be considered by the American House of Commons at this time, or else it would not have been given place by him in preference to all others." The bill, he explained, struck him as so important that every representative should be on record on it; thereafter, the Democrats set their record with twelve roll call votes in a day.[93]

89. Ibid., pp. 4326, 4978; Alexander, *History and Procedures of the House*, p. 210.
90. *St. Louis Republic* (March 28, 1908); *New York World* (April 6, 1906); *Louisville Courier-Journal* (April 20, 1908); *Baltimore Sun* (May 22, 1908).
91. *Independent* (May 29, 1908).
92. *Louisville Courier-Journal* (April 10, 1908); *Baltimore Sun* (April 30, 1908).
93. *Congressional Record*, Vol. 42, Part 7, pp. 6211, 6893–47.

"It is a curious situation, to be sure," noted the *Baltimore Sun*, "to find Democrats falling over themselves in their eagerness to carry out the wishes of a Republican President, and Republicans resisting bitterly." The word *curious* understates the case; the strange dance of Roosevelt and the Democrats finds no historic parallel before or after 1908.[94]

Since only Democratic efforts had saved Roosevelt's firm messages from drooping into irrelevance, Democrats might reasonably have hoped for more assistance from the president. Conducting his battle for reform legislation, Williams declared that "unless the President backs down, we will get it." But, one newspaper noted, the president's program "has not been pressed with the old-time vigor and aggressiveness of Mr. Roosevelt." He summoned no congressmen of either party to the White House; he never attempted to threaten the Republican leaders with a Democratic alliance; he certainly never attempted to recruit the thirty Republicans who could have joined with the Democrats to get his bills to the floor and passed.[95]

Roosevelt provided one instance of what he might have done. In a backhanded swipe at the Hepburn Act, House Republican leaders had omitted funds for railroad inspectors in the Sundry Civil Appropriations bill. Roosevelt swiftly put together a coalition of Democrats and administration Republicans, which by a vote of 83 to 78 inserted $350,000 for that purpose.[96]

Even though it led to little legislative accomplishment, the filibuster had its rewards. Williams "has forced the Republican side to repudiate the legislation asked for by a Republican President," noted the *Courier-Journal*. In the spring of an election year, when the Republicans would try to hold power by clinging to Roosevelt, Democrats might find that a useful achievement. And after twelve years in the wilderness of minority irrelevance, House Democrats had found a significant role. "The Democracy is standing solid," reported Williams proudly at the end of the session, "with less division than I ever knew in its ranks, still tending the full Democratic vote of the House."[97]

In Roosevelt's last Congress, as in the preceding one, only Democrats showed much enthusiasm for Roosevelt progressivism. He needed and used their votes for his limited congressional gains and might have gained more had not his partisanship prevented a closer working

---

94. *Baltimore Sun* (April 6, 1908).
95. Ibid. (April 20, 23, 1908).
96. Ibid (May 1, 1908).
97. *Louisville Courier-Journal* (April 20, 1908); *Baltimore Sun* (May 25, 1908).

arrangement. Whatever historical reputation Roosevelt retains as a legislative reformer he owes in good part to the Democrats of his era.

When Roosevelt imposed his will on the question of presidential succession, Democrats braced for more of the same. "So, I shall peg along, if life and health are granted me," wrote a Democratic senator as the Rough Rider's term ended, "helping, as I have with Roosevelt, to save Taft from the hostility of his own party: for knowing his progressive views and realizing the reactionary spirit of his party associates in the Senate, I am sure he will need help."[98]

98. Newlands to James Merriam (December 31, 1908), Newlands Papers, Yale University.

CHAPTER 2

The Election of 1908:
Defeat and Advance

Mark Sullivan, who observed the politics of the Progressive Era for *Collier's*, wondered afterward what would have happened if William Jennings Bryan had been born into a primitive society, "tending to exalt unusual personalities, susceptible to leadership, with a tradition of voices from on high." In such a situation, he implied, the three-time loser might have transcended politics entirely, rising instead to semidivine status.[1] Sullivan's description of the ideal setting for Bryan bears a striking resemblance to the turn-of-the-century Democratic party, which the Peerless Leader dominated as totally as any Rider Haggard heroine. According to a common saying of the time, most Democrats would rather lose with Bryan than win with anyone else. It often seemed that Bryan himself felt the same way.[2]

By 1908, William Jennings Bryan had symbolized reform in America for a dozen years. He could claim primacy in the fight for issues across the progressive horizon, including tariff reform, trust regulation, a federal income tax, labor reform, and direct election of senators. Opponents could call Bryan dangerous but not inconsistent. In 1904, when he could not control the party's nomination, he still managed to put his ideas in the platform. When Roosevelt emerged as a reforming rival, Bryan endorsed his efforts. If their platform satisfied him, he actively supported state candidates, such as Hearst in 1906 and John McLean in Ohio in 1899, who aspired to take the party leadership from him.[3]

Conversely, Bryan considered any disagreement with his policies as treason to reform. He would threaten to drive from the party all who disagreed with him or what he considered a reform issue, even if their stands appeared politically wise. "Win! Win! That's it!" he railed at

---

1. Mark Sullivan, *Our Times* 6 vols. (New York: Charles Scribner's Sons), I:112 n.
2. Paolo Coletta, *William Jennings Bryan, Political Evangelist*, 1909–1915 (Lincoln: University of Nebraska Press, 1964), p. 402.
3. Louis W. Koenig, *Bryan* (New York: Putnam's, 1971), p. 307.

a group of Democratic senators in 1907. "You want to win! You would sacrifice principle for success! I would not." He could see only one motive behind opposition: his attacker must be a tool of the Interests. To the *World*'s constant charge that Bryan had brought the party only disaster, he demanded that Joseph Pulitzer publish his stock portfolio.[4]

Moreover, Bryan worked for reform every day. He "had no other interests or attachments," remembered William Allen White. "He was a Liberal political orator, agitator, statesman . . . eating, walking, sleeping." Bryan neither practiced law, operated a business, nor maintained a farm. He supported himself as a political journalist and as an orator on the Chautauqua circuit, where he discoursed on reform and religion. He could bring in $25,000 in a single summer, and in 1907 at least 300,000 people paid to hear him conduct his perpetual presidential campaign.[5]

Bryan's oratory, which had raised him to political prominence, thus contributed greatly to keeping him there. His voice was "mellow, rather than strong or loud," noted a reporter, "but it has a thrilling quality." Later technicians working with recordings of Bryan's voice found that it contained no bass; it was pure treble, having a unique bell-like quality. But he could address an open-air crowd of 30,000 and without apparent effort be heard in the last row. Bryan's strength as a speaker, however, rested on more than just tonal quality. "Every point he makes is so easy to grasp," grumped a hostile observer, "that unskilled auditors are apt to infer that must be true which has been made so easy to understand."[6]

Besides his oratorial skills and recognized commitment to his cause, Bryan could call on an awesome vitality. Bryan "likes it all," wrote a Washington correspondent, "the early rising, the crowded days, the turmoil, the shouting and applause." He had the enviable ability of falling asleep immediately, rising to address a cheering crowd, and returning to his Pullman car to sleep an hour before the next town. "Living near him is like living near Niagara," commented a fellow Nebraskan, Willa Cather. "The almighty ever-renewed energy of the man drives one to distraction."[7]

4. Arthur Wallace Dunn, *From Harrison to Harding*, 2 vols. (New York: Putnam's, 1922), II:48–49; *Commoner* (February 14, 1908).
5. William Allen White, *Masks in a Pageant* (New York: Macmillan, 1928), p. 264; Edmund Vance Cooke, "Bryan as a Speechmaker," *Collier's* (July 11, 1908).
6. Henry J. Ford, "An Explanation of Mr. Bryan," *World's Work* (May 1908); Boyce House, "Bryan the Orator," *Illinois State Historical Society Journal* 53 (Autumn 1960): 277.
7. Edward G. Lowry, *Washington Close-ups* (Boston and New York: Houghton Mifflin, 1921), p. 34; House, ibid., p. 278; Koenig, *Bryan*, p. 317.

But behind this public Bryan, who has become a historic legend as a one-man reform movement, stood an effective, highly organized mechanism for party control. While the Peerless Leader barnstormed across the country, his younger brother, Charles Wayland Bryan, remained home in Lincoln, running the Bryan machine. The best-known cog in that machine was the *Commoner*, founded by Bryan after the election of 1900. Refusing all liquor and tobacco ads, the weekly newspaper was soon selling 140,000 copies. It employed as many as seventy-five people, and all profits went back into the organization. Bryan used the *Commoner* to praise friends, to chastise enemies, and sometimes to float trial balloons, causing newspapers often to treat the appearance of an issue as a news story. To attract nonpolitical readers, the *Commoner* offered a humor column, poetry, and a women's page, with features such as "Contributed Recipes" and "Keeping Weevils from Peas and Beans."[8]

Charles Bryan controlled another key instrument of political power, three-quarters of a century before it became common: a massive national mailing list of like-minded voters, compiled over a dozen years. To put pressure on a wavering Democratic congressman, the Bryans could put as many as 3000 letters into his district. Charles Bryan once told Colonel Edward House that 500,000 letters a year came into the Lincoln headquarters; House reflected that the volume dwarfed the White House correspondence. By the end of 1907, Charles was busily sending out a mailing of 600,000 urging Democrats to form Bryan Clubs and work to ensure proper delegate selection.[9]

Charles Bryan also served as his brother's closest political advisor, arranging his schedule and managing his money. Totally submerged in his brother's career, he was a more fanatical Bryanite than Bryan. Along with his dogmatism, Charles had a personality as obnoxious as his brother's was magnetic, combining a boorish authoritarianism with a "verbose arrogance." Occasionally, even William found the mixture a little rich. "I am sorry my course is not entirely satisfactory to you," he once wrote his brother coldly, "but I am doing the best I can."[10]

Because of the efforts of both Bryans, William stood in a commanding position as 1908 approached. "Mr. Bryan will be easily nominated,

8. Koenig, ibid., p. 354; Larry G. Osnes, "Charles W. Bryan, 'His Brother's Keeper,' " *Nebraska History* 48 (Spring 1967): 57; *Commoner* (October 7, 1910).

9. Edward M. House Diary (February 9, 1913), House Papers, Yale University; Charles W. Bryan to William Jennings Bryan (June 28, 1909), Bryan Papers, Occidental College.

10. Osnes, "Charles W. Bryan," pp. 51–53; William Jennings Bryan to Charles W. Bryan (undated 1911), Bryan Papers.

and that too without organized opposition," predicted Senate Minority Leader Charles Culberson of Texas in June 1907. Even Democratic politicians unenthusiastic about the front-runner were reluctant to take a stand that could lead to political problems at home. "To be suspected of disloyalty to Bryan in those days," recalled a reporter, "was almost like buying a ticket to private life."[11]

Long before the nomination, Bryan's opponents in the party had begun bowing to the inevitable. "I cannot see," wrote *World* editor Frank Cobb to Joseph Pulitzer, "that the effort to break Bryan's grip on the party has been very successful."[12] The idea of suggesting to Bryan that he withdraw voluntarily seemed no more promising, and there was no rush of volunteers. "He thinks he will be elected," Culberson warned House, "and consequently, if I were you, I would not attempt to dissuade him from the candidacy."[13] Besides, there seemed no reason to suspect anyone else would do better. Although there certainly were Democrats who would never vote for Bryan, at least an equal number would vote for no one else. "If he should withdraw," explained Senator Francis Newlands of Nevada, "it would be felt by his friends that his action was forced, and they would resent it accordingly." Within the party, Bryan was both totem and taboo.[14]

Conscious that 1908 would be his last chance, Bryan now looked beyond the convention to the election. By mid-1907, he was stressing the need for party harmony, a strange text for the firebrand of 1896. He declined an indirect suggestion from William Randolph Hearst that Bryan, Hearst, and Populist leader Tom Watson impose a radical dominion over the Democratic party, but blandly offered to support the defeated publisher, "if he is the choice of the party next year." The *Commoner* loudly assured the party, "Government Ownership Not an Issue" in the coming campaign. Bryan would not compromise his beliefs, but he saw no objection to muting some of them.[15]

In November 1907, Bryan declared himself a candidate and modestly turned aside talk of a voluntary withdrawal; as the *Commoner* explained,

11. Charles Culberson to Edward M. House (June 21, 1907), House Papers; Dunn, *From Harrison to Harding*, II:52.

12. David R. Francis to Henry Watterson (June 8, 1906), Watterson Papers, Library of Congress; Frank Cobb to Joseph Pulitzer (undated 1907), Pulitzer Papers, Columbia University.

13. Culberson to House (November 17, 1907), House Papers.

14. Francis G. Newlands to Henry I. Willey (February 27, 1908), Newlands Papers, Yale University.

15. Koenig, *Bryan*, p. 419; William Jennings Bryan to John Temple Graves (August 9, 1907), Bryan Papers; *Commoner* (July 26, 1907).

"He will not assume to decide the question of his availability." At a Washington banquet two weeks later, he outlined a platform of traditional Democratic issues, noting how Roosevelt had fallen short. Although the president had made some gestures toward an income tax, labor law reform, and railroad and trust regulation, said Bryan, "the Republican leaders do not support the President's position." Roosevelt, he continued, had failed to endorse tariff reform, Philippine independence, or direct election of senators. Bryan offered a platform that was demonstrably more reformist than the Republicans but would not alienate conservative Democrats. He remained in Washington to greet the incoming Democratic congressmen — most of whom, according to one poll, expected his to be the only name presented to the 1908 convention.[16]

Undeterred, the *New York World* began its anti-Bryan campaign early in January 1908 with a series of editorials entitled "16 to 1." The paper aimed to show that the Democracy possessed at least sixteen presidential possibilities besides Bryan, as well as to remind Democrats of Bryan's old, discredited silver policy. Taken together, the *World's* candidates illustrated why Bryan dominated the party. To reach sixteen, Pulitzer had gathered a gallery of unavailables, including southerners, elderly conservatives, unknowns who had once been governors, and Bryanites unlikely to challenge their leader.[17]

But among the sixteen, the *World* and other anti-Bryanites did feel that they had one legitimate candidate. In 1904, John A. Johnson won the governorship of Minnesota due to a Republican split, squeaking through the Roosevelt landslide by 8000 votes. Combining a competent progressive administration with a strong appeal to his fellow Scandinavians, Johnson won an overwhelming reelection in 1906 and became nationally known in his second term when he peacefully settled a miners' strike on the Mesabi Range, after refusing to send troops. Johnson could boast the solid reform record essential for any Democratic aspirant.[18]

To the anti-Bryanites, Johnson seemed the answer to a prayer. The son of immigrants, he had left school at thirteen to help support his family. As the editor of a Democratic newspaper, he had supported

16. *Commoner* (November 15, 1907); *New York World* (November 27, December 2, 1907).
17. *New York World* (January 2, 1908).
18. Winifred G. Helmes, *John A. Johnson, the People's Governor* (Minneapolis: University of Minnesota Press, 1949), pp. 148–62, 170, 197, 222–24. Russel B. Nye, *Midwestern Progressive Politics, 1870–1958* (East Lansing: Michigan State University Press, 1958), p. 230.

Bryan twice, thus fulfilling the Commoner's first requirement for a Democrat—but he had done it unenthusiastically, thus meeting the anti-Bryanites' preference. In a front-page statement in the *World*, he named the traditional Democratic issue of the tariff as the key to the campaign. Called by one magazine "the best-loved public man in the great Northwest," he might bring the Democrats the electoral votes of that section, the prosperous Upper Mississippi Valley that Bryan had never been able to carry. Further, the *World* predicted hopefully that Johnson's immigrant background and "sane" Democracy would be worth 100,000 votes in New York and New Jersey.[19]

The Johnsonians had newspapers, some interested Democratic leaders, and a reasonable case. They lacked only a candidate. When Johnson had made no move by January 1908, Henry Watterson, an early booster, announced, "it is too late. The time has gone by, the psychological moment has passed." As late as the end of February, he held back, unsure of even his own Minnesota delegation. "Poor John A. Johnson," a Pulitzer agent wrote his employer in disgust, "is almost daily thrusting away the Presidency."[20]

He was also thrusting away the torrent of abuse that would engulf any Democrat foolhardy enough to oppose the party's idol. Upon learning of Johnson's ambitions, Bryan was reported to have shaken his head and murmured, "Poor John, poor John." The *Commoner* limited itself to remarking, "Now it must be evident that the Bryan opposition cannot rally very enthusiastically around a man who refuses that honor." But other Bryanites, as soon as Johnson talk began, drew a line from the reform governor to James J. Hill, the nominally Democratic railroad boss of the Northwest, based largely on their mutual residence in Minneapolis. The *Public* announced that Johnson was "generally believed to be a political protege" of Hill. "One thing is certain," Senator Newlands noted; "no man can be nominated who is not progressive."[21]

Neither, given the odds, did it seem worthwhile for Johnson to undergo this purgatory. Bourke Cockran, of Tammany's congressional delegation, wrote Tammany boss Charles Murphy that he had studied the House, "and I am satisfied that there is no likelihood whatever that

19. Helmes, ibid., pp. 6–9, 19, 86–87, 105; *New York World* (January 3, 1908); William Hard, "John Johnson of Minnesota," *American Magazine* (October 1907).

20. *Louisville Courier-Journal* (January 11, 1908); Horatio Seymour to Joseph Pulitzer (February 26, 1908), Pulitzer Papers, Columbia University.

21. Frank A. Day and Theodore Knappen, *Life of John Albert Johnson* (Chicago: Forbes and Co., 1910), p. 167; *Commoner* (January 17, 1908); *The Public* (October 5, 1907); Francis G. Newlands to D. E. W. Williamson (January 20, 1908), Newlands Papers.

Mr. Bryan's nomination can be defeated." Others reached the same conclusion.[22]

But with or without a candidate, with or without a chance of victory, Joseph Pulitzer opened his campaign to save his party from Bryan and a fourth consecutive defeat. After twelve years of the Commoner's leadership, the *World* pointed out, "whole states in the North are without Democratic legislators in Congress, and from the Atlantic to the Pacific, North of the Ohio River, there are but six Democratic governors." The *World* accompanied this blast with "A Map of Bryanism," showing the Democratic party cornered in the South, with Republican black covering the rest of the country. To those who claimed the Commoner's time had come, the newspaper asked one question: what states would Bryan carry now that he had lost in 1896?[23]

But throughout February and March, while Johnson hesitated and the *World* fulminated, state after state instructed its delegates for Bryan. Democratic bosses Roger Sullivan of Chicago and Tom Taggart of Indiana, who had far more to lose than Joseph Pulitzer did, now came to terms with Bryan. Had they not done so, Bryan might easily have captured their delegations out from under them. He conceded nothing for their support and even exacted Sullivan's retirement from the National Committee.[24]

Inexplicably, Johnson now announced his decision to run. No American could refuse a presidential nomination, he declared, adding with unfortunate accuracy, "I have done nothing and will do nothing in the way of organization to bring this about." No groundswell resulted; it seemed the moment had passed. "I wish he could have been persuaded to do it sooner," one editor wrote to Pulitzer. "Evidently he is afraid of Bryan — that is, he is exceedingly careful not to give him offense." But even this modest ambition was doomed to be frustrated when his managers sent out an appeal against "supinely acquiescing in any nomination which guarantees defeat."[25]

Bryan responded with a charge that "Johnson money" had influenced the Michigan convention, and he continued to absorb state delegations. He swept fifty-one of sixty-four delegates elected to the Pennsylvania primary, in a state Johnson had counted on. By early May the

22. W. Bourke Cockran to Charles F. Murphy (February 21, 1908), Cockran Papers.

23. *New York World* (February 4, 1908).

24. Koenig, *Bryan*, p. 426; *Commoner* (April 3, 1908).

25. *Louisville Courier-Journal* (March 28, 1908); Horatio Seymour to Joseph Pulitzer (April 1, 1908); Pulitzer Papers; *Baltimore Sun* (April 6, 1908).

Baltimore Sun conceded, "It looks like Bryan." Only the *World* held out, informing its readers in a Sunday profile, "Feature by feature, the lines of John A. Johnson's face are remarkably like those of Lincoln."[26]

But even as the lopsided race continued, the two sides began to grope toward each other. The *World* began to transfer its fire to Republican front-runner William Howard Taft and Wall Street, and in June, Pulitzer sent editor Frank Cobb a "very confidential" cable, suggesting that he ease up on Bryan, in light of the "distinct possibility" that the paper would end up supporting him. By the end of that month Cobb could report back that attacks on Pulitzer had disappeared from the *Commoner*. Henry Watterson actively championed Bryan's candidacy, and the Peerless Leader solicited his advice on the vice-presidency.[27]

Behind all this unusual Democratic fraternity lay a suspicion that this time the party might just win. The Panic of 1907 had left a considerable recession in its wake. Roosevelt would not be the Republican candidate. And the Democrats thought they knew where they could pick up some additional support.

The American Federation of Labor had also had a bad year. Unfavorable Supreme Court decisions, high unemployment, and the strong antiunion policies of the National Association of Manufacturers had seriously sapped its strength. Entrance into a presidential campaign would be a more traumatic step than endorsing congressional candidates, but the membership demanded "something new, something extraordinary, something spectacular." Bryan may not have been very new, but he represented the federation's only chance.[28]

The Democrats also hoped for their first large inroads into the northern black vote. The intellectual activist, W. E. B. Du Bois, revolting against the Republicanism of Booker T. Washington, endorsed Bryan in March, later proclaiming, "If between two parties who stand on identically the same platform you can prefer the party who perpetrated Brownsville, well and good; but I shall vote for Bryan." (Booker T. Washington remained with Roosevelt's chosen successor, Secretary of War William Howard Taft.) One magazine estimated that there were more than 100,000 black voters in New York, Illinois, and Ohio

26. *Baltimore Sun* (April 18, 1908); *Commoner* (April 24, 1908); *Baltimore Sun* (May 4, 1904); *New York World* (May 17, 1908).

27. Joseph Pulitzer to Frank Cobb (June 1908), and Cobb to Pulitzer (July 1, 1908), Pulitzer Papers, Library of Congress; William Jennings Bryan to Henry Watterson (May 26, 1908), Watterson Papers.

28. R. F. Hoxie, "President Gompers and the Labor Vote," *Journal of Political Economy* 16 (December 1908):693–94.

and 60,000 in the swing state of Indiana. In a close election, black voters, who strongly opposed Taft for the Republican nomination, could make the difference by merely abstaining.[29]

"The labor vote might do it," mused Pulitzer about the chance of a Bryan victory, "and the negro vote and the discontented vote generally and the [un]employed vote particularly all combined might do it. And the *New York World* might do it — in all modesty."[30]

The Republican convention in June made the Democratic claim to the progressive vote look even more promising. Roosevelt did succeed in naming Taft as the GOP nominee, but not even the Rough Rider could see the convention as a forward-looking gathering. "They cheered the reactionary leaders," noted William Allen White. "Joe Cannon was their hero — not Taft." Roosevelt having given no orders about the vice-presidency, the convention happily named Cannon's lieutenant, James ("Sunny Jim") Sherman.[31]

Moreover, the Republicans seemed to have provided the ideal platform for Bryan to run against. Going through the motions of nonpartisanship, Gompers and two AFL vice-presidents dutifully trooped to Chicago to testify before the GOP platform committee. Roosevelt wired the committee urging some concessions to labor, but instead it followed the advice of National Association of Manufacturers President James Van Cleave and refused Gompers anything. La Follette's Wisconsin delegation launched floor fights to try to insert some reform measures into the platform; a resolution calling for popular election of senators lost, 886 to 114; three others, including publicity for campaign contributions, did even less well. A vague pledge to revise the tariff furnished "one of the few progressive spots in the whole platform."[32] "All

---

29. In August 1906, several black soldiers stationed in Brownsville, Texas, allegedly shot up the town, killing a bartender and wounding a policeman. When no trooper either confessed or identified the guilty, Roosevelt cashiered, without trial, three entire companies of black troops. William Henry Harbaugh, *Power and Responsibility, The Life and Times of Theodore Roosevelt* (New York: Farrar, Straus, and Cudahy, 1961), pp. 303–306. Elliott M. Rudwick, *W. E. B. Du Bois* (Philadelphia: University of Pennsylvania Press, 1960), p. 112; Louis R. Harlan, *Booker T. Washington, the Wizard of Tuskegee* (New York and Oxford: Oxford University Press, 1983), pp. 325–34; Francis L. Broderick, *W. E. B. Du Bois* (Stanford: Stanford University Press, 1959), pp. 83–85; *The Public*, (July 17, 1908); *Independent* (August 29, 1907).

30. Pulitzer Notes (July 11, 1908), Pulitzer Papers, Columbia University.

31. William Allen White, *Autobiography* (New York: Macmillan, 1946), p. 401.

32. Robert Wiebe, *Businessmen and Reform: A Study of the Progressive Movement* (Cambridge: Harvard University Press, 1962), p. 110; *The Public* (June 26, 1908); George Mowry, *Theodore Roosevelt and the Progressive Movement* (Madison: University of Wisconsin Press, 1946), p. 31.

the influences against which Roosevelt has pretended to be waging un-compromising war," sneered the *St. Louis Republic*, "are satisfied with the Chicago ticket and platform."[33]

Meanwhile, at the Democratic convention in Denver, Bryan rolled to his inevitable nomination. Opposition leaders tried hopelessly to amass the one-third that would stop him on the first ballot. "Gentle-men, you have not got the votes," pronounced Tammany boss Murphy at a meeting with the Johnson managers. "There seems to be nothing left for New York to do but vote for Bryan."[34]

Even without the votes of New York, Bryan had clearly established himself as national leader of the party, no longer just the candidate of the South and West. He had the solid support of the Ohio Valley; strong and enthusiastic backing from New England; and as a result of its primary, three-quarters of the Pennsylvania delegation. Bryanites, the *Baltimore Sun* commented sourly, now came from all parts of the country.[35]

Bryan now had to select a running mate, and he seemed particularly eager to cement his appeal to labor. Many Democrats, including Chi-cago boss Sullivan, wanted United Mine Workers President John Mitchell, but his repeated and vehement refusals killed the idea. Bryan then turned to federal Judge George Gray of Delaware, a favorite-son candidate who had finished slightly ahead of the luckless Johnson. (Bryan resented Johnson's campaign tactics, and ruled him out.) Gray, Bryan wrote a friend, was the best of "what might be called the Cleve-land Democracy" and had a strong reputation with labor. But Gray, too, refused, and Bryan then asked Murphy for suggestions, hoping to help his chances in New York. Murphy demurred, fearing that he would be held responsible if the ticket lost.[36]

Finally, Bryan named John W. Kern of Indiana, an old-time Bryanite who also was a protege of Indiana boss Taggart. In his last elected of-fice, as Democratic leader of the Indiana Senate, Kern had worked closely with the state Federation of Labor. The nominee, noted one magazine, was a good speaker, a wit, and "the possessor of one pair of the most picturesque whiskers that have ever been brought into American politics."[37]

33. *St. Louis Republic* (June 25, 1908).

34. *Baltimore Sun* (July 7, 1908).

35. *Baltimore Sun* (July 7, 1908); *New York World* (July 11, 1908).

36. *Cleveland Plain Dealer* (July 2, 1908); *Baltimore Sun* (July 1, 1908; July 2, 1908; July 10, 1908); William Jennings Bryan to Louis F. Post (June 30, 1908), Louis F. Post Papers, Library of Congress.

37. Claude G. Bowers, *Life of John W. Kern* (Indianapolis: Hollinbeck Press, 1918), pp.

Kern could only supplement the appeal already explicit in the platform. The Democrats accepted bodily the first six demands of the AFL, including limitations on injunctions, an eight-hour workday on all federal projects, and a separate Department of Labor. All wings of the party agreed on the labor plank; 1904 candidate Alton Parker had represented Gompers in a recent legal case, and Murphy had promised the AFL leader the full support of the New York delegation. Bryan personally contacted Gompers after the convention to make sure that the labor section was acceptable.[38]

The candidate took equal pains with the rest of the platform, careful to alienate no one in the party while staying well to the left of Taft. He personally wrote the Nebraska state platform to serve as a model and spent forty hours on a telegraph line to the Resolutions Committee at Denver. He rejected any single dramatic issue, such as free silver or imperialism, that might excite but also divide Democrats. Instead, the platform and the campaign concentrated on the traditional Democratic progressive issues, reforms that could be supported by all elements of the party: labor issues, tariff reduction, the income tax, and direct election of senators.[39]

Bryan had never rejected the tariff issue, but he had never stressed it. In 1908, however, opposition to high protective rates had forced even the Republicans to insert a tariff revision pledge into their platform. This time, Bryan made tariff reduction not only prominent in the platform, but he also emphasized it during the campaign: one issue of the *Commoner* featured six pages in boldface on the question. In every statement on the tariff, Democrats cited the income tax, a party cause since 1894, as a far more equitable means of raising revenue.[40]

Finally, the platform again featured a plank calling for election of senators by the voters instead of the state legislatures. Democrats expected to make major political gains with the increasingly popular proposal, especially after its overwhelming rejection by the Republican convention. In his acceptance speech, Bryan promised that his first act as president would be to call a special session of Congress to pass the necessary constitutional amendment.[41]

93, 136; Cleveland *Plain Dealer* (June 26, 1908); E. I. Lewis, "John Worth Kern," *Independent* (July 23, 1908).

38. Marc Karson, *American Labor Unions and Politics, 1900–1918* (Carbondale: Southern Illinois University Press, 1958), p. 59; Samuel Gompers, *Seventy Years of Life and Labor*, 2 vols. (New York: 1925), II:263-64.

39. Koenig, *Bryan*, pp. 436-39.

40. *Commoner* (August 21, 1908).

41. *The Public* (June 26, 1908; August 21, 1908).

Bryan moved quickly to strengthen his party consensus, arranging to have some of the hostile delegations stop by Lincoln on their way east from Denver. He praised Johnson to the Minnesota delegation, and in full view of photographers, shook hands with the boss of Tammany Hall, announcing, "I want to thank you, Murphy, for your good work at Denver." Bryan promised Watterson that free silver, government ownership of railroads, and other "issues on which Democrats differ" would have no part in the campaign.[42]

Early returns from Democratic newspapers indicated the success of Bryan's conciliatory policy. Although the *New York Times* could not swallow him this time either, predicting a "veritable reign of terror" for business were he elected, the *Cincinnati Enquirer* and the *Boston Post* came out for the ticket. Herman Ridder, whose *New York Staats-Zeitung*, the country's largest German newspaper, had deserted the party both in 1896 and 1900, came to Lincoln to pay homage. The *World* called the platform "unquestionably a great improvement," and Bryan confidently expected its eventual support. Watterson, guiding spirit behind the 1896 Gold Democrats, took charge of press relations for the campaign.[43]

One Democratic publisher, however, objected to the ticket. William Randolph Hearst had supported Bryan twice without receiving reciprocal aid for his own ambitions in 1904. Bryan's strong support of him in New York in 1906 had failed to mollify the grudge-holding publisher, and the candidate's dismissal of his earlier offer of alliance did not heal the breach. Hearst felt that he possessed the ideal weapon to accomplish two ends: destroy his erstwhile ally and simultaneously advance himself. Since his defeat for the governorship, large amounts of Hearstian energy and cash had been dedicated to maintaining the Independence League. Encouraging showings in the 1907 elections had rewarded his efforts; the IL had won 22 percent of the vote in Massachusetts, and 10 percent in New York state. Hearst clearly intended to name a presidential ticket, but Bryan hoped that the IL would nominate him, just as the Populists had in previous years. Pulitzer, without Bryan's faith in Hearst's underlying sincerity about reform, warned that the IL posed "a distinct danger to democracy in New York and New Jersey."[44]

42. *New York World* (July 12, 1908); Bryan to Watterson (August 4, 1908), Watterson Papers, Library of Congress.

43. *New York Times* (July 10, 1908); *Baltimore Sun* (July 13, 1908); *Cleveland Plain Dealer* (July 13, 1908); *New York World* (July 11, 1908); Bryan to Watterson (August 4, 1908); *Democratic Party Campaign Textbook* (Chicago: 1908), p. 199.

44. Richard M. Abrams, *Conservatism in a Progressive Era* (Cambridge: Harvard University Press, 1964), p. 172; Irwin Yellowitz, *Labor and the Progressive Movement in New York*

Pulitzer had the shrewder insight. Shortly after Bryan's nomination, Hearst cabled from Europe that the Democratic platform was "a sop of false promises," and his agents began preparing for an independent candidacy. They produced a platform slightly stronger than the Democratic but without the older party's opposition to militarism and imperialism. Rather than run himself, Hearst decided to risk the national reputations of Thomas Hisgen, a former IL candidate for governor of Massachusetts, and John Temple Graves, a columnist for the Hearst newspapers. "Hearstism without Hearst," sneered the *Cleveland Plain Dealer*, "cannot be taken seriously," and the Chicago reform magazine, *The Public*, derided the IL as a "privately owned, automatic, count-twenty-and-cheer party."[45]

Democrats tried not to worry about Hearst's defection; everything else looked so promising. Bryan selected a New Yorker, Norman Mack, for national chairman, after clearing it with Tammany Hall. (Because of his hopes for the black vote, he would not select a chairman from the South.) The makeup of the various campaign committees indicated that the Cleveland Democrats were coming home. "The members of the Advisory Committee," noted the *World* approvingly, "are practically all old-line democrats, of national fame, and many of them were not previously identified with Mr. Bryan in his two previous campaigns." Johnson, Parker, Sullivan, Taggart, and Josiah Marvel (Gray's campaign manager) all sat on some campaign committee, and by September, every living member of Cleveland's cabinet had publicly endorsed the Commoner.[46]

Bryan also found an effective means of dramatizing his plea for publication of campaign contributions. He directed the National Committee to announce that all contributions over $100 would be made public on October 15 and daily thereafter. No contributions over $100 would be accepted at all within three days of the election. In what was probably an unnecessary precaution, Bryan proclaimed that he would accept no individual contributions above $10,000. He would rely heavily on small contributions, collected by Democratic newspapers.[47]

State (Ithaca: Cornell University Press, 1965), p. 219; *Commoner* (June 3, 1908); Joseph Pulitzer to Ralph Pulitzer (May 28, 1908), Pulitzer Papers, Library of Congress.

45. *Commoner* (July 24, 1908; August 24, 1908); *Cleveland Plain Dealer* (June 30, 1908), quoted in *The Public* (August 7, 1908); *The Public* (July 31, 1908).

46. *St. Louis Republic* (July 21, 1908); *New York World* (July 25, 1908; August 1, 1908; September 3, 1908); Coletta, *Bryan, Political Evangelist*, p. 423. Not every Clevelandite supported Bryan. Simon B. Buckner, Gold Democratic candidate for vice-president in 1896, denounced him in a long, bitterly sarcastic letter. Buckner to E. A. McMillan, Buckner Papers, Huntington Library, San Marino, California.

47. *Commoner* (July 24, 1908).

The candidate now pulled all the strings together with a superb acceptance speech in early August. Bryan proclaimed "Let the People Rule" as his campaign slogan and repeated his pledge on direct election of senators. He emphasized his commitment to tariff revision and charged that Republicans had not supported Roosevelt's reform efforts. Finally, he restated the irrelevance of silver and government ownership of railroads. "A platform," Bryan stated righteously, "is binding as to what it omits, as well as to what it contains." Even Joseph Pulitzer was impressed, writing wonderingly, "It is a far better statement than I thought he could make."[48]

To supplement their success with old friends, the Democrats appeared to be doing equally well with their new friends of the AFL. The *American Federationist* for August announced to unionists, "Both Parties Have Spoken—Choose Between Them" and made it clear which it recommended. Gompers had formally endorsed Bryan immediately after the convention, and he would campaign for him in six large industrial states. The AFL chief particularly attacked GOP vice-presidential candidate Sherman, charging, "at no time has he either by voice or vote indicated a friendliness toward labor." AFL Vice-President Frank Morrison predicted "the great bulk of the labor vote" would go for Bryan, and 30,000 cheering unionists greeted the candidate in Chicago on Labor Day. Democrats put an endorsement by mine workers' leader John Mitchell at the front of their campaign textbook. Josephus Daniels, head of the Publicity Bureau, harbored "no doubt that the voters in the Federation of Labor are with us."[49]

State Democratic parties provided further encouragement. In Bryan's first two races, obscure or unattractive gubernatorial candidates in key states had dragged down the Democratic vote. Prominent Democrats had been unenthusiastic about his candidacy or unwilling to share his defeat. But in 1908, Bryan could look with satisfaction upon his running mates. In Indiana, the party enthusiastically named Thomas Marshall, an effective orator who had stood outside previous party battles. Cleveland Mayor Tom Johnson and the Ohio Bryanites had originally objected to the designation of Judson Harmon, Cleveland's last attorney general, but supported him after he accepted the progressive

48. *Democratic Campaign Textbook*, pp. 236–43; Pulitzer to Cobb (August 10, 1908), Pulitzer Papers, Library of Congress.

49. *American Federationist* (August 1908): 598; Karson, *American Labor Unions*, p. 60; Samuel Gompers to E. J. Shin (September 12, 1908), American Federation of Labor Letterbooks, Library of Congress; *St. Louis Republic* (August 27, 1908); *New York World* (September 8, 1908); *Democratic Campaign Textbook*, p. 4; Josephus Daniels to Addie Daniels (August 17, 1908), Daniels Papers, Library of Congress.

state platform. New York Democrats had a ready-made candidate in Lieutenant Governor Lewis Chanler, and Illinois Democrats dusted off their party icon, Cleveland's vice-president (and Bryan's 1900 running mate) Adlai Stevenson. Johnson refused to run again in Minnesota but relented after the state convention nominated him and adjourned.[50]

Across the nation, Bryanites and anti-Bryanites arrived at their own version of the Denver truce. "From 1896 to 1908 the Democratic party in Indiana had been torn into factions," wrote Marshall in words which could have applied to most states. "It was a somewhat difficult thing to find a man who was a Democrat — just a plain, unadorned, unterrified Democrat. You could find Jackson Democrats, Jefferson Democrats, Parker Democrats, and Bryan Democrats; the party was a party of hyphenated Democrats." Whatever the outcome of the election, erasing the hyphens marked a Democratic turning point.[51]

Early votes bolstered Democratic confidence. Republicans retained the governorship in Maine by only 7000 votes, far below the traditional GOP danger line. Five standpat Republican senators lost in primaries, although a Democrat would succeed only one of them. "The voice of the people is unmistakeable," explained the *Democratic Campaign Textbook*. "Whenever they have had a chance to speak, they have earnestly lifted their voices, saying: WE WANT A CHANGE!"[52]

By mid-September, even some Republicans had started to think that Bryan was about to break his jinx. "The Bryan 'scare' is on," Frank Cobb wired his boss. Louis Brandeis noted "quite a little uneasiness in Republican ranks East about the campaign." Taft, who had been planning a McKinleyesque front-porch campaign, now decided to go out campaigning, repeating the Republican themes of prosperity and Roosevelt. The spirit even infected anti-Bryan Democrats; Congressman Henry Flood of Virginia, who had predicted in June that Bryan would carry only the South and a few mountain states, now predicted Bryan's election. Uneasiness pervaded even Theodore Roosevelt's White House. "Bryan is making a wonderful campaign, and the Republicans are very anxious," observed Archie Butt, his military aide. "Mr. Roosevelt is the only person who can save the day."[53]

50. Clifton J. Phillips, *Indiana in Transition* (Indianapolis: Indiana Historical Bureau and Indiana Historical Society, 1968), pp. 93, 101; Hoyt L. Warner, *Progressivism in Ohio* (Columbus: Ohio State University Press, 1964), p. 215; Helmes, *Johnson*, pp. 270–75.

51. Thomas R. Marshall, *Recollections* (Indianapolis: 1925), p. 159.

52. *New York World* (September 14, 1908); *Democratic Campaign Textbook*, p. 3.

53. Cobb to Pulitzer (September 19, 1908), Pulitzer papers, Columbia University; Louis Brandeis to Alfred Brandeis (September 20, 1908), in Melvin I. Urofsky and David W. Levy, eds., *Letters of Louis D. Brandeis*, 4 vols. (Albany: State University of New York

An unlikely source now gave TR the chance to come to the rescue. Campaigning for the IL ticket, with the nominal candidates as curtain raisers, Hearst began releasing "the Archbold letters," stolen from a Standard Oil executive years before. The letters detailed political and in some cases financial ties between Standard Oil and various politicians, including Governor Charles Haskell of Oklahoma, treasurer of the Democratic National Committee. Hoping to deflect some votes to his own party, Hearst now began a sustained attack on Bryan in his newspapers, calling him "the Oil Trust candidate supported in the campaign by Oil Trust funds." He bludgeoned Gompers so viciously that the AFL chief contacted his attorneys about the possibility of a libel suit.[54]

But Hearst's direct assault hurt Bryan less than the opening it afforded Roosevelt. Once again, Bryan and the Democrats had left themselves open for such an attack by refusing to criticize the Rough Rider directly. Again and again, Bryan had condemned the Republicans for insufficient support of the president, ignoring the constant demands of the *World* that he take on the White House, as well as its warnings of the inevitable blow from that direction. "Both Taft and Bryan are trying to convince the people that each is better fitted to carry out the Roosevelt policies," noted Archie Butt. "That seems to be the only issue."[55]

With the release of the first letters, Roosevelt issued his first blast of the campaign. "Governor Haskell stands high in the councils of Mr. Bryan," he charged, which "casts a curious sidelight on the attacks made upon this Administration" by the Democrats. Although Bryan had despatched Josephus Daniels to procure Haskell's resignation, publicly he placed himself behind his treasurer. He demanded that Roosevelt substantiate Hearst's charges. "Bryan," mourned Frank Cobb, "being a plain damned fool, felt called upon to defend Haskell."[56]

Roosevelt seized this new chance in an open letter that must have caused all Democrats, even Bryan, to regret that the subject had been

Press, 1971–1975), II:207; Horatio Seymour to Pulitzer (September 7, 1908), Pulitzer Papers, Columbia University; Henry D. Flood to John H. Flood (June 24, 1908); Henry D. Flood to W. C. Warre (September 22, 1908), Flood Papers, Library of Congress; Lawrence F. Abbott, ed., *The Letters of Archie Butt* (Garden City: Doubleday and Co., 1924), p. 95.

54. *Los Angeles Examiner* (October 14, 1908; November 2, 1908); Gompers to Ralston and Siddons (November 5, 1908), AFL Letterbooks.

55. *New York World* (September 14, 1908); Abbott, *Letters of Archie Butt*, p. 96.

56. *New York Times* (September 22, 1908); Bryan to Daniels (undated, September 1908), Daniels Papers, Library of Congress; Cobb to Pulitzer (September 26, 1908), Pulitzer papers, Columbia University.

aired. "I regard it as a scandal and a disgrace that Governor Haskell should be connected with the management of any national campaign," he thundered virtuously, citing the Standard Oil letters and throwing in some other charges for good measure. As for Haskell's sponsor, Roosevelt termed Bryan impractical and extremist, a man whose current platform should be placed next to his demands for free silver and government ownership of railroads. "Let me repeat that no law-defying corporation has anything to fear from you," he sneered at the Commoner, "save what it would suffer in the general paralysis of business" that a Bryan victory would bring. "Bryan gave me a bully good chance to hit him," TR wrote smugly to Taft, "and I think I have hit him to some purpose."[57]

Incredibly, Bryan now wrote Roosevelt a second open letter, charging him with using the presidency for partisan purposes and convicting Haskell without a trial. Roosevelt responded with an eloquent defense of his own administration and a long, detailed account of the charges against Haskell. "Of all corruption," he wrote, "the most far-reaching for evil is that which hides itself behind the mask of furious demagogy." Haskellism, he informed Bryan, "was the natural result of the effort to apply in practice your teachings." Not even Bryan's capacity for this kind of punishment was unlimited. He announced that he might reply to Roosevelt in a speech sometime. Roosevelt, enormously pleased with himself, now proposed to "lapse into a condition of innocuous desuetude."[58]

The Democratic campaign never recovered. In the middle of October 1908, Charles Bryan wrote frantically from Nebraska, demanding that Democratic newspapers attack Roosevelt and Hearst together. Bryan tried to establish government insurance of bank deposits as a vote-getting issue, but that idea's time would not come for another twenty-five years. In Bryan's previous campaigns, he had identified himself totally with a single issue: silver in 1896, and anti-imperialism in 1900. But the *World* now noted a "complete absence of an issue of general value or vote-getting potency." In such a situation, voters might just follow the lead of Theodore Roosevelt.[59]

57. Theordore Roosevelt to William Jennings Bryan (September 23, 1908), in *Letters of Theodore Roosevelt*, VII:1252; Roosevelt to William Howard Taft (September 24, 1908), in ibid., VII:1255.

58. Roosevelt to Bryan (September 27, 1908), in ibid., VII:1268; Roosevelt to Taft (September 28, 1908), in ibid., VII:1268; *New York Times* (September 28, 1908).

59. Charles W. Bryan to Norman Mack (October 16, 1908), Elections File, Josephus Daniels Papers, Library of Congress; *New York World* (October 18, 1908).

For the third time in three campaigns, Bryan also faced the problem of campaign financing. "The Democratic party has never lost a Presidential campaign," its treasurer would tell a Senate committee in 1920, "where their campaign has not collapsed from a lack of finances." Josephus Daniels, busily creating publicity that the party could not afford to distribute, unhappily wrote in September, "the problem in this campaign is money." When, as promised, the Democratic books were opened to the public on October 15, they revealed the embarrassing total of only $248,567.55.[60]

Although this amount more than doubled (to $620,644) in the three weeks before the election, it still fell a million dollars short of the Republican total of $1,655,518. Republican contributions included $110,000 from the candidate's half-brother, Cincinnati capitalist Charles P. Taft; $55,000 raised at the Philadelphia Union League Club; and $30,000 from J. P. Morgan. Such donations, explained Senator-railroad chairman Chaucey Depew, were "like taking out an insurance policy." The GOP's success in selling insurance enabled it to pour money into doubtful states, pumping $284,000 into New York and $61,000 into Indiana.[61]

The detailed Democratic accounting revealed the unsurprising fact that the Democratic party—or at least Bryan—simply lacked wealthy contributors. Herman Ridder, named treasurer after Haskell's departure, combined with his sons to give $37,000. Fewer than ten other donations exceeded $1,000. Bryan had succeeded in financing his campaign from small instead of large donations; 74,000 contributions made up the Democratic fund, whereas only 12,300 donors filled the far heavier Republican strongbox.[62]

Despite their revelation of poverty, the party's accounts demonstrated Bryan's achievement in unifying the party. Tammany Hall gave the maximum, $10,000, and most of the $1,000 gifts came from well-heeled Democratic politicians. Bryan stressed this unity in his campaign, consulting with Sullivan in Chicago, campaigning in New York with Parker and David B. Hill, the gold leader of the 1896 convention. The Democrats regularly trotted out Cleveland's cabinet members and held the major Democratic newspapers—except the *Baltimore Sun*,

60. Testimony of Wilbur Marsh, *Hearings before a Subcommittee of the Committee on Privileges and Elections, U.S. Senate*, 2 vols. (Washington: 1921), I:537; Josephus Daniels to Addie Daniels (September 22, 1908); *New York World* (October 16, 1908).

61. *Testimony before a Subcommittee of the Committee on Privileges and Elections, U.S. Senate*, 2 vols. (Washington: 1912), I:62, 79, 450, 628; Louis Overacker, *Money in Elections* (New York: Macmillan, 1932), p. 73.

62. *Testimony*, ibid., I:63; Overacker, ibid., p. 132.

which was thought to have taken Maryland into the Republican column with it. For the first time since 1894, observed Cobb, the party was united.[63]

With little money and no paramount issue, Bryan relied heavily on the unknown quantity of the AFL. He met frequently with Gompers and detailed Kern to concentrate on the labor issues in his speeches. Bryan neglected his own strongholds in the mountain states and the plains to center his personal campaign in New York and the Ohio Valley, where labor should have been most potent. He emphasized labor questions increasingly as the campaign ended, denouncing the GOP in his election eve speech as "the open foe of labor."[64]

The AFL leaders mounted an equal effort. Gompers campaigned actively, and John Mitchell of the miners' union issued a strong endorsement on November 1. The *American Federationist*, the AFL's official magazine, denounced the Independence League as "Mr. Hearst's Political Toy" and the Socialist candidate as "Debs, the Apostle of Failure" and came out with a special election edition. Such activities gave Democrats their only hope: "If the labor vote is as good as it looks," Daniels wrote hopefully, "Bryan will carry [Illinois] and be elected."[65]

But, on November 3, Taft beat Bryan more decisively than McKinley ever had. The three-time loser received fewer electoral votes, fewer popular votes, and a smaller percentage of the vote than in either of his previous outings. He carried only the South, three mountain states, Kentucky and Oklahoma, and his home state of Nebraska. Very narrowly, he lost even Missouri and Maryland. Although he ran more than a million votes ahead of Parker's 1904 performance, he lost New York, the linchpin of his strategy, by even more than the hapless jurist had.[66]

The result stunned Bryan, who had apparently expected victory. "I can't understand how we were so badly beaten," he confided to a close friend three days after the election. "Am not yet able to measure the relative influences of various causes." The *Commoner* dubbed the result "The Mystery of 1908," claiming "neither political managers nor writers, neither candidates nor counsellors foresaw the result." (This was

63. *Commoner* (October 23, 1908; October 30, 1908); *St. Louis Republic* (October 20, 1908); *New York World* (October 21, 1908; October 29, 1908); *Baltimore Sun* (October 7, 1908); Cobb to Pulitzer (October 22, 1908), Pulitzer Papers, Columbia University.

64. Karson, *American Labor Unions*, p. 62; Bowers, *Kern*, pp. 182–83; Coletta, *Bryan, Political Evangelist*, p. 428; *Rocky Mountain News* (November 3, 1908).

65. *Louisville Courier-Journal* (November 2, 1908); *American Federationist* (September 1908): 734, 736; Special Edition (November 1908); Josephus Daniels to Addie Daniels (October 27, 1908), Daniels Papers.

66. *New York World* (November 4, 1908).

somewhat disingenuous; Bryanites had known of unfavorable polls but chose to disbelieve them.) Brother Charles immediately began sending out letters, asking Democrats across the country what had gone wrong.[67]

Bryan felt he knew one reason at the outset. "He lost heavily in many of the larger cities," noted the *Commoner*, "the democratic vote being out in a surprising and unprecedented manner." The candidate's massive defeat in New York stemmed largely from his extraordinary feat, for a Democrat, of losing New York City, which even he had won in 1900. His loss of Baltimore cost him Maryland, and he came within a few hundred votes of losing even Boston. Bryan saw only one explanation: the bosses had again played him false. If Tammany was not treacherous, charged the *Commoner*, then it was too weak to be of any use.[68]

If the first explanation of Bryan's fiasco was aggravating, the second was embarrassing to all concerned. "There is in America today no labor vote," one observer stated flatly. Both Bryan and Gompers maintained staunchly that the AFL–Democratic alliance had achieved a great deal, and both agreed that only coercion and intimidation by employers had prevented greater success. Yet, however understandingly the two partners treated each other, the votes had simply not materialized. Gompers had run up against his own long-standing tradition of nonpartisanship; the worker, explained an observer, resented the idea that "someone in authority is trying to deliver his vote." Moreover, during the long years of AFL neutrality, local union leaders had formed their own alliances. The entire effort, sneered one writer, was "Mr. Gompers' latest failure."[69]

Yet, more likely neither Gompers nor Tammany were guilty of failure or betrayal; Bryan simply did not appeal to their constituencies. Both the AFL and the urban Democratic vote were heavily Catholic and largely Irish. Such voters had never liked the evangelical Bryan, who exuded missionary Protestant rural attitudes. In past races, he had found this enmity a disagreeable fact of life. But in 1908, the identity of the Republican candidate made the situation far more serious. Taft was enormously popular among Catholics, having dealt generously

67. William Jennings Bryan to Louis F. Post (November 6, 1908), Louis F Post Papers, Library of Congress; *Commoner* (November 13, 1908); Thomas J. Pence to Josephus Daniels (October 27, 1908), Daniels Papers.

68. *Commoner* (November 6, 1908; November 20, 1908); *New York World* (November 4, 1908); *Baltimore Sun* (November 4, 1908; November 5, 1908); Abrams, *Conservatism in a Progressive Era*, p. 186.

69. Hoxie, "President Gompers and the Labor Vote," pp. 693, 697, 699, 700.

with the church as governor-general of the Philippines. Catholic voters, who recalled with anger and apprehension the hostile American Protective Association of the 1890s, appreciated such official cordiality. The missing votes had clearly gone to Taft. Hearst's ticket polled fewer than 100,000 votes, and Eugene Debs and the Socialists registered virtually no gain over 1904.[70]

Bryan had perceived the danger in the situation early. "The Republicans are making an effort to reach our Catholic Democrats," he nervously wrote Watterson in August. "I should not be surprised if we lost a little in this direction." Taft, he admitted to an admirer, was far stronger than his party among Catholics. By the end of the campaign, Treasurer Ridder, a prominent Catholic himself, was warning Bryan of problems among his coreligionists.[71]

Bryan, for obvious political reasons, never publicly suggested religious voting as a cause of his defeat. But in response to his request for explanations, Bryanites deluged him with accounts of Catholic desertions, in letters ranging from the analytical to the scurrilous. A correspondent from South Bend, Indiana, blamed Catholics for Bryan's narrow loss of the state: "You gained from 25 to 150 votes in every precinct in the country inhabited by Americans." Not only Democrats noticed the phenomenon; at one low point in his administration, Taft told Archie Butt that the Catholics had elected him in 1908, and they would do it again.[72]

Nor could Bryan blame his allies for other weaknesses in the Democratic appeal. To AFL members, whom Gompers had taught to consider themselves middle-class entrepreneurs, Bryan's labor policy did not efface his Populist reputation, whereas to businessmen, the AFL alliance reconfirmed his perniciousness. Besides Roosevelt's enormous popularity, Taft was also heir to the Republican connection with stability and prosperity that had bolstered the GOP majority status since 1894. "Doubtless," conceded Newlands, "cowardice regarding future business conditions prevented many from voting for Mr. Bryan."[73]

70. Karson, *American Labor Unions*, p. 221; Koenig, *Bryan*, p. 448; *New York Times* (November 5, 1908).

71. Bryan to Watterson (August 17, 1908), Watterson Papers, Library of Congress; Charles Weidler to Bryan (November 5, 1908), Bryan Papers, Library of Congress; Herman Ridder to Josephus Daniels (October 26, 1908), Daniels Papers.

72. Charles Weidler to Bryan (November 5, 1908), Bryan Papers, Library of Congress; Archibald Butt, *Taft and Roosevelt*, 2 vols. (Garden City: Doubleday, Doran and Co., 1930), II:757.

73. Karson, *American Labor Unions*, p. 66; Louis F. Post to Bryan (November 12, 1908), Louis F. Post Papers; Judson Harmon to Henry T. Rainey (November 15, 1908), Henry T. Rainey Papers, Library of Congress; Newlands to Edward E. Can (November 6, 1908), Newlands Papers.

Another projected Democratic gain, the hoped-for defection of black voters, never appeared either. Bryan had done little enough to encourage blacks to vote Democratic, and the young blacks urging the bolt, such as W. E. B. Du Bois and William Monroe Trotter, simply lacked the credibility to compete with Booker T. Washington and the historic black connections with the GOP on a national and local basis. Facing what Louis R. Harlan calls "a choice between the party of hypocrisy and the party of outright racism," blacks voted overwhelmingly for Taft.[74]

Finally, Bryan suffered from what the *World* angrily described as "the stupendous folly of posing as Roosevelt's heir." Although it was perfectly true for the Democrats to claim, as Bryan often did, that they had provided TR's major support, truth is not always the best offense. The policy again left the party wide open for an attack like the Roosevelt-Bryan correspondence, in which the president refused the Democrats any character reference at all, providing them instead with what the *World* called "the official assurance that they are unfit to be entrusted with power." Between two parties claiming to be Roosevelt's true heir, the voters logically chose the one named in the will.[75]

Bryan had led the party to its fourth consecutive defeat. Yet Democrats — except perhaps for Bryan himself — could find some comfort in the returns. For the first time since 1892, Democratic state victories had raised up potential national leaders. Although Taft swept his native Ohio, Judson Harmon won the statehouse by 19,000 votes. Although Bryan lost Indiana, Thomas Marshall nosed into the governorship, financing his own campaign on a broad reform platform. In Minnesota, Johnson turned an 86,000-vote Taft presidential majority into a 25,000-vote victory for himself. In New York, Illinois, and Michigan, Democratic candidates ran 50,000 to 100,000 votes ahead of the top of the ticket. Suddenly, the party had three plausible presidential candidates and a new vitality throughout the North. "Tuesday's election was a Bryan disaster," crowed the *World*, "rather than a Democratic disaster."[76]

Pulitzer's newspaper, which had proclaimed the inevitability of Bryan's defeat until his nomination, may have been entitled to gloat, but it had missed the point. Admittedly, the election had revealed hun-

74. Broderick, *W. E. B. Du Bois*, p. 85; Harlan, *Booker T. Washington, the Wizard of Tuskegee*, p. 337.

75. *New York World* (November 4, 1908; September 23, 1908).

76. *New York World* (November 5, 1908); *St. Louis Republic* (November 5, 1908).

dreds of thousands of voters who would vote for a Democratic candidate but not for Bryan. But the election of 1904 had shown hundreds of thousands of Democrats who would vote for Bryan and nobody else. "Bryan's return to leadership was very inspiring to the Democrats," recalled James Cox, the party's presidential candidate in 1920, who first went to Congress in 1908. "It was a factor in our carrying Ohio for the state ticket." If Bryan could not poll the full Democratic vote himself, he could, in the absence of an open party split, bring many votes to candidates below him on the ticket. Democrats who boasted that winning local candidates had run far ahead of Bryan failed to note that local candidates had also run far ahead of Parker—and far behind their Republican opponents.[77]

Similarly, Democrats rejoiced in a small but pleasant gain in Congress, mostly in the Ohio Valley. Picking up approximately ten seats, the party cut the GOP majority in the House to less than fifty. It even added two new northern senators, one from Indiana and another from Oregon—"the first gains in ever so long." When the total Republican congressional vote was compared with Taft's tally, predicted *Collier's*, "the results will speak plainly the country's discontent with the Republican Congress."[78]

An obscure representative named James Lloyd of Missouri could claim some credit for the party's congressional showing. Lloyd, the House Democratic whip, had refused the chairmanship of the Congressional Campaign Committee two years before. But he accepted in 1908 and soon made clear his intention to make some organizational changes. A staunch Bryanite who had once introduced a constitutional amendment limiting personal wealth to $10 million, Lloyd established his headquarters in Chicago, away from perfidious Wall Street. As financial chairman, he named Henry Flood of Virginia, an anti-Bryanite who had opposed him for the chairmanship, with the expectation that Flood would assess wealthy conservative Democrats. Although Lloyd actually amassed only $27,500—less than half the fund of his Republican counterpart—the fund still enabled him to offer some help to Democrats with reelection problems, and to dispense information and encouragement throughout the campaign.[79]

---

77. James M. Cox, *Journey through My Years* (New York: Simon and Schuster, 1946), p. 57.

78. Pulitzer to Cobb (November 6, 1908), Pulitzer Papers, Library of Congress; *Collier's* (December 19, 1908).

79. *St. Louis Republic* (December 3, 1905; February 22, 1906; February 25, 1906; February 4, 1908; February 8, 1908; April 19, 1908); *Baltimore Sun* (June 26, 1908); Lloyd

"A party that elects Governors in three major northern states, in the face of large majorities for the Republican Presidential candidate," admitted the *Independent*, which had endorsed Taft, "and that also at the same time reduces the Republican majority in the House, is very much alive." In the White House, Theodore Roosevelt uneasily noted the increase in Democratic strength. Nobody but Taft, he told the president-elect, could have won at all.[80]

Lloyd, Marshall, and Harmon had all had a unique advantage for Democratic campaigners — a united party. This odd amity carried over into the post-election period, which was singularly free of recriminations, aside from Bryan's obligatory shot at Tammany Hall. Bryanite congressman Henry Rainey of Illinois felt that the party was in its best shape in sixteen years; the editor of Pulitzer's *St. Louis Post-Dispatch* diagnosed "a better and more harmonious condition than it has been in since Cleveland's first term." Bryan's performance in unifying and strengthening the party in 1908 was an essential prelude to the Democratic victory in 1912.[81]

Both elements in the party saw reason for rejoicing. Bryanites saw the triumph of their issues if not their candidate. The *Rocky Mountain News* proclaimed that Bryan, though defeated, would rank with Washington and Lincoln; Senator Thomas P. Gore of Oklahoma claimed a "moral victory." Unlike the response to Bryan's second defeat in 1900, there was no widespread cry for reorganization of the party, for a return to "sound" Cleveland principles. When the Democrats finally took power, they brought Bryan's issues of 1908 with them. The Sixteenth and Seventeenth Amendments, the Underwood Tariff, and the Wilsonian labor laws stand as the least ambiguous reform achievements of the Progressive Era.[82]

The anti-Bryanites were also satisfied. With Bryan's third defeat, he could not hope to run again. Still, after twelve years of his domination of the party, they could not hope to name a candidate in 1912 who would be anti-Bryan. It would be enough if he were not Bryan.

to Henry Flood (June 13, 1908; November 1, 1908); *Testimony*, pp. 106, 110; Lloyd to William B. Wilson (September 12, 1908), Wilson Papers, Historical Society of Pennsylvania.

80. *Independent* (November 19, 1908); Roosevelt to Taft (November 20, 1908), in *Letters of Theodore Roosevelt*, VII:1340.

81. Rainey to Bryan (November 6, 1908), Bryan Papers; Horatio Seymour to Pulitzer (November 14, 1908), Pulitzer Papers, Columbia University.

82. *Rocky Mountain News* (November 4, 1908); Thomas P. Gore to Bryan (November 23, 1908), Bryan Papers.

CHAPTER 3

Democrats and Insurgents

Despite their bolstered strength and unity, and the long-awaited departure of their grinning antagonist, the Democrats found themselves upstaged almost from the moment the spring 1909 special session of Congress met. A floating coalition of insurgent Republicans, symbolized by the Democrats' old ally, Robert La Follette of Wisconsin, had captured the imagination of contemporary journalists. The eloquent midwesterners, rebelling against their party's power structure, seemed to have a far greater appeal than the Democrats, disdained by the middle-class reformers of the mass-circulation magazines.

The insurgents have remained the main attraction with historians as well. Thomas Dreier entitled his 1910 study of the rebellious group *Heroes of Insurgency*, and several later writers followed in his spirit and very nearly his terminology. In 1940, Kenneth J. Hechler provided a highly favorable portrait in *Insurgency*, and Russel Nye's *Midwestern Progressive Politics* offered a sympathetic portrayal in the 1950s. Not until James L. Holt's *Congressional Insurgents and the Party System*, in 1967, was there a critical discussion of the limitations of the insurgents' ideas and political strategies.[1]

The insurgents have done at least as well in biographical studies. La Follette, notes Gabriel Kolko, "has been spared the sort of comprehensive challenge to his reform and liberal reputation that Roosevelt and Wilson have been exposed to." The most recent biography, by David Thelen, spares him further. Richard Lowitt provides a strongly positive study of George Norris, further advancing the reputation developed in two previous biographies, *Integrity* and *Democracy's Norris*. Albert Beveridge, William Borah, Jonathan Dolliver, Joseph L. Bristow, and Irvine

---

1. Thomas Dreier, *Heroes of Insurgency* (Boston: Human Life Publishing Company, 1910); Kenneth W. Hechler, *Insurgency* (New York: Columbia University Press, 1940); Russel B. Nye, *Midwestern Progressive Politics* (East Lansing: Michigan State University Press, 1951); James L. Holt, *Congressional Insurgents and the Party System* (Cambridge: Harvard University Press, 1967).

Lenroot have all found generally laudatory biographers, with Howard Allen's study of Miles Poindexter a rare critical exception.[2]

Even some historians dubious about the entire progressive movement have found the insurgents the best of the lot. Kolko, although portraying La Follette as the foe of Wisconsin Socialists and a man of dim economic comprehension, conceded that he "spoke with indignation and passion for the cause of the small farmers and businessmen." James Weinstein found La Follette and the insurgents one of only two pockets of genuine radicalism in the Progressive Era, and their leader one "who consistently and courageously attacked special privileges."[3]

The insurgents first appeared as a major force during the special session of Congress in the spring and summer of 1909, called by William Howard Taft to revise the tariff. The high protective tariff rates set during William McKinley's administration had begun to stir opposition not only from Democrats, but also from others, who blamed the tariff for the rising cost of living and for fattening corporate profits. Demand for a revision had forced the Republicans to include such a pledge in their 1908 platform. The tariff, they told voters, should be revised by its friends, not by its enemies.

To many midwestern and western Republicans, partly inspired by the rhetoric of Theodore Roosevelt, the tariff provided the perfect example of the alliance between the congressional leadership of their party and corporate capital, especially eastern corporate capital. In Congress, and especially in the Senate, the reopening of the tariff issue would reveal the extent of the Republican party's divisions — especially in the absence of Roosevelt's genius for balancing both sides.

"We are in good shape in the House," wrote a Democratic congressman to William Jennings Bryan at the end of 1908, "and we are going to put the Republicans to the test in the next Congress." The outlook

2. Gabriel Kolko, *The Trimph of Conservatism* (New York: Free Press of Glencoe, 1963), p. 212; David P. Thelen, *Robert La Follette and the Insurgent Spirit* (Boston: Little, Brown and Co., 1976); Richard Lowitt, *George W. Norris, The Making of a Progressive* (Syracuse: Syracuse University Press, 1963); George W. Norris, *The Persistence of a Progressive* (Syracuse: Syracuse University Press, 1973); Richard L. Neuberger and Stephen B. Kahn, *Integrity: The Life of George Norris* (New York: Vangard Press, 1939); John Braeman, *Albert J. Beveridge* (Chicago: University of Chicago Press, 1971); Marion C. McKenna, *Borah* (Ann Arbor: University of Michigan Press, 1961); Thomas Richard Ross, *Jonathan Prentiss Dolliver* (Iowa City: State Historical Society of Iowa, 1958); A. Bower Sagesser, *Joseph L. Bristow, Kansas Progressive* (Lawrence: University of Kansas Press, 1968); Howard Allen, *Poindexter of Washington: A Study in Progressive Politics* (Carbondale: Southern Illinois University Press, 1981).

3. Kolko, ibid., p. 213; James Weinstein, *The Corporate Ideal in the Liberal State* (Boston: Beacon Press, 1968), p. 6.

did indeed look almost hopeful for House Democrats in the 61st Congress. Their numbers had increased slightly, and Williams's retirement had ended the feud between his faction and David De Armond's, producing a new leader highly popular with both sides.[4]

John Quincy Adams's famous injunction, "Preserve your papers," was never ignored at greater cost than by James Beauchamp ("Champ") Clark, Democratic leader of the House from 1909 to 1921, and Speaker for four sessions. With no significant body of Clark papers available to scholars and no biography published since 1912, Clark has appeared to history solely as the rural clown who almost beat Wilson at the 1912 Democratic convention. Generations of historians have gleefully reproduced his campaign song, "You Gotta Quit Kickin' My Dawg Around." Clark himself contributed mightily to this image with a two-volume autobiography mixing memoir, cliche, and gratuitous exhibitions of scriptural and historical knowledge. Historiographically, Clark remains, in Arthur Link's disdainful phrase, "the statesman from Pike County."[5]

Yet, despite a somewhat contrived countrified image, the real Champ Clark was a gifted politician with a reform record stretching back to the Missouri legislature in the 1880s. "A man of commanding presence, a ready, forceful and often witty speaker," wrote one reporter, "he has been steadily gathering strength and leadership in his party." Wilsonians such as William G. McAdoo and Albert S. Burleson respected Clark's abilities and appeal, as did most Democratic House members.[6]

Williams had chosen Clark as his assistant and successor, and the House Democrats considered no other candidate. (Had Clark not deferred to De Armond as a senior member of the Missouri delegation, he might have been elected minority leader earlier.) "Only those who knew Champ Clark," remembered one of his followers, "could appreciate the sweetness of his nature." As leader, and later as Speaker, Clark kept his fences mended and his eye on the younger Democrats;

4. Henry D. Clayton to William Jennings Bryan (December 6, 1908), Bryan Papers, Library of Congress.

5. Champ Clark, *My Quarter Century of American Politics*, 2 vols. (New York: Harper Bros., 1920); Arthur Link, *Wilson: The Road to the White House* (Princeton: Princeton University Press, 1947), p. 398.

6. Clark, ibid., I:115; W. L. Webb, *Champ Clark* (New York: Neale Publishing Co., 1912), pp. 62–71; Ray Stannard Baker, "What About the Democratic Party?" *American Magazine* (July 1910): 156; William G. McAdoo, *Crowded Years* (Cambridge: Riverside Press, 1931), p. 144; interview with A. S. Burleson, Baker Papers, Library of Congress.

he once called the freshman Sam Rayburn to his office and urged him to read more.[7]

Clark directed his first efforts as minority leader to seeking a working agreement with the House Republican insurgents, then chafed under Speaker Joseph Cannon and House rules that gave him almost absolute control. To the insurgents in the House, what they called "Cannonism" was an illustration of the ability of conservatives to control decisions by controlling the rules. Cannon's use of the House rules, including the Speaker's power to appoint House committees, to frustrate House reformers seemed to the midwesterners to parallel the way eastern corporate power frustrated the popular will in the nation. Cannon's firm control of the Republican caucus required the insurgents to take their grievances onto the floor of the House. Although the insurgents refused Clark's suggestion of alliance to block Cannon's reelection, Clark pledged after several conferences that the Democrats would vote solidly "for the liberalization of the House," as they had under Williams.[8]

In its first outing, the Democrat-insurgent coalition managed to defeat the adoption of the previous rules, but the surprise defection of twenty-three Democrats prevented the passage of Clark's amendment for a restructured Rules Committee without the Speaker. The bolters included Tammanyites, involved in a complex deal with Republicans in Washington and Albany; southerners, looking for tariff and committee appointment favors; and a Bostonian whose seat was being challenged. "Eastern so-called Democrats and 'sugar delegates,' " mourned the *Courier-Journal*, "went, as usual, back on the party."[9]

John J. Fitzgerald of Brooklyn, leader of the defectors and perhaps the House's foremost parliamentarian, then produced and passed more limited reforms calling for a Calendar Wednesday, when the Rules Committee could be bypassed, and regulating the Speaker's power of recognition.[10] Despite these gains, the Democratic defections humili-

7. James Hay to Henry D. Flood (June 24, 1908), Flood Papers, Library of Congress; W. Bourke Cockran to Clark (July 29, 1908), Cockran Papers, New York Public Library; Arthur W. Dunn, *From Harrison to Harding*, 2 vols. (New York: Putnam's, 1922), I:388; James M. Cox, *Journey Through My Years* (New York: Simon and Schuster, 1946), p. 58; C. Dwight Dorough, *Mr. Sam* (New York: Random House, 1962), p. 150.

8. Clark, *My Quarter Century*, II:4, 268–70; Claude M. Barfield, " 'Our Share of the Booty': The Democratic Party, Cannonism, and the Payne-Aldrich Tariff," *Journal of American History* 57 (September 1970): 310; *New York World* (March 15, 1909).

9. *Congressional Record* Vol. 44, Part 1, pp. 20–34; *Louisville Courier-Journal* (March 17, 1909). For a detailed account of the bolters' motives see Claude Barfield, "Congressional Democrats in the Taft Administration" (diss., Northwestern University, 1969), pp. 35–46.

10. *Congressional Record*, ibid., p. 26.

ated Clark, and he sought to prevent such lack of party loyalty in the future. The bolters were denounced in the Democratic caucus, and some of them temporarily expelled from it. Clark himself served notice that he would continue the struggle. "It does not make any difference," he told the Cannonites, "if you beat us by a few votes, or we beat you by a few votes. The jig is up with the House machine."[11]

The first, unsuccessful attempt at alliance revealed attitudes that would permanently characterize the relationship between the two groups. The Democrats, as they had since La Follette entered the Senate, praised the efforts of the insurgents, invited them into the Democratic party, and offered further alliances. "Here and now," avowed Clark, "I want to express my admiration for the courage and fidelity of the so-called insurgents who voted with us today." The insurgents, on the other hand, tended to treat the Democrats as political untouchables who happened to be voting the same way. "Mr. Speaker," stated one sharply, "the alliance between the insurgents and the Democrats goes merely to changing the rules." For the next four years, the insurgents would lose few opportunities to disparage the people whose votes gave them whatever influence they possessed.[12]

Clark opened the Democrats' fight with a strong attack on the Republican leadership's bill, denouncing it for five hours. His speech, appraised *Collier's*, "is not only well-informed as to tariff facts, but . . . has the flavor of a racy personality, and abounds in qualities which make even a tariff speech readable." Charging that the proposed Payne bill actually increased the current tariff rates, Clark repeated the Democrats' call for an income tax or an inheritance tax. He urged Democrats to avoid the temptation to seek protective benefits for their own districts: "I want to repeat, and we might as well settle it and be through with it, that I am not going to help any man plunder the American people because he happens to live in Missouri."[13]

Democratic theory held for a tariff set for revenue only, not for the economic advantage of any American industry or region. Holding Democratic congressmen to that standard on products of their own regions was always a challenge, and it appeared at the beginning of the struggle that Clark would fall short. Forty Democrats opposed an amendment to put lumber on the free list; slightly fewer voted against free hides. Such splits, along with the rules vote, led journalistic observers to declare the Democrats "a demoralized party."[14]

11. Cox, *Journey Through My Years*, p. 65; *Congressional Record*, ibid.; Hechler, *Insurgency*, p. 57.
12. *Congressional Record*, ibid., pp. 26, 27.
13. *Collier's* (May 8, 1909); *New York World* (May 24, 1909); ibid., p. 217.
14. *Congressional Record*, ibid., pp. 1293–98; *Collier's* (May 15, 1909).

Under the circumstances, keeping the Democrats together would have challenged the most adroit freshman floor leader. "I favor, as you know, a revision and reduction of the tariff," wrote Senator Francis Newlands of Nevada before Congress opened, speaking for numerous Democrats in both houses, "but . . . if there is to be a protective tariff, I shall endeavor to see that the West gets its fair share of protection." Many Democrats refused, as Carter Glass of Virginia did, "to sit in the House and, merely to exploit a theory [I] was powerless to make effective, see the industries of [my] state and section sacrificed to the rapacity and utter selfishness of another section." Still, the great majority of Democrats supported the lower tariff on each vote, often holding firm against the interests of their region.[15]

Democrats could claim more unanimity on questions that did not involve tariff rates. Asked how he wanted to pay for the government if tariff rates were cut sharply, Oscar Gillespie of Texas answered, "We want to pay a tax on our incomes." Few Democrats made tariff speeches without calling for an income tax, although Republican control of the House prevented any such amendment from coming to a vote.[16]

From the beginning, Clark had concentrated on the final vote rather than the amendments. Besides Clark, Democratic leaders such as Fitzgerald, Oscar W. Underwood of Alabama, Claude Kitchin of North Carolina, and Ollie James of Kentucky led the attack on the measure with relatively little insurgent assistance. In the final vote on the bill, not a single insurgent joined the Democrats in opposition.[17]

However divided and uncertain the Democrats appeared in their attempts to lower the tariff, the insurgent Republicans seemed to be aiming at something else entirely. No insurgent would begin a tariff speech without first affirming his belief in the protective system; behind their rebellion was, in Howard Allen's phrase, "a strong core of regional self-interest."[18] On two of the three schedules (lumber, barley, and hides) that the insurgents forced to a record vote on the final day, they wanted not to reduce the tariff rate but increase it. Kansas Republicans, taunted a standpatter, "voted for free lumber because their state does not produce any, and for a duty on hides because that was important to their

15. Francis G. Newlands to John Henderson (December 31, 1908), Newlands Papers, Yale University; Rixey Smith and Norman Beasley, *Carter Glass* (New York: Longmans, Green and Co., 1939), p. 71; *Congressional Record*, ibid., p. 272.

16. *Congressional Record*, ibid., p. 1098.

17. Ibid., p. 1301. Only four Democrats supported the bill.

18. Allen, *Poindexter*, pp. 40, 166.

pocketbooks." With the aid of regular Republicans (and a dozen Democrats) the insurgents increased the proposed tariff on barley by 60 percent. Far more than the derided Democrats, the insurgents believed that the tariff reduction should begin somewhere other than at home.[19]

The situation in the Senate only bolstered the insurgent advantage. "The ten insurgents in the Senate," commented *Collier's* at the end of the tariff debate, "comprise the only effective opposition to the present domination of national politics by the power of organized wealth." This indirect comparison of the performances of the Senate insurgents and Democrats was understandable; during the three-month fight on the Payne-Aldrich bill, while the Democrats appeared largely ineffectual, Senate insurgents delivered cogent, informed, and sometimes eloquent attacks on the measure.[20]

Partly—and least importantly—this development resulted from Democratic design. "The Democratic Senators," reported the *St. Louis Republic* in April, "think it good policy to allow Republicans to go on record as attacking a Republican bill." Democrats wanted the maximum public attention devoted to this pleasing spectacle. Within ten days of the tariff's final passage, Chairman James Lloyd of the Democratic Congressional Campaign Committee was planning publication of a pamphlet containing the speeches of the insurgents.[21]

Second, the sheer weight of numbers rendered Senate Democrats ineffectual. With a far smaller proportion of seats in the Senate than in the House (35 to 44 percent), Democrats had even less chance of hindering passage of the bill and even less reason to hold fast for purity. Accordingly, Senate Democrats proved even more eager to salvage some benefit for themselves than their House colleagues. Among the Democrats, eighteen voted against free iron ore, seventeen against free lumber, ten against free hides. "When we find ourselves confronted with a bill framed on protective lines," explained Joseph Johnston of Alabama, "we want to see it made equal and fair in its operations upon all sections of the country."[22]

Finally, even for Senate Democrats, there was no leadership. Four years after the Hepburn Act, Joseph Bailey's intellect and eloquence still made him the real leader of the party, "half accepted as such by

19. *Congressional Record*, ibid., pp. 1158, 1293–98.
20. *Collier's* (July 19, 1909).
21. *St. Louis Republic* (April 24, 1909); James T. Lloyd to Henry D. Flood (August 17, 1909), Flood Papers.
22. *Congressional Record*, Vol. 44, Part 2, pp. 2055, 2337, 1995; Part 4, p. 3667.

those democrats who are willing to follow any leader at all," in the sardonic appraisal of the *Chicago Record-Examiner*. But Bailey now led in the fight against including free raw materials (coming mostly from the South and West) in a generally protective tariff. "Remitting the manufacturers' taxes on their raw materials and still leaving them a duty on their financial products," he charged, was only additional "favoritism to the manufacturers." His efforts, rather than aiding party unity, gave a vague tinge of doctrinal legitimacy to the rebels.[23]

Such a division could hardly be overcome by the actual minority leadership. Charles Culberson of Texas, the titular minority leader, had grave health problems, which heavy drinking did not improve. His formal duties devolved largely upon Hernando de Soto Money of Mississippi, an elderly, near-blind Confederate, whose seat in the next Congress had already been awarded to John Sharp Williams. Searching for the reason for Money's rise to leadership, the *Independent* could suggest only that "there seemed to be needed additional places in which members of his family could be employees." Actually, although he was hardly a man to rally the troops, Money seems to have performed fairly well in debate. But real party leadership, such as it was, rested largely with Augustus Bacon, an elderly, earnest, and rather long-winded Georgian, and on Bailey, on those roll calls when he himself stayed with the party.[24]

Next to this picture of dullness and inconsistency, the image of the insurgents, courageously and ably battling their own party machine, with such dramatic leaders as La Follette and Jonathan Dolliver, has proven irresistible.[25] No one would have accepted this perspective more fully than the insurgents themselves. Democrats, to them, were unreliable and not very important adjuncts to their fight. "I have little doubt," sneered Albert Cummins of Iowa early on, "that many of them will stand before the country as delinquents." Dealing with such people, insurgents wanted only their votes. "I am not in a mood," snapped Norris Brown of Nebraska about one amendment, "to have much opposition from that side of the aisle to my proposition." Relations with the Democrats were not important anyway, explained Moses Clapp of Minne-

23. *Chicago Record-Examiner*, quoted in *Commoner* (July 2, 1909); *Commoner* (July 9, 1909).

24. James W. Madden, *Charles Allen Culberson* (Austin: 1929), p. 182; Lewis L. Gould, "Progressives and Prohibitionists, Texas Democratic Politics, 1911–1921," *Southwest Historical Quarterly* 75 (July 1971): 15; *Independent* (December 30, 1909); January 20, 1910).

25. See for example, George Mowry, *Theodore Roosevelt and the Progressive Movement* (Madison: University of Wisconsin Press, 1946), Chapter 2.

sota; they were just a matter of "here and there a point where one on the one side and another upon the other wishing a given tariff could vote together."[26]

In response, Senate Democrats praised the insurgents at every opportunity. Bailey commended their "obedience to their own convictions." The blind Thomas Gore of Oklahoma announced, "I hope the Lord will increase the tribe of the progressive Republicans," and urged Democrats not to run against them. "I am prepared to go along with them along the line of reform," said Newlands, virtually enlisting under the insurgent banner, "though perhaps they may not be willing to go as far as I may."[27] But in that last subordinate clause, Newlands provided a generally ignored clue to insurgent-Democratic relations. The insurgents, as both they and their sometimes allies realized, were not just Democrats with hayseeds in their hair.

"I am just as ardent a believer in and as faithful to the principle of protection as is the Senator from Michigan," Iowa insurgent Senator Albert Cummins correctly told one standpatter, and every insurgent paid homage to protection during the debate. Although the demand for tariff revision had arisen due to the high-protection levels of the current Dingley tariff, insurgents were generally willing to let rates stay at that level; they fought only proposed increases. The insurgents opposed not protection but excess protection, a term that they seemed to define anew with each vote. "Their idea is, when they strike down certain schedules, to maintain the great principle of the bill," observed Democrat Isidor Rayner of Maryland, "and I am against the principle of the bill."[28] In opposing only "excessive protection," the insurgents had created for themselves a rationalization that made attacks on their consistency, such as those that bedevilled the Democrats, nearly impossible. When La Follette voted to raise the barley duty still higher than the House-increased rate, he could explain that such protection was not excessive but essential. In the same argument used by noninsurgent Republicans on other schedules, he swore that without it, Americans would have to stop growing barley.[29]

The protection that the insurgents could agree was excessive, such as on lumber, rarely involved products of the Great Plains. William Borah of Idaho, normally an active insurgent, charged Knute Nelson

26. *Congressional Record*, Vol. 44, Part 2, pp. 1789, 1810; Part 4, p. 3382.
27. Ibid., Part 3, p. 2332; Part 4, p. 4313; Part 2, p. 1441.
28. Holt, *Congressional Insurgents*, p. 15; ibid., Part 2, p. 1927; Part 5, p. 4880; Part 3, p. 2580; *Independent* (May 20, 1909); *New York World* (May 16, 1909).
29. *Congressional Record*, Vol. 44, Part 3, p. 2701.

Table 3.1. Average Votes by Democrats and Insurgents on Tariff Roll Calls

	Democratic Reduction Amendments (28)		Insurgent Reduction Amendments (28)		Finance Committee Increases (22)		Regular Republican Reduction Amendments (7)		Regular Republican Increase Amendments (4)		Democratic Increase Amendments (2)		All Votes Average (91)	
	L	H	L	H	L	H	L	H	L	H	L	H	L	H
Democrats	20.75	1.18	20.61	1.54	18.68	2.68	14.29	7.57	19.25	1.0	15.0	5.5	19.51	2.24
Insurgents	3.39	5.36	8.54	1.04	7.27	2.1	8.71	.71	8.5	1.0	8.5	.5	6.66	2.58

Note: Insurgent votes are based on the ten insurgents voting against the final Senate bill.
L = Lower rate.
H = Higher rate.

of Minnesota with favoring free lumber only because Minnesota's supply was almost gone. In both the Senate and the House, the free lumber
amendments were introduced not by insurgents but by conservative
Republicans from the north central states.[30]

The insurgents' slippery tariff philosophy produced, on 91 roll-call
votes on tariff rates, a consistently higher tariff position that that taken
by the "demoralized" Democrats (see Table 3.1). On the average roll-
call, 10 insurgents produced more votes for the higher rate (2.58 to
2.24) than did more than 30 Democrats. From another perspective,
89.6 percent of the Democratic votes cast (1774 of 1979) were for the
lower rate, and only 72.1 percent of insurgent votes (606 of 841) were
on that side. Further, the figures do not include hundreds of Democratic votes paired against higher rates; insurgents, unable to pair with
fellow Republicans, had to record their votes.

The table also underscores the attitude of the two allies toward each
other. To Democratic senators, it made little difference whether an
amendment to reduce a rate was introduced by a Democrat or an insurgent; they supported it 20.75–1.18 in the first case, 20.61–1.54 in the
second. But insurgent senators, although voting overwhelmingly for reductions introduced by themselves (8.54–1.04), actually cast most of
their votes against Democratic reduction amendments (3.39–5.36).
Often La Follette alone crossed party lines to vote for the lower Democratic rate.

The relative commitment of Democrats and insurgents to tariff reduction is also reflected in Table 3.2. Based on all 129 votes taken during the special session, it lists how often each senator voted with or
against Nelson Aldrich of Rhode Island, Senate Majority Leader and
arch-protectionist. It shows that of thirty-two Democrats, only two —
the Louisianans, willing to exchange protection for rice and sugar for
their votes on everything else — voted with Aldrich more often than did
the leading insurgent, La Follette. Only four of the insurgents voted
against Aldrich two-thirds of the time, and two of them voted against
him less than half the time.

Watching the battle, the leading tariff authority of the time, F. W.
Taussig of Harvard, charged that insurgents had shown not courage
and dedication in the fight but "half-heartedness and inconsistency."
Yet popular attacks centered on the Democrats. Only five Democratic
senators, charged one magazine muckraker, were "really consistent
low-tariff men" who had voted for every reduction and against every

30. Ibid., Part 3, p. 2316; Part 2, p. 1880.

Table 3.2. Votes for and against Aldrich

Democrats	For	Against	Insurgents	For	Against
McEnery (La.)	66	25	La Follette (Wisc.)	18	106
Foster (La.)	29	63	Clapp (Minn.)	20	91
Martin (Va.)	18	87	Bristow (Kan.)	27	101
Chamberlain (Ore.)	16	85	Cummins (Iowa)	31	89
Daniel (Va.)	14	56	Beveridge (Ind.)	34	55
Taliaferro (Fla.)	14	87	Dolliver (Iowa)	45	73
Simmons (N.C.)	14	88	Nelson (Minn.)	53	69
Smith (Md.)	12	61	Brown (Neb.)	56	65
Fletcher (Fla.)	12	107	Burkett (Neb.)	70	58
Taylor (Tenn.)	11	64	Crawford (S.D.)	70	52
Bailey (Tex.)	11	69			
Money (Miss.)	11	74			
Bacon (Ga.)	11	111			
Bankhead (Ala.)	10	79			
Hughes (Colo.)	9	101			
Tillman (S.C.)	8	67			
Overman (N.C.)	8	106			
Newlands (Nev.)	7	87			
Stone (Mo.)	7	97			
Johnston (Ala.)	7	103			
Owen (Okla.)	6	62			
Davis (Ark.)	6	63			
Clay (Ga.)	6	81			
Culberson (Tex.)	6	83			
Rayner (Md.)	5	64			
McLaurin (Miss.)	5	67			
Paynter (Tenn.)	5	75			
Gore (Okla.)	5	118			
Shively (Ind.)	4	63			
Smith (S.C.)	3	57			
Frazier (Tenn.)	3	97			
Clarke (Ark.)	0	10			

Note: The 38 votes not included in Table 3.2 concerned the income tax, the Philippine tariff, the tax commission, and the final votes on passing the Senate and conference committee bills.

Source: *Collier's* (August 29, 1909).

increase. He did not note that by those criteria, not a single insurgent would have qualified.[31]

The Democrats managed more unity and had even more problems with insurgent lack of commitment in their struggle to attach an income tax rider to the tariff bill. Although a Democratic meeting on tariff schedules had collapsed in chaos, the caucus had agreed to push the income tax. Besides unity, the Democrats had another advantage they had lacked on rates: Bailey. The brilliant Texan strongly supported an income tax, thus ensuring that on at least one issue Democrats would not have to rely on insurgent leadership.[32]

As in the tariff fight in general, the Democrats and insurgents did not see the income tax issue the same way. Bailey's amendment called for taxing both individuals and corporations; Cummins proposed to tax only individuals. The Democrats supported an income tax as a partial, fairer alternative to the tariff; the insurgents only wanted an income tax available if the tariff failed to produce enough revenue. "It is a crime," explained Albert Beveridge of Indiana, "to put upon the people an emergency tax if the present bill will supply sufficient revenue."[33]

On this point, several insurgents were not too different from President Taft, who informed a Democratic senator, "I do not believe we need such a revenue except in time of war." When Bailey, at several points in the tariff debate, sought a vote on an income tax amendment—or at least an agreement to vote later—he drew the support of only three or four insurgents.[34]

Even after Bailey and Cummins reached an agreement, Aldrich won another postponement and called Taft to his rescue. The president responded with a plan for a corporation tax and a constitutional amendment permitting the government to pass an income tax some time in the future. "I shall vote for a corporation tax," declared Aldrich, "as a means to defeat the income tax." On two votes contrived by the Senate leader to substitute his amendment for Bailey's, thus avoiding a floor vote on the income tax alone, the Democrats voted unanimously

---

31. F. W. Taussig, *The Tariff History of the United States*, 5th ed. (New York: Putnam's, 1910), p. 375; Baker, "What About the Democratic Party?" p. 159.

32. Barfield, "Congressional Democrats," pp. 81–82, 132–33; *New York World* (April 16, 1909); *St. Louis Republic* (April 15, 1909).

33. Barfield, ibid., pp. 128, 1331–34; *Congressional Record*, Vol. 44, Part 2, pp. 1351, 1421, 1686.

34. William Howard Taft to Francis G. Newlands, May 14, 1909, Newlands Papers; Edward M. Silbert, "Support for Reform among Congressional Democrats, 1897–1913," unpublished dissertation, University of Florida, 1966, pp. 78–79.

against his maneuver. The insurgents split in half, opposing it only five votes to four.[35]

The Democrats disliked Taft's constitutional amendment strategy for two reasons; they felt the government already had the power to collect such a tax, and they doubted that such an amendment could pass. Citing conservative Republican control of eastern and far western legislatures, Money warned of twelve states "quite likely to defeat any amendment of this sort to the Constitution," a probability that doubtless also had occurred to Aldrich.[36]

For that reason, Bailey introduced a proviso that states call conventions to pass the amendment, rather than leave it to the legislatures. The Democrats supported his measure 24 to 1, but he could gain only 4 insurgent votes. The Democrats then joined all the Republicans in passing the constitutional amendment. "For a wonder," wrote Frank Cobb to Pulitzer, with grudging respect, "the damn fool Democrats did not repudiate their platform again, but all of them voted for the resolution . . . "[37]

In the House, where Democrats also supported the amendment unanimously, Clark predicted that it would be ratified, "very much to the disgust of the Republican leaders who are advocating it today." With two more Democratic tributes to the insurgents and another insurgent attack on the Democrats, the House passed the final tariff bill that had emerged from the conference committee and sent it to the Senate for approval.[38]

Champ Clark had other reasons to feel pleased when the Payne-Aldrich bill had passed. "The House Democrats," he told reporters, "came out of the tariff fight more united than they have been in a generation." He pointed out that on the House vote on the original bill, he had lost only four Democrats, all from Louisiana. On his motion to recommit the final conference committee version, only one Democrat had defected, and on final passage, only two. If the Democrats of both houses were hardly a smooth, well-oiled juggernaut in the special session, neither were they pathetically divided and ineffectual.[39]

---

35. *New York World* (May 22, 1909).

36. *Congressional Record*, Vol. 44, Part 4, pp. 3929, 4059–61.

37. Ibid., pp. 4115, 4120–21; Frank Cobb to Joseph Pulitzer (July 13, 1909), Pulitzer Papers, Columbia University. The Supreme Court had killed an income tax in 1894, but the Democrats felt that the current Court would support one.

38. *Congressional Record*, ibid., pp. 4371, 4392, 4440; Part 5, pp. 4467, 4749, 4754–55.

39. *New York World* (August 7, 1909).

"I have waited for five months," wrote Kansas insurgent editor William Allen White to Taft in early 1910, "to find some decent opportunity to tell you that if you will just let the insurgents alone they will come home like Little Bo-peep's sheep." White's "decent opportunity" was an unsolicited pledge by the House insurgents to support Taft's legislative program, an act that, the *World* disgustedly charged, "made their surrender to the White House complete." The insurgents took the action, although Taft had hardly "let the insurgents alone." In a fall tour he had identified himself closely with the regular wing of the party, and reports from both the White House and the Republican Congressional Campaign Committee warned of patronage cutoffs and primary opponents for insurgents.[40]

What had impelled the House insurgents to make this gratuitous pledge of fealty, to feed the mouth that had been biting them? It could hardly have been fear: the insurgents knew they were far stronger in the Midwest than was Taft. Indeed, the insurgents seemed to be rushing aboard a sinking ship. "Never have I seen such a debacle since Cleveland's second term," wrote Henry Adams, across the street from the White House. "Nothing can be done. The whole concern is going to pieces."[41]

Rather, what motivated the insurgents to attest so consistently the orthodoxy of their Republicanism was a distaste for the alternative. The insurgents, Bailey once complained, were "imbued with an inherent and traditional hostility to the Democratic party." Mostly small town midwesterners, they reflected the biases of their region. William Allen White, watching the 1912 Baltimore Democratic convention after the Republican chaos at Chicago, found it "a sinister exhibition . . . more unrestrained, more savage. . . . It was all Irish, and the rebel yell ripped through the applause like a knife."[42]

The Midwest, as much as the South, still fought the Civil War in the Progressive Era. Speculating on why insurgents had such difficulty allying with Democrats, one magazine noted, "In most of these states the name 'Democrat' still suggests 'rebel.'" When the midwestern

40. William Allen White to William Howard Taft (February 3, 1910), in Walter Johnson, ed., *Selected Letters of William Allen White* (New York: Henry Holt and Co., 1947), p. 105; *New York World* (February 2, 1910), *New York Times* (February 2, 1910); *New York World* (January 5, 1910); *St. Louis Republic* (January 11, 1910).

41. Henry Adams to Elizabeth Cameron (January 11, 1910), in Worthington Chauncey Ford, ed., *Letters of Henry Adams, 1892–1918* (Boston: Houghton Mifflin, 1938), p. 529.

42. *New York World* (March 19, 1911); William Allen White, *Autobiography* (New York: Macmillan, 1946), p. 478.

states turned insurgent, their antisouthern feelings evolved into an attack on the largely Bryanite South for its "conservatism." La Follette, who had worked closely with southern Democrats in the Senate and had based his Wisconsin railroad rate law on an earlier Texas model, announced during his 1912 presidential campaign, "I don't know of any progressive sentiment or any progressive legislation in the South."[43]

The insurgents felt no more comfortable with the other center of Democratic power, the city and its immigrants. "Things will only be better," prescribed Borah, "when the face of the American citizen turns from the crowded and congested conditions of the city to a more intensive life on the farm." In stronger terms than Bryan would ever use, George Norris of Nebraska charged bluntly, "The city has always been the breeding place of crime and immorality."[44] Social attitudes, therefore, combined with farm state political realities and policy disagreements to make the insurgents reluctant to identify too closely with the Democrats. When Congress returned for the regular session of the 61st Congress, the strains would persist.

Despite their own mixed performance in the tariff fight, Democratic congressmen were cheerful at the start of the regular session. Although they had drawn criticism from both Bryan and the party newspapers, the tariff debacle had hurt the Republicans more. As the House gathered, Champ Clark proposed to press the attack with another move against the House rules, the one area where Democrats and insurgents were in unqualified agreement. He designated Albert S. Burleson of Texas to continue as his permanent emissary to the insurgents. Clark had two reasons, he wrote later, for the rules fight: "First, because the rules, in my opinion, needed liberalizing; second, for political advantage."[45]

When insurgent George Norris obtained the floor on March 17, 1910 to introduce a motion removing the Speaker from the Rules Committee, Clark and the Democrats were ready. Oscar Underwood, Clark's assistant, was the first to support Norris, proclaiming, "The time has come, gentlemen, if you propose to amend these rules, to make a proposition to amend them in order." Clark, Ollie James of

43. *World's Work* (December 1909); Arthur Link, "The Progressive Movement in the South, 1870–1914," *North Carolina Historical Review* 23 (April 1946): 173; Thelen, *La Follette*, p. 45.

44. McKenna, *Borah*, p. 98; Holt, *Congressional Insurgents*, p. 9.

45. Bascom Timmons, *Garner of Texas* (New York: Harper and Bros., 1948), p. 60; Clark, *My Quarter Century*, II:259, 269.

Kentucky, and William Hughes of New Jersey followed swiftly; Henry Clayton of Alabama praised "the patriotic insurgents."[46]

Early procedural votes showed the insurgents and the now-unanimous Democrats in control of the House, and the Cannonites desperately postponed the rules vote, hoping to round up votes or reach an agreement with the insurgents. Twice, regular and insurgent Republicans combined to force recesses to try to reach a compromise, while Democrats watched nervously. Nor did the insurgents' statements on the floor suggest intransigence; they complained of their treatment on committee appointments, something that could be easily adjusted, and avowed their dedication to the Republican party. Edmund Madison of Kansas called the House to witness that the insurgents were voting for a Republican resolution, not one introduced by Democrats, and Henry Cooper of Wisconsin spoke movingly of his family's involvement in the antislavery movement. But when the regulars would not agree to remove the Speaker from the Rules Committee, negotiations collapsed, and Democrats and insurgents joined to dissolve the committee.[47]

Over two days of waiting, reported the *Courier-Journal*, "the superb generalship of such men as Clark . . . Underwood . . . James" held the Democrats tightly in line. Since his humiliation exactly one year before, Clark had worked diligently to avoid a repetition. He enlisted a network of whips, headed by young John Nance Garner of Texas, and he maintained personal ties throughout the Democratic delegation. Now, Cannon had no more committee or tariff favors to hand out, and even Taft conceded that Clark would likely be Speaker of the next House.[48]

But Clark could not prevent one party error, coming directly after the vote that established a ten-member Rules Committee without the Speaker. Cannon, in an ingenious move to salvage something, announced that he would entertain a motion to declare the Speaker's office vacant. Before Clark could stop him, Burleson made such a motion, which Cannon quickly put to a vote despite efforts by other Democrats to move adjournment. As both Clark and Cannon expected, most of the insurgents took the opportunity to avow their Republicanism, a bare nine (of forty-three) voting to oust the Speaker. The motion, scolded one magazine, was "an ungraceful and vindictive error of the Democratic minority, which promptly seized its first chance to make

46. *Congressional Record* Vol. 45, Part 3, pp. 3293–94, 3392.
47. Ibid., pp. 3304, 3318–23, 3415–16; Clark, *My Quarter Century*, II:276.
48. *Louisville Courier-Journal* (March 19, 1910); Timmons, *Garner*, p. 61; Clark, ibid., II:277.

a tactical error." Democrats, it seemed, not only lost clumsily but also won that way.[49]

Whatever disappointment the Democrats brought upon themselves, they received a heavier one at the hands of their allies. "Whether anything is gained," the *Commoner* evaluated the situation, "will depend on the character of the men chosen for the new committee." If the insurgents now entered the Republican caucus to select the six Republican members of the new Rules Committee, warned Underwood, "the Speaker will dominate legislation and control the situation just as he did before the changes in the rules." Only by keeping the selection on the House floor, and maintaining their alliance with the Democrats (who offered the insurgents two seats on the new Rules Committee as a reward for cooperation) could the insurgents have any influence.[50]

Horrified, the insurgents spurned such a course. "We are Republicans," explained the normally fiery Victor Murdock of Kansas. "If the majority of the Republicans in Congress wish to appoint again a lot of high-handed rulers to the Rules Committee that is their problem." In caucus, Norris himself nominated the arch-Cannonite, Sereno Payne, chairman of the Ways and Means Committee, to the new committee. Unsurprisingly, the caucus filled the GOP seats with six regulars.[51]

"Between us," Irvine Lenroot of Wisconsin, an insurgent who had voted to remove Cannon as Speaker, confided to a friend, "I do not think that anything substantial has been gained by the fight. Cannon controls the new Committee on Rules as effectively as if he were a member of it."[52]

In his autobiography, Norris explained that the alliance with the Democrats had limited the possibility of reform. The Democrats, he charged, did not wish to weaken the Speaker seriously, since they expected Clark to hold the office in the next Congress, and historians have accepted Norris's version. Yet, when Clark did become Speaker, he led the Democrats in stripping the Speaker of all power to appoint any committees.[53]

49. *Congressional Record*, Vol. 45, Part 4, p. 3437; *World's Work* (May 1910).

50. *Commoner* (March 25, 1910); *Louisville Courier-Journal* (March 21, 1910; March 22, 1910).

51. *New York World* (March 22, 1910); *Louisville Courier-Journal* (March 22, 1910); Hechler, *Insurgency*, p. 81.

52. Herbert L. Margulies, *Senator Lenroot of Wisconsin* (Columbia: University of Missouri Press, 1977), p. 96.

53. George Norris, *Fighting Liberal* (New York: Macmillan, 1945), p. 301; John D. Baker, "The Character of the Congressional Revolution of 1910," *Journal of American*

The day after the Democrats saw the limits of the insurgent commitment, they also learned they might not need the insurgents much longer. In a special election in Massachusetts, the party changed a 14,000 vote deficit into a 5,000 vote plurality. The Democrats' assault on Cannonism had also significantly boosted party morale—a major gain. In the future, when Payne mockingly asked when the Democrats had ever stood together, Clark could reply, "On the 19th of March."[54]

Whatever opinions the two forces expressed about each other privately, or not so privately, they still needed each other. With the Democrats gaining new confidence from election returns and the insurgents from their press clippings, they turned, in the spring of 1910, to their second great battle, which was against a railroad regulation overhaul supported by Taft and which would become the Mann-Elkins Act. That struggle closely paralleled the pattern of the Payne-Aldrich fight, except in one respect: on the railroad bill, the Democratic-insurgent alliance won.

Taft's original bill, fumed La Follette, was "in all the history of railroad legislation, the rankest, boldest betrayal of public interest ever proposed in any legislative body." Taft did not help the situation by ostentatiously consulting with railroad presidents (and ignoring the insurgents) while the bill was being prepared. Long before its introduction, correspondents predicted radical changes would be made in the bill. The forecasts came true in both the House and the Senate, with the Democrats and insurgents following their traditional roles. "You will find," Newlands told an audience that fall, "that the great progressive leaders of the Republican party furnished the oratory and the Democrats furnished the votes."[55]

Democrats and insurgents found Taft's bill to be partly good and mostly terrible. They favored its provisions for a uniform freight classification system, for shipper control over routing, and for giving the Interstate Commerce Commission power to initiate rate investigations— all things La Follette and the Democrats had tried to include in the Hepburn Act. They objected strongly to clauses legalizing certain traffic agreements among railroads, allowing a railroad owning 50 percent

History 60 (December 1973): 683; Charles O. Jones, "Joseph G. Cannon and Howard W. Smith: An Essay on the Limits of Leadership in the House of Representatives," *Journal of Politics* 30 (August 1968): 634 n.

54. *New York World* (March 23, 1910); *Congressional Record*, Vol. 45, Part 7, p. 6817.

55. Robert La Follette, *Autobiography*, p. 420; Gabriel Kolko, *Railroads and Regulation* (Princeton: Princeton University Press, 1965), p. 183; Horatio J. Seymour to Joseph Pulitzer (March 18, 1910), Pulitzer Papers, Columbia University; Francis G. Newlands, Speech at Tonopah, Nevada (October 20, 1910), in Newlands Papers.

of the stock of another railroad to buy the rest, and making the attorney general rather than the ICC the defendant in appeals from ICC rulings. (The identity of Taft's attorney general — George Wickersham, a conservative corporation lawyer — probably stiffened their resolve on this point.)

But the core of the bill, the section that raised the Democratic and insurgent hackles the highest, established a new Court of Commerce, staffed by federal circuit court judges, to hear appeals from ICC rulings. The railroads had been lobbying for such a tribunal since 1893. Such a body, charged the allies, would eventually make the ICC a nullity. "The whole tendency of this bill," charged Democrat Gilbert Hitchcock of Nebraska, "is to belittle the Commission." Moreover, they feared that such a small, centralized body would be easy for the railroads to control. "Sometimes," mused Rufus Hardy of Texas, "the ablest lawyers placed on railroad commissions seem after a while to absorb the railroad view of things."[56]

In the House, the Democrats carried the attack on the bill. Denouncing the measure as "a scheme of the reactionaries," William Adamson of Georgia, ranking Democrat on the Interstate Commerce Committee, led the fight to omit objectionable clauses and add new reforms. A united Democratic vote, plus some regulars and a dozen insurgents, attached another plan of La Follette's for basing rates on a physical valuation of railroad property, which Adamson had unsuccessfully tried to attach in committee. With the aid of fourteen insurgents, Adamson almost succeeded in killing the section making the attorney general the defendant, but had to settle for an amendment giving the ICC and shippers a role in the hearings, and forbidding the attorney general to abandon the suit. Sections 7 (permitting traffic agreements) and 12 (allowing purchase of stock in other railroads) were struck out entirely.[57]

On the critical issue of the Commerce Court, Democrats again tried to gain Republican support by having the amendment introduced by an insurgent, Elbert Hubbard of Iowa. But the insurgents still split, and the Commerce Court twice survived on tie votes. "Judge Hubbard lost," commented the *New York Times*, "solely through the refusal of some of his insurgent colleagues to support him." The Democrats did no better on a similar motion by Adamson, winning only thirteen insurgent votes.[58]

56. Kolko, ibid., p. 198; *Congressional Record*, Vol. 45, Part 5, pp. 5517, 5162.

57. *Congressional Record*, ibid., p. 4720; *New York Times* (April 29, 30, 1910; May 11, 1910).

58. *New York Times* (April 27, 1910; May 11, 1910); *Congressional Record*, Vol. 45, Part 6, p. 6032.

On the final vote, fourteen Democrats decided that the bill had been sufficiently improved to vote for it, along with all the Republicans. Clark refused to vote for the measure as long as the Commerce Court remained in it, but still claimed some credit. "When it was first brought into the house," he boasted, "it was a 'railroad' bill, pure and simple"; the Democrats had improved it.[59]

Such a prominent leadership role, of course, was beyond the capabilities of the anarchic Senate Democrats. Not only did formal accession to the leadership fail to heighten Money's charisma, but the party's expert on railroad questions, Tillman, was ill throughout the debate. Most of the Democrats still tried to follow Bailey, a difficult feat since they rarely knew where he was going. An illustration of the party's condition came at one point, when Aldrich wanted to fix a date for the vote. The Democrats saw no reason not to agree, but decided not to accept anything with Bailey absent.[60]

Because of their party's condition and because of the insurgents' ability, eloquence, and attitude toward Democrats, the minority decided to lie low and vote for insurgent amendments. The one point both Republican factions agreed upon, suggested Democrat William Stone of Missouri, "is that amendments proposed by Democrats would be voted down." The Democrats, explained Bailey, would take little role in the debate: "We are just going to say enough to keep you irritated." The minority showed another reason for this low-key policy when two Democrats ignored it and swiftly got into a more vituperative exchange than the divided Republicans had ever managed.[61]

Using this strategy, the muted minority joined with the insurgents to make major changes in the original bill, which came into the Senate and the House at the same time. As in the House, many insurgents followed a wavering path, but their numbers were augmented by several western regular Republicans who could not afford to seem conservative on a railroad issue. The alliance forced Aldrich to drop sections 7 and 12 without a vote and added the House limitations on the attorney general, although both the Democrats and insurgents preferred to try to remove him from the proceedings entirely.[62]

Of the major House additions, the Senate failed to adopt only physical valuation, despite unanimous Democratic and near-unanimous insurgent support. After one vote, Bailey rose and assured La Follette that

59. *Baltimore Sun* (May 11, 1910).
60. Barfield, "Congressional Democrats," p. 158; *New York Times* (May 19, 1910).
61. *Congressional Record*, Vol. 45, Part 7, p. 6966; Part 5, p. 5263; Part 6, p. 6450–54.
62. *New York Times* (May 14, 1910; May 19, 1910).

"the majority has no more chance to avoid the ultimate adoption of this amendment . . . than they have to repeal, from preamble to conclusion, the entire interstate commerce law."[63]

Both La Follette and the Democrats had several old railroad reform amendments left over from the Hepburn fight that they now tried to tack onto the Mann-Elkins bill. La Follette's amendment to keep judges owning railroad stock off the Commerce Court, a descendant of his 1906 effort to prevent such judges from ruling on railroad questions, failed despite a solid Democratic and near-solid insurgent vote. Lee Overman of North Carolina had better luck with his heirloom amendment, requiring three separate judges or a Supreme Court justice to enjoin an ICC rate.[64]

But as in the House, insurgent divisions reprieved the Commerce Court. The day before Cummins's amendment to eliminate the court came up, Taft invited the less committed insurgents, as well as several new railroad insurgents, to the White House. The next day, virtually all of them voted to save the court, which also survived a later amendment by Bacon. Still, citing improvements, six Democrats voted for the bill on Senate passage, and seven when it returned from conference committee.[65]

Insurgents had criticized the Democrats during the tariff fight for inconsistency and division, but the absence of those problems in the railroad debate did not change their attitude. Dolliver transcended the entire pattern of voting to announce, "it has been found quite as difficult to use the Democratic party to promote progressive government as it has been to use the Republican party," and proclaimed, "the insurgents seek no alliance." Cummins, after some rough handling by Republican regulars, pledged that he would "everywhere" campaign for Republican victory.[66]

Sometimes, the insurgent attacks were utterly gratuitous. When Democrat Robert Owen of Oklahoma asked a vote on a constitutional amendment for direct election of senators, Beveridge rose to say he was glad Owen had not called it a partisan issue, because "when the Senator brought up his resolution before . . . there were only nine Democratic Senators who voted for it — less than a third of the Democratic membership of this body. On the contrary, the majority of the Senators

63. *Congressional Record*, Vol. 45, Part 7, pp. 7196–99, 7213.
64. Ibid., pp. 7347, 7254–58; *Baltimore Sun* (June 3, 1910).
65. *New York Times* (May 16, 1910); *Congressional Record*, Vol. 45, Part 6, p. 6342; Part 7, pp. 6901, 7365, 7375; Part 8, p. 8391. See also Margulies, *Lenroot*, pp. 99–102.
66. *Congressional Record*, Vol. 5, Part 5, pp. 5445, 5128.

who did vote for it were Republican Senators." The comment was not only wholly unprovoked, it was an odd way to describe a roll call that saw the Democrats split 9 to 2 for the amendment, and the Republicans 30 to 11 against it.[67]

Although Democrats continued to support the insurgents' efforts with votes and speeches, they resented their allies' attitude. Democrats bridled not only at the condescension of the insurgents, but at their reluctance to go as far as the Democrats would. "I have the highest respect and admiration for the insurgents on this floor," complained Rayner of Maryland, but "I am becoming weary of being fondled and caressed only to be rejected and deserted when the supreme moment comes." On the last railroad bill, he recalled, Theodore Roosevelt had urged him to stand fast. "Mr. President, I took his advice and did not give up the ship, but the ship gave me up."[68]

The insurgents required Democratic support not only to exert power in Congress, but often to be there at all. In many plains states, a Democratic nomination meant little, and Bryanites often invaded the Republican primary to support insurgents. La Follette admitted that his early candidacies for governor of Wisconsin were aided by Democratic votes, and 10,000 Democrats provided insurgent Coe Crawford's margin of victory in the 1908 Republican Senate primary in South Dakota. The same year, a worried standpat Congressman tried to keep Democrats out of the Iowa Republican primaries. In Wisconsin, the Democrats demonstrated their importance when they returned to the Democratic primaries with the coming of Wilson. "With that defection," notes one historian of Wisconsin progressivism, "the makeup of the Republican party became more apparent" and La Follette's control diminished.[69]

Democratic votes would play a key role in the 1910 Republican primaries, when the insurgents resisted Taft's purge attempts and increased their numbers. "At the Wisconsin and Washington primaries," an ally wrote Charles Bryan, "our kind of Democrat went over almost bodily . . . to La Follette in the former and [Miles] Poindexter in the latter." In the insurgents' two most dramatic victories, Democratic votes helped Hiram Johnson win the nomination for governor of California and defeated James Tawney, chairman of the House Appropria-

67. Ibid., Part 7, pp. 7126, 7109.

68. *New York Times* (April 28, 1910); ibid., Part 5, p. 5443.

69. La Follette, *Autobiography*, p. 347; *New York World* (August 10, 1908); John Ely Briggs, *William Peters Hepburn* (Iowa City: State Historical Association of Iowa, 1919), p. 238; Herbert Margulies, *Decline of the Progressive Movement in Wisconsin* (Madison: Historical Society of Madison, 1968), p. 126.

tions Committee, in Minnesota. Even Democratic leaders supported the GOP insurgents; Bryan endorsed Norris in Nebraska, and the leading Democrat in Minnesota came out for Senator Moses Clapp. "It appears whenever there was a contest of insurgents against regulars, Democrats left their own primaries and voted the insurgent ticket," wrote the political expert of the *World*. "It was so in Wisconsin, Kansas, Iowa, California, and Minnesota."[70]

The insurgents also benefited from a friendly Democratic press. "Urge Democrats to vote for insurgent candidates in districts where Democrats cannot be elected," Joseph Pulitzer instructed his editor. "Support Bristow, Cummins, and Dolliver especially. They ought to be in the Democratic party. I wish to God they were." When Taft attempted to coerce the insurgents by cutting off patronage, they received warm endorsements from such Democratic papers as the *Baltimore Sun* and the *St. Louis Republic*, which editorialized, "The progressives did not insurge over differences in patronage or details of party management. Their stand, involving great sacrifices, was based on principle." Even so conservative a Democratic newspaper as the *New York Times* praised the insurgents as "that wing of the Republicans who have the sympathy and support of the people."[71]

Insurgents, however, liked Democrats no better on the hustings than in Congress. Campaigning for the conservative Republican House floor leader in 1910, Cummins proclaimed, "Anyone who reaches the conclusion that we ought to substitute for any Republican the best Democrat on earth badly needs an intellectual stimulant." Two years later La Follette, opposing Taft and loathing Theodore Roosevelt, could not bring himself to follow his close friend Louis Brandeis and support Woodrow Wilson. "Under no circumstances does he now expect to give you active support," a friendly Democratic senator wrote Wilson. "On the other hand, he does not want any conditions to arise that will cause him to attack you or your candidacy." Although La Follette did

70. Louis F. Post to Charles W. Bryan (September 20, 1910), Louis F. Post Papers, Library of Congress; Michael Rogin, "Progressivism and the California Electorate," *Journal of American History* 55 (September 1968): 303; Roger E. Wyman, "Insurgency in Minnesota, the Defeat of James A. Tawney in 1910," *Minnesota History* 40 (Fall 1967): 327–328; *New York World* (July 30, 1910); *The Public* (October 21, 1910); Joseph Pulitzer to Frank Cobb, quoting John L. McNaught (October 20, 1910), Pulitzer Papers, Library of Congress.

71. Notes on conversation with Grammarite (Cobb) (August 8, 1910), Pulitzer Papers, Library of Congress; *Baltimore Sun* (March 1, 1911); *St. Louis Republic* (October 23, 1910); *New York Times* (April 8, 1910).

tacitly support Wilson, by the end of the campaign *La Follette's Magazine* was denouncing the "reactionary Democratic House machine."[72]

The constant insurgent attacks on the Democrats, in and out of Congress, stemmed partly from aesthetic distaste, and partly from the open ambition of at least five insurgents (La Follette, Borah, Beveridge, Cummins, and Dolliver) for a Republican presidential nomination. But no issue did more to separate the two than a strong difference of opinion on the role of organized labor.[73]

Although labor issues had long had a high priority throughout the Democratic party, La Follette was the only insurgent to take much interest in them. Beveridge of Indiana, the insurgent whose state was most nearly industrial, was no more than "ambivalent" towards labor, and Norris, when on the House Labor Committee, was on the AFL's 1906 blacklist. Although the insurgents generally voted for better working conditions and shorter hours, they were uncomfortable with the idea of a strong organized labor movement. As White said of the Bull Moose convention, insurgency was "just as suspicious of Gompers and organized labor as it was of Rockefeller and organized capital."[74]

This division of interests became apparent after William Hughes of New Jersey, a union lawyer and the second-ranking Democrat on the Labor Committee, introduced an amendment to the Sundry Civil Appropriations Act of June 2, 1910. For years, the AFL had struggled against prosecutions under the Sherman Anti-Trust Act, and now Hughes introduced a simple but ingenious amendment providing that no money supplied by the act could be used for such prosecutions of labor unions. "Any man who knows anything about it at all," he explained earnestly, "knows that an organization of labor, a combination of laboring men, can never be very harmful." Conscious of the election five months in the future, the House adopted the amendment.[75]

In the Senate, Democrats fought to keep the Hughes Amendment in the bill. "There is no act of violence that would be protected by this provision," promised Bacon. "The effort in the United States to

72. *The Public* (October 28, 1910); Luke Lea to Woodrow Wilson (July 13, 1912), Wilson Papers, Series 2, Library of Congress; Holt, *Congressional Insurgents*, p. 87.

73. La Follette ran for the Republican nomination in 1908, 1912, and 1916; Cummins in 1912 and 1916; Borah in 1916. Dolliver died in 1910 and Beveridge lost his Senate seat, before they could strike for higher office.

74. Holt, *Congressional Insurgents*, p. 10; Braeman, *Beveridge*, p. 137; Lowitt, *Norris*, p. 110; White, *Autobiography*, p. 482.

75. John D. Buenker, *Urban Liberalism and Progressive Reform* (New York: 1973), p. 81; *Congressional Record*, Vol. 45, Part 7, pp. 7325, 7327.

prosecute laboring men for attempting to better their own conditions," cried Thomas Gore of Oklahoma, "is simply a relic of those darker times." Democrats supported the amendment 11 to 2 but drew only two insurgent and three regular Republican votes. Five insurgents, plus three more who had rebelled on the railroad bill, voted to kill the amendment. When the Sundry Civil Appropriations Act went to conference, the Senate conferees insisted on dropping the clause.[76]

On the first House vote to reconsider, on June 22, Democrats voted 116 to 2 to retain the Hughes Amendment, and with the aid of thirty-eight Republicans kept it in the bill. The forty-three insurgents who had voted against Cannon narrowly supported the Democrats, 22 to 15. Then Taft took an active hand as he had on the Commerce Court issue, and began summoning representatives to the White House. Two days later, the House voted to drop the provision, 138 to 130. The Democrats held virtually solid (109 to 3), but the insurgents, proving no less susceptible to White House pressure than their regular compatriots, now opposed the amendment 12 to 16. Madison, the only insurgent on the Labor Committee, spoke against it; his "sudden appearance as the champion of the House organization drew over many wavering members," commented the *Times*. Said Madison firmly, "Why, the laws of this country are liberal to the working man." Once again, the ship had given up the Democrats.[77]

Slowly, as historians examine the political history of the Progressive Era more intensely, the longtime image of the Democrats as a bumbling and divided band following after the insurgents is changing. Howard Allen, who once abandoned a quantification model that depicted Democrats as too progressive, has concluded that "the issues of the Progressive Era were fought out within the framework of traditional partisan alignment." His quantitative study of Senate Democrats in the 61st Congress, a group long derided for their divided stance on the Payne-Aldrich tariff, revealed the highest level of cohesion of fifteen selected Congresses, including the first Congresses of Woodrow Wilson and Franklin D. Roosevelt. "Almost all Democrats," he stated of that maligned contingent, "voted consistently in support of progressive reform measures."[78]

76. *Congressional Record*, ibid., pp. 7650–54.

77. Ibid., Part 8, pp. 8656, 8850–53; *New York Times* (June 24, 1910); *New York Tribune* (June 24, 1910).

78. Howard W. Allen, "Geography and Politics: Voting on Reform Issues in the United States Senate, 1911–1916," *Journal of Southern History* 27 (May 1961): 216–28; Howard W. Allen and Jerome Clubb, "Progressive Reform and the Political System," *Pacific Northwest Quarterly* 65 (July 1975): 133.

Why did contemporary observers fail to note this situation? To some extent, the Democrats' public relations problems derived from their obvious problems with organization, which led some observers to confuse lack of effectiveness with lack of progressivism. But another idea emerges from a look at the contemporary arbiters of progressivism. Middle-class reform magazines wielded great influence in the Progressive Era. Journals such as *Collier's*, the *American Magazine*, the *Outlook*, and the *World's Work* constituted the national media of the time. Their best-known writers, such as White, Lincoln Steffens, and Ray Stannard Baker, became national celebrities. The magazines praised La Follette and the insurgents and did much to arouse national interest in reforms. They also closely reflected the middle-class outlook of their readers.[79]

This meant, in part, unflinching opposition to Bryanism. When Ray Stannard Baker wrote in the *American Magazine* that Champ Clark was "a traditional radical rather than a constructive radical," he reflected this attitude. None of the magazines had supported Bryan in 1908, and many had printed favorable stories about Minnesota's John Johnson before the Democratic convention. In support of Taft, *Collier's* had featured William Allen White explaining, "He who errs on the side of the weak errs just as totally . . . as he who errs for the strong." Norman Mack, the Democratic national chairman, founded his own magazine in 1909, goaded "by the contemptible treatment our party received at the hands of nearly every magazine in the country during the campaign of 1908."[80]

The uplift magazines cared no more for the Democrats' northern constituents, immigrants and labor. In the Northeast, as Richard Abrams has pointed out, these groups, rather than disgruntled middle-class Republicans, were the true insurgents. The magazines were not overtly nativist, but when Mark Sullivan said of the insurgents in *Collier's*, "Wisconsin and Minnesota contain some of the best alien strains that have come to the American blood," the identity of the other less desirable (and more Democratic) types was clear. Although the magazines often sympathized with labor, they were horrified at its activities in 1908. The *World's Work* headlined "LABOR'S DANGEROUS PART IN POLI-

79. Eric Goldman, *Rendezvous with Destiny* (New York: 1952), pp. 171–76.
80. Baker, "What About the Democratic Party?" p. 156; William Hard, "John Johnson of Minnesota," *American Magazine* (October 1907); Winthrop B. Chamberlain, "A Great Democratic Governor," *World's Work* (April 1908); Richard Washburn Child, "John Johnson of St. Peter and St. Paul," *Collier's* (June 27, 1908); Charles B. Cheney, "A Labor Crisis and a Governor," *Outlook* (May 2, 1908); William Allen White, "Twelve Years of Mr. Bryan," *Collier's* (October 17, 1908); Norman Mack to Newlands (June 1, 1910), Newlands Papers.

TICS," and the *Outlook* warned that the resolutions of the AF of L convention that year showed a "distinctly Socialist character." When the AF of L entered the congressional campaign in 1906, *Collier's* had condemned its effort "to ruin some of our most high-minded office-holders because of honest differences in opinion."[81]

In this, the magazines and insurgents accurately reflected the middle-class reform outlook. "Most progressives were more comfortable espousing worker's rights than contemplating a strong union movement," notes one recent historian. "Liberals remained patronizing, arrogant and condescending in their attitude toward organized labor."[82] With such a world view, the influential uplift magazines found the insurgents highly congenial. They were reformers but reasonable, responsible, and from the American heartland. Several of the writers and editors became personal friends of the midwesterners. The magazines gave the insurgents valuable publicity, enviable reputations, and a leg up on history.

The insurgent movement ran from the genuine, if distinctly Republican, radicalism of La Follette, through the intensely partisan, and personally ambitious, progressivism of Cummins and Dolliver, down to numerous Republicans who broke with the leadership on one or two issues. Many of them were extremely able men, and most believed in the necessity for major reform. They played an important role in the politics of the Progressive Era. But they were rarely as radical, and never as numerous, as the Democrats whom they denounced, despised, and depended upon.

81. Abrams, *Conservatism in a Progressive Era*, pp. 132–33; *Collier's* (July 21, 1908); "Labor's Dangerous Role in Politics," *World's Work* (September 1908); *Outlook* (December 5, 1908); *Collier's* (September 24, 1906).
82. Eugene Tobin, *Organize or Perish* (Westport: Greenwood Press, 1986), p. 61.

CHAPTER 4

Trying on Power

Nineteen months before Theodore Roosevelt walked out of the 1912 Republican convention to launch his own party, the Democrats were already favored to win the White House that year. When the opposition party took over the House of Representatives in the off-year elections, a White House evacuation was expected two years later. It had happened in 1890 and 1894 (and would happen again in 1918 and 1930), and it was generally expected after the huge — but historically obscure — Democratic victory of 1910.[1]

"We are none of us writing very much on politics right now," one *World* correspondent informed Pulitzer in November 1909, after Taft had signed his unpopular new tariff bill, "but it is a foregone conclusion that in the near future there is to be such big politics in this country that no one can keep out of it." By February, Taft and the Republican leaders feared a Democratic landslide, and their only hope seemed to be the Democratic urge toward self-destruction. "You Republicans think you dare do anything now," Bailey had charged during the tariff fight, "because you think the country is afraid of the Democratic party," and Democratic congressmen could easily have revived those fears. When Democrats reached the end of the session without catastrophe, the *Baltimore Sun* described the departing party members as "jubilant."[2]

Almost a year earlier, even before the 1909 special session adjourned, House Democrats had reelected James Lloyd of Missouri chairman of the Congressional Campaign Committee because of his impressive performance in 1908. By campaign time, Lloyd could offer Democratic candidates textbooks, literature, and speakers, including several speaking in foreign languages.[3] Lloyd's *Campaign Textbook* devoted its first 176

1. Cortez A. M. Ewing, *Congressional Elections, 1896–1944* (Norman: University of Oklahoma Press, 1947), p. 24.
2. John McNaught to Joseph Pulitzer (November 23, 1909), Pulitzer Papers, Columbia University; *New York World* (February 6, 1910); *Congressional Record*, Vol. 44, Part 4, p. 4252; *Baltimore Sun* (June 26, 1910).
3. *National Monthly* (September 1909); James T. Lloyd to Henry D. Flood (August 2, 1909; January 29, 1910), Flood Papers, Library of Congress; *Louisville Courier-Journal*

pages to the tariff and the economy. "The real cause of this political unrest in this country," Cobb had written Pulitzer in March, "is the cost of living," and Democratic newspapers and politicians — even those running for state office — pounded home the issue throughout the campaign.[4]

Democrats also attacked Republican congressional leaders, whom they accused of bending Taft to their reactionary will. The *World* published a series on "Senators of Privilege," relating the business holdings of various senatorial millionaires to their tariff votes. Above all, the Democrats continued their attacks on House Speaker Cannon, an issue particularly attractive to the uplift magazines. But where *Collier's* suggested voting for Republican candidates who pledged to oppose Cannon in caucus, the Democrats successfully extracted partisan advantage from the issue. "Any person who votes for the Republican candidate for Congress," warned Lloyd, "may as well understand that he is casting his vote for Cannon to remain in power."[5]

Strong, reformist gubernatorial and senatorial campaigns in the major northeastern and midwestern states complemented the national effort. In Ohio, Governor Judson Harmon, running for reelection, drew both his platform and his running mates from the Tom Johnson forces in the state party. In New Jersey, the state convention gave Princeton President Woodrow Wilson a progressive platform, which he built on throughout the campaign. Governor Thomas Marshall of Indiana, in the middle of a four-year term, forced the state party convention to pledge support for Bryan's 1908 running mate, the bewhiskered radical, John Kern, for the Senate. Eugene Foss, a low-tariff businessman just elected to Congress, ran for governor in Massachusetts, calling for regulation of business and labor. Even in New York, where Tammany named the "clean" upstate businessman John Dix for governor, the *World* conceded grudgingly that the platform was "singularly free of corporation influences."[6]

(March 1, 1910); James T. Lloyd, "The Present Outlook," *National Monthly* (February 1910); James T. Lloyd to William B. Wilson (September 6, 1910; September 13, 1910), William B. Wilson Papers, Historical Society of Pennsylvania.

4. *Democratic Campaign Book* (Washington and Chicago: 1910); Frank Cobb to Joseph Pulitzer (March 26, 1910), Pulitzer Papers, Columbia University. For the importance of the tariff in at least one state race, see Frederick H. Jackson, *Simeon Eben Baldwin* (New York: King's Crown Press, 1955), p. 164.

5. See for example, *New York World* (September 5, 1910); *Collier's* (March 26, 1910); James T. Lloyd, "The People vs. the Interests," *National Monthly* (September 1910).

6. Hoyt L. Warner, *Progressivism in Ohio* (Columbus: 1964), pp. 252–53; *New York World* (April 27–29, 1910; September 16, 1910; October 1, 1910); *Independent* (September

Not only the platforms, but the quality of the Democratic gubernatorial hopefuls struck observers. "The challenge of the Democratic
party is . . . notable," commented the *Independent*. "They seemed to
have learned the lesson that for success . . . they must put the very best
men at the head of their tickets."[7]

The party's 1908 ally, the AFL, played a reduced role in the 1910
campaign, having burned its fingers badly the preceding time. But Samuel Gompers still sent out lists of friendly and unfriendly congressmen,
and most of the friends turned out to be Democrats. For an especially
good friend of labor, such as William Hughes of New Jersey, he could
also provide literature and a personal endorsement. He also published
an editorial, "Labor's Political Opportunity," in the October *American
Federationist* that, although mentioning no parties, urged union voters
to strike against Cannonism.[8]

The improved party prospects also caused people once active in the
party to revalidate their old allegiances. The thought occurred to numerous Grover Cleveland Democrats, who scented not only victory but
also the possibility of new leadership under such men as Harmon and
Wilson, and also to a more recent apostate. William Randolph Hearst's
1908 disaster had not slaked his thirst for high office nor reduced the
power of his newspapers. He had partially resurrected his political identity with a strong independent run for mayor of New York in 1909,
and as early as April 1910, a Pulitzer editor noted Hearst's efforts to
"ride on the rising Democratic wave." In November, his newspapers
supported the party everywhere but in New York, where Hearst continued his feud with Tammany.[9]

The Democratic landscape disclosed only one spot of discontent, but
it was the largest spot on the horizon: William Jennings Bryan. He had
expected victory in 1908 and was overwhelmingly rejected. Bryan still
could not understand why. Throughout 1909, the *Commoner* printed
ever more virulent attacks on Bryan's enemies in the party: against
Tammany, the *World*, Bailey. Bryan's frustration did not decrease at the
prospect of party victories in 1910 and 1912, success in which he would

22, 1910); Robert F. Wesser, *A Response to Progressivism: The Democratic Party and New
York Politics, 1902–1918* (New York: New York University Press, 1986), p. 37.

7. *Independent*, September 22, 1910.

8. Samuel Gompers to William Hughes (October 28, 1910), AFL Letterbooks, Library
of Congress; "Labor's Political Opportunity," *American Federationist* (October 1910).

9. Frank Cobb to Joseph Pulitzer (December 4, 1909), *New York World* Papers,
Columbia University; Horatio J. Seymour to Joseph Pulitzer (April 20, 1910) *New York
World* Papers; *Los Angeles Examiner* (November 9, 1910).

have no share. By 1910, he openly attacked Harmon of Ohio, already considered a likely presidential possibility. Bryan wanted to run for the Senate from Nebraska in 1910, and his followers set out to gather 15,000 signatures. They collected only 2,000, Bryan did not run, and his candidate, the business manager of the *Commoner*, lost badly in the primary.[10]

But, by then, Bryan had taken up the issue that no politician with national prospects would willingly go near: prohibition. He began to blame the liquor lobby for his 1908 defeat and demanded action against it. He wrote Watterson in May 1910 that the liquor industry had beaten him in Missouri and Indiana and had hurt him in Ohio and New York. (The letter alarmed Watterson greatly. "I have had a long letter from Mr. Bryan explaining his 'attitude' as to the liquor question," he wrote Norman Mack. "The real point was and is, that he should have no 'attitude' at all.") He now demanded that the Democratic governor of Nebraska call a special session of the legislature to pass a county option bill. When the governor refused, Bryan defeated him in the primary by backing the aggressively "wet" mayor of Omaha, whom Bryan then piously refused to support in the election. That November, Nebraska proved a dry well of Democratic defeat, and Bryan had served notice on Democratic victors in other states that any would-be reorganizer of the power had better conciliate its titular leader.[11]

The dominant figure of the Republican party also had his difficulties. Theodore Roosevelt, having tangled with lions and been lionized by kings, returned from his yearlong vacation in June 1910 to find his party in shambles. Throughout his presidency, the Rough Rider had managed to keep the GOP together by a combination of radical words and conservative actions. He now sought to do it again. Seizing control of the New York party, he named Henry Stimson, a personal friend and Taft appointee, as the party's candidate for governor, with a good deal of progressive rhetoric and a platform that endorsed the new tariff and did not mention labor legislation or the income tax amendment. In Ossawottomie, Kansas, Roosevelt proclaimed his New Nationalism, a program of legalizing and regulating trusts, and he campaigned for Republicans from all wings of the party.[12]

10. *Commoner* (November 20, 1908; May 14, 1909, July 9, 1909; May 27, 1910); Louis W. Koenig, *Bryan* (New York: Putnam's, 1971), p. 470; *Commoner* (July 22, 1910).

11. *Commoner* (December 10, 1909); William Jennings Bryan to Henry Watterson (May 13, 1910), Bryan Papers, Occidental College; Henry Watterson to Norman Mack (May 28, 1910), in Isaac Marcosson, *Marse Henry* (New York: Dodd, Mead, 1951), p. 181; Koenig, ibid., pp. 471–72.

12. *New York World* (October 1, 1910); *Commoner* (September 9, 1910).

But Roosevelt's brand of politics was ill-suited to the atmosphere of 1910. Never very comfortable with issues, he remained particularly apathetic about the tariff. He had taken no interest in it as president, and wrote Lodge from Africa that only the mental condition of the people required its revision. Campaigning in 1910, he mentioned it rarely and tried to dismiss it as a minor issue. "Mr. Roosevelt's fine moral fervor," sneered the *World*, "oozes out of his fingers when it comes to the tariff." Unconcerned with the issue himself, he could not see what others were so excited about, nor why people should deride his speaking for both the rebel Beveridge in Indiana and the Aldrich supporter Lodge in Massachusetts. In a typical speech, Roosevelt would declare, "the Democratic party has forfeited its right to respect and support of decent men," and would remind his hearers that the Republican party had saved the Union. In 1910, this was not enough.[13]

Few Republicans could join Roosevelt in rising above the issues that divided the party. Party regulars, in control from Illinois eastward, clearly demonstrated in 1910 that they feared the Democrats far less than they did losing party control to insurgents—a view that the Taft administration appeared to share. In New York, where Roosevelt's aura gave the ticket an insurgent tinge, many regulars defected. The Ohio convention, which the conservatives controlled, virtually read progressive Republicans out of the party. (To such charges, Ohio gubernatorial candidate Warren Harding would point out, plaintively and accurately, that he was running on virtually the same platform as the "progressive" New York ticket.) Regulars in Indiana, where Beveridge was running for reelection, openly knifed the ticket. "I can't see how any self-respecting Republican can vote for a single candidate on the Beveridge ticket in Indiana," stated a party congressional leader. "It is not a Republican ticket." In all three states, the key swing states of the country, Democrats won sizable victories.[14]

New York, Ohio, and Indiana were the brightest triumphs of a national victory that exceeded Democratic expectations. Lloyd had predicted a House majority of thirty-five seats; the Democrats controlled the new House by sixty-three. Harmon won reelection by a "very avalanche" of 100,000 votes, carrying in the entire ticket. Wilson and Foss, expected to win narrowly, chalked up convincing victories. The party

13. *New York World* (September 5, 1910); *Commoner* (October 21, 1910); *St. Louis Republic* (October 12, 1910).
14. George Mowry, *Theodore Roosevelt and the Progressive Movement* (Madison: University of Wisconsin Press, 1946), p. 154; *Independent* (August 4, 1910); *Cleveland Plain Dealer* (October 5, 1910); John Braeman, *Albert J. Beveridge* (Chicago: University of Chicago Press, 1971), p. 194.

also gained governorships in Connecticut and Maine, and the results in the legislatures showed it in line for a gain of eight seats in the Senate. "Democratic gains in yesterday's election," commented a dazed *Baltimore Sun*, "especially in the great pivotal states, assumed the proportion of a political earthquake." The *Courier-Journal* covered its front page with seven crowing and contented Democratic roosters.[15]

Moreover, the Democrats had fought and won as a party committed to reform. "In turning to the Democratic party," Charles Bryan wrote Newlands, "[voters] undoubtedly had in mind the principles that were paramount in the 1908 campaign, as embodied in the Denver platform." For once, the *World* agreed with a Bryan on the party's course, saying, "Never before, since the civil war, has there been so general an agreement about leaders and issues and opportunities." The election, observed the *Independent*, had been won by "Democracy more progressive and radical than the most advanced Republicans."[16]

Given this widespread agreement, Democrats looked hopefully toward their coming encounter with power. "Frank, I believe there is a great future for our party," wrote one New York Democratic Congressman to another, "and if we can only do that which the people demand, it will be impossible to defeat us in a great many years.[17]

Richard V. Oulahan, new president of the Gridiron Club, was about to open the February 1911 dinner of the Washington correspondents' club when fifteen members demanded that he turn the dinner over to them. "But fifteen men cannot preside over this dinner," protested Oulahan.

"Fifteen men are to preside over the next House of Representatives," they pointed out.[18]

Historians, when they touch on the subject at all, tend to accept George Norris's statement that the Democrats lost interest in House rules reform in 1910 when it became clear that they would control the next House. Actually, Democratic victory signalled a sweeping restructure of the operation of the House of Representatives. The removal of the House Speaker from the Rules Committee only began what Charles

---

15. *Louisville Courier-Journal* (November 6, 1910; November 10, 1910); *New York World* (November 7, 1910; November 9, 1910); *Baltimore Sun* (November 9, 1910); *Louisville Courier-Journal* (November 9, 1910).
16. Charles W. Bryan to Francis G. Newlands (December 1, 1910), Newlands Papers, Yale University; *New York World* (December 19, 1910); *Independent* (November 24, 1910).
17. Daniel A. Driscoll to Francis Burton Harrison (November 30, 1910), Harrison Papers, Library of Congress.
18. Arthur W. Dunn, *Gridiron Nights* (New York: Frederick A. Stokes, 1915), p. 242.

O. Jones calls "the most significant changes in this century—perhaps in the history of Congress."[19]

First, Democrats had to elect a progressive as House Speaker. Immediately after the election, some Democrats suggested that the election of Champ Clark, a Bryanite, might repeat the problems of the immediate past, and a few congressmen diffidently suggested themselves as alternatives. The reaction was swift. Any Democrat voting against Clark, wrote Louis F. Post of *The Public*, was "playing the game of the plutes." Clark's supporters moved swiftly to wrap up his selection and, within a week, opposition had vanished. At the January caucus, Clark became the first Democratic Speaker ever elected to his first term unanimously.[20]

The Speaker-designate and his followers now faced the one single issue at the core of Cannonism. The 120-year-old power of the Speaker to name committees was now considered, in the words of House insurgent leader Victor Murdock, "the greatest source of the outrageous control of the House by its presiding officer." Clark, as minority leader, had often stated that he did not want the power, and Democrats now made a historic shift: committee selection would be made instead by the Democratic members of the Ways and Means Committee, the most prestigious committee in the House.[21]

At the first caucus in January 1911, the Democrats elected fourteen members to the now ultra-powerful body. "A number of the older members who, by the rule of seniority, would be entitled to the most important places," the *Baltimore Sun* had predicted a month earlier, would find themselves "supplanted by younger men who more nearly represent the views of the progressive element." Probably to a greater extent than it might have wished, the *Sun* proved accurate.[22]

Democratic leaders carefully selected reliable progressives, especially on the tariff. Two holdover committee members, Robert Broussard of Louisiana and Edward Pou of North Carolina, were purged as unreliable. The new Ways and Means Committee members included labor ad-

19. Richard Lowitt, *George W. Norris, The Making of a Progressive* (Syracuse: Syracuse University Press, 1963), p. 209; Charles O. Jones, *The Minority Party in Congress* (Boston: Little, Brown and Co., 1970), p. 15.

20. *Baltimore Sun* (November 11, 12, 1910); Louis F. Post to William Kent (November 26, 1910), Kent Papers, Yale University; *Louisville Courier-Journal* (November 13, 1910); Champ Clark, *My Quarter Century of American Politics*, 2 vols. (New York: Harper, 1920), II:29.

21. Victor Murdock, "After Cannonism—What?" *Independent* (September 22, 1910); *Baltimore Sun* (November 16, 1910); Arthur W. Dunn, *From Harrison to Harding*, 2 vols. (New York: Putnam's, 1922), II:118.

22. Harold Syrett, ed., *The Gentleman and the Tiger*, p. 134; James M. Cox to Francis Burton Harrison (December 31, 1910), Harrison Papers, Library of Congress; *Baltimore Sun* (December 24, 1910).

vocate William Hughes of New Jersey; Ollie James of Kentucky and Henry Rainey of Illinois, skilled debaters and close friends of Bryan; Cordell Hull of Tennessee, the party's income tax expert; Claude Kitchin, the only North Carolina Democrat to oppose the lumber tariff, who had made one of the most admired Democratic speeches during the Payne-Aldrich debate; Dorsey Shackelford of Missouri, an active foe of Cannonism and old Hearst ally; and A. Mitchell Palmer of Pennsylvania, who had impressed party leaders with a tariff speech in the preceding Congress. Oscar Underwood of Alabama, Clark ally and firm low-tariff advocate, would serve as committee chairman and majority leader.[23]

Progressive Democrats exulted in both the decisions of the caucus and its startling harmony. The meeting "disclosed an almost unanimous determination to 'make good' this time," cheered *The Public*; its actions were "a great victory for popular government," gushed the *Commoner*. Even *Collier's*, normally given to comparing Democrats unfavorably with insurgent Republicans, proclaimed *"the fourteen men appointed to the committee are men who can be depended upon to write a tariff bill in the interests of the people."*[24]

But before proceeding, the new committee had to name other standing committees. It expanded the majority positions on thirteen major committees from twelve to fourteen, and on the Rules Committee from six to seven, and stipulated that no Democrat could be on more than one of the fourteen committees. This step provided 189 of 227 Democrats, including many freshmen, with significant committee assignments. It also ended such Cannonite practices as depositing insurgents on the Committee on the Census, while a promising young standpatter

23. William Jennings Bryan to Henry T. Rainey (September 8, 1906), Rainey Papers, Library of Congress; William G. McAdoo, *Crowded Years* (Cambridge: Riverside Press, 1931), p. 266; *St. Louis Republic* (March 6, 1906; January 17, 1910); Marvin Block, "Henry T. Rainey of Illinois," *Illinois State Historical Society Journal* 65 (Summer 1972): 142–157; Robert A. Waller, *Rainey of Illinois* (Urbana: University of Illinoies Press, 1977), pp. 102–03; Cordell Hull, *Memoirs*, 2 vols. (London: Hodder and Stoughton, 1948), I:48, 58, 62; Alex M. Arnett, *Claude Kitchin and the Wilson War Policies* (Boston: Little, Brown and Co., 1937), pp. 21, 37; *Congressional Record*, Vol. 44, Part 1, pp. 583–601; Stanley Coben, *A. Mitchell Palmer, Politician* (Princeton: Princeton University Press, 1963), p. 17. Another indication of the quality of the committee is the striking political success its members enjoyed afterward. The fourteen Democrats on the committee produced four senators (Underwood, James, Hull, and Hughes); one governor (Hammond of Minnesota); one mayor of Boston (Peters); two cabinet members (Hull and Palmer); a governor-general of the Philippines (Harrison); and the Speaker of the House during Roosevelt's Hundred Days (Rainey).

24. *The Public* (January 27, 1911); *Commoner* (January 27, 1911); *Collier's* (February 4, 1911).

like George Malby, described by *Collier's* as "promoted to Congress from the Twenty-Sixth New York for eminent service to corporations in the State Senate," sat on both the Appropriations and Judiciary Committees in his second term.[25]

The Democratic changes amounted to "a vast improvement on previous methods," conceded one Republican insurgent. "The whole spirit of committee appointments was changed. A far greater fairness of selection resulted." When the Republicans recaptured Congress, they retained the practice of appointment by committee.[26]

The members of Ways and Means Committee, however, made their choices carefully. "If we had the least doubt about a prospective member's attitude," recalled Hull, "we sent for him beforehand, cross-examined him, and pledged him unequivocally to do teamwork." The erratic William Sulzer of New York was denied the chairmanship of the money-granting Military Affairs Committee and put at the head of the then somewhat ornamental Foreign Affairs Committee. (The ranking Democrat on the Foreign Affairs Committee was consoled with the chair of the Territories Committee.) They took particular pains with the Rules Committee, installing as chairman the Bryanite, prolabor Robert Henry of Texas.[27]

Several of the more activist Democrats urged supplanting John J. Fitzgerald, the Tammanyite who had led the bolt in the 1909 rules fight, from the chair of the Appropriations Committee. But Fitzgerald let it be known that he would fight such an effort and might carry enough northern Democrats to block organization of the House. Fitzgerald also had influential friends. He had "rendered exceptionally valuable aid to labor," testified Gompers, and had "proven his worth on many occasions."[28]

25. *Report of the Majority Members of the Ways and Means Committee Nominating the Majority Members of the Standing Committees of the House of Representatives in the 62nd Congress,* in Claude Kitchin Papers, University of North Carolina; *Baltimore Sun* (January 13, 1911); *Collier's* (December 1, 1906); *Congressional Directory* 61st Congress (Washington: 1909).

26. William Kent, "Circular Letters to District Number Three," (August 17, 1914), Kent Papers, Yale University.

27. Hull, *Memoirs,* I:63; Henry D. Flood to E. G. Brantley (October 21, 1912), Flood papers; George Rothwell Brown, *Leadership in Congress* (Indianapolis: Bobbs-Merrill, 1922), p. 175; Samuel Gompers, *Seventy Years of Life and Labor,* 2 vols. (New York: E. P. Dolton, 1925), I:542; Michael F. Conry to Francis B. Harrison (March 6, 1911), Harrison Papers.

28. *New York World* (December 5, 1910); Dunn, *From Harrison to Harding,* II:150; Samuel Gompers to T. F. O'Toole (October 31, 1910), AFL Letterbooks; *Collier's* (April 15, 1911).

The AFL chief had a more direct concern about committees. Cannon, Gompers often complained, "took special delight in so constituting the Committee on Labor that bills referred to it were never reported." Making up their Labor Committee, Democrats named as chairman William B. Wilson of Pennsylvania, former international secretary-treasurer of the United Mine Workers; and added a national treasurer of the United Hatters of North America; a former international president of the Bridge and Structural Iron Workers' Union; and a former coal miner who had put himself through law school. In a notable switch, President John A. Kirby of the National Association of Manufacturers would attack the Democrats for "so constituting the important committee on Labor of the House as to place it under the domination of present or ex-labor union officials who sit in Congress."[29]

The Democrats also altered some other rules. The Speaker's power of recognition was "much impaired," and such means of escape from regular order as Calendar Wednesday and the discharge calendar were strengthened. "The Democratic party," boasted Rainey with some hyperbole, "has taken from the Speaker of the House every one of his powers."[30]

To maintain discipline, the Democrats would rely not upon the Speaker's power but on the binding caucus. Such a body, the *Rocky Mountain News* had said in 1906, was "a thing of the past and will not be resumed for a generation, if ever." But the new masters of the House saw it as a form of Democratic discipline. A two-thirds vote in caucus would bind a congressman, but "no member shall be bound upon questions involving a construction of the Constitution . . . or upon which he made contrary pledges to his constituents prior to his election." Mindful of their record and reputation, Democrats were resolved that the end of Cannonism would not bring chaos.[31] The Democrats had reorganized the rules, the functioning, and the committees of the House. Now all they had to do was legislate.

"When prospects looked good for the election of a Democratic

29. Samuel Gompers to John H. Walker (October 17, 1916), AFL Letterbooks; *Congressional Directory*, 62nd Congress (Washington: 1911); Open Letter from John A. Kirby (July 31, 1912), in William B. Wilson Papers.

30. Brown, *Leadership in Congress*, p. 181; *Congressional Record*, Vol. 47, Part 1, pp. 11–21; Henry T. Rainey to H. N. Wheeler (December 6, 1911), Rainey Papers.

31. *Rocky Mountain News* (March 14, 1906); *Preamble and Rules Adopted by Democratic Caucus*, 62nd Congress, in Claude Kitchin Papers, University of North Carolina; Wilder H. Haines, "The Congress and Caucus of Today," *American Political Science Review* 9 (November 1915): 696; Adrian Anderson, "President Wilson's Politician: Albert Sidney Burleson of Texas," *Southwest Historical Quarterly* 77 (January 1974): 342.

House," Judson Harmon told the Democrats of the Ohio legislature, "men who . . . hoped for nothing more than Democratic success felt like praying that we wouldn't get control of the House of Representatives, lest we do something to mar the prospects of the party." Yet, within a month after the new House convened, the *National Monthly* boasted exuberantly, "Democracy Is Making Good," and *Collier's* cited "the splendid record of the Democrats in the lower House."[32]

To the surprise of most political observers—and themselves—the perennially disorganized Democrats, after sixteen years out of power, began immediately to create a momentum that would last until November 1912. The new Democrats got their chance at power eight months early, thanks to the man they intended to displace. William Howard Taft had presented his own variety of tariff reform (limited reciprocity with Canada) to the lame duck session of the departing Republican Congress. Opposed by the majority of Republicans, the measure passed the House due to Democratic support but failed to come to a vote in the Senate. Standpatters opposed any reductions, and insurgents feared that the largest effect of reciprocity would be to admit Canadian agricultural products, injuring and angering their Farm Belt constituents. "There does not appear to be a single Republican in the Senate," observed the *Baltimore Sun*, "who is enthusiastic over the Administration's measure."[33]

Taft, determined to show a disaffected electorate that he too could reform tariffs, decided to seek the assistance of a Democratic House. He called in Clark and Underwood, who agreed to pass reciprocity but refused to pledge to consider no other issues. The president, showing the political ineptitude that had gotten him into this situation, called a special session anyway.[34] On April 4, 1911, Champ Clark—"big, picturesque, emotional . . . with just a touch of the flamboyant, just a tinge of the actor when the scene becomes dramatic"—opened the first session of a Democratic House since 1895. To a chorus of rebel yells, he intoned, "We are this day put on trial."[35]

The new House began by passing, in its first day of deliberation, the constitutional amendment for direct election of senators. The measure

32. "A Speech and Special Message by Governor Judson Harmon that Helped to Obtain Progressive Legislation in Ohio," in Newlands Papers; Frank B. Lord, "Democracy is Making Good," *National Monthly* (May 1911); *Collier's* (April 29, 1911).
33. *Baltimore Sun* (February 24, 1911).
34. Clark, *My Quarter-Century of American Politics*, II:7; Oscar W. Underwood, *Drifting Sands of Party Politics* (New York: Century, 1928), p. 167.
35. *New York World* (April 5, 9, 1911).

had passed the previous House but had been killed in the Senate when conservative Republicans attached the Sutherland amendment, providing for federal control of the elections, thus scaring off important southern Democratic votes. The House now repassed the original bill, opposed only by fifteen Republicans, including much of the party's House leadership, and one Democrat, who later admitted to a state of parliamentary confusion. The next day, the Democrats added the Rucker bill, requiring preelection publication of presidential campaign contributions.[36]

Those tasks accomplished, Underwood now led his troops to reciprocity. He, and other Democratic speakers, stressed that they supported Taft's bill only as "the first step toward breaking down the system of monopolistic protection," and that further bills would follow. But they refused all motions to tack other tariff measures onto the reciprocity bill, wishing to give Taft no reason to veto it. Democrats spent a scant four days defeating amendments, passing the bill, and enjoying the discomfiture of the insurgents.[37]

In the preceding Congress, the insurgents had enjoyed the reputation of standing firm and waging courageous rebellion against the party establishment. Now, with tariff revision threatening their own constituents, they appealed to Republican orthodoxy. "This bill cannot be defended from a Republican standpoint," pleaded Irvine Lenroot of Wisconsin, a close ally of La Follette. Others showed deep bitterness against both parties. Had not the Republican leaders failed to revise the tariff properly, complained one newly elected insurgent, "Tammany and Dixie would not have been given an opportunity to combine against the country."[38]

The Democrats could now turn to their own plans for the tariff. "The tariff ought to be so reformed," demanded Henry Clayton of Alabama, new chairman of the Judiciary Committee, "as not to afford shelter to its evil progeny, the trusts and unlawful combinations." Shortly after reciprocity passed, the Democrats began by putting through a "farmer's free list," removing tariffs from farm machinery, equipment, and materials, a clear but defined compensation for the possible effects of the earlier bill on farmers. It received the unanimous support of the Democratic majority, plus the votes of twenty-four Republicans and the House's lone Socialist, Victor Berger of Milwaukee.[39]

36. *Baltimore Sun* (March 1, 1911), *Congressional Record*, Vol. 47, Part 1, pp. 239, 242–43, 268–69.
37. Ibid., pp. 534–35, 537–60.
38. Ibid., pp. 431, 424, 559–60.
39. Ibid., pp. 858, 916, 932; Part 2, pp. 236–309.

By now, Congress watchers beheld a political phenomenon: Democratic efficiency. They were most impressed by a large, balding person in the third row of the majority desks. Oscar W. Underwood had come to Congress in 1895 as a strong supporter of labor, free silver, and an income tax and rapidly rose to leadership positions. If his later marriage to a Birmingham steel heiress seemed to have taken the edge off his reformism, he was still far from a standpatter and closely followed the party line on most issues.[40]

His conservative image may have derived largely from his appearance and manner. Unlike his predecessors, John Sharp Williams and Champ Clark, Underwood was no orator: he spoke, and dressed, like a quiet, prosperous executive in one of the trusts he disliked. The majority leader, commented the *World*, "suggests of those Anthony Hope heroes in his first books . . . who faced the conspirators on the palace steps so quietly and courteously, and ran them through with his rapier with such suavity."[41]

Underwood employed a variety of rapiers to run legislation through the House. As chairman of the Ways and Means Committee, he now exercised much of the committee appointment power previously held by the Speaker. He worked closely with Clark and benefited greatly from the latter's substantial influence in the House. He shared none of the insurgents' fondness for unlimited debate and amendment. "I am glad to see that the Democrats are not going to take any nonsense from [Minority Leader James] Mann," wrote one atypical insurgent, "but will apply gag rule when needed to pass measures upon which there is common consensus of opinion in the country."[42]

Underwood used all of this—as well as the general progressive consensus among Democratic congressmen—to revive and master the party caucus. "The Democratic caucus was more or less a joke," wrote George McClellan, a Tammany congressman in the early years of the century, "and I never knew it to agree on anything except a motion to adjourn." Underwood, aided by Clark and Caucus Chairman A. S. Burleson, now brought major and minor issues in, worked out agree-

40. Ann Firor Scott, "A Progressive Wind From the South," *Journal of Southern History* 29 (February 1963): 69; Claude Barfield, "Congressional Democrats in the Taft Administration" (diss., Northwestern University, 1969), p. 283; Evans C. Johnson, "Oscar W. Underwood: A Fledgling Politician," *Alabama Review* 13 (April 1960): 120–25; Johnson, *Underwood*, pp. 100–104.

41. "Men We Are Watching," *Independent* (June 29, 1911); *New York World* (March 26, 1911).

42. Brown, *Leadership in Congress*, p. 185; Chang-wei Chiu, *The Speaker of the House of Representatives since 1896* (New York: Columbia University Press, 1928), p. 304; William Kent to Elizabeth Kent (April 12, 1911), Kent Papers.

ments, and then bound the members to support the bills and oppose amendments. "The House majority is working with machine-like precision in great harmony," a *World* political correspondent wrote Pulitzer. "The secret seems to be good management in caucus." The rank and file supported the new approach, although insurgent and standpat Republicans joined in deriding the caucus as the "tell-me-how-to-vote club." Retorted John Nance Garner, "Under a Republican House, you had a one-man caucus, where under the Democratic House we have a 227-man caucus."[43]

Despite substantial gains, Democrats did not control the Senate. But if forty Democratic senators still constituted a minority, they were no longer a hopeless one. Indeed, combined with the old (and new) insurgents, they made up a comfortable majority of the upper house. Moreover, the new arrival showed heartening solidarity and considerable ability.

Several old-line Democrats, who for several years had prudently avoided national affairs, reviewed the 1910 election returns and rediscovered senatorial ambitions. John McLean again hoped to parlay the power of his Cincinnati *Enquirer* into a Senate seat from Ohio. In New Jersey, former senator and current boss James Smith, who had pledged Woodrow Wilson that he would not run for the Senate, reassessed his position after the Democrats unexpectedly won control of the legislature. Tammany boss Charles Murphy endorsed the aspirations of William F. ("Blue-Eyed Billy") Sheehan, lieutenant-governor in the 1880s and Parker's manager in 1904. As the party prepared to elect its first senators from these states since 1893, many Democrats viewed the prospects more with alarm than rejoicing. "For three great States of the North to send Democratic Senators of Privilege to Washington," warned the *World*, "would destroy popular confidence in the good faith of a whole party."[44]

But all three would-be legislators, as well as the rest of the country, now learned how much the party had changed since 1893. Among the thoroughly Johnsonized Ohio Democrats, McLean did not even offer his name, and the conservative candidate received but ten of eighty-nine votes in caucus. Woodrow Wilson, to national applause, faced

43. Syrett, *The Gentleman and the Tiger*, p. 154; James S. Fleming, "Re-establishing Leadership in the House of Representatives: The Case of Oscar W. Underwood," *Mid-America* 54 (October 1972): 240; Brown, *Leadership in Congress*, p. 185; Horatio J. Seymour to Joseph Pulitzer (April 18, 1911), *New York World* Papers; *Congressional Record*, Vol. 48, Part 3, p. 2212; Vol. 47, Part 3, p. 2201.

44. *New York World* (December 17, 1910).

down Smith and forced the election of the Bryanite nonentity who had won the advisory primary. In New York, two dozen young progressive legislators, led by freshman State Senator Franklin D. Roosevelt, refused to vote for Sheehan and caused Murphy to name a more acceptable Tammanyite.[45]

Perhaps the progressivism of the new recruits spurred a new interest in the upper house on the part of William Jennings Bryan. Senate Democrats had rejected Joseph Bailey's ambition to become leader, instead, compromising on Thomas Martin of Virginia. Martin, a former railroad lawyer, may have been "thoroughly conservative in his beliefs and ideals" as well as his associations, but he had followed a moderate course on the tariff and had brilliantly organized the party in Virginia. Many Democrats were already committed to him by the time Bryan, figuring on "somewhere between twenty and twenty-five who will act together in favor of a progressive organization," descended upon Washington.[46]

After several refusals from other senators, Benjamin Shively of Indiana agreed to stand as Bryan's candidate. But he received only sixteen votes to twenty-one for Martin. Senators denied that Martin was a reactionary and resented Bryan's injecting himself into the situation. They, and other Democrats, could only have been more alarmed at Bryan's reaction to defeat. Although the radical Senator Robert Owen of Oklahoma stated that he expected to be "agreeably disappointed" in Martin, Bryan fumed, "Most of [the Democratic senators] who voted for him voted for him because they are themselves reactionary." A disgruntled and quarrelsome Bryan could blight the most favorable Democratic prospects.[47]

But as the Senate moved to deal with reciprocity, its Democrats had a behavior problem closer to home. Bailey opposed the bill, and party leaders feared the havoc he could create. The Texan had been growing ever more erratic: in March he had telegraphed his resignation to the governor of Texas, then allowed his colleagues to talk him out of it.

45. *New York World* (January 6, 1911); *Baltimore Sun* (December 28, 1910); *New York World* (February 10, 1911); *Commoner* (April 7, 1911).
46. Wythe W. Holt, Jr., "The Senator from Virginia and the Democratic Floor Leadership: Thomas S. Martin and Conservatism in the Progressive Era," *Virginia Magazine of History and Biography* 83 (January 1975): 4–5; Allen W. Moger, *Virginia, Bourbonism to Byrd, 1870–1925* (Charlottesville, 1968), pp. 96–99, 112; William Jennings Bryan to William Allen White (March 22, 1911), Bryan Papers, Occidental College.
47. Francis G. Newlands to Robert L. Owen (April 8, 1911), Newlands Papers; *Baltimore Sun* (April 7, 8, 1911); *Louisville Courier-Journal* (April 8, 1911); *Commoner* (April 14, 1911).

He claimed to be protesting Democratic radicalism, but observers felt he was more upset over his own declining influence among Senate Democrats. Now he called reciprocity "an abandonment of the doctrines of both parties," and prepared to attack the bill, and its sponsors, in his usual slashing style.[48]

Four of the freshmen Democrats, however, had brought particularly useful qualities to their new position. They were firmly progressive, they were strong debaters, and they were not afraid of Bailey. John Sharp Williams had finally arrived in the Senate after his two-year vacation on his Yazoo County plantation; Gilbert Hitchcock, a prominent House Democrat, had been raised to the Senate from Nebraska; Bryan's running mate, Kern, had ousted Beveridge in Indiana; and the acid-tongued James Reed had arrived from Missouri. All four shortly crossed swords with Bailey, something veteran Democrats did only reluctantly. "The Senator from Texas must remember that he cannot freely attack the position of his Democratic colleagues," warned Williams, "without expecting them, in their ineffective and frequently helpless way, as compared with his own great ability, to attack the attacker."[49]

The quartet, along with some newly emboldened veterans, rapidly succeeded in exorcising Bailey's power over the party, an essential prerequisite to the Senate Democrats' functioning as an effective reformist bloc. Only three Democrats ultimately voted against reciprocity, a sign of change that led the *Courier-Journal* to muse on "the pitifully shrunken forces of Senator Bailey."[50]

Besides the fall of their former idol, the vote also reflected the new spirit and effectiveness of Senate Democrats. Considering reciprocity at best a slight step toward general tariff reform, they supported it almost as a body. "It is our duty as Democrats," explained Ellison Smith of South Carolina, "to vote for everything that is moving in a Democratic direction." Their ranks even held on a long series of votes on insurgent efforts to attach broader tariff reform amendments to Taft's bill. "The Democrats, for the most part," stated Newlands, "believe it will imperil this reciprocity bill if they allow it to be amended." Insurgents not dependent upon agricultural constituents agreed. "I have voted against the amendments," said John Works of California, "because I am in favor of the bill."[51]

48. *New York World* (March 5, 6, 7, 1911); *Independent* (March 9, 1911); *Congressional Record*, Vol. 47, Part 3, p. 2294.
49. *Congressional Record*, ibid., p. 2812.
50. *Louisville Courier-Journal* (July 23, 1911).
51. *Congressional Record*, Vol. 47, Part 3, pp. 3123, 2526, 3035.

Insurgents with strong agricultural constituencies were undergoing a decline in popular favor as rapid as the Democrats' rise. Even *Collier's*, faithful house organ of the movement, conceded, "there is some chance that the movement they started has gone ahead faster than they have." Socialist congressman Victor Berger observed from his uniquely impartial position, "The insurgents by opposing reciprocity have lost their opportunity and are disintegrating day by day." House insurgent leader Victor Murdock agreed glumly, "It does not look near so good for us as it did a few months ago."[52]

Democrats, after two years of invidious comparisons with insurgents, chortled openly over the new situation. Williams quoted Dolliver's speeches of the previous Congress to the insurgents and asked, "Did you mean what you said then, or were you fulminating in the air?" Rainey taunted the House Republican contingent, "There are no insurgent members any longer. You are all together and we know it." In their first months of their resurgence, the Democrats were triumphing not only over their enemies, but also their former allies.[53]

The congressional Democrats still had one conquest to make, however, and it could prove easily the most difficult. The Ways and Means Committee began its broader look at the tariff issue with the wool schedule, the one Aldrich had boasted had the most powerful political alliance behind it. Although a majority of the Democrats originally favored putting wool on the free list, Underwood, stressing the advantages of gradual reduction and pointing out that the Senate would never accept free wool, persuaded them to recommend cutting the rate in half to 20 percent. Unfortunately, William Jennings Bryan, expressing a sentiment he had never previously associated himself with, chose that moment to proclaim, "Without free wool, tariff reform would not amount to much."[54]

Goaded on by his brother Charles, who urged him (in a striking choice of language for a private citizen to use about the Speaker of the House) "to notify Clark that you would not consent to gradual reduction," Bryan decided to make a fight in caucus. He contacted the free wool members of the committee and put pressure on Clark, who was trying to hold the Democrats together and avoid getting entangled in

52. *Collier's* (July 15, 1911); *Independent* (June 29, 1911); *Louisville Courier-Journal* (June 19, 1911).

53. *Congressional Record*, Vol. 47, Part 3, p. 2389; Part 2, p. 1289.

54. Ida Tarbell, *The Tariff in Our Times* (New York: Macmillan, 1911), p. 355; F. W. Taussig, *The Tariff History of the United States* (New York: Putnam's, 1910), p. 240; *Baltimore Sun* (February 25, 1911); *Louisville Courier-Journal* (May 3, 1911); *New York World* (May 16, 1911); Koenig, *Bryan*, p. 475; *Commoner* (May 12, 1911).

the fight himself. Bryan reminded his old supporter, rapidly becoming a strong contender for the 1912 nomination, that "Wilson is making friends because he *fights*. . . . You won your position by fighting and must continue to fight to hold it." But, as one Bryan biographer points out, the course advised by the Commoner, for Clark to declare open war on Underwood and bring the Democrats' record of achievement to a halt, would not help but hurt the Speaker's presidential chances. Bryan was angry, Clark remembered later, because Clark "would not help him split the party on the infinitesimal difference between a small tariff on wool and no tariff on wool."[55]

Even without Clark's help, the acrimonious caucus session almost accomplished that end, running all day and into the night. Finally, Clark, Underwood, and the free wool leaders compromised: the caucus would pass the 20 percent rate but affirm its commitment to eventual free wool. The result seemed to satisfy everyone but Bryan; he denounced it as "a step backward" and opened a continuous attack on Underwood in the *Commoner*.[56]

Bryan now charged that the majority leader was a secret protectionist, striving to keep tariff reform away from his wife's holdings. Underwood rose in the House to deny the charges and attack Bryan, and called upon Kitchin, a close friend of Bryan, to confirm his version. After his speech, the *Congressional Record* noted "loud and continuous applause on the Democratic side."[57]

Once again, the brunt of Bryan's frustration fell upon the luckless Speaker. In a letter to "My Dear Mr. Clark," Bryan demanded to know how closely Clark agreed with Underwood. Clark answered twice, trying to get the right conciliatory tone. He argued that Bryan and Underwood were not that far apart on the tariff and defended his tactics on the grounds that they had led to success in the 1910 election.[58]

Three years' worth of bitterness spilled from Bryan's final response. "You give the Democrats in the last Congress credit for the election of a Democratic Congress, Senators & Governors," he wrote angrily. "It is strange that you overlook the influence of three progressive

55. Charles W. Bryan to William Jennings Bryan (May 25, 1911), Bryan Papers, Occidental College; William Jennings Bryan to Francis B. Harrison (May 28, 21, 1911), Harrison Papers; William Jennings Bryan to Champ Clark (May 30, 1911), Bryan Papers; Koenig, *Bryan*, p. 475; Clark, *My Quarter-Century of American Politics*, II:397.

56. Claude Kitchin to R. G. Allsbrook (April 9, 1915), Kitchin Papers, University of North Carolina; *Commoner* (June 9, 1911).

57. *Commoner* (August 4, 1911); *Congressional Record*, Vol. 47, Part 4, pp. 3511–13.

58. William Jennings Bryan to Champ Clark (August 7, 1911); Champ Clark to William Jennings Bryan (August 30, 1911), Bryan Papers, Occidental College.

national campaigns (1896, 1900 & 1908) especially as you are now engaged in carrying out the platform of 1908."[59]

By then, Bryan must have felt his lessened public position keenly. "Mr. Bryan is not easily pleased in these days," noted the *Independent*, "and is too fond of denouncing as traitors those Democrats who refuse to be guided by him." By October, a friend wrote that Bryan's influence "is not really so great as it was a year ago. His fight with Underwood has done him very great harm." Twice bloodied, Bryan withdrew from congressional politics. His turn would come next year, in the presidential nomination politics he had mastered long before. "When the time comes to name the man for the candidacy," he pledged ominously, "I will not be silent."[60]

Underwood had been right in his prediction that the Senate would not accept free wool; but he was wrong in thinking that it might accept 20 percent wool. On each of the three tariff bills sent up by the House, the insurgents, vital to Senate passage, demanded major increases in exchange for their support. To get any wool reduction at all, for example, Democrats had to accept La Follette's proposed rate of 35 percent.[61]

The insurgent role here has rarely been noted by historians. In fact, La Follette's most recent biographer has maintained that the insurgent leader "partially restored the insurgents' reputation as consumer champions by securing enough Democratic votes in July 1911 to enact laws that lowered duties on cotton, wool, and products purchased by farmers."[62] In his new role as champion of protection, La Follette was named to the first conference committee of his Senate career; it produced a rate of 29 percent. Underwood told the House that he wished it had been lower; La Follette assured the Senate that there was no real loss of protection.[63]

The insurgents were no fonder of the House cotton bill, which cut duties on cotton goods an average of 43 percent. But, at this point, Republican Senate leader Boies Penrose of Pennsylvania, angry at his own inability to control the situation and furious at the insurgents, an-

59. William Jennings Bryan to Champ Clark (September 5, 1911), Bryan Papers, Library of Congress.

60. *Independent* (June 8, 1911); Franklin K. Lane to Francis G. Newlands (October 7, 1911); *Louisville Courier-Journal* (August 15, 1911).

61. *Congressional Record*, Vol. 47, Part 4, pp. 3431–35; *Louisville Courier-Journal* (July 25, 1911); *Congressional Record*, ibid., 3277–79.

62. David P. Thelen, *Robert La Follette and the Insurgent Spirit* (Boston: 1976), p. 85.

63. *Congressional Record*, Vol. 47, Part 4, p. 3879; Claude Barfield, "Congressional Democrats," pp. 347–48; *New York World* (July 30, 1911); *Louisville Courier-Journal* (August 10, 12, 1911); *Congressional Record*, Vol. 47, Part 4, pp. 3916, 3953.

nounced, "I have concluded to leave this measure to this body and to the so-called insurgents, to perfect it in any way they may desire." With most of the regulars refusing to vote, Democrats easily passed their own bill, tacking onto it revisions of the metal and chemical schedules.[64]

The Democrats had shown that they could devise and pass low tariff bills in the House and get some version through the Senate. They could also claim some success with the other concerns of the session. The Rucker bill, requiring publication of campaign contributions, after being bottled up in committee throughout most of the session, finally passed the Senate toward the end of it. Somewhat earlier, the Democrats (minus Bailey and one other) led the Senate in admitting Arizona and New Mexico as states. Conservatives objected that Arizona's draft constitution contained a judicial recall clause; as Cannon piously explained, this made it "not republican in form." Taft agreed and vetoed the bill. Democrats, although unhappy, agreed to admit the state without the offending item, reasoning that Arizonans could repass it after statehood.[65]

Direct election of senators had failed during the previous Congress due to the insistence of regular Republicans, against the opposition of Democrats and insurgents, on attaching the Sutherland amendment for federal control of the elections. Since the forces against the amendment now controlled the Senate, Democrats were stunned to see it reappear as the Bristow amendment, sponsored by Kansas insurgent Joseph L. Bristow. "I am a little surprised," said John Sharp Williams, "that the Senator from Kansas . . . should push his natural allies upon the subject, Southern Senators, into this unnatural position." Five insurgents who had opposed the amendment in February now reversed their position and, along with regular Republicans who openly declared their opposition to direct election, managed by one vote to amend the House bill. All but eight Democrats then voted for the resolution anyway, but the House refused to accept it. Finally, eleven months later, the House surrendered, realizing, in the words of one Alabama Democrat, "It is clearly a question of whether we will have it as it comes to us now or not have it at all."[66]

Even though Taft vetoed all three of their tariff bills, Democrats

64. *Louisville Courier-Journal* (July 26, 1911); *Congressional Record*, ibid., pp. 4065, 4049–67.

65. *New York World* (August 14, 1911); *Congressional Record*, ibid., p. 4141; Part 5, p. 4234; *Commoner* (September 1, 1911).

66. *Congressional Record*, Vol. 47, Part 2, pp. 1485, 1923–24; Part 3, pp. 2433–37, 2544; Part 7, pp. 6348–67.

were exultant at the close of the session. (Many, such as Joseph Pulitzer, felt the vetoes made the Democratic position even better.) "At this session," boasted Clark, "the Democrats have made a record which has surprised our friends and dumbfounded our enemies." The record also made two of its authors, Clark and Underwood, prominent presidential candidates. "The Republicans can no longer charge that the Democratic Party is not in favor of constructive legislation," rejoiced Clayton, "nor can it any longer be charged that the Democratic party is composed of conflicting factions." There was even an extra satisfaction for the party. "The extra session may be said to have marked the passing of the insurgents from public confidence," claimed the *Courier-Journal*, "and the establishment in it of the Democrats."[67]

In March 1912, four months after Congress had returned for the regular session, the *Independent* remarked wonderingly, "We have been expecting the Democrats to make some stupendous blunder, as they usually do." Instead, warmed by the new and pleasant feeling of popular favor and anticipating a presidential victory in November, the Democrats, if anything, were more effective than in the special session.[68]

Underwood began with bills slashing tariff rates on metals and chemicals and then met one of the party's most explosive issues head-on by putting sugar on the free list against the objections of the Democrats from Louisiana and Colorado. To replace the projected $50 million loss in revenue, Cordell Hull presented a solution more clever than ingenuous. As the start of an attack on "the present hideous, monstrous system of taxation," he introduced an excise tax extending the corporate income tax to individuals with incomes over $5000 by treating their professions as businesses. The Democratic caucus accepted the measure unanimously, and two-thirds of the Republicans felt forced to vote for what they were assured was a constitutional income tax.[69]

Finally, the Democrats repassed their original wool bill of the previous session, while the Republican members of the Ways and Means Committee offered their own bill embodying the conclusion of Taft's Tariff Board that the wool rates would safely be cut by an average of

67. Joseph Pulitzer to Frank Cobb (August 21, 1911), *New York World* Papers; *Commoner* (September 1, 1911); *Congressional Record*, Vol. 47, Part 5, p. 4333; *Louisville Courier-Journal* (August 21, 1911).
68. *Independent* (March 7, 1912).
69. Archibald Butt, *Taft and Roosevelt* 2 vols. (Garden City, Doubleday, Doran and Co., 1930), II:162; *Baltimore Sun* (December 6, 1912); *Congressional Record*, Vol. 48, Part 2, pp. 1456, 1502; Part 3, pp. 2294–95; Part 4, pp. 3457, 3503, 3637; *St. Louis Republic* (March 2, 1912)

40 percent. "It is unfortunate for the party," commented one magazine acidly, "that this was not known by its leaders three years ago."[70]

When the first House tariff bills reached the Senate floor, after spending months in committee, insurgent leader Albert Cummins of Iowa announced openly, "I do not want the foreign manufacturer to be able to enter our markets." Again, insurgents joined regular Republicans in substituting their own higher sugar and wool bills, attaching reciprocity repealers to the metal and excise tax bills, and meeting Democratic tariff reform speeches with lurid tales of depression under Grover Cleveland. In July and August 1912, with Underwood refusing to let Congress adjourn or any Democrats leave, the two houses agreed on compromise bills. (By then, with the Republican party shattered, some Democrats opposed any concessions. New York's Francis Burton Harrison, a fervent low-tariff advocate, proclaimed, "I am in favor of waiting until we get a Democratic administration and can pass Democratic tariff bills.") Taft vetoed them all, and just before adjournment the House, in Ollie James's words, "punched up the Republican animals some" by passing the wool bill over his veto.[71]

Even before Underwood called up his first tariff schedule, William B. Wilson's Labor Committee began pouring out bills blocked by previous Republican committees. Once the measures reached the floor, reelection-conscious Republicans often supported them overwhelmingly. Virtually the first major legislation of the session limited work on all government contracts to eight hours a day, a long-time AFL objective. After the bill passed the Senate, with only one Democrat and ten Republicans in opposition, and was signed by Taft, Wilson boasted, "It will reduce the hours of labor of hundreds of thousands of workers." Just to make sure, the House attached eight-hour workday clauses to bills for naval construction, purchase of coal, and dredging rivers. The House passed nineteen prolabor measures, ranging from the prohibition of the manufacture of phosphorus matches (for worker safety), to extending second-class mailing privileges for labor newspapers, to the creation of a Department of Labor. Despite Republican warnings that the bill would "provide a sinecure for those who preach labor and do not practice it," the bill passed the Senate in February 1913, and the

70. *Congressional Record*, ibid., Part 4, p. 4127; *Independent* (March 28, 1912).
71. *Congressional Record*, ibid., Part 7, pp. 7312, 7378; Part 10, pp. 9631–9638, 9709, 9755, 9613, 9908. Edward Pou to Woodrow Wilson (August 3, 1912); Ollie James to Woodrow Wilson (August 14, 1912), Woodrow Wilson Papers, Series 2, Library of Congress.

president-elect named William B. Wilson the first secretary of labor.[72]

But the bills most important to the AF of L, limitation on labor injunctions and guarantee of jury trials in contempt of court cases, had to come from the Judiciary Committee. Before the session began, party leaders planned such legislation and assigned West Virginia's John W. Davis, a freshman with a reputation as a deft legal draftsman, to the committee. Both bills passed the House with heavy Republican support, but the Republicans in opposition included the highest ranking minority leaders. Democratic changes, grumbled one Republican, made laborers "at liberty not only to strike but to boycott and destroy their employer's property at will, and beat him up and destroy him personally to their hearts' content." The Senate buried both measures in committee, but Wilson could read the 1908 Democratic labor plank to the House and boast, "The present Democratic House of Representatives has redeemed every one of those pledges."[73]

Under unfinished business, the Democratic House again tried to attach the Hughes amendment to the Sundry Civil Appropriations Act, and again met Senate rejection. Democrats enjoyed more success with two issues left over from the Mann-Elkins fight. Aligned with the Democrat-insurgent coalition of the Senate, the House Democrats finally empowered the ICC to physically evaluate railroad property. And they disposed of the Commerce Court (which had amply borne out fears that it would prove obstructive and had been rebuked by the Supreme Court for exceeding its powers) by refusing to appropriate funds for its continuation.[74]

Control of the House allowed the Democrats not only to pass legislation but to launch investigations. After fourteen years of exclusion from the executive branch of the government, the new majority had several things it wanted to investigate. A special committee on the Sugar Trust, appointed during the special session, reported nine months later that a trust did indeed exist and manipulate prices; shortly thereafter, the House passed its free sugar bill. And, in February 1912, the House in-

72. *Congressional Record*, ibid., Part 1, p 396; Part 7, p. 7455; Part 10, pp. 10680–681; Part 4, p. 4007.

73. *New York World* (November 14, 1911); William Henry Harbaugh, *Lawyer's Lawyer, The Life of John W. Davis* (New York: Oxford University Press, 1973), pp. 69–72; *Congressional Record*, ibid., Part 7, pp. 6470–71, Part 9, p. 8903; Part 4, p. 3589; Part 10, p. 10679.

74. *Congressional Record*, Vol. 49, Part 5, pp. 4852, 4256; Part 4, pp. 3806, 3083; Gabriel Kolko, *Railroads and Regulation 1887–1916* (Princeton: Princeton University Press, 1965), pp. 199–201.

structed the Banking and Currency Committee to examine financial
power in America and gave it the powers of a special committee. The
Pujo Committee held open hearings for eight months, demonstrating
the narrow control of the country's money and providing propaganda
for Democratic campaigners. "I think you will be surprised," committee counsel Samuel Untermyer wrote Colonel Edward House when its
report was issued, "at the vast and perilous extent of the concentration
of credit in this country."[75]

But, for at least ten years, Democrats had yearned to get a good look
at United States Steel and its relationship with Republican administrations. In May 1911, the House chartered a special committee on the
biggest trust under Augustus Owsley Stanley, a cultivated Kentuckian
who recruited Robert Woolley from the *New York World* as chief investigator. "If the Steel Trust can be convicted of greedy and oppressive tactics," encouraged the *Courier-Journal*, "the influence for restraint
in other combinations will be most salutary." Stanley's own position
was clear. "I have no doubt," he wrote Watterson, "that in its creation
and operation the United States Steel Corporation is in open and absolute contravention of the Sherman Anti-Trust Act."[76]

Although denied cooperation by the Bureau of Corporations, the
committee attempted "to make a minute, thorough study of the methods employed by the Steel Corporation in conducting its business." In
open hearings, Martin Littleton, a freshman Democrat and New York
corporate attorney, caused Elbert Gary of U.S. Steel to admit that the
corporation had maintained close ties with the Roosevelt administration and had probably deceived the Rough Rider during the Panic of
1907 by telling him that Tennessee Coal & Iron would collapse if the
trust were not permitted to acquire it. Stanley and Woolley then called
in reform attorney Louis Brandeis, who demonstrated that 42 percent
of the corporation's labor force worked a 72-hour workweek and wrote
a bill forbidding specific trust practices as unfair competition. "I find
that Stanley has taken the bill I drew for him hook, line, and sinker,"

75. *St. Louis Republic* (February 18, 1912); *Congressional Record*, Vol. 48, Part 3, pp.
2389–2418; Part 6, pp. 5336–46; Gabriel Kolko, *The Triumph of Conservatism* (New York:
Free Press of Glencoe, 1963), p. 220; Samuel Untermyer to Edward M. House (March
13, 1913), House Papers, Yale University.
76. *New York World*, April 6, 1911; Robert Woolley, "Politics is Hell," unpublished
autobiography, Chapters 13 and 15, Woolley Papers, Library of Congress; *Louisville
Courier-Journal* (May 5, 1911); Augustus O. Stanley to Henry Watterson (June 17, 1911),
Watterson Papers, Library of Congress; Nicholas C. Burckel, "A. O. Stanley and Progressive Reform," *The Register of the Kentucky Historical Society* 79 (Spring 1981): 141.

the reform lawyer wrote his brother. The La Follette–Stanley Anti-Trust bill failed to become law, but bore some similarity to the Wilson administration's Clayton Anti-Trust Act.[77]

Democratic House investigations helped shape legislation in the next administration, and the public hearings helped the party elect that administration. Moreover, they may help explain the most paradoxical question of the Progressive Era: why the conservative Taft filed so many antitrust suits. Two-thirds of Taft's suits were filed in the last year and a half of his administration, after power in Congress had shifted. The administration sued for dissolution of U.S. Steel, citing its acquisition of Tennessee Coal & Iron, in October 1911, well after Gary's testimony before the Stanley Committee. If Taft out-prosecuted his trust-busting mentor, Roosevelt, it may be partially because Roosevelt never felt the pressure of a Democratic House.[78]

Throughout the session, Bryan continued to snipe at the leadership. In November, the *Commoner* printed an editorial, "Wanted: A Leader," demanding that Clark do more fighting and less conciliating. Bryan continually attacked Underwood, charging, on minor matters, that the majority leader "is not losing many opportunities to show himself a reactionary." By the end of May, however, he conceded privately. "Congress is making a splendid record. . . . Concessions have to be made from time to time, and Clark has made but a few concessions compared with the number of times he has held out for real radical legislation."[79]

Looking back at the 62nd Congress, James Cox recalled thirty-five years later, "It was exhilarating to be in Congress at that time." The Democrats used their House control to demonstrate not only their progressive commitment but, far more importantly, their ability to handle power. To an electorate whose last experience with Democratic power had come in Grover Cleveland's days, the lesson was essential. "We have a Democratic national administration and a Democratic State Ad-

77. *New York World* (July 21, 1911); Robert M. Woolley to Edward M. House (March 7, 1914), House Papers, Yale; *New York World* (June 8, 1911); *St. Louis Republic* (January 30, 1912); Louis D. Brandeis to Alfred Brandeis (July 28, 1912), in Melvin I. Urofsky and Daniel W. Levy, eds., *Letters of Louis Brandies*, 4 vols. (Albany: State University of New York Press, 1971–1975), II:652. Burckel, ibid., pp. 143–44. Roosevelt defended his action in a brief appearance before the Stanley Committee during which, according to the *World*, he used the first person singular 101 times.

78. *New York World* (October 27, 1911); James Weinstein, *The Corporate Ideal in the Liberal State* (Boston: Beacon Press, 1968), p. 83; Marc Sullivan, *Our Times* 6 vols. (New York: Charles Scribner's Sons, 1926–1933), IV:406.

79. *Commoner* (November 24, 1911; February 2, 1912); William Jennings Bryan to E. W. Rankin (May 29, 1912), Woodrow Wilson Papers, Series 2.

ministration in Illinois." Rainey wrote the governor of Illinois in 1914, "principally on account of the work of a Democratic Congress."[80]

Rainey, as he often did in his attacks on the Watch Trust, had put the matter strongly. The performance of the Democratic Congress had been important, but the party also gained progressive credentials, public confidence, and presidential candidates from another source. In three stages — Ohio and Indiana in 1908; New York, New Jersey, and Massachusetts in 1910; and Illinois in 1912 — Democrats won the governorships of the major two-party states. The performance of the Democratic governors brought progressive legislation to the most conservative parts of the country and made four of them presidential contenders.

Despite several studies of particular states in the Progressive Era, state reforms have rarely been seen as a partisan issue. A partial explanation for this outlook may be that early and influential studies concentrated on states dominated by one party, such as California, Wisconsin, or Mississippi, where political battles were generally fought out within that party. "In the one party states where national views are not discussed on the stump," a South Carolina editor explained to Wilson, "the personality of candidates is the controlling factor." But from New England to Illinois, where the two parties contended on more equal terms, reformers generally found Democrats supporting them and Republicans opposed.[81]

Just as La Follette's Wisconsin served as the insurgent ideal, Ohio became the Democratic reform showcase. Governor Judson Harmon, despite Bryan's constant attacks on him as a reactionary, signed a sizable amount of progressive legislation. Johnsonian Democrats in the legislature may have fought harder for the bills than did the management-minded governor, but Harmon supported their efforts, and appeared before the party caucus to remind it of its obligations to the platform. In his first term Ohio reorganized its tax structure, raising the valuation of railroad property from $166 million to $580 million. In his second term, a more Democratic legislature set up a Public Utilities Commis-

80. James M. Cox, *Journey through My Years* (New York: Simon and Schuster, 1946), p. 116; Henry T. Rainey to Edward F. Dunne (May 9, 1914), Rainey Papers.

81. W. E. Gonzales to Woodrow Wilson (January 3, 1911), Wilson Papers Series 2. For example, see George Mowry, *The California Progressives* (Berkeley: University of California Press, 1951); Robert S. Maxwell, *La Follette and the Rise of the Progressives in Wisconsin* (Madison: State Historical Society of Wisconsin, 1956); and Albert Kirwan, *The Revolt of the Rednecks; Mississippi Politics 1876–1925* (Lexington: University of Kentucky Press, 1951).

sion and passed a strong corrupt practices act, a ten-hour maximum workday and a fifty-four-hour workweek for women workers, and an optional worker's compensation bill. The latter, and other labor legislation, was introduced by William Green, a Democratic state senator from the coal districts who would later succeed Gompers as the head of the AFL. "It would be unfair to Judson Harmon," argued his successor, "to assert that he was not a constructive liberal."[82]

That successor, James Cox, had shown himself to be a zealous progressive activist in Congress and would continue that course in Columbus. He took office in 1913 after a constitutional convention, composed mostly of Democrats, had greatly strengthened the state legislature's power to pass labor reforms and "direct democracy" measures. Cox recommended fifty-six reform bills to the legislature, which passed them all. They included a ban on child labor, a nine-hour workday for women, mine and railroad safety regulation, the initiative and referendum, and a new mandatory worker's compensation program. Under the latter, Cox boasted to Bryan: "Compensation is paid within two weeks after the accident occurs. Four hundred claims are settled daily. Labor and capital are out of the courts." Cox's program, estimates Hoyt Warner, was far in advance of Wilson's New Freedom.[83]

In Indiana, the other key state won by the Democrats in 1908, the party was thought to be under the complete control of Tom Taggart of French Lick, one of the old-time bosses particularly disliked by reformers. His successful candidate for governor, Thomas Marshall, was a small-town lawyer who had never held public office and whose previous distinction was being one of only five members of the party state committee to stay with Bryan in 1896. But Marshall rapidly proved himself to be a gifted campaigner, politician, and governor. Hampered by a Republican state senate in the first half of his term, he managed during the second to enact a set of labor reforms, a corrupt practices act, and a bill empowering the state railroad commission to fix rates.

82. William Bayard Hale, "Judson Harmon and the Presidency," *World's Work* (May 1911); *Independent* (February 8, 1912); "A Speech and Special Message by Governor Judson Harmon that Helped to Obtain Progressive Legislation in Ohio," in Newlands Papers; Warner, *Progressivism in Ohio*, pp. 227, 268–83; John D. Buenker, *Urban Liberalism and Progressive Reform* (New York: Charles Scribner's Sons, 1973), pp. 56–60; Cox, *Journey*, p. 138.

83. Warner, ibid., pp. 386–405; Ernest I. Antrim, "The Ohio Constitutional Convention," *Independent* (June 27, 1912); James E. Cebula, *James M. Cox, Journalist and Politician* (New York: 1985), pp. 39–53; James Cox to Francis B. Harrison (October 1, 1915), Harrison Papers; James Cox to William Jennings Bryan (April 7, 1914), Bryan Papers, Library of Congress.

He even gained a national reputation by blocking Taggart's bid for the Senate in 1910.[84]

Even after a close ally of Taggart won the governorship in 1912, the boss made no attempt to block reform legislation; he asked only that he be consulted on appointments. With his approval, and with election results that gave the party every seat in the state senate and 95 of the 100 seats in the assembly, Indiana acquired an inheritance tax, a Public Utilities Commission, worker's compensation, an antilobbying law, and statewide primaries.[85]

Governor Woodrow Wilson broke with his sponsor somewhat more violently. He used the momentum and acclaim of his fight with James Smith over the Senate seat to induce a Democratic assembly and a Republican Senate to pass a direct primary bill, corrupt practices legislation, a strong Public Utilities Commission, and a worker's compensation bill, "which is said to be the most radical in the United States." In early 1913, before leaving for Washington and after the election of a Democratic state senate, he used unanimous party support to pass the "seven sisters" bills, altering New Jersey's long-time status as a haven for trust headquarters.[86]

Besides his own persuasiveness and charm, Wilson could call upon a growing reform spirit among New Jersey Democrats. When they last controlled the assembly, in 1907, Democrats had passed a Public Utilities Commission bill only to see it killed by the Senate. Led by the delegation from industrialized Hudson County, Democratic legislators had agitated for the bill and worker's compensation ever since. They strongly supported Wilson's measures and, with little help from the governor, put through a large number of labor regulation bills of their own.[87]

In New York, Charles Francis Murphy of Tammany was not a man to be upstaged by his creations. He completely dominated the feeble

84. Thomas R. Marshall, *Recollections* (Indianapolis: Bobbs-Merrill, 1925), p. 243; Matilda Henderson Wheelock, "Magnetic Tom Marshall," *National Monthly* (August 1910); Clifton J. Phillips, *Indiana in Transition* (Indianapolis: Indiana Historical Bureau and Indiana Historical Society, 1968), pp. 108–10; *New York World* (April 29, 1910).

85. Norman Hapgood, *The Changing Years* (New York: 1930), p. 278; Phillips, ibid., pp. 118–20.

86. Arthur Link, *The Road to the White House* (Princeton: 1947), pp. 239–64; Cornelius Ford to Woodrow Wilson (May 1, 1912), Wilson Papers, Series 2; Buenker, *Urban Liberalism and Progressive Reform*, p. 98.

87. Buenker, ibid., pp. 94–135; John D. Buenker, "Urban, New-Stock Liberalism and Progressive Reform in New Jersey," *New Jersey History* 87 (Summer 1969): 79–104; Link, ibid., p. 266; John Morton Blum, *Joe Tumulty and the Wilson Era* (Boston: Little, Brown and Co., 1951), pp. 15, 17.

John Dix, elected in 1910, and impeached and removed from office William Sulzer, elected in 1912. Sulzer's successor, Martin Glynn, turned out to be an able and progressive governor, but New York's reforms were identified most closely with a group of young Tammany legislators, led by Senator Robert F. Wagner and Assemblyman Alfred E. Smith.[88]

Between 1907 and 1910, Republican Governor Charles Evans Hughes had produced, with Democratic support, some business regulation bills, but for labor "progress during these years was slow indeed." After the Triangle Fire of 1911, Dix appointed Wagner, Smith, and Gompers to a Factory Investigation commission, and Frances Perkins guided the legislators through the industrial conditions of the state. The efforts produced a three-year burst of labor legislation, pushed by Wagner, Smith, and Glynn, which created an enduring alliance between New York Democrats and social reformers. "I never was so gratified over anything in my life as the splendid conduct of Gov. Glynn," cheered Frank P. Walsh, labor lawyer and chairman of Wilson's Industrial Commission. "His work was not alone for the state of New York but for humanity." The state AFL announced happily, "We doubt if any state in the union can now compare with our Empire State in its present code of labor law."[89]

New York's political alignments became even clearer in 1915 when the Republicans recaptured the state and attempted to undo the Democrats' work. "This is such a dreadful legislature," moaned one social worker, "that it is no use asking anything of them, except that they stop sinning a little."[90]

In Massachusetts, Connecticut, and Illinois, Democratic governors never enjoyed the luxury of Democratic legislatures. But Bay State Governor Eugene Foss was able to add enough Republicans from labor

88. J. Joseph Huthmacher, "Charles Evans Hughes and Charles Francis Murphy: The Metamorphosis of Progressivism," *New York History*, 66 (January 1965): 25–40; Nancy J. Weiss, *Charles Francis Murphy* (Northampton: Smith College, 1968), pp. 78, 89.

89. Huthmacher, ibid., p. 29; Robert F. Wesser, *Charles Evans Hughes, Politics and Reform in New York, 1905–1910* (Ithaca: Cornell University Press, 1967), p. 314; J. Joseph Huthmacher, *Robert F. Wagner and the Rise of Urban Liberalism* (New York: Atheneum, 1968), pp. 5–8, 30; Frances Perkins, *The Roosevelt I Knew* (New York: Viking Press, 1946), pp. 22–23; Frank P. Walsh to Jeremiah Lawler (December 22, 1913), Industrial Commission Papers, Frank P. Walsh Papers, New York Public Library; David M. Ellis, James A. Frost, Harold C. Syrett, and Harry J. Carman, *A History of New York State* (Ithaca: Cornell University Press, 1957), pp. 389–90; Wesser, *A Response to Progressivism*, pp. 112–40.

90. Irwin Yellowitz, *Labor and the Progressive Movement in New York State* (Ithaca: Cornell University Press, 1965), pp. 119, 238.

districts to his own alliance of Boston ward bosses, labor unions, and reformers to pass a substantial package of reform legislation, much of which had failed to pass earlier, more heavily Republican legislatures. Under his tenure, Massachusetts gained worker's compensation, the direct primary for state legislators, a fifty-four-hour workweek for women, a minimum wage commission, and jury trials for contempt of court in labor cases. "There are few, if any, of his acts as Governor that I should be disposed to criticize," wrote Louis Brandeis after Foss's first year, and the *Commoner* praised "his positive and aggressive stand for remedial legislation."[91]

Connecticut's legislature was so badly malapportioned that even a statewide victory in 1910 left the Democrats in a hopeless minority. Governor Simeon E. Baldwin, a seventy-year-old Mugwump, barely managed to get a Public Utilities Commission (PUC) against the determined opposition of J. Henry Roraback, state Republican chairman and New Haven Railroad lobbyist. After two terms, Baldwin could claim only the PUC, a plain ballot law, a corrupt practices act, and a weak worker's compensation bill.[92]

Edward F. Dunne of Illinois, elected in 1912, was perhaps the most radical of the progressive Democratic governors. He also enjoyed strong support from Roger Sullivan's Chicago machine legislators (although Sullivan did try to prevent his renomination in 1916). But the minority Democrats could pass only bills approved by the Bull Moose delegation and renounced their ambitions for an eight-hour workday for state employees, a minimum wage for women, and a child labor law. They did manage to improve railroad and mine safety laws and initiate old-age pensions for public employees. Besides his labor measures, Dunne obtained a Public Utilities Commission and legislation allowing municipal ownership of utilities, his main interest during an earlier term as mayor of Chicago.[93]

91. Buenker, *Urban Liberalism and Progressive Reform*, p. 66; Richard B. Sherman, "Foss of Massachusetts: Demagogue or Progressive?" *Mid-America* 43 (April 1961): 87–91; Leslie G. Ainsley, *Boston Mahatma* (Boston: William M. Predible, 1940) pp. 110, 120; Abrams, *Conservatism in a Progressive Era*, pp. 257–59; Michael E. Hennessey, *Four Decades of Massachusetts Politics* (Norwood: Norwood Press, 1935), pp. 151–60; Louis D. Brandeis to Mark Sullivan (October, 9, 1911), in Urofsky and Levy, *Letters of Louis Brandeis*, I:503; *Commoner* (November 17, 1911).

92. Buenker, ibid., pp. 13, 137–38; Frederick H. Jackson, *Simeon Eben Baldwin* (New York: King's Crown Press, 1955), pp. 84, 176; *New York World* (June 4, 1911); "The Democratic Party of Connecticut to the Independent Voters of Connecticut," in Baldwin Family Papers, Yale University.

93. John D. Buenker, "Edward F. Dunne: The Urban New Stock Liberal as Progressive," *Mid-America* 50 (January 1968): 11–15; *The Public* (September 22, 1916); Buenker, *Urban Liberalism and Progressive Reform*, pp. 62–65.

West of the Mississippi, where the party was less numerous but thoroughly Bryanized, Democrats also managed to write and pass a large amount of reform legislation. Nevada and Colorado, the most consistently Democratic states of the Rocky Mountains, were the progressive pacesetters of the region. When the Democrats finally captured Bryan's Nebraska in 1908, they promptly put bank deposit guarantee and physical valuation of railroad laws on the books. John Burke, Democratic governor of North Dakota from 1907 to 1913, merged progressive Republicans with the few Democrats in the legislature to pass primary laws, the initiative and referendum, a corrupt practices act, and a child labor bill.[94]

"In the direction of progressive social and political legislation, the present year has been one of extraordinary activity," rejoiced the editor of *World's Work*, a middle-class uplift magazine, in April 1911. But Democratic state victories not only led to state reform legislation, they dramatically improved prospects for the constitutional amendments providing for an income tax and direct election of senators. When the former passed the Senate, the Democratic *National Monthly* suggested, "The Senate ring so complacently passed the resolution that it is apparent that they see no possible hope of the amendment becoming a part of the Constitution." Republicans and businessmen relied on their control of Western and Northeastern state legislatures to block the amendment.[95]

Eight of the first nine states to ratify the amendment were southern and border states, soon joined by four more southern states and Nebraska and Nevada. Then the results of the 1910 elections began to take effect. Ohio and Indiana ratified, and the newly Democratic states of New York and Maine, which had rejected the amendment the year earlier, now reversed themselves. But despite two special messages from Wilson, the Republican New Jersey state senate refused. By the time the Democrats captured that house and ratified the amendment, a com-

94. Francis G. Newlands to Theodore Roosevelt (March 29, 1911), Newlands Papers; Percy Stanley Fritz, *Colorado, the Centennial State* (New York: Prentice-Hall, 1941), pp. 263–66, 379, 381–84; Fred Greenbaum, *Fighting Progressive* (Washington: Public Affairs Press, 1971), p. 32; Arthur Mullen, *Western Democrat* (New York: Wilfred Funk, 1940), p. 139; Russel B. Nye, *Midwestern Progressive Politics* (East Lansing: Michigan State University Press, 1959), p. 217; Charles N. Glaab, "The Failure of North Dakota Progressivism," *Mid-America* 39 (October 1957): 199–204.

95. Walter Hines Page to all Governors (April 19, 1911), Woodrow Wilson Papers, New Jersey State Library, Trenton; *National Monthly* (August 1909).

bination of Democratic and insurgent states had already written it into the Constitution.[96]

The Seventeenth Amendment, providing for direct election of United States senators, had a similar history. In a survey of state platforms of 1910, the *Commoner* found that the Democrats of twenty-six states, not counting the southern and border states, favored such an amendment; only ten Republican platforms, none east of Illinois, supported the idea. Republican State Chairman William Barnes of New York openly argued that the Senate "should be a check on the popular mind." Considered by the states during 1913, the year when the Bull Moose split had given the Democrats their greatest representation in state legislatures, the amendment passed quickly and easily.[97]

According to a widespread historical impression, the Democratic party spent the Progressive Era passively awaiting the coming of Woodrow Wilson. In reality, Democrats at both the state and federal levels, inspired by Bryan and their newspapers and supported by organized labor, occupied themselves during the Roosevelt and Taft administrations in agitating and organizing against the problems of the new industrial society.

Congressional Democrats played a major role in obtaining the reform legislation of the period, and they laid the groundwork for most of Wilson's measures. State Democrats launched a number of "Little New Freedoms" that largely antedated the national program. Their efforts brought the Progressive Era to the industrial states, where the Gilded Age lasted until 1910. The Democratic party was not simply the tool of Woodrow Wilson; he carried out a program that the party had long supported. It was largely the performance of earlier Democrats in Congress and in the states that gave him the chance to do it.

96. *Commoner* (January 13, 1911; March 31, 1911; April 7, 1911); *New York World* (July 13, 1911); Link, *Road to the White House*, p. 267; John D. Buenker, "Urban Liberalism and the Federal Income Tax Amendment," *Pennsylvania History* 26 (April 1969): 194.
97. *Commoner* (November 25, 1910); *New York World* (December 22, 1911).

CHAPTER 5

On to the White House

As his supporters always claimed, Woodrow Wilson, the Democratic candidate for president in 1912, was the most persuasive argument for the Democratic party's commitment to reform. This may well be true, but not for the reasons they suggested. Wilson demonstrates the progressivism of his party, not from the steadfastness of his progressive principles, but rather from their sudden appearance.

From the time, two years earlier, that the perceptive Princetonian took aim at the presidential nomination, he moved rapidly to acquire advanced standing as a progressive. Wilson's calculation, that such a change was essential to his candidacy, reveals the nature of the Democratic position more strikingly than volumes of the *Congressional Record*.

As a convert, Wilson had a long way to go. Although always a Democrat, he despised Bryan and had consistently aligned himself with the right wing of the party. Wilson voted the Gold Democratic ticket in 1896 and had supported John Johnson for the nomination in 1908. Because the presidency of Princeton University was a position of rare prominence for a Democrat, George Harvey, a former editor on the *World*, then editing J. P. Morgan's *Harper's Weekly*, had persuaded Pulitzer to include Wilson as one of the sixteen possible alternatives to Bryan that year. But, as the *Louisville Courier-Journal* pointed out, there was no reason to think that the conservative Wilson would run any better than the conservative Alton Parker had. After 1908, Wilson began taking a marginally more progressive position, but it consisted mostly of advocating the short ballot and urging businessmen to behave themselves.[1]

As late as 1909, his politics tended in the opposite direction. In a baccalaureate address at Princeton in June, Wilson charged labor unions with the "economically disastrous" policy of forcing the worker "to give as little as he may for his wages." The next year, contemplating his own candidacy, the would-be party leader assured a friend, "I do

---

1. Arthur Link, *Wilson: The Road to the White House* (Princeton: Princeton University Press, 1947), pp. 25, 96, 116, 122; *New York World* (January 6, 1908); *Louisville Courier-Journal* (March 17, 1906).

not in the least despair of seeing the Democratic party drawn back to the definite and conservative principles which it once represented."[2]

When New Jersey Democratic boss James Smith, seeking a respectable candidate who could help him ward off the mounting pressure of young progressive Democrats, offered Wilson the nomination for governor in 1910, many reformers reacted with alarm. The radical magazine, *The Public*, called the private conference that brought the academic into the race "a midnight meeting of prominent connoisseurs of poultry under a henroost." New Jersey reformers very nearly blocked Wilson's bid at the state convention.[3]

Had Wilson desired only to be governor of New Jersey, he might have run on the tariff and on his character, downplaying his conservatism, and he might have won. But he never regarded Trenton as more than a way station on the road to Washington. "Of course," he wrote on July 14, 1910, "the men who are planning my nomination for the governorship look forward to putting me up for the presidential nomination later." To make these plans realistic required a different Woodrow Wilson from the one James Smith thought he had nominated. "It was an excellent time," recalled an associate of Wilson, "for an outstanding Democrat to become a progressive."[4]

Fortunately for Wilson, the progressives who failed to prevent his nomination succeeded in writing him a reformist platform. The White House hopeful now warmly embraced all of it and attacked the conservatism of the Republicans. In response to a challenge from one of New Jersey's few progressive Republicans, he even began attacking boss rule.[5]

On labor issues, however, Wilson's transformation could not have come with such ease. The Essex Trades Council opposed his nomination, accurately charging that he "has publicly shown his antagonism to organized labor." Achieving neither candor nor persuasiveness, Wilson now explained, "The criticisms I uttered in those addresses were meant entirely as criticisms of a friend. . . . My own position is consistent with the friendliness and sympathy I have always felt with the labor organizations." Even this response proved more ingenuous than

2. *New York World* (June 14, 1909); Woodrow Wilson to H. S. McClure (April 9, 1910), Wilson–McClure Correspondence, Princeton University.

3. Willis F. Johnson, *George Harvey, "A Passionate Patriot"* (Cambridge: Riverside Press, 1929), p. 139; James Kerney, *Political Education of Woodrow Wilson* (New York: 1926), p. 25; *The Public* (July 22, 1910); Joseph Tumulty, *Woodrow Wilson as I Know Him* (Garden City: Garden City Publishing Co., 1925), p. 14; Link, *Road to the White House*, pp. 165–66.

4. Woodrow Wilson to Henry B. Thompson (July 14, 1910); Link, ibid., pp. 193–98.

5. *New York World* (September 16, 1910; November 2, 1910); Link, ibid., pp. 193–98.

his answer to Gompers's request for a copy of the baccalaureate speech; he wrote the AFL chief that he had no copies left. Gompers wrote back that if Wilson would send him the speech, he would make copies of it.[6]

Aside from such embarrassments, Wilson strengthened himself (and the self-esteem of academics) with a dazzlingly effective campaign. He gathered 54 percent of the vote (to 42.5 percent for his Republican opponent) and immediately became a leading presidential contender for 1912. In the three days after his victory, Wilson heard from Bryan, Alton Parker, Roger Sullivan, Judson Harmon, Joseph Pulitzer, and many others who were (or hoped to be) important in the Democratic party.[7]

For Joseph Pulitzer, the rise of Woodrow Wilson meant the end of a fourteen-year search for an alternative to Bryan. "Unless already assigned," he had ordered in July, "pick out the very best man you have for specially striking interview with Woodrow Wilson." Throughout the campaign the *World* praised Wilson extravagantly, calling him "New Jersey's Man of the Hour." (Such support was more important than that of an out-of-state newspaper might appear; then as now, northern New Jersey was a media colony of New York City and depended heavily on the metropolitan press.) After Wilson's victory, the blind publisher paid his last best hope the ultimate compliment, instructing his editors, "As to the Presidency, build up Woodrow Wilson on every possible occasion. . . . I think he is an abler man than Tilden was." He even gave Wilson his own entry in the *World's* private code book: Melon.[8]

James Smith performed two vital services for Wilson's presidential hopes: he ran Wilson for governor, and he ran himself for the Senate. Before the momentum from Wilson's election victory had abated, the governor-elect had an opportunity to show himself at once independent

6. Resolution of Essex Trades Council (August 10, 1910), in Wilson Papers, Princeton; Samuel Gompers to Woodrow Wilson (October 20, 1910), Wilson Papers, Library of Congress.

7. Franklin K. Lane, Josephus Daniels, Roger Sullivan, Thomas B. Love to Wilson (November 8, 1910); William Jennings Bryan, Theodore Bell, Charles Culberson, Eugene Foss, Francis Burton Harrison, Thomas Marshall, A. Mitchell Palmer, Alton Parker, Brand Whitlock, Edwin Wood to Wilson (November 9, 1910); Simeon E. Baldwin, Judson Harmon, John Walter Smith, John J. Fitzgerald to Wilson (undated); all in Wilson Papers, Library of Congress.

8. Joseph Pulitzer to J. J. Spurgeon (July 18, 1910), Pulitzer Papers, Columbia University; *New York World* (August 20, 1910); Joseph Pulitzer to George S. Johns (December 5, 1910); Pulitzer Papers, Library of Congress; Joseph Pulitzer memo (December 2, 1910), *New York World* Papers, Columbia University.

of the boss and progressive as a crusader. Citing a pledge that Smith denied making and an advisory primary for which Wilson had little regard, the governor fought and defeated Smith in the Democratic legislative caucus.[9]

The effect was everything a presidential aspirant could hope for. "Wilson vs. Smith," trumpeted the *Baltimore Sun*. "The one spells Democracy, the other, privilege." From Washington, New Jersey's Congressman William Hughes of New Jersey reported that Democrats in both houses were watching developments closely. *The Public*, so distrustful of Wilson earlier, enthusiastically noted that the action "puts him further to the front in the democracy of the Democractic party than ever before."[10]

Most heartening of all was a letter Wilson received in early January. "I am expecting to come East early in March and would like to see you for an hour or so on political matters," wrote William Jennings Bryan. "The fact that you were against us in 1896 raised a question in my mind in regard to your views on public questions, but your attitude in the Senatorial cause has tended to reassure me."[11]

Wilson spent most of 1911 reassuring the Nebraskan and his followers. "Bryan will be a power in the next National Convention," wrote Wilson's campaign aide and future son-in-law, William G. McAdoo. "In fact, I think he will hold the 'balance of power' absolutely." By March the swiftly moving governor had, in Champ Clark's sardonic phrase, "gone the whole hog" and endorsed virtually all of Bryanism.[12]

After the adjournment of the New Jersey legislature, Wilson headed west on a speaking tour and made his new discipleship even more apparent. In early May in Kansas City, he repudiated a lifelong position by endorsing the initiative and referendum, Bryan's current pet issue. Shortly thereafter, Wilson announced that he was willing to run for president, "although I have not the audacity to seek the nomination." The reception given Wilson's characteristic eloquence and uncharacteristic radicalism was encouraging: the New Jersey governor, Charles Bryan informed his brother, "has been leaving a trail of fire throughout the west."[13]

9. Link, *Road to the White House*, pp. 205–37.

10. *Baltimore Sun* (December 28, 1910); William Hughes to Woodrow Wilson, (December 9, 1910), Wilson Papers, Library of Congress; *The Public* (December 16, 1910).

11. William Jennings Bryan to Woodrow Wilson (January 5, 1911), Wilson Papers, Library of Congress.

12. William McAdoo to Byron P. Newton (April 8, 1911), Newton Papers, Yale University; Francis Fisher Kane to Woodrow Wilson, (March 8, 1911), Wilson Papers, Library of Congress.

13. *Louisville Courier-Journal* (May 6, 1911); *New York World* (May 19, 1911); Charles W. Bryan to William Jennings Bryan (May 25, 1911), Bryan Papers, Occidental College;

As might be expected, Wilson's new departure worried some of his original supporters. "I fully appreciate the importance of Bryan," warned George Harvey, "but I also appreciate the danger of being regarded as . . . 'the Bryan candidate.'" Pulitzer told Frank Cobb, "The man is a great artist, a great genius, but is leading himself astray and should be brought back to his senses." He tried to lure his candidate back from the primrose path with an editorial asking, "Is Woodrow Wilson Bryanizing?"[14]

But Wilson had a powerful, built-in defense against such charges. Whatever he might say to a group of Bryanites in Missouri, the former president of Princeton University could not be stigmatized as a wild-eyed Populist. In 1911, Woodrow Wilson could supply something the Democratic party had needed for fifteen years—respectability. "The fatal weakness of the Democratic party in the last ten years," mourned the *World* in one of its frequent Cassandra-like pronouncements on the Future of the Party, "has been that when it was radical the people distrusted its intelligence, and when it pretended to be conservative they distrusted its honesty." Woodrow Wilson, Ivy League radical, respected by businessmen but with no financial ties to them, could single-handedly resolve that paradox. In him, the Democrats had found a presentable progressive.[15]

Throughout the country, influential figures who despised Bryan could accept Bryanism with a Princeton accent. Pulitzer, detesting the initiative and referendum, could console himself with the likely thought that Wilson "probably does not believe it but . . . has only thrown it out for western consumption." Henry Watterson, who shared not only Pulitzer's political outlook but also his long memory, declared in August, "I shall do my best for Woodrow Wilson because I believe him as clearly to be the intellectual leader of Democracy as Mr. Tilden was thirty-six years ago." Even Adolph Ochs of the *New York Times* found Wilson to be a respectable reformer, something he rarely discovered.[16]

Wilson made another conquest denied his Nebraska predecessor: the middle-class uplift journals. *Collier's* and the *American Magazine*,

---

John Milton Cooper Jr., *The Warrior and the Priest* (Cambridge: Belknap Press of Harvard University Press, 1983), p. 180.

14. George Harvey to Woodrow Wilson (March 1, 1911), Wilson Papers; Joseph Pulitzer, memo to Cobb (June 22, 1911), *New York World* Papers; *New York World* (July 31, 1911).

15. *New York World* (January 23, 1906).

16. Joseph Pulitzer to *World* (September 6, 1911), Pulitzer Papers, Library of Congress; Henry Watterson to Desha Breckenridge (August 22, 1911), Watterson Papers, Library of Congress; Gerald W. Johnson, *An Honorable Titan* (New York: Harper and Bros., 1946), p. 233.

although never moderating their enthusiasm for Roosevelt and La Follette, found in Wilson virtues that they rarely perceived in a Democrat. Walter Hines Page of *World's Work* exemplified the magazine response, praising his fellow southerner as "the best example in present public life of the old-fashioned Democrat who has applied his activities to present conditions with refreshing and convincing clearness."[17]

It is accurate but misleading to say, as Gabriel Kolko does, that Wilson enjoyed the support of "important financiers."[18] Such businessmen as Cleveland H. Dodge, Thomas Jones, and Cyrus McCormick supported Wilson for Princetonian, rather than political reasons, and they remained generous throughout his various ideological incarnations. Dodge donated $51,500 to the 1912 campaign, and the others donated a total of $33,500. They enabled Wilson to spend $193,500, more than any other Democratic hopeful.[19]

Another group of pro-Wilson financiers was more significant for the future. Through McAdoo, a southerner who had come North and become successful in business in New York, Wilson became the first Democratic candidate to attract Jewish contributors. American Jews had adored Theodore Roosevelt, and Jacob Schiff, head of the Kuhn, Loeb banking house, had been a well-publicized advisor of the Rough Rider. They supported Roosevelt's chosen successor until 1911, when Taft refused to abrogate the passport treaty with Russia over the limitation of travel rights for American Jews. McAdoo, chairman of the national citizens' committee against the treaty, brought Wilson to address a Carnegie Hall protest meeting. Clark, Hearst, and other politicians also spoke, but on such an occasion Wilson could easily outclass the Democratic field. Several days afterward Schiff, a lifelong Republican and perhaps the most influential Jewish leader in the country, sent McAdoo a check for $2,500. Wilson, whose scholarly qualities also appealed to the Jewish community, further received $20,000 from Henry Morgenthau (father of FDR's treasury secretary), $7,000 from Samuel Untermyer (counsel for the Pujo Committee), and $12,500 from Abram Elkus, another Wall Street figure.[20]

17. *Collier's* (March 11, 1911); Ray Stannard Baker, "Our Next President and Some Others," *American Magazine* (June 1912); Gregory Ross, *Walter Hines Page* (Lexington: University of Kentucky Press, 1970), p. 16; *World's Work* (November 1911).
18. Gabriel Kolko, *Triumph of Conservatism* (New York: Free Press of Glencoe, 1963), p. 211.
19. *Testimony before a Subcommittee of the Committee on Privileges and Elections*, U.S. Senate (Washington: 1912), p. 866.
20. Lawrence H. Fuchs, *The Political Behavior of American Jews* (Glencoe: Free Press, 1956), pp. 42–54; Simon Wolf, *Presidents I Have Known from 1860–1918* (Washington:

Such evidence hardly demonstrated, however, that Wilson was the favored candidate of business. Most non-Jewish (and non-Princetonian) major donors remained Republican; Wilson was well-financed only in Democratic terms. Roosevelt spent $611,118 in his attempt on the republican nomination, against Taft's $499,527.[21]

Still, the Wilson money did not go unnoticed. "There must be somebody (or several somebodies) with a lot of money who consider Wilson 'safe,' to judge from the campaign that is being made," groused one western Democrat. The Wilsonians opened a New York headquarters in July 1911 and a Washington office in December. They sent the passionately pro-Wilson *Trenton True American* to 27,159 politicians and journalists each week. After Wilson's nomination, Dodge feared that a Senate committee investigating campaign spending "might bring up the matter of that newspaper, which would be unpleasant." But not until a year later was Dodge forced to reveal that he had lent the friendly journal $25,000.[22]

Finally, Wilson's supporters, especially young college alumni, "saw him so vividly and brightly that they were wonderful missionaries." At the end of 1911, he was sufficiently in the lead to consider the strategy that perpetually tantalized Democratic front-runners: abolishing the rule requiring two-thirds to nominate. He disliked the rule, he wrote House, but "I feel there would be a certain impropriety in my urging a change because it would be so manifestly in my favor."[23]

The Wilson movement even survived two minor crises in January 1912, when a dinner in Washington officially opened the campaign. Just before the event, the conservative *New York Sun* released a 1907 letter in which Wilson expressed the wish that Bryan be knocked "into a cocked hat," but Josephus Daniels managed to reassure the Commoner. A longer and more complicated dispute over Wilson's break with George Harvey, whose support was now hurting him among

---

Press of Byron S. Adams, 1919), p. 309; William G. McAdoo, *Crowded Years* (Cambridge: Riverside Press, 1931), pp. 117–22; Kerney, *Education of Woodrow Wilson*, p. 155; Nathan Straus to McAdoo (February 1, 1912), McAdoo Papers, Library of Congress. See Fuchs, p. 57, for the attitude of American Jews toward Wilson as a scholarly candidate.

21. George Mowry, *Theodore Roosevelt and the Progressive Movement* (Madison: University of Wisconsin Press, 1946), p. 255 n.

22. W. F. Hudson to James D. Finch (August 29, 1911), Newlands Papers, Yale University; Link, *Road to the White House*, pp. 330, 336; White, Blue, Yellow, Pink Lists in Newton Papers, Yale University; Cleveland Dodge to Woodrow Wilson (September 5, 1912), Wilson Papers; *Testimony Before . . .* , (Washington: 1912), pp. 948–50.

23. Henry Breckenridge, *Reminiscences*, Oral History Research Office, Columbia University, p. 144. See *New York World* (January 9, 1912), for an account of Wilson's success at the dinner; see Link, ibid., pp. 347–78, for Wilson's problems at the time.

Bryanites, probably ended up helping Wilson slightly, although it cost him Watterson's support. Neither problem dimmed Wilson's triumph at the dinner itself, when a burst of Wilsonian eloquence "made other candidates realize that the man each of them had to beat was Wilson."[24]

One year earlier, that happy position had been occupied by Governor Judson Harmon of Ohio. Harmon's election as governor in 1908 had immediately set off speculation about his presidential chances, and a poll of Democratic editors in May 1910 found him as popular as Bryan and far ahead of other possibilities mentioned. "If Harmon is re-elected Governor of Ohio," commented Watterson, "it is perfectly certain that he will be our nominee for the Presidency." Wilson's advisors, contemplating his chances for the presidency before he decided to run for governor, considered the Ohio governor his major opposition. After Harmon's overwhelming reelection in 1910, Congressman Francis B. Harrison, of the Ways and Means Committee and Tammany Hall, invited selected congressmen to meet Harmon for lunch at Washington's Metropolitan Club.[25]

No Democratic hopeful, however, could withstand open and constant attacks from Bryan, who steadily pounded Harmon through 1910 and 1911. Bryan, according to reports, regarded Harmon's refusal to support him in 1896, when the Ohioan was Cleveland's attorney general, as being in a different class from that of Wilson; one was "a trained officer in the Democratic army," the other "a scholarly recluse." By early 1911, the impact of the Commoner's opposition was making itself felt. "Harmon is losing strength every day," reported an Indiana party leader. "If nominated, he can never be elected; the influence of the Bryan following will be against him." In October, House noted many Harmon people were abandoning him as a "sinking ship." The once-promising candidate of the anti-Bryanites never became much more than a favorite son, who could not even claim the full vote of his state; Mayor Newton Baker of Cleveland snagged two-fifths of the delegation for Wilson.[26]

24. Henry Morgenthau, *All in a Lifetime* (Garden City: Doubleday, Page and Co., 1922), p. 144. See *New York World* (January 9, 1912), for an account of Wilson's success at the dinner; see Link, ibid., pp. 347–78, for Wilson's problems at the time.

25. *Chicago Tribune* poll, reprinted in *Commoner* (May 6, 1910); Henry Watterson to Norman Mack (May 28, 1910), Watterson Papers, Library of Congress; David B. Jones to Woodrow Wilson (July 29, 1910), Wilson Papers, Library of Congress; Francis Burton Harrison to Henry D. Flood (December 6, 1910), Flood Papers, Library of Congress.

26. See, for example, *Commoner* (May 27, 1910), for Bryan's attacks on Harmon. *Independent* (January 11, 1912); William C. Liller to Woodrow Wilson (January 26, 1911), Wilson Papers, New Jersey State Library; *Louisville Courier-Journal* (April 26, 1911);

As Harmon sank slowly in the Midwest, anti-Bryanites began to look for another vehicle for their hopes. Some turned to Oscar Underwood, a certifiable anti-Bryan figure whose candidacy had been created from nothing by the surprising record of the Democratic House. "If Underwood does as well the next nine months as he has the last four months and keeps going," wrote Pulitzer at the close of the special session, "he would seem the natural beneficiary of the situation he has so largely created." The businesslike majority leader was admired by many of the eastern Wilsonians, including the candidate himself. But his feud with Bryan was open and festering, and intensified by Underwood's opposition to the initiative and referendum, described by Charles Bryan as "the acid test of a man's democracy these days." Although Underwood tried to sharpen his reform image as the campaign progressed, he sought the backing of wealthy New York Democrats. Like Harmon, he received most of his financial support from Thomas Fortune Ryan, Virginia and New York entrepreneur, regarded by Bryanites as a good example of everything wrong with the party.[27]

Underwood's real strength and weakness, however, rested less on politics than on his accent. No southerner had made even a semiserious run for the presidency since the Civil War, and Underwood relied on regional loyalty to provide his convention votes. The Underwood forces made little or no effort outside the Southeast and centered their hopes on a deadlocked convention. This strategy dismayed the Wilson managers, who had counted on their candidate's Dixie origins to supply delegates from the region. Underwood could not win, McAdoo wrote desperately to southern Democrats; the South must be united for someone who could.[28]

The political capital of Joseph W. Folk, former governor of Missouri, consisted entirely of the useful but insufficient fact that Bryan liked him. Folk had been running for president ever since leaving the governorship in 1909 and had won several favorable references in the

---

Edward M. House to Thomas H. Gregory (November 19, 1911), House Papers, Yale University; C. H. Cramer, *Newton D. Baker* (New York: World Publishing Co., 1961), pp. 64–65.

27. Joseph Pulitzer to Cobb (August 23, 1911), *New York World* Papers; Link, *Road to the White House*, pp. 328–29; Charles W. Bryan to William Jennings Bryan (February 29, 1912), Bryan Papers, Occidental College; Evans C. Johnson, *Oscar W. Underwood: A Political Biography* (Baton Rouge: Louisiana State University Press, 1980), pp. 166–74; *Testimony Before . . .* (1912), pp. 931, 938.

28. Arthur S. Link, "The Underwood Presidential Movement of 1912," *Journal of Southern History* II (May 1945): 236–37, 242; William G. McAdoo to Colonel J. R. Gray (March 27, 1912), McAdoo Letterbooks, McAdoo Papers, Library of Congress.

Commoner. In July 1910, when he and Harmon were the two prominent candidates, *The Public* had called him the only acceptable prospect. Perhaps dazzled by such praise, he agreed not to run for the Senate in 1910 in exchange for the state convention's endorsement for the presidency.[29]

Folk was not only an inept politician; he was also an anachronism. Ten years earlier, as district attorney of St. Louis, he and Lincoln Steffens made each other famous with Steffens' article on Folk's battle against the local machine. Despite his four years as governor, a term that produced reform legislation on the railroad and trust issues, Folk still seemed a relic from progressivism's earlier period, when honesty versus corruption seemed the only issue. After leaving the governorship, he lectured on civic righteousness, and the *New York World* featured "A Talk with Graft-Hunting Candidate for the Presidency."[30]

With no issue, no organization, and no association with recent party triumphs, Folk was helpless when the Champ Clark movement began to sweep Missouri. He hoped that local Wilson men might support him in order to injure Clark, and he eagerly accepted Bryan's suggestion that he and the Speaker split the delegation. When Clark refused, and early primary returns showed the Speaker heading for an overwhelming victory in the state, Folk gave up.[31]

Champ Clark's presidential campaign has provoked much scholarly derision. Probably, this is the inevitable fate of anyone running for president on the slogan, however symbolic, "You Gotta Quit Kickin' My Dawg Around." But as McAdoo conceded, "The ideas and driving power behind the Clark effort were neither foolish nor trivial." Clark's long congressional career had brought him a wide friendship among party politicians. His solid progressive record and close friendship with Bryan appealed to many Democrats, especially in the West, and won him the support of Samuel Gompers. He had skillfully managed the Democratic minority, negotiated the alliance with the insurgents, and could claim a share of the credit for the effective organization and procedure of the new House. "How could all of this have been possible," asked the *St. Louis Republic*, responding to the attacks of the eastern journals, "if the Speaker had been the amiable mountebank sketched in *Collier's*?[32]

Clark's strategy, which made a virtue of necessity, called for total

29. *Commoner* (July 14, 1911); *The Public* (July 28, 1910); Louis G. Geiger, *Joseph W. Folk of Missouri* (Columbia: University of Missouri Press, 1953), p. 94, 137–43.
30. Geiger, ibid., pp. 135–36; *New York World* (May 1, 1910).
31. Geiger, ibid., pp. 147, 150; *St. Louis Republic*, (January 28, 1912; February 11, 1912).
32. McAdoo, *Crowded Years*, p. 144; *St. Louis Republic* (June 21, 1912).

identification with the Democratic House. He did not go out campaigning as Wilson did, but carried out his duties as Speaker. To questions on his platform, he cited the positions taken by the House, for which his supporters gave him credit. (Others, especially Wilsonians, gave Underwood virtually all the laurels.) He relied heavily on his personal connections in the House. The *World* cited a poll showing Clark's lack of support in the Senate as proving that the Speaker was "not now taken seriously" but failed to mention that he was the leading choice among his fellow House members. Democratic congressmen, especially western progressives, played key roles in winning the delegates of many states to Clark and in persuading local leaders already dubious of Wilson's views on party organization. Clark's House ties also brought him the useful support of former congressman William Randolph Hearst, who disliked Wilson and realized sadly that 1912 could not be his own year.[33]

The Clark movement rapidly seized the attention of Democrats. In March, in the first state conventions, the Speaker won Kansas and half the delegates from Oklahoma, two states where the Wilson forces had expected victory. He became the unquestioned front-runner the next month, humiliating Wilson by better than 2 to 1 in both the Illinois and Massachusetts primaries. Alarmed, the Wilson forces launched the attacks on Clark that have so largely shaped his historical image.[34]

The eastern Democratic press, rejoicing in having outlasted one rural radical, now watched unhappily the rise of another. "We had hoped that it would not be necessary to treat Mr. Clark's candidacy seriously," sighed the *World*. "That was a compliment we paid to the intelligence of Western and Southern Democrats." Not only was Clark not of presidential size, the newspaper argued, but he would carry nothing Bryan had not carried. In *Collier's*, Mark Sullivan attacked Clark almost weekly, complaining that "although, in fact, he is nothing, he is scheduled as a progressive."[35]

33. *Louisville Courier-Journal* (May 7, 1911); *St. Louis Republic* (February 21, 1912); Clyde H. Tavenner, "Speaker Champ Clark," *National Monthly* (October 1911); *New York World* (January 7, 1912); *Commoner* (September 1, 1911). Among the congressmen who were crucial in bringing their states to Clark were Ollie James (Kentucky), Joseph T. Robinson (Arkansas), and Scott Ferris (Oklahoma). *New York World* (September 29, 1911); Link, *Road to the White House*, p. 382; *Baltimore Sun* (February 25, 1912).

34. *St. Louis Republic* (February 24, 1912; March 15, 1912; April 10, 1912); Edward M. House to William McCombs (March 17, 1912), House Papers.

35. *New York World* (April 25, 1912); *Collier's* (March 9, 1912; June 1, 1912). While western Wilsonians listened to Bryan's proscription of Underwood and generally favored Clark as second choice, the anti-Bryan eastern Wilson press ran friendly accounts of Un-

Such attacks baffled and frustrated the Speaker; after twenty-five years, he was being asked to prove himself as progressive as this new convert. His reform record, commented *The Public* sympathetically, "must be repeated like ancient history, to a generation of voters who know him only as a democratic politician." Occasionally Clark's frustration would surface, making him seem somewhat less than presidential. To a printed questionaire sent to all candidates by the Reform Club, asking in part, "Do you favor the present protective tariff?" Clark wrote back, "How in the name of Heaven do you think that I would be in favor of the present protective duties when I led the fight against the Payne-Aldrich Tariff Bill, and came within five votes of recommitting it, which would have killed it as dead as the men who lived before the flood?"[36]

The Wilsonians directed much of their fire at Clark's ties with Hearst, especially after the Illinois primary. Hearst's two newspapers in Chicago had been active for Clark, and McAdoo blamed the size of Wilson's defeat on him. The day after the vote, Wilson declared himself confident that Democrats were "unwilling to see their party delivered over to the domination of William Randolph Hearst." The *New York World* and *Collier's*, Hearst's bitterest journalistic opponents, constantly attacked his presence in Clark's campaign, and a Wilson pamphlet, "The Enemies of Woodrow Wilson," was concerned almost entirely with the publisher, barely mentioning Clark. Whether or not Hearst created new enemies for Clark, his presence clearly further embittered many already opposed to the Speaker.[37]

Throughout the spring, the Democratic race grew more fevered as the Democratic nomination shot up in value. At the start of 1912, Theodore Roosevelt raised the banner of revolt against Taft's renomination, and the Republican fight rapidly became far more poisonous than the Democratic battle. State by state, the president of the United States

derwood, considering them their second choice. See *Collier's* (January 6, 1912), and the *New York World* (December 3, 1911). The anti-Clark blasts of the *World* were written by the strongly anti-Bryan Frank Cobb, who had voted for Taft in 1908 and took over editorial direction after Pulitzer's death in October 1911.

36. *The Public* (October 12, 1911); "Position on Tariff of Candidates for the Presidential Nomination," pamphlet of Reform Club, in William Kent Papers, Yale University. Late in May, Bryan conceded privately, "I believe that much of the criticism directed against Clark is unfair. I have known him for a great many years, and he has been on the right side of all the reform questions." William Jennings Bryan to E. W. Rankin (May 29, 1912), Wilson Papers, Library of Congress.

37. William G. McAdoo to W. H. Osborn (April 13, 1912), McAdoo Letterbooks, McAdoo Papers; *New York World* (April 27, 1912); *Collier's* (June 1, 1912); "The Enemies of Woodrow Wilson," in *New York World* Papers.

and the country's most popular politician denounced each other in terms harsher than any of the Democrats would use about them. In Roosevelt's new social justice progressive posture, he was challenging Taft not simply over the leadership of the party, but over the identity of the party. Against a Republican party that seemed to be tearing itself apart, it appeared that any Democrat could win.

As Wilson's fortunes ebbed, his managers began to charge ever more loudly that the other candidates were combining against Wilson, that he was the victim of "a vast network of schemes, intrigues, and propaganda attacks" directed by "a curious mixture of editors, reactionary politicians and Wall Street financiers, demagogues and former Populists, and self-styled radicals." Clark, Underwood, and Harmon, they charged, were all being funded from Wall Street, were responsible for a vast number of scurrilous attacks on Wilson, and had divided the country among them, each opposing him in his own section.[38] "The Wilson management seems to be attacking every other candidate," noted Underwood. "[They] started out with the idea that they were going to have a runaway race. . . . They are losing their temper and attacking everybody."[39]

The *St. Louis Republic* responded that the charges showed only the "persistent assumption by Gov. Wilson's agents that no one could prefer another Democrat without being in some respects 'reactionary' or a servant of the interests." The Wilson forces never produced any evidence that Clark was being financed by Wall Street, and nobody seemed to consider the Speaker's campaign very prosperous. In May, a Wilson leader relayed a rumor that the Speaker was about to run out of money, and Roosevelt's campaign manager noted afterward that he had heard scandalous stories about the campaign fund of every Democratic candidate except Clark. Clark's campaign did cause Wilson to undergo a large amount of typical Hearstian abuse, but the Wilsonians gave back as good as they got.[40]

If, as Arthur Link says, there is "much circumstantial evidence" that the other candidates had agreed each to oppose Wilson in his own section, there is also evidence that they did not. Harmon's collapsing campaign included a full-scale effort in only one state outside Ohio: Ne-

38. Link, *Road to the White House*, p. 347; Woodrow Wilson to Edward M. House, (March 15, 1912), House Papers; *Collier's* (March 23, 1912).

39. Underwood to J. H. Woodward, (March 25, 1912), in Johnson, *Underwood*, p. 176.

40. *St. Louis Republic* (March 16, 1912); Thomas B. Love to Edward M. House (May 5, 1912), House Papers; *Testimony Before . . .*, p. 428.

braska, where he faced both Wilson and Clark. Underwood never had the support to mount an effort outside the Southeast; his strategy had always been to win that and hope for the best. Far from being part of an anti-Wilson cabal, most of Clark's delegates favored Wilson as their second choice. Clark, although to some extent a western candidate (his campaign biography explained, "Mr. Clark believes in the West as Benton believed in it"), sought and won delegates from southern and eastern states as well. Although Clark's managers made little or no effort in states seemingly locked up for any of his opponents, he was a national candidate, not one-third of a stop-Wilson committee.[41]

Wilson and Clark met in one other important primary in April, in a state where both the eloquent governor and the rough-hewn speaker tried to step lightly. William Jennings Bryan had long regarded the Nebraska Democratic party as his private preserve, and neither candidate wanted to incur his displeasure. At the moment, Bryan was contenting himself with denouncing Harmon and Underwood, stating "as between Mr. Wilson and Mr. Clark he does not care to express a preference, regarding them both as progressive."[42]

The candidates also feared the emergence, at any time, of Bryan's own candidacy. Bryan deprecated the possibility in careful statements that did not quite close the door, such as, "I cannot conceive of any condition that could arise which would make me a candidate this year." But Bryan, after three painful disappointments, now faced the best Democratic opportunity in twenty years, and his brother, at least, wanted him to consider running again. In March, a Wilsonian warned his candidate that Bryan wanted the nomination, and House wrote in April that only Wilson "can keep Bryan or Clark from being nominated." Others thought they saw a subtle rebirth of ambition in the Commoner. "When the conservative Harmon has been brushed aside," predicted the *Independent*, "and Wilson and Clark have eliminated each other, and the minor candidates have been crowded aside, who will be left but William J. Bryan for a fourth time."[43]

As the Nebraska primary approached, Bryan's "neutrality" between

41. Link, *Road to the White House*, p. 380 n; Link, "The Underwood Presidential Movement," p. 244 n; W. L. Webb, *Champ Clark* (New York: 1912), p. 87.

42. *Commoner* (March 29, 1912).

43. *Independent* (January 11, 1912); Charles W. Bryan to William Jennings Bryan (August 26, 1911), Bryan Papers, Occidental College; William Jennings Bryan to Charles W. Bryan (December 1, 1911), Bryan Papers, Occidental College; James F. Williamson to Woodrow Wilson (March 19, 1912), Wilson Papers, New Jersey State Library; Edward M. House to Thomas H. Gregory (April 23, 1912), House Papers; *Independent* (May 9, 1912).

Wilson and Clark was ebbing fast. He (and his brother) resented Clark's attitude on congressional matters and his refusal to accept Bryan's plan on the Missouri delegation, and their pique rendered them susceptible to Wilson's ingratiating letters. "How often," wrote the candidate to the Commoner, "I would like to take counsel with you on these matters in these critical times."[44]

Wilson's efforts were augmented by those of a far more experienced intriguer, Colonel Edward House of Texas. House, a small catlike man, the most skilled sycophant of the Progressive Era, had attached himself to a succession of Texas governors and to Bryan himself before entering Wilson's camp. In late 1911, he began to try to influence his former patron in the interest of his new one. House wrote letters playing upon all the Commoner's fears, dislikes, and vanity, warning him about the efforts of Morgan, Hearst, and Underwood, subtly cautioning Bryan about Clark. "My main effort was in alienating him from Champ Clark," House wrote Wilson after spending some time with Bryan, "and I believe I was successful there."[45]

For whatever reason, Bryan clearly preferred that Wilson oppose Harmon alone in Nebraska. He tried to get Clark to leave the primary and resented the efforts of two old allies for the Speaker. He did not expect Clark to make much of a showing, he told his brother; if the Speaker outpolled Wilson, they would owe him an apology. But after Clark won handily, with 20,000 votes to 14,000 for Wilson and 12,000 for Harmon, no apology was forthcoming.[46]

Even without it, the Speaker now began to sweep all before him. Throughout May, he seemed to win states almost daily. "Clark was running like a prairie fire," McAdoo shudderingly recalled. He picked up delegates in all parts of the country, and defeated Wilson in primaries in Maryland, Rhode Island, and California, where the dimensions of his victory shocked the state's Wilsonians. The Clark strength, wrote

44. Louis W. Koenig, *Bryan*, (New York: 1971), p. 482; *Baltimore Sun* (February 12, 1912); Woodrow Wilson to William Jennings Bryan (March 15, 1912; April 3, 1912), Bryan Papers, Library of Congress.

45. Jonathan Daniels, *The End of Innocence* (Philadelphia: Lippincott, 1954), p. 50; House Diary (September 26, 1914), House Papers; Edward M. House to William Jennings Bryan (October 25, 1911; November 25, 1911; December 6, 1911), House Papers; Edward M. House to Woodrow Wilson (November 18, 1911), House Papers. For House's skill at ingratiating himself, see Alexander George and Juliette George, *Woodrow Wilson and Colonel House* (New York: 1956), esp. pp. 123–28.

46. Arthur Mullen, *Western Democrat* (New York: Wilfred Funk, 1940), pp. 164–65; William Jennings Bryan to Charles W. Bryan (April 15, 1912; undated), Bryan Papers, Occidental College.

a dazed congressman, "is a matter of surprise to his closest friends." The Speaker would go to Baltimore as the Democratic front-runner.[47]

The Wilsonians had other problems to occupy them. They had counted on their southern-born candidate picking up delegates in the Southeast, but Underwood and local pride were proving too much for them. Although Wilson's supporters claimed that Wilson was more southern than Underwood, the Alabama candidate flooded the section with buttons reading, "Vote for the South," and defeated Wilson in Georgia, Florida, Mississippi, and Alabama. Even South Carolina, where Wilson had long and solid support, refused to instruct its delegates for him. Underwood gathered some surprising allies on the sectional issue. Tom Watson, whose Populism had now fused with virulent racism, helped in Georgia; the racist radical senator-elect James Vardaman delivered Mississippi to him; Underwood enlisted men in North Carolina "who have been preaching the progressive ideas for years."[48]

Wilson was being hurt by the first law of politics, that a candidate in decline tends to continue to decline. "I think it is becoming apparent to all close observers that Wilson cannot possibly be nominated," wrote a Virginia congressman, arguing against instructing the delegation for him. Yet, Wilson won just enough to remain a major candidate. In April, he defeated Clark in Wisconsin, after a heavy investment, and won Pennsylvania against little opposition. The next month he swept Texas, where his forces had been organized for a year and Harmon's and Clark's hardly at all, and held New Jersey against James Smith's vindictive support of Clark. At the end of the month, he gained the open endorsement of the *New York World*, which McAdoo claimed "is doing immense good."[49]

In a Democratic convention, the Wilsonians realized, anything

47. McAdoo, *Crowded Years*, p. 129; *St. Louis Republic* (May 27, 1912); Robert E. Hennings, *James D. Phelan and the Wilson Progressives of California*, (New York: Garland, 1985), pp. 43–45.

48. Obadiah Gardner to L. F. Hemans (June 15, 1912), Wilson Papers, Library of Congress; *St. Louis Republic* (May 19, 1912); C. Vann Woodward, *Tom Watson, Agrarian Rebel* (New York: Macmillan, 1938), p. 427; Wayne Flynt, *Duncan Upshaw Fletcher* (Tallahassee: Florida State University Press, 1971), p. 62; Albert Kirwan, *Revolt of the Rednecks: Mississippi Politics 1876–1925* (Lexington: University of Kentucky Press, 1951), p. 235; W. H. Osborn to William G. McAdoo, (May 17, 1912), McAdoo Papers.

49. Henry D. Flood to Captain J. M. Harris (April 20, 1912), Flood Papers; Link, *Road to the White House*, pp. 407–408; Lewis Gould, *Progressives and Prohibitionists: Texas Democrats in the Wilson Era* (Austin: University of Texas Press, 1973), pp. 59–75; C. Richard King, "Woodrow Wilson's Visit to Texas in 1911," *Southwestern Historical Quarterly* 47 (October 1944), 169–85; *New York World* (May 30, 1912); William G. McAdoo to W. E. Gonzales (June 7, 1912), McAdoo Letterbooks, McAdoo Papers.

might happen, especially when there would be present a man who specialized in making things happen. House wrote to Bryan again in May. He assured the Commoner that Clark, Harmon, and Underwood were now in coalition and many of the Clark delegates were anti-Bryan: "On the other hand, where you find a Wilson delegate you will usually find one friendly to you." The week before the convention opened, McAdoo went out to meet Bryan in Chicago to stress the point.[50]

Bryan was in Chicago as a journalist covering the Republican national convention, where he watched the year's political calculus dramatically shift. The Taft forces, combining the support of Republican conservatives with the administration's firm control of the patronage-dependent southern GOP delegations, claimed a narrow but immovable majority of the convention, rejecting the delegate challenges that Roosevelt needed to change the odds. Charging that one nomination had been stolen from him, Roosevelt and his supporters marched out of the convention and made their own. Suddenly, there were not one but two Republican tickets in the field, and a Democratic candidate who did no more than hold the party's basic vote could expect to be the next president.

The Democratic convention of 1912, historians agree, was not the story of the man who was expected to win nor even of the man who eventually did win. The convention belonged instead to a man who was not even a candidate: William Jennings Bryan. Bryan's vigorous role, according to his biographers, managed "to prevent the nomination of anyone who represented the Morganization of America" and "made the Democratic gathering progressive." Even Arthur Link writes of Bryan "smashing the plan of a few conservatives to control the convention."[51]

Although Theodore Roosevelt located the Armageddon of 1912 at the Republican gathering in Chicago, accepted accounts depict another one at Baltimore, with a death struggle over the nomination between armies of progressive and reactionary Democrats. Yet, no such division existed. In forty-six ballots, no conservative candidate developed significant strength. Baltimore witnessed a battle of personal ambition, conducted exclusively among three progressive candidates. "Underwood was no more of a possibility at that convention than were Harmon, Marshall, Foss, Baldwin and others," wrote one reporter. "Only

50. Edward M. House to William Jennings Bryan (May 6, 1912), House Papers; McAdoo, *Crowded Years*, p. 134.
51. Paolo Coletta, *William Jennings Bryan, Progressive Politician and Moral Statesman, 1909–1915* (Lincoln: University of Nebraska Press, 1966), p. 72; Koenig, *Bryan*, p. 496; Link, *Road to the White House*, p. 435.

Champ Clark, Woodrow Wilson, and William Jennings Bryan had a chance to be named." All three made powerful efforts.[52]

Few historians have believed that Bryan was seeking the nomination, quoting him to the effect that he did not want it. Yet, between Bryan's ambiguous denials of the winter and spring and the opening of the convention in late June, the situation had changed utterly. Roosevelt had walked out of the Republican convention to launch his own ticket, and the Democratic nomination had suddenly become a letter of transit to the White House. Bryan "will not want the nomination," House predicted in early June, "unless two republican tickets are in the field." As soon as there were, Bryan's view understandably changed.[53]

Bryan went directly from the shambles of the Republican convention at Chicago to Baltimore, launching his campaign against the designation of Alton Parker as temporary chairman of the convention. He sent telegrams to all "progressive" candidates urging them to join him in the fight. If Parker were selected, he declared, reactionaries would control the convention. But the temporary chairmanship hardly meant control of the convention; its function consisted primarily of making the keynote speech and handing the gavel to the permanent chairman. Bryan had been offered the position himself and had refused it.[54] Still, it might provide an issue to disrupt the developing pattern of the convention. Only with such a disruption might Bryan hope for his fourth opportunity.

Many progressives resented Bryan's action, doubting both his motives and his argument. Gompers, a Clark supporter, rode the train to Baltimore with Bryan and "emphatically called Mr. Bryan's attention to the injustice and inconsistency of his position," citing Parker's active support of Bryan in 1908. Governor Marshall of Indiana, one of the progressives contacted by Bryan, wired back, "Parker came to Indiana in 1908 to advocate your election and mine. I do not see how his selection as temporary chairman will result in a reactionary convention."[55]

But for the Wilson forces, also in desperate need of anything that might derail the Clark bandwagon, Bryan's action came as a godsend. Although they realized that "Bryan . . . and his brother, with their keen

52. Arthur W. Dunn, *From Harrison to Harding*, 2 vols. (New York: 1922), II:192.

53. Coletta, *Bryan*, p. 37; Edward M. House to Woodrow Wilson (June 7, 1912), House Papers.

54. *New York World* (June 20, 1912); Norman Mack to Edward M. House (May 2, 1913); *National Monthly* (August 1912).

55. Samuel Gompers, *Seventy Years of Life and Labor*, 2 vols. (New York: 1925), p. 280; Josephus Daniels, *The Wilson Era, Years of Peace, 1910–1917* (Chapel Hill: University of North Carolina Press, 1944), p. 551.

political sense, were playing exactly the same game as we were," the Wilsonians had to play along. They had nothing to lose but a second-place finish. "It was felt that Woodrow Wilson had played his only chance when he joined Mr. Bryan against Judge Parker," reported the *Courier-Journal*. To a suggestion that Wilson could not afford a fight, McAdoo replied with perfect accuracy, "The Governor can't afford anything but a row. The bigger the row the better for us."[56]

The Clark forces faced a more complicated situation. According to ex-Senator Fred Dubois of Idaho, Clark's manager, their strategy had been to alienate nobody and emerge as acceptable to everybody. Now, with everything to lose, they faced a threat to the strategy.[57]

They handled it badly. Clark's response to Bryan's telegram asked harmony and urged that nothing be done to hurt the party's chances. Such a statement, which seemed to show not progressive principle but a front-runner's caginess, played directly into Bryan's hands. In Baltimore, Clark's bungling managers did even worse. Whether due to an agreement with Tammany or a real fear of Bryan's candidacy, they either encouraged or permitted a majority of the Speaker's delegates to oppose Bryan and support Parker in the election of the temporary chairman.[58]

Bryan now had an issue — corporate domination of the convention — with which he might overthrow all existing probabilities. "I do not know of any ground on which a progressive could have voted against me," he trumpeted, and he thereby deduced that many of Clark's delegates were not true progressives. The interests, he charged the next day, clearly controlled the convention, although "many of them came masquerading as progressives."[59]

Bryan refused all offers of compromise, including suggestions that he be either permanent chairman or chairman of the Resolutions Committee, which would write the platform. Since the interests controlled the convention, he explained, they should name the officers: when he controlled a convention, he had never sought their services. This posi-

56. Morgenthau, *All in a Lifetime*, p. 145; *Louisville Courier-Journal* (June 25, 1912); McAdoo, *Crowded Years*, p. 139.

57. *Louisville Courier-Journal* (May 30, 1912).

58. *St. Louis Republic* (June 23, 1912; June 25, 1912); William Jennings Bryan, *A Tale of Two Conventions* (New York: Funk and Wagnalls, 1912), p. 128; Henry F. Ashurst, *A Many-Colored Toga*, ed. George F. Sparks (Tucson: University of Arizona Press, 1962), p. 17, June 25, 1912. It should also be noted that the diversity of Clark's support made it impossible for his managers to deliver his votes solidly to one side or the other. *New York World* (June 23, 1912).

59. Bryan, ibid., pp. 128, 147.

tion, while stirring, was not quite accurate; at the Bryan-controlled 1908 convention, Alton Parker had taken a major role in writing the platform.[60]

As rumors of his own candidacy grew more persistent, Bryan pressed his issue. He introduced a resolution that the party declare itself opposed to "J. Pierpont Morgan, Thomas F. Ryan, August Belmont, or any other member of the privilege-hunting and favor-seeking class" and demand the withdrawal from the convention of any delegates representing them. Significantly, the resolution was the idea of Bryan's brother, who had always favored a fourth campaign. "We reporters," recalled William Allen White, "all knew that someone, maybe it was brother Charlie—it might have been Bryan—was promoting a rather futile cabal to nominate Bryan again." Even the Wilsonians were becoming alarmed at Bryan's maneuverings.[61]

"To say the Commoner threw a bomb into the big gathering is expressing it entirely too mildly," reported the *Republic* of the reaction to the resolution. "It was an indescribable turbulent chaos," recalled McAdoo, "a cacaphony of howls, groans and yells, punctuated by futile attempts to obtain some sort of order." Such a scene resembled the kind of chaos out of which a Bryan candidacy might arise, but the New York and Virginia delegations, of which Belmont and Ryan were members, neatly squelched Bryan by voting for his resolution after the second part had been dropped. Despite Bryan's public statement that "this vote eliminates all of the reactionaries," he gained little by his strategem.[62]

By this point, several observers were noticing that the years of disappointment were beginning to show on the Commoner, that his charisma had lost some of its force, that his magnificent political timing was now just slightly off. The *World* noticed it, and Ellen Maury Slayden, the wife of a Texas congressman, wrote in her diary, "W. J. B. is much changed. His head is a shining bald crown with a fringe of dull, lank hair, and the fine, strong features that made him so handsome twenty years ago have hardened and grown coarse. . . . His neck is thick

60. William Jennings Bryan and Mary Baird Bryan, *Memoirs of William Jennings Bryan* (Chicago: John C. Winston, 1925), p. 170.

61. *St. Louis Republic* (June 28, 1912); William Allen White, *Autobiography* (New York: Macmillan, 1946), p. 477; *New York World* (June 26, 1912; June 17, 1912); *Louisville Courier-Journal* (June 28, 1912).

62. *St. Louis Republic* (June 28, 1912); McAdoo, *Crowded Years*, p. 149; *Louisville Courier-Journal* (June 28, 1912).

and his jaw has an iron rigidity. I still feel he might be a power for good if he could ever believe that anyone but himself could be right."[63]

Somewhat more unsettled than they had been a week before, but still confident that they were naming the next president, the delegates began voting. Clark held a strong lead over Wilson through the first nine ballots. On the tenth, New York deserted Harmon (leaving him with little outside Ohio) and switched to the Speaker, giving him a majority. Clark expected to be named on the next ballot, and Wilson considered withdrawing.[64]

The Wilson forces at Baltimore, however, rallied and held their ground. After six months of charging a Clark-Harmon-Underwood alliance, they quickly negotiated an agreement with the Underwood delegates, pledging that neither would break to Clark. Numbering well over one-third of the delegates, the Wilson-Underwood forces could prevent any other nomination.[65]

The chances of the coalition improved on the fourteenth ballot, when Bryan led Nebraska out of the Clark camp to Wilson. Amid a chaos almost comparable to the one he had created two days earlier, the Commoner announced that he could not support Clark, or anybody else, as long as that person enjoyed New York's support. Such backing would taint the nominee, he warned, and he developed the point unctuously in his daily newspaper column: "Few, if any, can entirely fortify themselves against the unconscious influence exerted by favors received." Bryan apparently included himself among the few. In 1908, he had eagerly sought Tammany support after his nomination, offering it the vice-presidency, naming a New York national chairman acceptable to Murphy, and publicly thanking the embarrassed Tammany boss for "your good work at Denver."[66]

The Clark managers had put their candidate into an impossible position. Whether or not they had actually made a deal with Tammany,

63. *New York World* (June 26, 1912); Ellen Maury Slayden, *Washington Wife, 1897–1919* (New York: Harper's Press, 1962), p. 179, July 3, 1912.
64. Memo on conversation with William Adamson (October 26, 1912), Ray Stannard Baker Papers, Library of Congress.
65. House Diary (March 19, 1916), House Papers; *St. Louis Republic* (June 30, 1912); Frank P. Glass to Woodrow Wilson (July 6, 1912); Wilson Papers, Library of Congress. Henry Morgenthau has suggested that the Clarkites lost because they demonstrated for an hour after New York's switch, giving the Wilson forces time to shore up their lines (*All in a Lifetime*, p. 147).
66.. Bryan, *A Tale of Two Conventions*, p. 128, June 29, 1912; *Commoner* (July 5, 1912); *Baltimore Sun* (July 5, 1908); *New York World* (July 12, 1908; July 25, 1908).

their support of Parker, followed by New York's votes for Clark, identified their candidate with Murphy. (The presence of Hearst, generally believed capable of anything, fueled reports of a deal.) Actually, Murphy's main priority at the convention was to avoid another Bryan candidacy; Tammany's support of the Speaker was probably explained, in large part, by a comment Murphy made about Wilson, the machine-wrecker: "The boys don't want him." For the Tammany boss, that was a very lengthy and revealing public statement.[67]

Link has argued persuasively that Bryan did not stop Clark, citing the few Clark votes that switched to Wilson. But what Bryan did, and what probably did stop the Speaker, was to give any switches to Clark the appearance of conniving with Tammany. With this situation, Underwood's determination to stand fast, and the statement of Taggart of Indiana (master of thirty votes then going to Marshall) that he would never support anybody backed by Hearst, Clark's candidacy was dead even as it polled a majority. The necessary two-thirds remained a flat impossibility.[68]

Bryan's charges stunned Clark, who demanded that Bryan prove or retract them, and the Speaker steamed into Baltimore eager to defend himself before the convention. His advisors dissuaded him, perhaps wrongly. "There were people who knew what kind of language Clark could use under great provocation," recalled one reporter, "and they seemed to feel that if he spoke from the convention platform grave consequences might result." Locked in a Baltimore hotel room, Clark watched his chances die.[69]

The Wilsonians, meanwhile, abandoning their own hopes for New York's support, slowly and skillfully developed their position. They papered the convention with the *World*'s angry editorials; the *Baltimore Sun*, read daily by the delegates, strenuously argued Wilson's case. (This situation particularly angered Clark, who claimed to have agreed to Baltimore as the convention site only after receiving pledges of the *Sun*'s neutrality.) Local Princeton alumni worked and demonstrated for

67. *New York World* (June 30, 1912); Richard Pettigrew, *Imperial Washington* (Chicago: Charles Kerr and Co., 1922), p. 213; Robert F. Wesser, *A Response to Progressivism* (New York: New York University Press, 1986), pp. 84–88; Mrs. J. Borden Harriman, *From Pinafores to Politics* (New York: Henry Holt and Co., 1923), p. 103; *Louisville Courier-Journal* (March 16, 1908).

68. Link, *Road to the White House*, p. 464; *New York World* (June 30, 1912).

69. Memo on conversation with William Adamson (October 26, 1926), Ray Stannard Baker Papers; *New York World* (July 1, 1912); *Louisville Courier-Journal* (July 1, 1912); *Louisville Courier-Journal* (July 1, 1912); Robert Woolley, "Politics Is Hell," Chapter 17, Woolley Papers, Library of Congress; Dunn, *From Harrison to Harding*, II:190.

Wilson. Ballot by ballot, from the fifteenth to the forty-fifth, the Wilsonians chipped away at Clark's strength, gaining slightly on each. On the twenty-seventh, they gained the support of Taggart's Indiana, in exchange for the vice-presidency for Marshall. They maintained communications with the Underwood forces, and could count on the eventual support of Roger Sullivan of Illinois, committed by primary for Clark but an opponent of Hearst in Chicago politics.[70]

"I saw that my man Clark was dead," explained Virginia senator Claude Swanson of his strategy at this point. "I wasn't going to lie down on that ice and get political pneumonia. No sir! I got up and cut some fancy didoes and came out for Wilson."[71]

During Wilson's long march toward the nomination, the most likely alternative to him was Bryan. Although he was voting for Wilson, Bryan had never endorsed him; in fact, he made it clear that he would oppose Wilson if New York were to support him. Since New York's delegation numbered almost a tenth of the convention, Bryan was demanding that a candidate win nearly three-quarters of the remaining votes. The *St. Louis Republic* reflected a widely held belief when it headlined, "Nebraskan's Stand Indicates Deadlock Cannot Be Broken." Bryan fueled reports of his own ambitions by refusing, despite demands from both the Wilson and Clark camps, to say that he did not want the nomination himself.[72]

Wilson's forces viewed the Commoner with growing apprehension. "He was reported to have said things having an ominous meaning, that indicated he was planning his own nomination," remembered Robert Woolley, a Wilson press aide. After several days of voting, Bryan suggested five new candidates who the convention should consider. "All these men have high character and fine ability, but not one of them had the remotest chance of nomination," wrote one observer; perhaps Bryan was thinking of some other undeclared candidate. After the forty-second ballot, when the Wilsonians had begun to smell victory, Bryan infuriated them by suggesting that the convention take a month off and return after talking to the people. According to James Kerney, a close advisor of Wilson, Bryan told an emissary of Roger Sullivan

70. Gerald W. Johnson, Frank R. Kent, H. L. Mencken, and Hamilton Owens, *The Sunpapers of Baltimore* (New York: Alfred A. Knopf, 1937), p. 305 n; Link, *Road to the White House*, p. 458; Tumulty, *Woodrow Wilson as I Know Him*, p. 121.

71. Henry C. Ferrell, *Claude Swanson of Virginia* (Lexington: University of Kentucky Press, 1985), p. 103.

72. *New York World* (June 38, 1912; July 1, 1912); *St. Louis Republic* (July 1, 1912; July 5, 1912).

"that if the convention should regard his nomination as needful, the regular party leaders would find him easier to deal with than Wilson."[73]

Bryan's hopes collapsed on the forty-sixth ballot, when the Underwood delegates, following Roger Sullivan's example, went to Wilson and nominated him. "Beyond rising [Bryan] did not participate in the concluding Wilson demonstration," reported the *St. Louis Republic*. "His face seemed to have frozen and apparently he had aged ten years. . . . Many who studied his expression in the closing minutes believe they saw there the emotions of hope lost and a lifetime ambition again defeated."[74]

Strikingly, so bitterly fought a convention produced virtually no party division. Clark and all his supporters came immediately to the support of Wilson, although the Speaker would hate William Jennings Bryan for the rest of his life. Gompers, although "disheartened" at the nomination, consoled himself with the thought that the platform "goes as far as a great political party can declare under present industrial and political conditions." Murphy, publicly branded a party pariah, conceded, "This has been a remarkable and interesting convention," but pledged that Wilson "will have the enthusiastic support of the Democrats of New York." He later offered to name any candidate for governor that Wilson wished. In September, the *National Monthly* commented happily, "The party has rallied as one man to Wilson and Marshall."[75]

Such a result further demonstrates that the Democrats struggled over different candidates, not different philosophies. At Chicago, Theodore Roosevelt stood, even if temporarily, for a different idea of government than did William Howard Taft, and he split his party. At Baltimore, Woodrow Wilson and Champ Clark agreed on all major issues. Either could have run on the Democratic platform, called by Bryan " the most progressive platform ever adopted by a great party" and closely resembling that of 1908. Either would have inherited the backers of the other,

73. Woolley, "Politics Is Hell," Chapter 17, Woolley Papers; *St. Louis Republic* (July 5, 1912), Thomas W. Gregory to Edward M. House (July 9, 1912), House Papers; Kerney, *Political Education of Woodrow Wilson*, p. 218, 228. Bryan's five choices were Senators John Kern of Indiana, Isidor Rayner of Maryland, James O'Gorman of New York, and Charles Culberson of Texas, and Senator-Elect Ollie James of Kentucky. None of them had been seriously suggested previously: three were southerners, including one Jew; and O'Gorman was an Irish Catholic.

74. *St. Louis Republic* (July 3, 1912).

75. Gompers, *Seventy Years of Life and Labor*, p. 282; *St. Louis Republic* (July 11, 1912); *New York World* (July 3, 1912); Wesser, *A Response to Progressivism*, p. 90; *National Monthly* (September 1912).

with the possible exception of Wilson's Cleveland Democrats and uplift magazines.[76] "Neither side," reported the *Republic* at the hottest point of the fight, "talked of a bolt and a separate kingdom." The *Independent* found one thing apparent: "the Democrats propose to keep their party together."[77]

Despite Bryan's warnings and machinations, the convention did what it had intended from the start: it wrote an explicitly progressive platform, nominated an explicitly progressive candidate, and rallied around him. One year later, House was surprised to find Underwood still disappointed at the result. "I thought this did not speak well for his political sagacity," he reflected, "for he never had a chance to win since the logic of the situation demanded a progressive, and there were enough progressive votes in the convention to make it impossible for a conservative to be nominated."[78]

Probably the best-known fact about the Progressive Era is that Woodrow Wilson was elected because the Republican party split. Wilson, historians point out, received more than a million votes less than the Republican and Bull Moose tickets combined, and won a majority only in the South, Kentucky, and Arizona. The only Democratic president between Grover Cleveland and Franklin Roosevelt, they conclude, took office on a fluke, in a "deviating election."[79]

Such an interpretation, however, overlooks the political history of the preceding eight years. Since 1905, the Democrats had been developing their issues and strengthening their party and, in 1910, had become the majority party in Congress and in statehouses. Their conduct in office had improved their prospect, and in 1912 their issues — the tariff, trusts, and labor questions — were at least as vital and appealing as they had been two years before. For many reasons, a flat comparison of the Bull Moose–Republican vote with that of Wilson does not provide a reliable result for a hypothetical two-party race. Given the prospects and condition of both political parties in 1912, Wilson probably would have defeated either Taft or Roosevelt.

The Democrats stressed throughout the 1912 campaign the issue that had brought them victory in 1910: the tariff. Shortly after the nomination, Wilson pronounced the tariff the key question, and repeated this position in his acceptance speech and pre-election state-

76. *Commoner* (July 12, 1912).
77. *St. Louis Republic* (June 29, 1912); *Independent* (July 4, 1912).
78. House Diary (September 5, 1913), House Papers.
79. V. O. Key, Jr., "A Theory of Critical Elections," *Journal of Politics* 17 (February 1955): 3–101.

ment. His correspondents approved his course and urged him to continue. "The tariff is the only thing [voters] really care to hear," Walter Hines Page assured House. Democrats not only pounded home the tariff issue in speeches, they produced millions of pamphlets, such as "The High Tariff Primer," which began, "A is for Adam. He did not have to pay a tariff on Apples."[80]

Wilson, as Link points out, had no real position on the trust issue, which the Democrats considered closely related to the tariff, until Louis Brandeis gave him one. But Wilson made no bold departure in accepting Brandeis's ideas on spurring competition and preventing monopoly; Democrats in the House had already recommended them in the La Follette–Stanley Anti-Trust bill, written by the Boston lawyer.[81]

Wilson absorbed this policy in an exchange of letters with Brandeis early in the fall and began to speak on the difference between the Democratic plan, of specifying unfair practices and moving against companies in violation, and the Bull Moose plank, of regulating rather than attacking the trusts. Wilson warned of Bull Moose "paternalism" and "a government of experts" in terms that paralleled the *World's* warnings that under Roosevelt's plan, government would not control the trusts but be controlled by them.[82]

Two of the Democrats' traditional issues, the income tax and direct election of senators, had passed Congress as constitutional amendments and were no longer national issues. But the party's labor plank, which Kern reminded Gompers had been adopted from an AFL draft "without the dotting of an 'i' or the crossing of a 't', " remained a major party issue. Despite the power of the platform and the record of the Democratic House, Gompers sulked for a few weeks after the naming of Wilson. But an August meeting with the nominee won him over, and the Democratic National Committee paid the expense of several AFL and railroad union organizers who rallied strength for the ticket.[83]

80. *St. Louis Republic* (July 7, 1912; August 7, 1912); *Louisville Courier-Journal* (November 2, 1912); Walter Hines Page to Edward M. House (September 6, 1912), House Papers; "High Tariff Primer," in Newlands Papers.
81. Link, *Road to the White House*, pp. 488–92.
82. Woodrow Wilson to Louis D. Brandeis (September 27, 1912); Brandeis to Wilson (September 30, 1912); both in Arthur Link, ed., *Papers of Woodrow Wilson* (Princeton: 1966–), Vol. 25, pp. 272, 289–304; Cooper, *The Warrior and the Priest*, pp. 192–205; *New York World* (October 30, 1912).
83. John W. Kern to Samuel Gompers (August 10, 1912), Wilson Papers, Library of Congress; memo on interview with Robert S. Hudspeth (November 3, 1927), Ray Stannard Baker Papers; Martin J. Wade to Josephus Daniels (November 4, 1912), Daniels Papers, Library of Congress; Karson, *American Labor Unions and Politics* (Carbondale: Southern Illinois University Press, 1958), pp. 70–72.

In addition to appealing issues and a united party, the Democrats had an extraordinarily attractive candidate. Wilson was not only "clean," with a good record and broad acceptability, he was a gifted and sometimes inspiring speaker and writer. One dazzled journalist, William Bayard Hale, wrote that Wilson had shown "a trained and skillful handling of the resources of the language, a sureness, an accuracy, a power, and a delicacy surpassing anything ever heard before on the political platform in America." Although differing greatly from the usual political oratory of the time, his eloquence often had a striking effect. "I am just a common laborer at $75.00 a month, the prices on the commodities of life are so high you can easily see that a man of my position can never amount to anything financially," ran one letter that came into campaign headquarters. "After reading your address to the American people, I felt that I was included."[84]

Throughout the campaign, Democrats largely ignored Taft and concentrated their fire on Roosevelt and the Bull Moose. The Progressive party, because of the presence of a smattering of apolitical social reformers like Jane Addams and its own propaganda, has often been considered more radical than either of the major parties. But many of the Bull Moosers, a diverse group of Republicans who found Roosevelt more progressive, more inspiring, or simply more electable than Taft, did not see it that way. "We believed that the reactionary element was represented by the old Republican party, and that the extremists were then represented by the Democratic party," recalled Roy S. Durstine, Bull Moose press chief. "We believed that there was a middle path down which a man like Theodore Roosevelt could lead the country."[85]

Both the platform and the public leadership of the new party rebutted accusations of radicalism. "If we're not careful," worried ex-Senator Albert Beveridge, "we'll be labelled a Wall Street promotion." The prominent role played in the Progressive party by George W. Perkins, of U.S. Steel and J. P. Morgan Co., alarmed contemporary reformers as much as it has subsequent historians. "I know of no man in the Democratic party," wrote Brandeis, "who is a greater menace to the country than the gentleman who the new party has named as Chairman of its Executive Committee." Rumors spread that the Steel Trust was backing Roosevelt, that he would have all the money he wanted. Democrats drew a direct line between such support and Roosevelt's unique

84. William Bayard Hale, "Friends and Fellow Citizens," *World's Work* (April 1912); C. R. Palaway to Woodrow Wilson (November 6, 1912), Wilson Papers, Library of Congress.

85. Roy S. Durstine, *Reminiscences*, Oral History Research Office, Columbia University, p. 30.

new trust plank. "Naturally," scoffed the *World*, "the Steel Trust believes in the sort of Federal regulation that gave it the Tennessee Coal & Iron Company and suspended the Sherman Act for its benefit." Bull Moosers made little effort to refute charges that they were too close to the trusts: Beveridge on the stump denounced Democratic attacks on big business as "a campaign trick to excite the prejudices of the unthinking."[86]

Certainly, businessmen could find nothing to dislike in the Bull Moose tariff plank, which supported a strong protective tariff, adjusted by a permanent tariff commission to control the cost of living. "It would be discourteous, we think," remarked the *Independent* mildly, "to ask Mr. Roosevelt just now to explain this tariff in detail, and tell us how it will go about its benign performance." Democrats charged that there was no difference between Taft and Roosevelt on the tariff; the *World* cartooned them as the Gold Dust Twins. "I confess I do not know what the debate between Mr. Roosevelt and Mr. Taft is," charged Mayor William J. Gaynor of New York. "Mr. Roosevelt was President for seven years. Just what did he 'do' about the tariff or any other living issue?" Roosevelt's own campaign pronouncements on the issue were purest McKinleyism: he told a Providence audience that the Democratic platform would close their factories, and warned another audience that it would usher in "a period of commercial disorder such as we have not seen in a lifetime."[87]

Aside from those two issues, and Roosevelt's habitual call for more battleships, the Bull Moosers offered an advanced progressive platform, with strong planks on labor, direct democracy, and social issues. The platform, in the eyes of Democrats, contrasted sharply with Roosevelt's conduct in office. Bryan, campaigning actively for the ticket, argued that Roosevelt was eighteen years late on direct election of senators, was still not very active for the income tax, and had never mentioned the tariff nor supported labor while in the White House. "I wish I could believe," wrote one reformer, "that he intended to do a single

86. Walter Johnson, *William Allen White's America* (New York: Henry Holt and Co., 1947), p. 203; Louis Brandeis to Arthur Kingsley Stone (September 4, 1912), in Melvin I. Urofsky and Daniel W. Levy, eds., *Letters of Brandeis* 4 vols. (Albany: State University of New York Press, 1971–1975), II:666; W. W. Marsh to W. D. Jamieson (August 9, 1912), House Papers; Josephus Daniels to Addie Daniels (August 17, 1912), Daniels Papers, Library of Congress; John Braeman, *Albert J. Beveridge* (Chicago: University of Chicago Press, 1971), p. 225.

87. *St. Louis Republic* (August 8, 1912); *Independent* (September 19, 1912); *New York World* (September 29, 1912); Lately Thomas, *The Mayor Who Mastered New York* (New York: William Morrow, 1969); *New York World* (September 29, 1912).

honest thing, or that he would carry out a single plank in the platform if elected. . . . I cannot."[88]

For all these reasons, Roosevelt's party drew strikingly little support from established reform politicians. Congressional insurgents, in particular, distrusted Roosevelt and would not leave the Republican party for him. Many simply sat out the election; some endorsed Roosevelt but would not join his party. Senator John Works of California, supporting Wilson, charges that the Rough Rider was "in no proper sense a tried and true progressive. He had never until now stood openly for progressive principles." Rudolph Spreckels, another California leader, attacked Roosevelt's "open political alliance with trust builders like Perkins and political bosses like [Pennsylvania's William] Flinn." Robert La Follette, whom Wilson often praised in his speeches, could not bring himself to endorse the Democratic candidate but provided tacit support.[89]

Despite its claims to be a new party rather than a Republican faction, the Bull Moose party drew virtually no support from Democrats. From bitter experience, Democrats too distrusted Roosevelt, and the party made no effort to conciliate them. It nominated few ex-Democrats for office, and ex-Congressman Bourke Cockran, the only Democrat of any stature who supported Roosevelt, complained that he could not persuade party leaders of the importance of actively recruiting Democrats. "The result," commented one Republican leader after the election, "shows that practically none but former Republicans joined the Roosevelt movement."[90]

The new party failed to impress the leaders of organized labor, despite its attractive labor plank. Gompers remembered the frustrations of Roosevelt's incumbency and preferred to stick with the likely winners: the Democrats. Roosevelt may have pleaded for those oppressed, commented his supporter, William Allen White, "But Roosevelt's underdog was not proletarian. He was a middle-class, white collar dog."[91]

88. *National Monthly* (September 1912); *New York World* (November 4, 1912); Link, *Road to the White House*, p. 478.

89. Mowry, *Theodore Roosevelt and the Progressive Movement*, p. 257; James L. Holt, *Congressional Insurgents and the Party System* (Cambridge: 1967), pp. 53–54; *New York World* (October 14, 1912); *Louisville Courier-Journal* (November 4, 1912); Luke Lea to Woodrow Wilson (July 13, 1912). William Flinn of Pittsburgh was an old-line boss whose presence in Roosevelt's crusade struck many as inappropriate.

90. Donald Richberg, *My Hero* (New York: Putnam's, 1954), p. 80; Mowry, ibid., p. 262; Bourke Cockran to Bernhard Black (October 1, 1912), Cockran Papers, New York Public Library; *Louisville Courier-Journal* (November 6, 1912).

91. Karson, *American Labor Unions and Politics*, pp. 70–72; White, *Autobiography*, p. 465.

By October, the Bull Moose party showed signs of following the traditional route of American third parties, of proving less potent in November than in August. Three weeks before the election, however, the party received a figurative and almost literal shot in the arm, when a would-be assassin wounded its candidate during a Milwaukee speech. Roosevelt, with his unfailing sense of the dramatic, finished the speech before going off for a two-week stay in the hospital. In an election already decided, his gallantry doubtless reaped a large sympathy vote. "This shooting will help TR directly and indirectly by stopping his talking," assessed Brandeis. "There seemed to be very strong evidence of an ebbing tide before." In a probably exaggerated estimate, one Democrat suggesting that the assailant, "instead of murdering the intrepid Teddy . . . shot about a million votes into him."[92]

Roosevelt's shooting is only one reason why the 7.5 million votes polled by Roosevelt and Taft are as deceptive a statistic as Wilson's 435 electoral votes. A second reason is the extremely low turnout of voters. If Wilson received fewer votes than Bryan in 1908, Taft and Roosevelt together polled fewer than Taft did in 1908. Based on population increase, the admission of two new states, and the extension of suffrage to women in two others, Edgar E. Robinson has suggested an increase in the electorate of approximately one million from 1908 to 1912. Yet, the total vote increased by only 150,000, and in most states voter turnout dropped. Faced with an election already decided — gamblers offered 5 to 1 on Wilson — almost one million voters from both parties stayed home and another one-half million voted Socialist for the first time. (A similar situation had occurred in the lopsided elections of 1892 and 1904.) In a closer bout between two candidates, many absentees might well have turned out to vote for one of the two. It might also be argued that many who voted Socialist might have voted for Wilson if the race had appeared close, as most of the new 1912 recruits apparently did in 1916.[93]

Finally, it must be remembered that the figure of 7.7 million votes, arrived at by adding the Taft and Roosevelt totals, is an imaginary number. Neither candidate alone could have reached that figure. "The 4,200,000 and the 3,500,000 could not have been brought together under Mr. Taft or Mr. Roosevelt," the Independent pointed out after the election. The gulf between the two sides, politically and personally, was

92. Louis Brandeis to Alfred Brandeis (October 15, 1912), in Urofsky and Levy, Letters of Louis Brandeis, II:703; Woolley, "Politics Is Hell," Chapter 17, Woolley Papers.
93. Edgar Eugene Robinson, The Presidential Vote 1896–1932 (Stanford: Stanford University Press, 1934), p. 15; New York World (October 31, 1912).

far too broad, after the bitterest preconvention campaign in American history.[94]

The fight for the 1912 Republican nomination was a battle for the soul of the party, waged between its most colorful, dynamic figure and the president of the United States. The two candidates denounced each other in terms so strong that the nation was stunned, terms far stronger than anything the Democrats were using about each other. If any part of what Roosevelt was saying about Taft were true, commented an awed Democrat, the president should immediately be impeached. The angry feelings of the principals permeated their supporters: violence erupted at many Republican state conventions. By the time the national convention met, the two sides had almost forgotten the Democrats entirely. "If Taft is named the Roosevelt partisans will make their protest on Election Day," predicted the Republican *New York Tribune*, "and if Roosevelt is nominated, the Taft men will do the same thing."[95]

If the election of 1912 appeared to be decided by Republican weakness and division, the situation had been created by Democratic strength and unity. A large and persuasive demand for Roosevelt to oppose Taft emerged because of the clear likelihood that the Democrats would defeat the incumbent for reelection. Taft had been repudiated in the 1910 elections and had hardly improved his position since then: the few elections held in 1911 saw new Democratic gains. "The fates were against him from the first, for the Democratic tide had not ebbed," admitted the *Independent*, which supported Taft for reelection on the race issue, "and the secession of Theodore Roosevelt only made sure what was before scarcely doubtful." After Taft had won the worthless GOP nomination, the *Nation* commented, "It scarcely needed the open split in his party to accentuate the general belief that the chances are enormously against his being elected in November."[96]

Against Wilson, Taft would have had great difficulty in winning the large part of the Roosevelt vote that sincerely favored reform. Louis H. Bean has argued persuasively, based on the congressional returns of 1912, that the Bull Moose vote for president would have split evenly between the two old parties. In that event, Wilson would have received almost 60 percent of the two-party vote.[97]

94. *Independent* (November 21, 1912); William Manners, *TR & Will* (New York: 1969), p. 272.

95. Frank B. Lord, "Taft and Roosevelt," *National Monthly* (June 1912); Mowry, *Theodore Roosevelt and the Progressive Movement*, pp. 231–32; *New York Tribune* (June 20, 1912).

96. *Independent* (November 17, 1912); Manners, *TR & Will*, p. 211; *World's Work* (January 1912); *Nation* (June 27, 1912).

97. Louis H. Bean, *How to Predict Elections* (New York: Alfred A. Knopf, 1948), p. 68.

Theodore Roosevelt, a superb campaigner, a progressive, untouched by the failures and unpopularity of Taft's administration, might appear to have had a better chance against Wilson. The feeling that Roosevelt might win, while Taft certainly could not, motivated many Republicans to demand that he run again. But even as Roosevelt prepared to enter the race, the *Nation* commented prophetically, "It is confidently said that Roosevelt could be elected, but could he? Could he, that is, if he first had to go out and make open war upon Taft ... with his party torn asunder in the process and with countless Republican enemies eager to pay off old spites? Under the circumstances, it would be a cool judgement that maintained he would win." Senator Elihu Root, a friend of both men, expressed the same idea more succinctly. After Roosevelt had fought Taft for the nomination, he predicted, neither could win the election.[98]

Theodore Roosevelt had enjoyed great success in Republican politics by smiling at the progressives while winking at the conservatives, occasionally reversing the process. But in 1912, he could not rely on such caginess. If he were to persuade his party to reject an incumbent president on the grounds of Taft's extreme conservatism, he himself had to be overtly progressive. Moreover, the Rough Rider had to lure away the supporters of Robert La Follette's candidacy, many of whom already distrusted his sincerity. Roosevelt had no choice but to lurch leftward. "If that is revolution," he told the Massachusetts legislature, "make the most of it."[99]

From the entire record of the Republican party since 1896, it can be seen that Roosevelt could not possibly have united the party behind the program he was advocating in 1912. The majority of Republican leaders, especially in the East, could never have supported a platform of recall of judicial decisions, labor benefits, and close governmental regulation of big business. In 1910, when Roosevelt had forced a much milder program (and candidate) upon the Republicans of New York, they abandoned him in droves. Beveridge had the same experience in Indiana, and the regular Republicans of Ohio showed themselves no less implacable.[100]

Organization leaders would have had an even stronger motivation to knife Roosevelt had he somehow obtained the presidential nomination.

98. *Nation* (January 11, 1912); Mowry, *Theodore Roosevelt and the Progressive Movement*, p. 211.

99. Mowry, ibid., pp. 216–17, 229.

100. William Barnes to Joseph Pulitzer (October 7, 1910), Pulitzer Papers, Columbia University.

In state after state, including New York, Pennsylvania, Ohio, and Indiana, Roosevelt had allied himself closely with minority factions in the party. His election would make them the dominant factions. Had Roosevelt been nominated, the conservative leaders in power would have been forced to choose between losing the presidency to Wilson or losing control of the party of Roosevelt and his allies.

Based on both their concepts of government and their previous behavior, it seems likely that they would have chosen to write off an election. "They know with Roosevelt, they lose everything," observed the *New York Tribune* from the Chicago convention. "They are fighting for themselves, and for their particular personal kind of Republican party."[101]

The intense bitterness between the two Republican parties was the most striking feature of the fall campaign. "In my opinion," House wrote Wilson in late August, "The greatest asset we have is the scare that Roosevelt is giving the conservative republicans." A Democratic governor reported from the Midwest, "The Taft men would rather see you elected than Roosevelt, and the Roosevelt men would rather see you elected than Taft." The president himself, reflecting the views of his dwindling band of followers, hoped that Wilson would win if he could not.[102]

The election results in California may provide some idea of how Taft supporters might have reacted to a Roosevelt-Wilson contest. Governor Hiram Johnson, Roosevelt's running mate, controlled the Republican party in the state, and awarded its ballot line to Roosevelt, keeping Taft off entirely. Refusing to mount a write-in campaign, fifteen Republican county committees and forty Republican newspapers endorsed Wilson. In a state not carried by a Democrat since 1894 and where Taft had received 62.7 percent in 1908, the result was a virtual tie, Roosevelt winning 283,610 to 283,436. Preferring a Democratic president to a renegade Republican—especially one running on a reform platform— tens of thousands of conservative California Republicans refused to support Roosevelt, voting for Wilson instead.[103]

By running separately, Taft and Roosevelt may have destroyed any chance their party had, but they also maximized the "Republican" vote. Each won votes that the other would have lost to Wilson. No single

101. *New York Tribune* (June 16, 1912).
102. Edward M. House to Woodrow Wilson (August 21, 1912), House Papers; John Burke to Woodrow Wilson (August 7, 1912), Wilson Papers, Library of Congress; Manners, *TR & Will* (New York: Harcourt, Brace and World, 1969), p. 272.
103. *Los Angeles Times* (November 1, 1912); *World Almanac* (New York: 1913).

Table 5.1 Comparison of Voting for the Roosevelt and Taft National Tickets and State Coalition Tickets

	Democratic Vote	%	Republican Vote	Progressive Vote	Total	%
Kansas:						
President	143,670	42.4	74,844	120,123	194,967	57.6
Governor	167,540	50.0			167,509	50.0
Maine:						
President	51,113	40.5	26,545	48,493	75,038	59.5
Governor	67,748	48.8			71,043	51.2
Nebraska:						
President	109,109	46.2	54,348	72,776	127,124	53.8
Governor	124,000	50.7			120,572	49.3
West Virginia:						
President	113,917	45.4	56,754	79,112	135,866	54.6
Governor	119,173	48.2			127,942	51.8
Wisconsin:						
President	164,409	46.6*	130,878	58,661	189,539	53.4
Governor	167,316	48.3			179,360	51.7

*The relative closeness of the two Democratic votes in Wisconsin results from a unique situation: Robert La Follette, the leading state Republican, supported Wilson.

Republican candidate could have been at once progressive enough to win in 1912 and conservative enough to hold his party's organization and power base.

The effect of this maximization can be seen in Table 5.1. In five states outside the South, Republicans and Bull Moosers ran separate presidential tickets but combined on a candidate for governor, generally a Republican who had endorsed Roosevelt. In all five states, numerous Republicans who supported Roosevelt or Taft spurned the unity candidate and voted Democratic for governor. Kansas Taft supporters organized the Taft Republican League for the specific purpose of cutting the pro-Roosevelt gubernatorial candidate off the ticket. The defections allowed the Democrats to win two state houses in the five normally Republican states and to come surprisingly close in others. The 3,000-vote Republican margin in September's gubernatorial election in Maine, for example, could strike Democrats only as good news: any Republican margin under 15,000 in Maine supposedly indicated national trouble for the GOP.[104]

Had Wilson faced either of his two opponents alone, he would not have scored the same kind of electoral vote landslide, of course, but he would probably have added enough of the disaffected from either side to win the election. Although Wilson carried only the South, Arizona, and Kentucky with a majority of the three-party vote, he won a total of 24 states with at least 45 percent of the vote. In these states, with 258 electoral votes — only 8 short of a majority — the bitterly divided halves of the Republican party would have had to merge with near unanimity to defeat him. In three more states, with 62 electoral votes, including New York, which contained the most committed partisans on both sides, Wilson did only slightly less well, with 43 percent. The two Republican factions were unable to merge cleanly in support of gubernatorial candidates acceptable to both. They could hardly have united in support of a Republican presidential candidate unacceptable to half his party.

"Had kind fortune spared Mr. Taft the disaster of the Roosevelt assault and bolt, the result would have been the same," claimed the *New York Times* after the election. "Had Mr. Roosevelt instead of Taft been nominated at the first Chicago convention, the result would have been the same, for then multitudes of Republicans would have reinforced the Democratic."[105]

104. Robert Sherman La Forte, *Leaders of Reform, Progressive Republicans in Kansas, 1900–1916* (Lawrence: University of Kansas Press, 1974), p. 292; *Nation* (September 12, 1912).
105. *New York Times* (November 6, 1912).

Speculation, however, gives way to the compelling fact of Democratic momentum. Ever since their victory in 1910 made their 1912 victory probable, the Democrats had done far better than anyone expected. The party strengthened itself by its performance in both Congress and the states and had won three special elections in Republican congressional districts.

For eight years, under relentless pressure from Bryan and its newspapers, the Democratic party had fought its image of being divided and ineffectual. It had supported Republican reform initiatives; it had allied itself with the labor movement; and it had reorganized and reshaped itself. "The Democracy," boasted the *National Monthly*, "has made bone of its bone and flesh of its flesh the legitimate progressivism of the country." The inauguration of Woodrow Wilson in 1913 would mark the culmination, not the birth, of Democratic progressivism.[106]

106. *National Monthly* (September 1912).

CHAPTER 6

The Theory and Practice of Democratic Power

In what may be a rare example of job solidarity, historians have tended to look for the roots of Woodrow Wilson's legislative success in the works of Wilson the historian. In this view, Wilson, as he had always advocated in his writings, functioned as President–Prime Minister, providing party leadership and using his followers to put his own program through Congress. Historians may differ on the value of the legislative achievements of the New Freedom, but they tend to agree on who gets the credit. "Wilson," explains Lewis L. Gould in a synthesis of the politics of the period, "did not so much work with the Democrats in Congress has through them." Wilson is frequently viewed as the figure who told Democrats in Congress not only what to do, but also when they should do it, breaking through the party's antebellum thinking. "Led by Woodrow Wilson," says Richard L. McCormick, "the Democrats gave up their rigid insistence on limited government."[1]

This vision tends to overlook, as Wilson himself did not, the other side of the model: that a prime minister is not simply the master of his party, he is also the creature of it. It also downplays two other vital elements in the legislative success of the New Freedom: what Democrats had already done, and what Democrats thought government should do. Drawing some lines between the New Freedom and the old Democratic policies reveals the persistence of the party's pre-Wilson patterns. In a party still largely dominated by Bryan, the paths of Democratic intellectuals are a bit harder to trace, but they did exist — and they led to the same place.

To many historians of the period, as well as to many contemporaries, Democratic political thinking is almost a contradiction in terms. To the extent that the party is thought to have any guiding principles at all,

---

1. Lewis L. Gould, *Reform and Regulation: American Politics, 1900–1916* (New York: John Wiley, 1978), p. 150; Richard L. McCormick, *The Party Period of Public Policy* (New York: Oxford University Press, 1986), p. 180.

they are often seen as outdated and unequal to dealing with a modern industrial democracy.[2]

Moreover, the basic tenet of Democratic political thinking — a fundamental distrust of concentrations of power — caused the party to be rejected by the foremost political intellectuals of the day, whose reputations have endured through this century. Shortly after Herbert Croly, Walter Weyl, and Walter Lippmann, all enthusiastic supporters of Theodore Roosevelt and the Progressive Party, founded the *New Republic* in November 1914, the new magazine explained that the Democratic party "has the vitality of a low organism. It can not only subdivide without losing the continuity of its life, but it can temporarily assume almost any form, any color, and structure without ceasing to recognize itself and without any apparent sacrifice of collective identity."[3]

In the twentieth century, reform presidents have usually enjoyed support from intellectuals; Wilson's difficulties with the most prominent political intellectuals of the period caused him some problems at the time and with historians later. The absence of comparable Democratic theoreticians has tended to reinforce the *New Republic*'s image of the party as based more on prejudices than ideas.

Yet the various components of the Democratic party did indeed share some ideas, as expressed most cogently by Louis Brandeis, and the Democrats' thinking offered more of a critique of the Progressive outlook than the intellectuals would ever concede. A comparison of the two reform world views suggests that not all the prejudices were on the Democratic side.

Like Roosevelt, their political idol, Croly, Weyl, and Lippmann began with a fundamental contempt for the Democratic party. This was especially true of Croly, who was a fervent Republican at least until 1912, originally sent to Roosevelt by Henry Cabot Lodge. "By 1909, Republicanism had become one of Croly's strongest prejudices," according to Charles Forcey, who points out that to Croly and other New York intellectuals the Democratic party would always be exemplified by Tammany Hall.[4]

Like the men of the middle-class magazines, the *New Republic* intellectuals also bore a distaste for the image and the components of the Democratic party; as Christopher Lasch suggests, "Perhaps the intel-

2. See, for example, Richard L. McCormick, "The Discovery that Business Corrupts Politics," *American Historical Review* 86 (April 1981): 258, or George Mowry, *The Era of Theodore Roosevelt* (Madison: University of Wisconsin Press, 1946).

3. *New Republic* (January 15, 1916).

4. Charles Forcey, *The Crossroads of Liberalism* (New York: Oxford University Press, 1961), p. 42.

lectuals retained more of their middle class prejudices than they realized." The *New Republic* could dismiss Governor David Walsh of Massachusetts as "a capable, honest, industrious Irish-Catholic politician, progressive in purpose but weak of will, and unconsciously limited by his narrow traditions and environment," and then make the point more explicitly a year later: "The Roman Church has purposes to fulfill, has positions to maintain that seem incompatible with the progress of the community."[5]

The magazine shared the Republican insurgents' skepticism about the existence of southern progressivism. When the Kern-McGillicuddy bill for worker's compensation for federal employees appeared to be stuck in committee, the *New Republic* suggested that the chairman's southern roots explained the difficulty. (Actually, Wilson's own lack of interest was more the problem.) That a party composed of Tammany, Jeffersonians, Bryanites, Catholics, and southerners could stand for anything significant seemed self-evidently absurd to Croly, Lippmann, and the early *New Republic*.[6]

Walter Lippmann, whose insight sometimes cut through his ideology, once noted some of the roots of the attitude. "I know how bogeys are made," he mused in his second book, *Drift and Mastery*. "I was a child of four during the panic of '93, and Cleveland has always been a sinister figure to me. His name was uttered with monstrous dread in the household. Then came Bryan, an ogre from the West, and a waiting for the election returns of 1896 with beating heart. And to this day I find myself with a subtle prejudice against Democrats that goes deeper than what we call political conviction."[7]

For Croly, Weyl, and Lippmann, the better choice was clear: Theodore Roosevelt. Croly had been under Roosevelt's spell since 1910, and the campaign of 1912 brought him together with Lippmann and Weyl. Henry May points out the attraction of the Bull Moose party's "demand for leadership, its occasional use of the language of scientific management," but notes that "few of the Young Intellectuals could resist TR's charm and versatility." Forcey also suggests that Roosevelt's personality may have been the decisive factor, that the Bull Moose platform was not so close to the intellectuals as they liked to think.[8]

5. Christopher Lasch, *The New Radicalism in America, 1889–1963* (New York: Alfred A. Knopf, 1965), p. 149; *New Republic* (January 16, 1915; November 6, 1915; September 2, 1916).
6. *New Republic* (June 10, 1916).
7. Walter Lippmann, *Drift and Mastery* (New York: M. Kennerly, 1914), pp. 240–41.
8. Henry May, *The End of American Innocence* (New York: Alfred A. Knopf, 1959), p. 304; Forcey, *The Crossroads of Liberalism*, pp. 130–51.

Roosevelt's unique ability to convince different groups that he sympathized with them entirely and that he dealt with others only because circumstance required seemed to work as well on intellectuals as on eastern businessmen and midwestern insurgents. In *The Promise of American Life*, Croly rejoiced, "It is fortunate . . . that one reformer can be named whose work has tended to give reform the dignity of a constructive mission"; five years later, in *Progressive Democracy* (1914), he eulogized Roosevelt in terms at least as warm. Roosevelt pervaded Lippmann's first book, *A Preface to Politics*, as both inspiration and example, much as Cesare Borgia pervaded Machiavelli's *The Prince*. "I have Roosevelt in mind," Lippmann explains. "He haunts political thinking." Later, he praises the Colonel for "attempting to make himself and his followers the heroes of a new social myth."[9]

The three editors went on pilgrimage to Oyster Bay two weeks after starting the magazine, and the *New Republic* of the first year sounded as though the campaign of 1912 were still being fought. "It looks as if we should have to depend during the coming winter upon ex-President Roosevelt to make political controversy interesting," predicted the magazine in September 1915. Roosevelt, it explained, had "a gift for leadership – a gift which is rendered the more conspicuous because of the almost complete lack of competition." One of the magazine's sharpest editorials of its first year responded to a comment by Wilson that the Republican party had not had a new idea in thirty years. Wilson, bristled the magazine, was "palpably and inexcusably distorting the facts. . . . During Mr. Roosevelt's second administration the Republican party was bursting with new ideas, while at the same time the Democratic party, not excluding Mr. Wilson, was laboring with old ones."[10]

One new idea of Roosevelt's that the *New Republic* particularly admired – and Democrats particularly objected to – was his muscular foreign policy. In *The Promise of American Life*, Croly had made approving noises about both militarism and colonialism; he had decried the American "superstition about militarism" and suggested that "disorganized peoples" might require "forcible pacification." This would benefit both the pacified and the pacifiers: an active national policy abroad

9. Herbert Croly, *The Promise of American Life* (Cambridge: Belknap Press of Harvard University Press, 1965) p. 167; Herbert Croly, *Progressive Democracy* (New York: Macmillan, 1914), p. 11; Walter Lippmann, *A Preface to Politics* (New York: M. Kennerly, 1913), pp. 98, 184.

10. Forcey, *The Crossroads of Liberalism*, pp. 3–4; *New Republic*, September 4, 1915; January 16, 1915.

would tend to mean an active national policy at home, as well as providing international peace.[11]

Accordingly, the *New Republic* called for a strong policy of preparedness and sympathy for the Allies in World War I. As Lasch has written, the *New Republic* was more sure that it wanted a strong policy than exactly what strong policy it wanted. But it did feel that it was not getting the policy it wanted from Wilson, whom it considered a "somewhat confused though entirely well-meaning amateur" in foreign affairs. Even after the magazine had become skeptical about Roosevelt's declining interest in domestic reform, foreign developments returned it to old allegiances.[12]

Democrats also saw in foreign policy a test of the national fiber and an issue with domestic reverberations. In 1900, Cleveland and Bryan Democrats had united to campaign against imperialism, and congressional Democrats had strongly opposed Roosevelt's naval expansion plans. On a list of reasons why he might reluctantly support Bryan in 1908, Joseph Pulitzer had placed first "Bryan's long and continued and consistent hostility to militarism and colonialism." He outlined his reasons a month later in a note on instruction to Frank Cobb: "Give estimate of total cost of this Philippine shame. Only possible excuse for it was commercial financial that it would pay. But even if it did it would remain completest stultification of all pretense of liberty."[13]

The Democrats agreed with Croly on all but his conclusion: expansionist foreign policy would indeed create a different kind of domestic state — one that might be as careless of the liberties of Americans as of those of Filipinos. Moreover, Democrats suspected that such policies might strongly benefit foreign business expansion, thus strengthening the same trusts they wished to weaken. In World War I, the coincidence of Wall Street loans to the Allies and demands for preparedness seemed to underscore the point. When House Democrats agreed to follow Wilson on preparedness, they demanaded that the program at least be paid for with higher income taxes, paid by the people they saw as benefiting from the program.[14]

But the fundamental issue dividing the Democrats and the *New Re-*

11. Croly, *The Promise of American Life*, pp. 54, 259.

12. *New Republic* (October 23, 1915); Lasch, *The New Radicalism in America*, p. 138; *New Republic* (February 19, 1916; January 1, 1916).

13. Memo from Joseph Pulitzer (undated, 1908), Joseph Pulitzer Papers, Columbia University.

14. Claude Kitchin to William Jennings Bryan (September 10, 1915; December 13, 1915), Kitchin Papers, University of North Carolina (microfilm).

public editors was domestic: the issue of bigness in general and trusts in particular. What Democrats found alarming, Croly, Weyl, and Lippmann found exciting.

"The new organization of American industry," wrote Croly in *The Promise of American Life*, "has created an economic mechanism which is capable of being wonderfully and indefinitely serviceable to the American people." This could be accomplished if the trusts were no longer hampered by what Lippmann called the "egregious folly of a Sherman Anti-Trust Law" and were permitted to operate with the efficiency that size could permit. "Whenever the smaller competitor of the large corporation is unable to keep his head above water," pronounced Croly, "he should be permitted to drown." The answer was not to break or hobble the trusts but to regulate them with a commission and a federal incorporation law. Their way to do this, as Henry May phrases it, was "an instrumental state run by experts."[15]

Expertise, efficiency, and administration tended to figure prominently in the solutions Croly, Weyl, and Lippmann offered to all problems, even those of an ostensibly political or legal nature. In the new government, explained Lippmann, "there will be merely much less use for lawyers and a great deal more for scientists." Those scientists, he explains in a later book, could deal with business in its most efficient incarnation: "The fact is that administration is becoming an exact science, capable of devising executive methods for dealing with tremendous units." Social and political questions, therefore, could be dealt with by the creation of a trained, expert class of administrators, insulated from popular and political pressures.[16]

The examples they offered of successful systems are revealing. Lippmann cited U. S. Steel ("management is autocratic . . . administrators are highly paid, and given power adequate to their responsibility"); Croly cited the nineteenth-century British system of an aristocratic ruling class and a professional civic service. The reason Americans might be skeptical of such a concentration of power, the *New Republic* explained crisply, was that "the mass of men never administer anything — so they are complacently oblivious to the importance of administration."[17]

The first Democratic objection to the idea of an expert-administrator

15. Croly, *The Promise of American Life*, pp. 115, 359; Lippmann, *A Preface to Politics*, p. 28; May, *The End of American Innocence*, p. 322.

16. Lippmann, ibid., p. 301.

17. Lippmann, *Drift and Mastery*, pp. 42, 62; Croly, *The Promise of American Life*, p. 231; *New Republic* (November 13, 1915).

state was its implicit elitism, an objection that Wilson, under the tutelage of Brandeis, stressed in the campaign of 1912. Croly's first book, *The Promise of American Life*, had made that elitism explicit, charging that "the average American is morally and intellectually inadequate to a serious and consistent conception of his responsibilities as a democrat." The intellectuals consistently attacked Jefferson and Jackson (much as Theodore Roosevelt did) for their positions on egalitarianism and popular government — burdens that, they argued, still crushed the Democratic party. "To men like Mr. Bryan," Croly complained in an early issue of the *New Republic*, "the expert is as suspect as he would have been to Andrew Jackson."[18]

But the strongest Democratic objection was not to the identity of the experts but to the impossibility of their jobs. Against the Roosevelt-Croly vision of efficiency of scale regulated by scientific government, the Democratic position was explicit: there were no good trusts, because concentration of wealth and power was dangerous by definition. According to this attitude, shared by Robert La Follette, the answer to the trust question was to enforce the laws, particularly the criminal provisions of the Sherman Act.

This seemingly simplistic stance has been attacked as anachronistic and unrealistic by both contemporary and recent critics. Roosevelt derided such a position as "sincere rural Toryism," and Croly dismissed Bryan as "a Democrat of both Jeffersonian and Jacksonian tendencies, who has been born a few generations too late."[19]

Yet the Democratic position was something more than knee-jerk negativism, barren of intellectual backing. The Democratic attitude toward the trusts was based upon experience with and perceptions about power and a consciousness of the limitations of structure. Moreover, the position was held throughout the party, from Bryan to the eastern newspapers to the congressional leaders, and formidably argued by the attorney who advised both Wilson and Democratic congressmen, Louis Brandeis.

Brandeis was not only an intellectual force capable of dueling with Lippmann and Croly; he was also an active and influential figure on the Democratic party scene who left a particular imprint on the New

18. John M. Cooper, Jr., *The Warrior and the Priest* (Cambridge: Belknap Press of Harvard University Press, 1983), pp. 192–205; Lippmann, *A Preface to Politics*, p. 316; *New Republic* (February 3, 1916). Lippmann, his most recent biographer notes, was "not much of a democrat." (Ronald Steel, *Walter Lippmann and the American Century* [New York: Atlantic Monthly Press, 1980], p. 56).
19. Mowry, *The Era of Theodore Roosevelt*, p. 295; Croly, ibid., p. 156.

Freedom. Brandeis first met Wilson, who had no particular trust position, shortly after Wilson's nomination for president; soon, as Roosevelt campaigned on his new trust plank, Wilson was writing the lawyer,
"Please set forth as explicitly as possible the actual measures by which
competition can be effectively regulated." Brandeis responded in detail,
and the candidate suddenly had a position. "Wilson, you can see from
his speeches, has swallowed Brandeis' theory without knowing much
about it," one Democrat complained to another at the end of the 1912
campaign, but the infusion had been crucial in meeting Roosevelt's attack.[20]

Wilson's new adviser had his own ties with Democrats in both Massachusetts and Congress. Close to organized labor, Brandeis had been
mentioned as a Democratic possibility for governor of Massachusetts;
when he temporarily changed his registration to support his close
friend La Follette in the 1912 presidential primary, he dashed hopes
that he would write the state Democratic platform that year. Later, he
would be offered the party's nomination for state attorney general.[21]

Brandeis had become a figure in national Democratic affairs in 1910,
when he worked with Democratic congressmen in the House investigation of Secretary of the Interior Richard Ballinger, a probe that improved the national standing of both the Democrats and Brandeis.
Later, Brandeis took part in the Stanley Committee's investigation of
U.S. Steel. After gathering information about U.S. Steel, the committee's chief investigator later recalled, he "then invited Mr. Brandeis to
digest it and make a presentation. . . . His statement . . . attracted the
widest attention, and was used liberally by the Democrats in the late
national campaign." The investigation also provided material for the
La Follette–Stanley Antitrust bill, the Democratic congressional remedy for the trusts, which Brandeis wrote. The other major investigation
conducted by the Democratic House majority, the Pujo Committee's
study of the concentration of credit resources, provided most of the material for Brandeis's best-known work, *Other People's Money*, published
in 1913. When Brandeis was under consideration for a spot in Wilson's

20. Wilson to Brandeis (September 17, 1912); Brandeis to Wilson (September 30,
1912); in Arthur Link, ed., *Papers of Woodrow Wilson* (Princeton: Princeton University
Press, 1966–), 25:272, 289–304; Franklin K. Lane to Francis G. Newlands (October 28,
1912). Newlands Papers, Yale University; Cooper, *The Warrior and the Priest*, p. 194.

21. Allon Gal, *Brandeis of Boston* (Cambridge: Harvard University Press, 1980), pp.
55–64; Alpheus T. Mason, *Brandeis: A Free Man's Life* (New York: Viking, 1946), pp. 124,
260, 369, 395; John N. Minton to Edward E. Moore (February 24, 1913), Wilson Papers,
Library of Congress.

cabinet, he drew a ringing endorsement from Bryan, who wrote the president-elect, "I do not know that a better man can be found."[22]

As Thomas K. McCraw notes, although Brandeis was "the most influential critic of trusts during his generation," economics was not a particular interest or concern. His highest priorities were social and political, and as Allon Gal argues, his views grew out of direct experience in the Massachusetts legal and political world.[23]

Unlike Croly, Weyl, and Lippmann, Brandeis was not interested in the efficiency of structures. Although he insisted in *Other People's Money* that trusts were in fact no more efficient, he also argued that that efficiency was not the point: "Even more important than efficiency are industrial and political liberty," endangered by the size and power of the trusts. "The key to Brandeis's thought," observes Richard B. Abrams, was "in his belief that the trusts represent a threat to democratic processes and, above all, to the institutional bases of individual liberty and sound national character. He took for granted that economic power was readily translated into political power, and that concentrated economic power necessarily jeopardized the political safeguards of liberal society."[24]

The question of national character was a very real one to Brandeis, whose distinctly Puritan views on life and work were bolstered by his own struggle upward as a Jew in pre-1900 Boston. In *Other People's Money*, he charged that interlocking directorates, one big business practice, "offends laws human and divine" by "substituting the pull of privilege for the push of manhood." American character and American freedom both hung on the preservation of competition and opportunity. "You cannot have true American citizenship, you cannot preserve political liberty, you cannot secure American standards of living," Brandeis told the Senate Interstate Commerce Committee, "unless some degree of industrial liberty accompanies it."[25]

Among Progressive Era Democrats, Brandeis found ready agreement

22. Mason, *Brandeis*, pp. 353–57; Robert M. Woolley to Edward M. House (March 7, 1914), House Papers, Yale University; Louis D. Brandeis to Woodrow Wilson (September 30, 1912), Wilson Papers, Library of Congress; Louis D. Brandeis, *Other People's Money, and How the Bankers Use It* (New York: Harper Torch books, 1967), ed. Richard B. Abrams; Bryan to Wilson, in Link, *Papers of Woodrow Wilson*, 25:622.

23. Thomas K. McCraw, *Prophets of Regulation* (Cambridge: Harvard University Press, 1984), pp. 82, 96; Gal, *Brandeis of Boston*, p. 177.

24. Brandeis, *Other People's Money*, pp. 48, xxxvi.

25. Ibid., 50; Melvin I. Urofsky, *A Mind of One Piece: Brandeis and American Reform* (New York: Charles Scribner's Sons, 1971), p. 56.

for his doctrine of the inevitable connection between economic and political power. "They are unable to understand," the *New York World* complained of the Bull Moosers in 1912, "that these thousands of millions of capital which they propose to regulate will as certainly seize the government as the slave-holding oligarchy seized the government." As on few other issues, Joseph Pulitzer's newspaper and William Jennings Bryan were in agreement. Concerning one Roosevelt proposal for centralized regulation of railroads, the *Commoner* warned, "It is impossible to exaggerate the extent to which the railroads will enter politics if the president's plan is carried out." Their agreement on the trust issue was another reason given by Pulitzer for eventually supporting Bryan in 1908. Democrats' consciousness of the power of business in government led some to contemplate going beyond even trust-busting. "I hope the day will never come when we have to own them," Rufus Hardy of Texas told the House about railroads, "but if the day comes when we cannot control them, I would rather own the roads than have them own Congress."[26]

With their certainty that economic power brought political power, the Democrats could never accept Roosevelt's distinction between "good" trusts, to be left unmolested, and "bad" trusts, to be prosecuted. When House Minority leader John Sharp Williams pledged support to Roosevelt's program in his second term, Williams specifically exempted Roosevelt's plans for modifying the Sherman Act: there were, he explained, no "good" trusts.[27]

Democrats protested angrily after the distinction was seemingly legalized by the Supreme Court in its 1911 "Rule of Reason" decision, distinguishing between "reasonable" and "unreasonable" dominations of the market. The decision of the Supreme Court seemed to confirm all the Democrats' worst fears about rooted trust domination. "I am anxious for you to speak out against the 'rule of reason' decisions," Bryan instructed the presidential hopeful Woodrow Wilson. "They repeal the criminal clause of the anti-trust law." Wilson's opponent, Champ Clark, proclaimed, "To my mind to talk about a 'reasonable' restraint of trade is preposterous."[28]

26. *New York World* (October 30, 1912); *Commoner* (May 22, 1908); memo from Joseph Pulitzer (undated, 1908), Pulitzer Paper, Library of Congress; *Congressional Record*, Vol. 45, Part 5, p. 5168.
27. *Congressional Record*, Vol. 47, Part 1, p. 769; *Louisville Courier-Journal* (March 27, 1908).
28. *New York World* (October 8, 1912); William Jennings Bryan to Woodrow Wilson (August 11, 1911), Wilson Papers, Princeton University; *Commoner* (April 26, 1912).

The situation would only get disastrously worse, Democrats believed, if the federal government were to take over chartering corporations, the remedy urged by Roosevelt and Croly. Behind such a policy, argued the *Commoner*, was "the corporations' demand [for] federal protection from state legislation," an argument recently readvanced by revisionist historians of the Progressive Era. Not only, agreed the *World*, would federal incorporation "further strip the states of their control over Big Business," but it would make it easier for Wall Street to take control of the entire process.[29]

Democrats believed that they had already seen a model of how such a system might work. Federal incorporation, wrote Congressman Augustus Owsley Stanley, investigator of U.S. Steel and sponsor of the La Follette–Stanley Anti-Trust bill, would "inevitably mean not federal control of great corporations, but federal control by great corporations.- ... A bureau saturated with fraud and corruption will traffic in privileges to great corporations as tariff duties are now bargained."[30]

Just before Wilson took office, one clear statement of Democratic policy came from the Pujo Committee, which was set up by the House to investigate the concentration of credit resources. Beginning in the summer of 1912, the committee, in Gabriel Kolko's words, "for eight months frightened the nation" with disclosures of interlocking directorates, the omnipresence of J. P. Morgan and Company, and the vast resources of financial and corporate power controlled or influenced by Wall Street banking houses. "The committee took the view that its duty was to ascertain whether, and if so to what extent, there was a concentration of the control of credit in a few hands," explained its counsel, "and not to go into the question of whether this power had been abused." Croly might suggest that the committee had thus missed the entire point, but to Democrats, its logic was clear: concentration had to mean abuse.[31]

It was the strength of Democratic resolve on this issue, as well as his own brilliance, that gave Brandeis influence in the Wilson administration. At the end of 1913, when he thought new anti-trust legislation was emerging too slowly, Brandeis warned the Secretary of the Interior that such an act was "politically necessary to satisfy the demands of the very large numbers of progressive Democrats and the near Democrats

29. *Commoner* (August 30, 1907); *New York World* (November 14, 1911).
30. Augustus Owsley Stanley to Henry Watterson (August 14, 1912), Watterson Papers, Library of Congress.
31. *Congressional Record*, Vol. 48, Part 3, pp. 2389–2418; Part 6, pp. 5345–46; Gabriel Kolko, *Triumph of Conservatism* (New York: Free Press of Glencoe, 1963), p. 220; Samuel Untermyer to Edward M. House (March 7, 1914); House Papers.

who are already beginning to express some doubt whether the administration will have the courage . . . to carry out the policy which it has hitherto declared."[32]

In *The Promise of American Life*, Croly recognizes the Democratic objection to his vision but distorts its point. Jeffersonians, he charges, wanted "a democracy of suspicion, discontent, of selfish claims, of factious agitation, and of individual and class aggression. A thoroughly responsible and efficient national organization would be dangerous in such a democracy, because it might well be captured by some combination of local individual or class interest." But that would be impossible, Croly assures his readers, in his commonwealth of cooperation, administered by disinterested experts.[33]

Croly had dealt with the power of special interests to overcome government by treating it not as a proven reality but as a nightmare of a fevered Jeffersonian imagination. The *New Republic* reflected this attitude; as John Chamberlain says of Lippmann's image of business in the new society, "He ignored his own advice entirely; he looked at carnivorous teeth and called them herbivorous." As a more recent critic notes, Croly's vision was fatally susceptible to "easy transformation into serving the interests of large corporations."[34]

The ostensibly rational response to emotional Bryanism actually came down to faith: the *New Republic's* faith in experts and Roosevelt's faith in himself. If the Democrats could offer no foolproof answers themselves, their suspicion of the Progressive vision was neither intellectually shallow nor anachronistically Jeffersonian. If anything, their questioning of the disinterested purity of federal regulation may mark them as more ahead of their time than behind it. The Democratic world view itself may have been inadequate to the task facing the party in 1913. But it was not the outlook of a party constricted by a commitment to a limited national power and looking blankly to Woodrow Wilson for an agenda.

In the first issue of the *New Republic*, which appeared after the congressional elections of 1914; after the special session of Congress that revised the tariff; and after the extended regular session that passed the Federal Reserve Act, the Clayton Anti-Trust Act, and the Federal Trade Commission bill; the editors explained, "The association of pro-

32. Louis D. Brandeis to Franklin K. Lane, in Mason, *Brandeis*, p. 400.
33. Croly, *The Promise of American Life*, p. 173.
34. John Chamberlain, *Farewell to Reform* (Chicago: Quadrangle, 1965), p. 230; Douglas Walter Jaenicke, "Herbert Croly, Progressive Ideology, and the FTC Act," *Political Science Quarterly* 93 (Fall 1978): 493.

gressivism with partisan democracy has made it more efficient for certain limited purposes, but less interesting and significant."[35] What was striking about the assessment was not the magazine's predictable dismissal of the Democratic spirit; it was the previously inconceivable idea of referring to a Democratic Congress as efficient.

Yet Wilson's first Congress had been efficient. In striking contrast to the last time Democrats had controlled both houses and the White House, which was under Grover Cleveland twenty years earlier (a specter that hung over the party from the day of the 1912 election), the party followed its leaders and carried out its platform. The record of Congress, admitted the *Baltimore Sun*, "has so far surpassed its own expectations as it has dumbfounded it opponents."[36]

The traditional hero of this triumph, of course, has been Wilson, delivering his messages in person, regularly traveling to Capitol Hill, keeping the pressure on the Democratic legislators. Seeing him as their only chance of staying in power, Democrats in Congress, in this view, fell in line and accepted his reform wishes.[37]

Certainly, Wilson was a vital and probably essential figure in the Democrats' legislative achievements. But the bulk of those achievements were hardly innovations of his own; they were completions of efforts congressional Democrats had mounted under Taft and advocated before that. When Wilson intervened, it was more often an effort to tone down reform legislation than force it upon unwilling congressmen.

Congressional Democrats followed him, said Wilson at the time, "because they see that I am attempting to mediate their own thoughts and purposes. . . . They are using me; I am not driving them." As Congress wound down, the *New York Times* discovered more concrete evidence of party unity of purpose, the surprising fact that "with Mr. Wilson well into his second year, there should be no anti-Administration faction in his party."[38] Another sign of the general party consensus was not visible until some years later, when Howard Allen found that congressional Democrats in the New Freedom years had an extraordinarily high party cohesion rating.[39]

Democratic party discipline in Congress, so surprising to observers

35. *New Republic* (November 7, 1914).
36. *Baltimore Sun* (October 8, 1914).
37. See, for example, Gould, *Reform and Regulation*, p. 150.
38. Cooper, *The Warrior and the Priest*, p. 236; *New York Times* (October 6, 1914).
39. Howard W. Allen, *Poindexter of Washington: A Study in Progressive Politics* (Carbondale: Southern Illinois University Press, 1981), p. 86.

and so important to a party with only a narrow edge in the Senate, was enforced with tools forged in the previous Congress. The use of the caucus to keep Democrats in line not only remained effective in the House, but also spread to the Senate. In an unsubtle warning, committee appointments were postponed until after tariff reform had passed, an extension of the leadership's 1911 strategy of packing the Ways and Means Committee with tariff reformers. And with the aid of the numerous freshman senators, Senate Democratic leader Thomas Martin of Virginia was rejected as insufficiently progressive and replaced by the Bryanite, John Kern, of Indiana.[40]

In the special session called by Wilson in April 1913, the first priority was a new tariff, which included all the reductions Democrats had previously sought. Rates were cut by more than 26 percent overall, with many food items, sugar, and wool going on the free list. Instead of raising the rates first passed by the House, the Senate cut them further. In the Senate, the Democrats lost only the votes of the Democrats from Louisiana, but gained only the votes of La Follette and Miles Poindexter. Poindexter was the sole senator to identify himself as a Progressive, and had been given a committee chairmanship by the Democrats.[41]

With the ratification of the Sixteenth Amendment, the Democrats could finally add to the tariff an income tax. With no encouragement from the administration, Democrats, first in the House and then in the Senate, adjusted the first proposed rates to make them more progressive and higher on upper incomes.[42]

Democratic party leaders and congressmen also left their mark on the administration's Federal Reserve proposal. Seventeen years after his "Cross of Gold" speech to the 1896 Democratic convention, Secretary of State William Jennings Bryan still considered himself an expert on currency issues, and together with Brandeis and western and southern Democrats in Congress redrew Wilson's plan to provide more public and less private control and disperse credit control more widely around

40. Evans C. Johnson, *Oscar W. Underwood: A Political Biography* (Baton Rouge: Louisiana State University Press, 1980), p. 199; Henry C. Ferrell, Jr., *Claude Swanson of Virginia* (Lexington: University Press of Kentucky, 1985), p. 105.

41. Gould, *Reform and Regulation*, pp. 151–53; Allen, *Poindexter*, pp. 87–92; Wilson Press Conference (June 16, 1913), in Link, ed. *Papers of Woodrow Wilson*, 27:524; Herbert Margulies, *Senator Lenroot of Wisconsin: A Political Biography* (Springfield: University of Missouri Press, 1977), pp. 161–62.

42. Gould, *Reform and Regulation*, p. 152; Allen, ibid., p. 92; Johnson, *Underwood*, pp. 217–18; Joseph P. Tumulty of Wilson (September 2, 1913), in Link, *Papers of Woodrow Wilson*, 28:247.

the country.[43] At the insistence of the administration, however, a rural credits plan, involving the government directly in extending credit to farmers, was removed from the plan. It took Wilson's direct intervention, and his insistence that the federal government should not directly aid any particular group in society, to delete the program, which would come up again.[44]

The proposed antitrust program of the Democrats in Congress was a lineal descendant of the previous session's La Follette–Stanley bill. Originally a specific enunciation of unfair practices and criminal penalties, described by Arthur Link as "Draconian," the Clayton Act was forcibly weakened by Wilson, who now preferred to place his emphasis on a Federal Trade Commission. The revised bill was less clear and harder to enforce, but Democrats in Congress followed along, with some grumbling.[45]

They did manage a limited victory over Wilson in one aspect of the bill — its treatment of labor. Republicans' use of the antitrust law to prosecute labor unions had been a long-standing grievance of the AFL, which congressional Democrats had responded to with the Hughes Amendment, forbidding the Department of Justice from spending any money on such prosecutions. Now, Samuel Gompers and most Democrats preferred to take the direct route of simply exempting labor and farm organizations from such prosecutions.[46]

Wilson, again seeing federal favoritism to one group, was dubious. When he received the first appropriations bill containing a Hughes Amendment, he announced that if it were possible he would have vetoed that section. His original plans for antitrust legislation envisioned no mention of labor at all, and House Democrats forced the inclusion of a labor exemption that was not as explicit as they and Gompers would have liked. When Attorney General Thomas Gregory told Wilson that he still thought the bill's labor section too broad, Wilson agreed, but said that the administration had better leave it alone.[47]

43. Ferrell, *Swanson*, p. 106; Dewey Grantham, *Southern Progressivism: The Reconciliation of Progress and Tradition* (Knoxville: University of Tennessee Press) p. 362.
44. Johnson, *Underwood*, pp. 211–12; Woodrow Wilson to Carter Glass (May 12, 1914), in Link, *Papers of Woodrow Wilson*, 30:24; see also Wilson to Elsworth Raymond Bathrick (December 14, 1914), 31:462.
45. Link, ibid., 30:vii; A. O. Stanley to Wilson (December 9, 1913), 29:25–30. McCraw, *Prophets of Regulation*, pp. 119–24.
46. Gompers to Wilson (March 14, 1913), in Link, ibid., 27:180–87.
47. Wilson statement on Sundry Civil Appropriations bill (June 23, 1913), in ibid., 27:558; Wilson Press Conference (March 16, 1914), 29:346; Wilson Press Conference

The record of Wilson's first Congress was substantial, and it was at least as much a party record as a Wilson record. The president, writes John Milton Cooper, Jr., "sought to temper, guide and restrain an excited following of reformers. After sixteen years of Bryan's leadership, the majority of Democrats required no prodding to support measures to curb the power of big business."[48]

On at least one issue, Wilson was leading his party backward. A southern president, southern cabinet members, and southern congressmen now moved to expand the hardening segregation system of the South into Washington, D.C. and the federal service, widening a gap between Democrats and blacks that would not be narrowed again for another twenty years.

The same discontent with Republican lip service that had led W. E. B. Du Bois to endorse Bryan in 1908 had led him in 1912 to urge black voters to take "a leap in the dark" and support Wilson. Wilson made efforts to encourage the switch; he met with black leaders shortly after his nomination and made further promises of evenhanded treatment in letters. Following one meeting, Oswald Garrison Villard, editor of the *Nation* and grandson of William Lloyd Garrison, felt "quite delighted" with Wilson's racial attitude.[49]

After the election, Bishop Alexander Walters, a leading black Democrat, claimed that Wilson had received 30 to 40 percent of the black vote. Although this was probably a considerable exaggeration — at Booker T. Washington's Tuskegee, feelings were split between Taft and Roosevelt, but there was no Wilson support in evidence — Wilson seemed to draw more black support than previous Democratic candidates.[50]

The honeymoon was brief. A few months after Wilson's inauguration, one observer commented, "It looks like a quick shoving of Ham down the shute." Segregation of white and black clerks was instituted in several departments, notably the Treasury and the Post Office. Even the few presidential appointments traditionally reserved for blacks —

(March 19, 1914), 29:356; *New York World* (April 13, 1914), 29:425; Thomas W. Gregory to Wilson (September 11, 1914), Wilson to Gregory (September 14, 1914), 31:24–26, 29.

48. Cooper, *The Warrior and the Priest*, p. 230.

49. Francis L. Broderick, *W. E. B. Du Bois* (Stanford: Stanford University Press, 1959), p. 86; William Monroe Trotter to Wilson (July 18, 1912), in Link, *Papers of Woodrow Wilson*, 24:558; Wilson to Alexander Walters, 25:448–449; Diary of Oswald Garrison Villard, 25:25.

50. Walters to Wilson, in Link, ibid., 25:606–608; Louis R. Harlan, *Booker T. Washington: Wizard of Tuskegee* (New York: Oxford University Press, 1983), p. 355.

minister to Haiti, registrar of the Treasury, recorder of deeds in the District of Columbia — were denied them; when southern senators objected to one appointment, Wilson quickly withdrew it, and not until 1915 did he appoint a black, J. L. Curtis, as minister to Liberia. By the end of summer 1913, complaints from blacks and their supporters were pouring into the White House, and Washington wrote Villard, "I have never seen the colored people so discouraged and bitter as they are at the present time."[51]

Wilson was not about to alter his course. He assured Villard of his concerns about the welfare of the black population but told him that the situation was too delicate for Wilson to name the commission that Villard requested. At a meeting with protesting black leaders at the White House, he responded to their complaint that "never in their history did [blacks] so overcome traditional fear of party and section as they did last year in voting for you" by insisting that his administration had "but very slightly altered the conditions." Other claims, he assured them, were "gross misrepresentations."[52]

In the face of directly contradictory evidence, however, blacks were hardly mollified. A year later, a second meeting essentially ended relations between Wilson and the black community. "If the colored people made a mistake in voting for me," the president told the delegation crisply, "they ought to correct it and vote against me if they think so." He professed himself offended by the mention of politics by William Monroe Trotter, one of the black leaders, and said that he would not receive Trotter again and that the black delegation had better find another spokesman. To complaints that his administration's policies humiliated blacks, he assured them that nobody could humiliate anyone else against that person's will.[53]

Blacks had hoped for treatment at least as benign as they had received from Grover Cleveland, but the situation was different. Not only was Wilson himself far more southern in his attitudes, but also the views

51. Harlan, ibid., p. 406; W. E. B. Du Bois, *Dust at Dawn*, (New York: Harcourt, Brace, 1940), pp. 234–37; Kathleen Long Wohlgemuth, "Woodrow Wilson's Appointment Policy and the Negro," *Journal of Southern History*, 24 (November 1958): 462–65; Oswald Garrison Villard, *Fighting Years* (New York: Harcourt, Brace, 1939), p. 239; Villard to Wilson (July 23, 1913), in Link, *Papers of Woodrow Wilson*, 28:65; A. E. Patterson to Wilson (July 30, 1913), 28:97–98; Robert N. Wood to Wilson (August 15, 1913), 28:115–19; Moorfield Storey to Wilson (August 15, 1913), 28:163–65; Booker T. Washington to Villard (August 10, 1913), 28:186–87.

52. Wilson to Villard (August 21, 1913), in Link, ibid., 28:202; meeting with blacks at White House (November 6, 1913), 28:491–500.

53. Remarks by Wilson and a dialogue (November 12, 1914), in Link, ibid., 31:301–308.

of the southern progressive Democrats in his administration and Congress reflected the segregation and black disenfranchisement that had spread throughout the South in the two decades between Cleveland and Wilson. Southern Democrats were not only more assertive in spreading the practice into Washington, D. C. and the North, but they were also prepared to claim that the change was a reform which was of benefit to both races.

Although it could hardly be called an issue that split the party, some northern Democrats did object to Wilson's practices. Congressman Robert Bulkley of Cleveland tried to fight the introduction of segregation onto Washington streetcars. Governor David Walsh of Massachusetts, in a letter whose timing suggested that it was aimed more at Boston's black voters than Wilson, declared that he was "decidedly opposed to any condition existing in Washington that could be interpreted as discriminating against our colored population." In what might have had more effect, the *New York World* called for "No Jim-Crow Government," calling the administration's program "a small, mean, petty discrimination."[54] But, except for a few local areas in the North, the Democratic party had clearly turned its back on blacks and would make little effort to win their support. Not until the next Democratic president would the bridges begin to be rebuilt.

In November 1914, in the first midterm elections of the Wilson administration, the Democrats lost sixty-one seats in the House of Representatives. "The Democrats made such a poor showing in the state and Congressional elections," Arthur Link explains, "that their defeat in 1916 seemed almost certain." Other historians have accepted this view of the Democratic performance as dismal; Carl Degler cites it as the beginning of the end, demonstrating the freakish nature of the 1912 results.[55]

Such retroactively plausible gloom, however, seems not to have possessed contemporary Democrats, except perhaps sixty-one of them. According to the more common view, the Democratic party had done rather well against a largely reunited GOP, after a tariff revision. "That we should have elected a majority of twenty-five or thirty in the House of Representatives, in an off year and with little help from the Progres-

54. William D. Jenkins, "Robert Bulkley: Progressive Profile," *Ohio History* 88 (Winter 1979): 62; David I. Walsh to Wilson (October 26, 1914), in Link, ibid., 31:237–38; "No Jim-Crow Government," *New York World*, 31:328 n–329 n.

55. Arthur Link, *Wilson: The New Freedom* (Princeton: Princeton University Press, 1956), p. 468; Carl Degler, "American Political Parties and the Rise of the City: An Interpretation," *Journal of American History* 51 (June 1964); 50.

sives," wrote one party stalwart to Bryan, "and at the same time increased our majority in the Senate so as to practically insure the complexion of that august body for the next four years, is, it seems to me, a cause for thankfulness." The old Bryanite politician Josephus Daniels, now secretary of the Navy, exulted, "The results of Tuesday's election were very satisfactory, and we think we did wonderfully well." More cautiously, and perhaps more accurately, Senator William Stone of Missouri wrote the president, "All things considered, I feel that the result is a great endorsement of the administration."[56]

Such assessments may sound less like political analysis than graveyard whistling, but the complete election picture would seem to have permitted some restrained rejoicing among Democrats. The party gained Senate seats in Wisconsin, Kentucky, South Dakota, and California, and only in the last was the Progressive vote a factor. If the Democrats lost five governorships, mostly in the East, they also gained five, mostly in the West, thus retaining their 3-to-2 margin in statehouses. Even in the sizable loss in the House, administration supporters found no reason to panic.

Democrats, as well as less partisan observers, could count votes and realized that their House majority was somewhat artificially inflated. "If the Democrats . . . lose fifty seats in the next Congress," conceded the *Baltimore Sun*, "they will have lost nothing that they are not fully entitled to." Only an actual loss of control, the newspaper suggested, would indicate a rejection of the party by the voters. "We could not have expected more," explained Representative Frank Doremus of Michigan, perhaps calmed by his own re-election. "Various districts that have never been Democratic and would not have elected Democratic Congressmen two years ago but for the Roosevelt strength, have returned to their former allegiance."[57]

The two million votes cast for congressional candidates on Roosevelt's ticket that year had returned Democrats from many "districts that had never been Democratic" and were unlikely to remain so. This kind of displacement has been a factor in all the great landslides of the twentieth century: with the exception of 1932, all—1912, 1920, 1936, 1964, 1984—have seen sizable readjustments in the next

56. George Fred Williams to William Jennings Bryan (November 9, 1914), Bryan Papers, Library of Congress; Josephus Daniels to Joshua A. Graham (November 11, 1914), Daniels Papers, Library of Congress: William J. Stone to Woodrow Wilson (November 10, 1914), Wilson Papers, Library of Congress.

57. *Baltimore Sun* (November 2, 1914); Frank E. Doremus to William G. McAdoo (November 19, 1914), McAdoo Papers, Library of Congress.

election, in which districts "returned to their former allegiance." The reason Democrats rejoiced — or claimed to — after the election of 1914 was the number of districts that were left.[58]

"The very prop upon which the large majority in the last House was based was completely destroyed," complained Joseph Tumulty, Wilson's private secretary, speaking of the Bull Moose vote. Although a few Bull Moose candidates for the Senate ran strong (if losing) races, the Progressive congressional vote fell beneath a million, with almost half (43 percent) from the four states of California, Illinois, Kansas, and Washington. Elsewhere, the collapse was resounding. In New York, on Roosevelt's ticket in 1912, the Progressive candidate for governor had received 393,000 votes; the 1914 candidate won barely 40,000. The party's congressional vote in Connecticut dropped from 29,737 to 6,834; in Rhode Island, from 8,844 to 1,666; in Michigan, one of its strongest states, from 191,067 to 47,700. "The Bull Moose party," wrote Arthur Krock, in the *Louisville Courier-Journal*, "is wiped off the earth." Soon, Democrats were hearing that "there had been a constant pilgrimage to Oyster Bay since the election and that Roosevelt had turned his followers loose, advising them to use their own inclination as to future party affiliations."[59]

Unsurprisingly, at the funeral of the Progressive party, some of the most sorrowful mourners were Democrats. "The Bull Moose vote this year is going to fall off, and that means heavy Democratic losses," a correspondent warned Tumulty in July 1914. The Democrats even made efforts to stave off the collapse; Illinois Democrats tried to maintain a full Progressive ticket in that state, and an Iowa Democrat had his own reasons for wanting his president to campaign there: "unless the President comes to Iowa, my information is that Mr. Roosevelt will not come, and his presence is imperatively necessary to vitalize the Progressive Party." Wilson did not come, and the Progressive state vote dropped from 15.6 percent for governor in 1912 to 5.7 percent for senator in 1914, a development that the Democratic candidate for the Senate blamed for his defeat.[60]

58. In 1922, the Democrats gained seventy-four seats; in 1938 and 1966, the Republican added seventy-five and forty-seven seats, respectively. In 1986, the Democrats, already in a majority in the House, won ten Senate seats and recaptured the upper house.

59. Joseph P. Tumulty to James R. Kerney (November 6, 1914), Tumulty Papers, Library of Congress; *Louisville Courier-Journal* (November 4, 1914); Edward M. House to Woodrow Wilson (November 9, 1914), House Papers.

60. E. S. Underhill to Joseph P. Tumulty (July 16, 1914), Tumulty Papers; J. M. Page to Joseph P. Tumulty (July 7, 1914) ibid.; Louis Murphy to William G. McAdoo (September 1, 1914), McAdoo Papers; Maurice Connolly to Edward M. House (November 7, 1914), House Papers.

Given their general awareness of both the Progressives' role and imminent collapse, the Democrats could claim to be, if not pleased, at least neither surprised nor greatly distressed by their showing. "The havoc wrought by the Republicans . . . was very great," conceded the *World*, but it noted that "the new majority represents a Democratic victory over a Republican party once more acting in essential harmony."[61]

But the election of 1914 revealed not only the weakness of the Progressive party, it also illuminated its nature — or rather, its two separate natures. As Progressives reacted to Wilsonian reform, many of the eastern leaders and spokesmen recoiled and reconsidered their attitude toward Republicanism: Frank Munsey spoke of "the patriotic duty of the forces opposed to the democratic party to work together as a unit," and George W. Perkins urged upon Roosevelt "the chance to elect a Republican Congress this fall, and in this way put a stop to this jamming through Congress of Wilson policies." The party itself seemed to be changing: former Congressman Bourke Cockran, one of the few prominent Democrats who had joined, heard in September that "all the Democrats (all the former Democrats) have either withdrawn from the party or been forced out of it. The same is true of most of the radicals." Ex-Senator (and insurgent) Albert Beveridge, leading the Progressive ticket in Indiana, now ran a probusiness, anti–tariff reduction campaign. *Collier's*, a major supporter of Roosevelt in 1912, criticized "a certain apparent defiance and distrust on the part of the Administration toward business under circumstances where sympathy was more called for." Throughout the East, from New Hampshire to Ohio, the Progressive vote virtually vanished, with Republicans the apparent beneficiaries.[62]

West of the plains, the situation — and the Progressive response — differed radically. Utah Progressives nominated a joint ticket with state Democrats, electing a congressman from Salt Lake City; and Progressive endorsements elected Democratic governors in Wyoming and Idaho. ("The time was ripe," boasted a Utah Democrat, "for a Democratic victory in this section.") Edward Costigan, Progressive candidate for governor of Colorado, bolted his own ticket to endorse Democratic Congressman Edward Keating for reelection. Minnesota and South

61. *New York World* (November 5, 6, 1914).

62. Frank A. Munsey to Theodore Roosevelt (June 30, 1914) George W. Perkins Papers, Columbia University; George W. Perkins to Theodore Roosevelt (April 14, 1914), ibid.; Ernest Harvier to W. Bourke Cockran (September 23, 1914), Cockran Papers, New York Public Library; John Braeman, *Albert J. Beveridge* (Chicago: University of Chicago Press, 1971), p. 237; *Collier's* (November 21, 1914).

Dakota, both for Roosevelt in 1912, elected a Democratic governor and senator, respectively. California, with its new wide-open primary system, reelected three Democratic congressmen, as well as one Prohibitionist, all of whom were expected to support Wilson. In the same state, James D. Phelan was elected senator — on the slogan "Give Woodrow Wilson a seat in the Senate" — at the same time Progressive Hiram Johnson won overwhelming reelection as governor.[63]

"Democratic policies have taken hold upon the conviction and approval of the West as never before," boasted Wilson, and other Democratic observers also rejoiced — and, privately, marvelled — at the returns from that region. Tumulty, in a lengthy memorandum, pointed out the meaning of the vote; it suggested an entirely different way Wilson might be reelected. Well before the war became a major national issue, the election returns — and Progressive political behavior — of 1914 suggested a Democratic West two years later.[64]

Beckoning western horizons, however, did not entirely compensate for setbacks in traditionally crucial states such as New York, Illinois, Ohio, and Connecticut. Aside from Bull Moose homesickness, four factors appear to have affected the Democratic showing in 1914. Two of them dealt with traditional party issues and makeup; two dealt with the tactics of the Wilson administration.

"The democratic majority in 1914," rejoiced the *Commoner*, "was the greatest majority ever received by any party in an 'off-year' following a tariff revision." Although this may appear rather tortured comfort, 1914 was the latest, though not the last, in a series of postrevision elections penalizing the revising party. The vote took place during a recession, ascribed by Republicans to the new tariff and by Democrats to the war, and the party losses centered, as the *Commoner* suggested, in the states "in which are located the large industrial centers and which were more affected by the business depression."[65]

Such an effect had been foreseen even before the tariff's passage. In May 1913, William Kent, a pro-Wilson independent congressman from California, rejoiced that the new tariff would have a four-year

63. William H. King to William G. McAdoo (November 13, 1914), McAdoo Papers; Fred Greenbaum, *Fighting Progressive* (Washington: Public Affairs Press, 1971), p. 67; James D. Phelan to Woodrow Wilson (November 13, 1914), Wilson Papers, Library of Congress; Robert E. Hennings, *James D. Phelan and the Wilson Progressives of California* (New York: Garland, 1985), p. 93.
64. Woodrow Wilson to Anne MacIlvaine (November 19, 1914), Wilson Papers, Library of Congress; Joseph P. Tumulty to James Kerney (November 6, 1914). Western Democrats had closely connected their campaigns to Wilson; C. C. Dill had won a House seat from Washington with the slogan, "The Woodrow Wilson Man." C. C. Dill, *Where Water Falls* (Spokane: Author, 1970), p. 47.
65. *Commoner* (November 1914).

trial, "in spite of the fact that there will be lots of Democrats beaten in the next Congressional elections." Less lightheartedly, Secretary of the Interior Franklin Lane suggested to Wilson that the reductions might be made over a three-year period; tariff reform, he warned, would not be worth it if it prevented the administration from doing anything else.[66]

By mid-1914, Democratic senators and congressmen viewed business conditions from a posture of personal as well as public alarm. Republican candidates swiftly picked up the issue, and after the vote, Democrats ranging from Tumulty and House to David Fitzgerald, the boss of New Haven, cited the slump as decisive. Most, however, took the position advanced by the *World*, that the economic situation was already adjusting itself and would be fully recovered by 1916.[67]

The second phenomenon had roots in American politics even deeper than the tariff issue. For years, Catholic Democratic organizations in cities such as New York, Boston, Jersey City, Cleveland, and Chicago had pragmatically nominated Protestants for statewide office, certain that no Catholic could win. But, with the coming of the party boom years, they grew less cautious. The entire Illinois state ticket in 1912 had consisted of Irish Catholics, and two years later Irish Democrats were running for the Senate from Illinois and Ohio and for governor of New York and Massachusetts.

That fall all four candidates, and others, suddenly found themselves engulfed in a tide of anti-Catholicism. "About the middle of October . . . the religious frenzy hit the state," explained Governor James Cox of Ohio, running for reelection on the same ticket with Senate candidate Timothy Hogan. "Churches and fraternal organizations, particularly in the rural parts, had meetings weekly." The newly revived anti-Catholic American Protective Association put out its own newspaper, urging voters to

Read *The Menace* and get the dope
Go to the polls and beat the Pope.

Pius X was not actually on the ballot in Ohio, but voters did beat Hogan and, for good measure, Cox, although he ran 70,000 votes ahead of his running mate.[68]

66. William Kent to Francis J. Heney (May 5, 1913), Kent Papers, Yale University; Franklin K. Lane to Woodrow Wilson (June 10, 1913), Wilson Papers, Library of Congress.
67. David E. Fitzgerald to Simeon E. Baldwin (November 6, 1914), Baldwin Family Papers, Yale University; *New York World* (November 2, 1914).
68. James M. Cox to Francis Burton Harrison (October 1, 1915), Harrison Papers,

In New York, the anti-Catholic Guardians of Liberty opposed the reelection of Governor Martin Glynn; and rumors spread that Senate candidate (and Presbyterian) James W. Gerard was also Catholic. The situation was particularly intense in Buffalo's Erie County, where all three Democratic congressmen elected in 1912 were Catholic: the only Democrat to carry the county in 1914 was also the only one with Guardian endorsement. The *New York Times* objected, "It is humiliating to have to make a protest against this kind of campaigning," but the issue was exacerbated by the independent candidacy of William Sulzer, elected governor in 1912 and impeached in 1913, who proclaimed that "if I had not been a 32nd degree Mason; that if I had not been a Protestant . . . the bosses . . . would never have removed me." In New York as well, the Catholic candidate for state office was swamped; the Protestant ran ahead but also lost.[69]

Chicago boss Roger Sullivan, and other observers, credited his defeat for the Senate from Illinois partly to his Catholicism, and modern scholars have agreed. David Walsh was strong enough personally to win reelection as governor of Massachusetts, but the religious issue may have defeated his running mate for lieutenant governor. The anti-Catholic wave did not affect Democrats exclusively; in the Wisconsin Republican primary, it helped to knock out Robert La Follette's candidate for governor.[70]

Both the New York and Illinois defeats, however, also traced to another party problem, that of progressivism and bossism. Wilson, like national Democratic leaders before and after him, was fascinated by the idea of creating a non-Tammany Democratic organization in New York state. His strongest personal supporters in the state, men such as Secretary of the Treasury William G. McAdoo, Dudley Field Malone, and Franklin D. Roosevelt, came from the anti-Tammany wing and looked to his administration for aid and comfort. McAdoo and the

---

Library of Congress; Francis G. Russell, *Shadow of Blooming Grove* (New York: McGraw-Hill, 1968), p. 250; James M. Cox, *Journey through My Years* (New York: Simon and Schuster, 1946), p. 179; Hoyt L. Warner, *Progressivism in Ohio 1897–1917* (Columbus: Ohio State University Press, 1964), p. 474.

69. James W. Gerard, *My First Eighty-Three Years in America* (New York: Doubleday and Co., 1951), p. 216; *New York Times* (October 23, 1914); *New York Tribune* (October 29, 1914); Thomas D. McCarthy to E. M. House (November 16, 1914), Tumulty Papers, Library of Congress.

70. Howard Zink, *City Bosses in the United States* (Durham: Duke University Press, 1930), p. 298; John D. Buenker, *Urban Liberalism and Progressive Reform* (New York: Charles Scribner's Sons, 1973), p. 20; Josiah Quincy to Edward M. House (October 22, 1914), House Papers; *New York Tribune* (November 4, 1914); David P. Thelen, *Robert La Follette and the Insurgent Spirit* (Boston: Little, Brown and Co., 1976), p. 119.

ubiquitous Colonel House planned strategy, beginning with overt support of an anti-Tammany Democrat's successful Fusionist campaign for mayor in 1913. They then began work on a challenge to Tammany in the statewide elections of 1914.[71]

"I may be wrong," wrote Governor Glynn, a Tammany ally, to Tumulty in May 1914, "but I think there is need—great need—of cooperation between your friends and my friends in this state. . . . I am willing to do anything but commit political suicide to bring it about." The administration (with the exception of Tumulty) apparently did think him wrong; it continued to develop and support primary opposition to Tammany, to the extent of recruiting Roosevelt to run for the Senate nomination. Even after Glynn and the organization swept the primaries, Wilson withheld his support. Both House and the *New York World*, seemingly unaware of Glynn's qualms about political suicide, wanted him to publicly denounce Tammany boss Murphy. Eventually, Wilson did endorse Glynn, who had a strong progressive record, but numbers of Wilsonians, including the administration's primary candidate for governor, bolted the losing ticket.[72]

The same conflict figured in the defeat of Roger Sullivan, Democratic candidate for the Senate from Illinois. As Chicago boss, Sullivan had long been a particular red flag to the Bryanites of the party, and his desire to ascend to the Senate—his last public office had been clerk of the Cook County Court in the 1890s—elicited opposition not only from them but from Illinois's other senator, the governor, and the mayor of Chicago, all members (or leaders) of other Democratic factions. Sullivan had already been complaining about the administration's patronage policies, and even after his plurality victory in a crowded primary, no endorsement from Wilson appeared. The *Baltimore Sun* objected that Sullivan had, after all, been decisive in nominating Wilson at Baltimore and was campaigning as a progressive: "In politics, as in

71. Frank Freidel, *Franklin D. Roosevelt: The Apprenticeship* (Boston: Little, Brown and Co., 1952), pp. 176–83; James Kerney to Woodrow Wilson (May 8, 1913), Tumulty Papers; William Prendergast, *Reminiscences*, Oral History Research Office, Columbia University, p. 532; Woodrow Wilson to John Purroy Mitchel (November 6, 1913), Wilson Papers, Library of Congress; Woodrow Wilson to William Jennings Bryan (April 2, 1914), ibid.; Edward M. House Diary (March 9, 1913; April 18, 1913; May 14, 1914), House Papers; Wesser, *A Response to Progressivism*. pp. 141–45.

72. Martin Glynn to Joseph P. Tumulty (May 18, 1914), Tumulty Papers; Edward M. House to Woodrow Wilson (October 9, 1914), House Papers; *New York World* (October 3, 1914); Woodrow Wilson to Martin Glynn (October 15, 1914), Wilson Papers, Library of Congress; William Gorham Rice to William G. McAdoo (November 13, 1914), McAdoo Papers; George F. Peabody to Edward M. House (November 11, 1914), House Papers.

religion, the wicked man who turneth away from the wickedness that he hath committed may save his soul alive." Wilson, still dubious about Sullivan's soul, produced only a weak statement urging Democrats to support the winner of the primary.[73]

In a three-way race, Sullivan might have overcome either hostile Wilsonians or the religious issue; facing both, he lost narrowly. Tumulty and Postmaster General Albert Burleson, who campaigned for Sullivan, were "appalled" by Wilson's course. "You know, Wilson never appreciated politicians," Burleson would remember later. "He used them, and knew he needed them, but he never appreciated them."[74]

The final component, another Wilsonian contribution, involved the ability, or rather the inability, of Democratic congressmen to campaign. As early as July 18, House Majority Leader Underwood wrote of his flock, "The ones who are up for re-election in doubtful districts are anxious to go home, and it is difficult to keep them here." On September 1, as the session stretched into the longest in history, he promised adjournment by October 1, a promise he was unable to keep. By early October, neither Underwood nor Senate leader John W. Kern could go on the floor without being "besieged every few minutes in the day by colleagues with inquiries about the plans for adjournment." Speaker Champ Clark, not normally noted as an ironist, wrote Wilson, "If we are to have any vacation I hope yours will be pleasant." Not until October 24, ten days before election, were congressmen permitted to leave for the hustings. The conclusion of the *Los Angeles Examiner*—"the upset of the great Democratic majority in the House appears to be due almost as much to the failure of the sitting members to get home to campaign as to any other one feature"—was doubtless somewhat exaggerated, but the situation could not have helped the chances of the large number of Democratic freshmen, thirty-seven of whom were defeated for reelection.[75]

73. Edward F. Dunne to William Jennings Bryan (June 12, 15, 23, 1914), Bryan Papers; Roger C. Sullivan to Joseph P. Tumulty (April 3, 1914), Tumulty Papers; "Statement of Edward F. Dunne, Carter Harrison, and James Hamilton Lewis to the Democrats of Illinois" (July 16, 1914), Tumulty Papers; *Baltimore Sun* (October 12, 1914); *New York Times* (October 6, 1914); J. M. Page to Henry T. Rainey (September 26, 1914), Wilson Papers, Congress; Robert A. Waller, *Rainey of Illinois* (Urbana: University of Illinois Press, 1977), pp. 38–39.

74. John Morton Blum, *Joe Tumulty and the Wilson Era* (Boston: Little, Brown and Co., 1951), p. 83. Memo on interview with Albert S. Burleson (March 17–19, 1927), Ray Stannard Baker Papers, Library of Congress.

75. Oscar W. Underwood to Francis Burton Harrison (July 18, 1914); Harrison Papers; *St. Louis Republic* (September 2, 1914), *Louisville Courier-Journal* (October 5, 1914); Champ Clark to Woodrow Wilson (October 17, 1914); *Los Angeles Examiner* (November

Several of these factors figured in Joseph Tumulty's lengthy, generally contented memorandum on the election's meaning. "Even under the adverse conditions," he wrote, "the only places which seemed to repudiate us were the states of New York, Pennsylvania, Rhode Island, and Connecticut." Moreover, within New York itself, the party showed "special strength in New York City and Brooklyn." (In twenty-three congressional districts entirely or mostly within the city, Democrats won seventeen seats, Republicans four, and Progressives and Socialists one apiece, and the Democrats won a significant majority of the popular vote.) Elsewhere, wherever Tumulty looked — the Midwest, the West, the border — he found only encouragement.[76]

Tumulty might have congratulated himself, not only on the result of the campaign but also on the nature of it. The Wilsonian strategy, as later expressed by one observer, was "to establish the Democratic party as the liberal party, and to force the republicans to accept a conservative role." Such an alignment appeared to emerge explicitly from the campaign of 1914. Democrats everywhere ran on the Underwood Tariff, the Clayton Anti-Trust Act, the Federal Trade Commission, and the rest of the record of the 63rd Congress, and were united in support of the administration. "In most contests," the Republican *New York Tribune* noted disgustedly, "all issues have been subordinated to an endorsement of President Wilson."[77]

The Republicans seemed only too eager to take up their role in the administration scenario. With the departure of numbers of progressive Republicans to be Bull Moosers, standpatters had no difficulty sweeping the Republican primaries of 1914. "The master machinists of the stolen convention," complained Raymond Robins angrily, "are in full control of what remains of the Republican party." Discussing the primary defeat of insurgent Senator Joseph Bristow of Kansas by conservative ex-Senator Charles Curtis, the *Commoner* noted acidly, "Thus we see how thoroughly progressive the Republican party, even in standpat Kansas, has become." The precise position of the surviving insurgents was also becoming difficult to discern; among them, Wilson had received consistent congressional support only from La Follette, and the others' statement about Wilson, before and during the campaign of 1914, bore little signs of insurgency. Bryan complained of Cummins

---

4, 1914). Underwood had only kept representatives from going home by a resolution denying salaries to absentees. Johnson, *Underwood*, p. 213.

76. Joseph P. Tumulty to James Kerney (November 6, 1914), Tumulty Papers.

77. Donald Richberg, *My Hero* (New York: Putnam's, 1954), p. 81; *New York Tribune*, (November 3, 1914).

of Iowa, "No standpat senator representing protected interests has assailed the president more vehemently or misrepresented him more unscrupulously."[78]

No candid Democrat could regard the election of 1914 as a ringing endorsement. The party had taken substantial, if not unexpected, losses in major states, and the Bull Moose, becoming an endangered species, served notice that victory would not again be easy. But if the party's aim for 1916 and beyond was to establish itself as the progressive alternative to a conservative GOP, it had made heartening progress. It had also discovered large areas of the country, not usually Democratic, that could be responsive to such an image.

The reform intellectuals of the *New Republic*, among others, viewed the 1914 results as a heartening prelude to the party's replacement in power. Yet, by November 1916, the magazine was one of the Democrats' most enthusiastic supporters. Its switch, and that of other Progressives, has been attributed to a bold shift toward the New Nationalism by Wilson, dragging his party along. Wilson did make a bid for Progressive support in 1916 with a series of actions that he and the congressional Democrats would not have taken before. The question, however, is who was dragging whom.

In *Progressive Democracy* (1914), Croly complained that because of Wilson's success, "people are deceived as to the real nature and effect of his leadership upon the Democratic party." Wilson, he explained, had only been nominated and elected because of the Bull Moose bolt and had received Democratic congressional support because of the party's hunger for "the privileges, emoluments, and prestige of office." He concluded, as Walter Lippmann did in *Drift and Mastery*, published the same year, that Wilson could never effectively reconcile democracy and progressivism. Worst of all, the magazine would point out, Wilson's partisan strategies, using appointment and the caucus to pass bills, tended to mislead the public and prevent true, nonpartisan, efficient progressive government, which was "sacrificed on the altar of Democratic resurrection."[79]

It is thus not surprising that even the *New Republic's* infrequent praises might have chilled Democratic bones. Admiring the Underwood Tar-

---

78. *St. Louis Republic* (September 19, 1914); *Commoner* (September 1914); *St. Louis Republic* (October 30, 1914). See also J. Lawrence Holt, *Congressional Insurgents and the Party System* (Cambridge: Harvard University Press, 1967), pp. 83–161, and A. Bower Sagesser, *Joseph L. Bristow* (Lawrence: University of Kansas Press, 1967), p. 129.

79. Croly, *Progressive Democracy*, pp. 345–46, 337; Lippmann, *Drift and Mastery*, p. 133; *New Republic* (February 5, 1916).

iff, the Federal Trade Commission, and the Federal Reserve, it sniffed that the 63rd Congress was "a body of men who did not intend to do as well as they did." The Federal Reserve Act, wrote Croly, marked the "adding to the statutes for the first time in the history of the Democracy a sound measure of constructive financial legislation." More often, even while the *New Republic* soured on Roosevelt and became fonder of Wilson, its comments on his party were more contemptuous: the Democrats had "shown little interest as a party in some indispensable phases of a progressive political and social policy"; they were "as inept in performance and as bankrupt in principle as they were at the time of the Alton B. Parker campaign." As late as June 1916, the magazine described the Democratic party as "an exclusively political organization whose members are associated for the purpose of getting and keeping control of the government."[80]

This belief, that Wilson's virtues hardly extended to other Democrats, who had to be whipped to the passage of progressive legislation, also found expression in less cerebrally Progressive sources. *Collier's*, which had commented of Wilson's first Congress that "The real trouble is the low average tone of intelligence and responsibility throughout the House," carefully explained after passage of the Child Labor bill in 1916 that "the bulk of the Democrats in Congress and the Senate, and of the Democratic leaders throughout the country, are following Wilson, not because they believe in his program, but because he is a winner. He means offices and power." The *Independent* commented on Wilson just before his reelection, "*He* is progressive, but we are not so sure that his party is anywhere near so progressive as he." Sometimes, Progressives clung to this idea to the point of self-delusion. Supreme Court nominee Louis Brandeis, William Allen White assured the readers of the *Emporia Gazette*, "won't get within ten votes of confirmation. There has been no time since the death of McKinley that the organized forces of evilly aggrandized capital have had such an immortal stranglehold cinch on the Congress of this country as they have today."[81]

Wilson managed to bring so many independent progressives to his cause in 1916 with a burst of new progressive legislation, a move especially dramatic considering his earlier statement that his program was finished. Progressives admired such legislation as a bill banning the products of child labor from interstate commerce, a rural credits measure, a federal worker's compensation act, the steeply graduated income

80. *New Republic* (March 6, 1915; August 7, 1915; February 5, 1916; June 24, 1916).
81. *Collier's* (June 27, 1914; September 16, 1916); *Independent* (October 9, 1916); *Emporia Gazette* (May 25, 1916) quoted in *The Public* (June 2, 1916).

tax rates of the 1916 revenue act, and the Adamson Act for an eight-hour workday for railroad workers. The bills, they assumed, had been forcibly extracted by Wilson from unwilling Democrats.

That view of the burst of reform measures of 1916 prevails today. Before 1916, according to Arthur Link, "Wilson and a majority of Democrats in Congress had drawn the line sternly against national legislation to give special advantage to classes and groups," such as child labor and rural credits bills. Wilson, however, motivated by Progressive pressures and the need to win their votes, then reversed himself; and the Democratic party, "under his leadership and goad," became a national reform party.[82]

Many of the strategies that rehabilitated Wilson in Progressive eyes were indeed his own doing: a much stronger preparedness program and a number of bold appointments, notably that of Brandeis to the Supreme Court. Preparedness was an explicitly Wilsonian policy, implemented largely over Democratic protests. Wilson could also claim credit for the nomination of Brandeis, although the Boston lawyer had more Democratic ties than are sometimes remembered. (Senate Democrats also voted to confirm Brandeis 39 to 1, despite the morbid predictions of White.) The other nominations praised by the *New Republic*, Newton Baker for Secretary of War and John H. Clarke for the Supreme Court, were products not of independent progressivism but of Tom Johnson's Democratic organization in Ohio.[83]

But the greatest impact was made by the 1916 congressional achievements, which in Link's terms turned the Democrats into a national reform party. And it is by no means clear that the credit for those bills, and for that act of party prestidigitation, rested so largely at the presidential end of Pennsylvania Avenue.

Limitations on child labor had been a Democratic interest, despite some southern opposition, well before Wilson decided he needed Progressive votes for his reelection. Back in the Roosevelt administration, congressional Democrats had generally supported the limited Beveridge Child Labor bill, which covered the District of Columbia and territories, and the *Commoner* had called child labor "The Burning Shame of the Age." Southern Democratic senators Ben Tillman and Hoke Smith were honorary members of the National Child Labor Committee, whose secretary sought the aid of Democratic Senator Francis

82. Arthur Link, *Wilson: Confusions and Crises* (Princeton: Princeton University Press, 1964), pp.322–23.
83. *New Republic* (August 19, 1916).

Newlands of Nevada, "knowing the friendship you have manifested in support of legislation for the protection of children." When Democrats won control of the House in the 62nd Congress, the House passed its own Child Labor bill, with Democratic representatives supporting it 114 to 62.[84]

In Wilson's first Congress, reform Democrats continued to press for the bill, despite clear administration opposition. "No child labor bill yet proposed," Wilson wrote Tumulty, "has seemed to me constitutional." Still, in February 1915, at a time when Wilson had publicly stated that all his major measures had been passed, a bill sponsored by A. Mitchell Palmer and written by the National Child Labor League passed the House 233 to 43, with Democrats in favor 163 to 42. Even southern Democrats supported it 44 to 38, including Majority Leader Underwood. According to Palmer's biographer, Senate Democrats expected a Wilson veto: "The bill's failure probably resulted more from Wilson's antipathy than from Southern threats."[85]

In February, 1916, despite such fears, the next House swiftly repassed the bill 337 to 46. But, when Postmaster General Albert Burleson, the administration's congressional liaison, wrote Wilson concerning the administration's must list in March, child labor was not on it. Wilson grew more interested only after Senator Robert Owen of Oklahoma, a cosponsor, urged him on political grounds to endorse the bill in the Democratic platform and the Republicans had announced their willingness to support it. In mid-July, Wilson heard from Secretary of the Navy Josephus Daniels ("I strongly feel that it is necessary to protect child labor and that such protection is the very basis of the social legislation which gave the Progressives hold of that portion of their party that cannot be controlled by Perkins"); John F. Fitzgerald, candidate for the Senate from Massachusetts ("Its abandonment by a democratic senatorial majority would cost us enough votes to lose more than one doubtful state, and the chastisement would be deserved"); and Senator Joe T. Robinson of Arkansas ("I reported this bill from the committee, and am anxious to secure its passage"). It appears that Democrats actively supporting the bill were obliged to use political arguments to per-

---

84. *Commoner* (December 28, 1906; January 11, 1907); Herbert J. Barrie to Francis G. Newlands (July 26, 1911), Newlands Papers; Edward M. Silbert, "Support for Reform among Congressional Democrats, 1897–1917," unpublished dissertation, University of Florida, 1966, p. 267.

85. Wilson to Tumulty (January 28, 1914), in Link, *Papers of Woodrow Wilson*, 29:170; *New York Times* (February 16, 1915); Stanley Coben, *A. Mitchell Palmer, Politician* (Princeton: Princeton University Press, 1963), pp. 87–89.

suade Wilson to join what was already Democratic congressional policy.[86]

The Rural Credits bill followed the same pattern. In 1914, only Wilson's opposition had killed the idea. Sounding like Croly's worst Jeffersonian nightmare, Wilson crisply wrote Carter Glass of Virginia, House Banking Committee chairman, that although he knew many senators and congressmen disagreed, "I have a very deep conviction that it is unwise and unjustifiable to extend the credit of the Government to a single class of the community."[87]

If Wilson thought he had settled the question, his subsequent correspondence may have unsettled him. By the time the next Congress met, in December 1915, Wilson had heard from Democratic Senators John Sharp Williams of Mississippi, Henry Hollis of New Hampshire, and Duncan Fletcher of Florida, the last reminding Wilson that Fletcher had "written for magazines and newspapers, and spoken in the Senate, and at numerous conventions urging legislation," as well as preparing the 1912 Democratic plank on the issue. Meanwhile, Claude Kitchin of North Carolina, new House majority leader, had also heard from his troops. Joe Eagle of Texas told him that the subcommittee and the great majority of the House would approve the bill, that "In my opinion any rural banking system without government aid is a farce." Asbury Lever of South Carolina, chairman of the House Agriculture Committee, insisted that "some form of government aid is necessary."[88]

As Link makes clear, Wilson's late embrace of rural credits also stemmed from political calculation. Again, the Democrats in Congress hardly needed his goad and, in fact, seemed rather to be goading him. "I entered earnestly into the work for a good Rural Credits bill," Wil-

86. Arthur Link, *Wilson: Campaigns for Progressivism and Peace* (Princeton: Princeton University Press, 1965), p. 56; Albert S. Burleson to Woodrow Wilson (March 4, 1916), Wilson Papers, Library of Congress; Jonathan Daniels to Woodrow Wilson (July 17, 1916), Wilson-Daniels Correspondence, Daniels Papers, Library of Congress; John F. Fitzgerald to Woodrow Wilson (July 19, 1916), Wilson Papers, Child Labor File, Library of Congress; Joe T. Robinson to Joseph P. Tumulty (July 20, 1916), ibid. See also Alexander J. McKelway to Woodrow Wilson (August 25, 1916), suggesting which congressmen and senators to invite to the bill's signing, ibid.

87. Wilson to Carter Glass (May 12, 1914), in Link, *Papers of Woodrow Wilson*, 30:24.

88. Link, *Wilson: Confusion and Crises*, p. 346; Carter Glass to Woodrow Wilson (May 9, 1914), Wilson Papers, Library of Congress; Woodrow Wilson to Carter Glass (May 12, 1914), Tumulty Papers; John Sharp Williams to Woodrow Wilson (February 15, 1915), Wilson Papers, Library of Congress; Henry Hollis to Woodrow Wilson (December 11, 1914); ibid; Duncan Fletcher to Woodrow Wilson (October 21, 1916), Wilson Papers, Rural Credits File, Library of Congress; Joe H. Eagle to Claude Kitchin, March 16, 1915, Kitchin Papers (microfilm); Asbury S. Lever to Claude Kitchin (June 28, 1915), ibid.

son was told by Jouett Shouse of Kansas, "because to my constituency it is the most important measure of the present Congress."[89]

One of the most radical achievements of the 64th Congress, in fact, had virtually nothing to do with Wilson at all. Three months before Congress met, Kitchin assured Bryan of his agreement that if there had to be a new revenue act to pay for preparedness, "I will insist that we raise a large portion of the revenue by an increased tax of whiskey and incomes." Kitchin received not only strong public support from Bryan but a barrage of demands from southern and western Democrats that new revenues should come from "accumulated wealth or large income derived therefrom."[90] Accordingly, Kitchin's Ways and Means Committee ignored the administration's proposals and reported instead a bill sharply raising tax rates on high incomes. After the bill emerged from the House, the Senate Democrats actually increased the progressivity of the rates, as Wilson stood by silently.

The result, according to Link, was "a landmark in American history, the first really important victory of the movement . . . or a federal tax policy based upon ability to pay. . . . Wilson, insofar as we know, had no part in this, one of the most significant achievements of the progressive movement."[91] Contemporaries also had a strong reaction to it. "The income tax as it stands now," huffed *World's Work*, "is purely class legislation aimed at the rich." Perhaps more important in the context of 1916, the reformers of the *New Republic* were enchanted by the new tax structure. "The schedule of income tax rates elaborated in the bill," the magazine explained warmly, "represents a powerful equalitarian attack on the swollen income."[92]

Worker's compensation for federal employees and the Adamson Act, the remaining two elements in the 1916 reform package, were both products of Wilsonian demands, but in neither case did he have to demand very persistently. Worker's compensation had figured prominently in many Democratic state reform programs and had appeared

89. Link, *Wilson: Confusion and Crises*, p. 348; Jouett Shouse to Woodrow Wilson (May 25, 1916), Wilson papers, Library of Congress.

90. Claude Kitchin to William Jennings Bryan (September 10, 1915; December 13, 1915); Kitchin Papers (microfilm); *Commoner* December 1915; Ashton C. Shallenberger to Claude Kitchin (January 20, 1916); Carl C. Van Dyke, Clyde Tavenner, Isaac Sherwood, Walter Hensley, William Gordon, Warren Worth Bailey to Claude Kitchin (all January 27, 1916); Dan V. Stephens to Kitchin (January 29, 1916); Carl Hayden to Kitchin (January 31, 1916); Scott Ferris to Kitchin (February 1, 1916); all in Kitchin Papers (microfilm); *The Public* (August 11, 1916).

91. Link, *Wilson: Campaigns for Progressivism and Peace*, p. 65.

92. *World's Work* (October 1916); *New Republic* (August 26, 1916).

in national party agendas as well; Speaker Champ Clark had urged it
in early 1912, as did the Democratic platform later that year. Congressman William Brantly of Georgia, widely considered a conservative, had
written Wilson before his inauguration about the importance of such
a bill; it was "a reproach to our civilized nations of the world that has
not adopted it." Wilson showed little interest, however; it did not appear on Burleson's March 1916 must list, and the House passed it without executive urging. Only when its importance to labor voters became
clear did Wilson develop a strong interest and request Senate leaders
to push the bill, which they promptly did.[93]

It took the threat of a national railroad strike, and a strong push from
Wilson, to produce the Adamson Act, mandating an eight-hour workday for railroad workers. But the president submitted the bill to congressional Democrats who had long fought for reduced hours for railroad workers and the eight-hour workday in general. Long before,
Democratic senators had supported a La Follette railroad hour-
limitation amendment to the bill establishing the Commerce Court,
and after the party captured the House, it added an eight-hour clause
to many government appropriations bills. Both the House and Senate,
with overwhelming Democratic support, had mandated the eight-hour
workday for all government contractors. Secretary of Commerce William Redfield had called for a railroad eight-hour workday in 1913, for
reasons of passenger safety as much as labor relations, and William
Adamson of Georgia, chairman of the House Interstate Commerce
Committee, later claimed to have been developing such a bill before
Wilson demanded it. Bryan, allegedly the embodiment of anachronistic
Jeffersonianism, responded to the railroad crisis by saying that he saw
no problem: certainly Congress had the power to fix hours of labor for
the workers.[94]

From this background, Democrats in both Houses supported the bill
virtually unanimously. Admittedly, few wanted to be responsible either

93. Champ Clark, "The Duty of the Democrats," *Independent* (January 25, 1912); W.
J. Brantley to Woodrow Wilson (January 24, 1913), Wilson Papers, Library of Congress;
Albert S. Burleson to Woodrow Wilson (March 4, 1916), ibid.; Virginia Haughton,
"John W. Kern: the Senate Majority Leader and Labor Legislation 1913–1917," *Mid-
America* 57 (July 1975): 189–90.

94. *Congressional Record*, Vol. 45, Part 7, pp. 7327; 7650–54; Vol. 48, Part 1, pp.
376–96; Part 6, pp. 5345–46; Part 8, p. 7455; Part 10, 10681; Siebert, "Support for Reform among Congressional Democrats," p. 261; *Commoner* (January 1914); W. C.
Adamson to R. S. Baker (February 9, 1927), Ray Stannard Baker Papers; William Jennings Bryan to Francis G. Newlands (August 27, 1916), Bryan Papers, Library of
Congress.

for a rail strike or for embarrassing Wilson two months before election, but a struggle for the soul of the party might be thought to leave at least some wreckage behind.

Of the five major measures constituting the party's metamorphosis, therefore, congressional Democrats were ahead of Wilson on two, completely independent of him on one, and required little, if any, persuasion on the remaining two. This box score reveals them to be neither Wilson's reluctant Jeffersonian accessories nor ideologically indifferent placemen. "President Wilson's leadership has been useful, even indispensable, but much that is good in the work of Congress has been achieved not because of the President's insistence, but on the initiative of Congress itself," declared the *New Republic* in September, sounding rather surprised. Speaking of both Wilson's first and second Congress, the magazine now explained, "They have builded better than they knew largely because they were building in good faith. In almost every case the bills originally introduced were substantially improved during transit through House and Senate."[95]

By the next month, of course, Lippmann was praising "the Wilson who is temporarily at least creating, out of the reactionary, parochial factions of the Democracy," a national reform party, and the creation has remained historiographically to Wilson's credit. Certainly, Wilson was a key progressive leader, but he also had the advantage of having determined progressive followers, who sometimes had to wait for their leader to catch up with them. Wilson's leftward shift in 1916, like similar shifts he made in 1910 and 1912, was toward positions already held by the rest of his party.[96]

Whoever was present at the creation, and whenever it had happened, in 1916 the Democratic party stood before the country as the party of progressive reform. Observations on the meaninglessness and imminent collapse of party identity, so often heard in the Taft period, had now almost disappeared. One by one, many of the advanced progressives, the social workers, and the troubled Bull Moosers would slip into the Wilson column.

The Democratic performance in passing the New Freedom legislation not only declared the Democrats' identity, it helped redefine the other parties. The Progressives, unable to appear as the only sincere, effective reform party, found themselves with no identity at all, and nearly vanished in 1914. Some, particularly in the West, began the trek

95. *New Republic* (September 2, 1916).
96. *New Republic* (October 14, 1916).

toward Wilson. Others, especially those who had envisioned a progressivism friendlier to large businesses, turned back to the GOP.

They would find it unwelcoming; the primaries of 1914 had revealed the new unbreakable hold of the standpatters on the party. In states won by the Republicans in 1914, particularly in New York, their subsequent policies redoubled the impression. Progressive Republicans in Congress, with a few notable exceptions such as La Follette, had emerged by 1914 as strident partisan opponents of Wilsonian reform, while still failing to gain leadership in their own party. The Republican party accepted its identity as a conservative foil to the Democrats, and the Adamson Act, opposed heavily by conservatives and insurgent Republicans, would draw the lines yet more firmly.

The fact of Democratic success was so unexpected and astounding to some observers that they ascribed it excessively to Wilson's influence in Congress. Democrats, in this view, had always been only a negative force, who although opposing Republican administrative efficiency seemed equally unable to get along with each other. Yet, during its years in the wilderness, the party had developed a legitimate body of progressive doctrine, heavily influenced by Bryan, the *World*, and later Louis Brandeis. Although this was hardly a comprehensive platform to which all Democrats subscribed — the three had sufficient differences among themselves, even before taking into account the objections of other Democrats — it did provide a general attitude toward business and government that contributed to the party's surprising legislative productivity.

Democrats, before and during the Wilson administration, were consistently willing to use government to curb the power of wealth: by taxing it, by curbing its control of credit, by attempting structural reforms to weaken its influence on government, and by encouraging the development of opposing power centers among the party's labor allies. Many Democrats, including Wilson, never quite lost their suspicion of bigness, but the party increasingly turned from a rejection of government to an effort to curb corporate power.

This rough consensus meant, to the frequent surprise of observers such as the *New Republic*, that congressional Democrats were entirely ready to use the federal power to aid groups such as credit-short farmers, children in textile factories, and railroad workers on duty for long hours. When they warned of the paralyzing Jeffersonianism possessing the Democratic party, the editors of the *New Republic*, like many at that time and since, were talking about Democrats but thinking about Wilson.

The election of 1916 would turn largely on the question of progressivism, with Democrats and Republicans offering a relatively clear choice. If Democrats themselves could not provide enough votes to re-elect Wilson, the party had helped construct the record on which he could appeal to others. In Wilson's reelection campaign, his party was not only a unified force behind him, but also a force building his appeal to other voters.

CHAPTER 7

The Wilson Coalition

Narrow elections tend to be accorded narrow explanations. Only sweeping, decisive triumphs are expected to tell us much about the geography of the electorate, whether it is reaffirming or realigning its political attitudes. Closer decisions are attributed to campaign blunders, unique situations, and the various elements that produce an aberrant episode.

Wilson's victory in 1916 was certainly narrow, with the Democrats losing nearly all of the East, and then, to general astonishment, snaring victory by winning virtually all of the West. Since it was followed by three sweeping Republican triumphs, the election of 1916 has been dismissed as a "deviating" election, with Republican candidate Charles Evans Hughes the luckless victim of circumstance. Our image of the election is shaped by the slogan "He Kept Us Out of War" and the long wait to hear from California, with the accompanying story of Hughes's snub of Progressive Governor Hiram Johnson during the candidate's visit to the state. According to legend, due to the temporary phenomenon of the war and the errors of the Hughes campaign, Wilson slipped through to remain Democratic president of a Republican country.

Yet, contemporary observers, denied our awareness of the subsequent Republican landslides, did not see the election quite like this. Several noted that not all the breaks had favored Wilson, and that, if the president had achieved a narrow victory, he had also narrowly missed a ringing one. Wilson "destroyed the normal Republican plurality in Minnesota . . . even in New England he was dangerous," observed Walter Lippmann, a Wilson supporter but hardly a Democratic wheelhorse. "Had it not been for the power and money of the Republican organizations, the economic superstitions about the Republican tariff, and the accumulation against Mr. Wilson of personal, nationalistic, and even religious feuds, the defeat of Mr. Hughes would have been stupendous."[1]

1. Walter Lippman, "A Progressive's View of the Election," *Yale Review* (January 1917).

In stern reality, of course, Hughes's defeat was not stupendous, and he could exhibit a fair collection of his own "what-ifs." But Lippmann had noticed something crucial: 1916 was not simply a story of odd bounces of the electoral ball but a display of substantial (and often surprising) Democratic strength, hampered by considerable ethnic Democratic defections over the war issue. Although many historians have tended to dismiss them, "personal, nationalistic, and even religious feuds" hurt Wilson seriously in a number of states, helping to keep his victory well below the stupendous level.[2]

Wilson survived those defections by winning the support of many non-Democrats in many non-Democratic places. While these gains are often attributed to the war, many of them were prefigured in earlier elections, and some persisted into later ones. West of the Alleghenies in particular, any voters ostensibly lured to the Wilson who had kept them out of war may actually have been thinking about the president— and party—who had enacted two great waves of progressive legislation. Kansas Progressives who supported Wilson on the war had other issues in mind as well; Wisconsin Germans who deserted him were more single-minded. World War I, instead of narrowly rescuing Wilson in 1916, may have prevented the kind of decision that Lippmann might well call "stupendous" and we might call "critical."

Two weeks after the election of 1914, Interior Secretary Franklin K. Lane wrote Colonel House that he had been speaking to various Progressives about Wilson and 1916. There were, he thought, possibilities for "very informal diplomatic relations," and House should speak to some leading Progressives. House thanked him for the suggestion but assured him that "I have already taken [these ideas] up in a quiet way, and have been seeing what could be done along those lines."[3]

House did not tell Lane how much earlier he had begun thinking "along those lines," but a good guess might be the morning after the election of 1912. It had been clear since then, and reaffirmed in 1914, that Wilson's chances for reelection depended largely on his ability to hunt Moose.

2. For arguments dismissing the importance of ethnic defection, see Arthur Link, *Wilson: Campaign for Progressivism and Peace* (Princeton: Princeton University Press, 1965), p. 161; William M. Leary, Jr., "Woodrow Wilson, Irish-Americans, and the Election of 1916," *Journal of American History* (June 1967): 57–72; Carl Wittke, *German-Americans and the World War* (Columbus: Ohio State Archaeological and Historical Society, 1936), pp. 110–11; Thomas J. Kerr, "German-Americans and Neutrality in the 1916 Election," *Mid-America* 43 (April 1961): 103.

3. Franklin K. Lane to Edward M. House (November 20, 1914); Edward M. House to Franklin K. Lane (November 23, 1914), House Papers, Yale University.

But except for some areas in the West, the 1914 congressional elections did not show the Democrats attracting Progressive support in large numbers. And even after that election had shown that the Progressive party itself had little future, few of its leaders seemed interested in discussions with the administration. Although some, such as Albert Nortoni of Missouri and Winston Churchill of New Hampshire, appeared friendly, many Progressives were sounding more like William Prendergast, comptroller of New York City and nominator of Roosevelt at the 1912 Progressive convention. In a speech at Boston in 1915, Prendergast grouped Progressives and Republicans together as "friends of protection" and warned, "It is impossible to expect strong business government from a Democratic administration."[4]

Watching these developments, Democrats could only express the hope that the Bull Moosers would soon learn who their real friends were. "That Democracy is the party of progress," predicted the *National Monthly* in September 1915, "is a truth which is bound to loom continually larger on the Progressive horizon in the interval between now and 1916." Sounding the note that they would trumpet until the election, Democrats warned that the Republican party the Progressives were considering a return to was the same as the one they had rejected in 1912.[5]

Early response to this tactic was not, however, heartening. "It now looks as if the Progressives were determined to return to the Republican party almost without conditions," complained Bryan in April 1916. "The number of recruits thus far won from the progressive Republicans is not encouraging, in fact it is disappointing."[6]

Although Progressives were aware of Republican shortcomings — both the *New Republic* and *Collier's* expressed themselves forcefully on the subject — three factors seem to have limited their responsiveness to Wilson. The first, of course, was an inherent distrust of his party. Second was the fact that the Progressive party's concerns, or at least its official concerns, appeared to be shifting, following the new preoccupations of its leader and idol. "I did not hear much really progressive doctrine at the Kansas [Progressive] convention yesterday," one party member complained to William Allen White in May 1916. "I heard

4. Edward M. House to Woodrow Wilson (November 24, 1914); Winston Churchill to Woodrow Wilson (February 19, 1915), Wilson Papers, Library of Congress; William Prendergast, *Reminiscences*, Oral History Research Office, Columbia University, p. 765.
5. *National Monthly* (September 1915).
6. William Jennings Bryan, "The Democrats Should Win," *Independent* (April 3, 1916).

a great deal about Preparedness, Protection, Roosevelt, and the crimes and weaknesses of the democratic party." Finally, Progressives were biding their time until their second national convention, due to meet in June in Chicago, simultaneously with the Republican gathering.[7]

"With the personnel of the Republican Convention in Chicago next week fully made up," admitted *Collier's* glumly, "it is quite certain that within certain limitations the convention will be controlled by the Old Guard." Those Progressives not simply determined to oust Wilson at any cost could only cling to the hope that the threat of another independent Roosevelt campaign might bring the GOP to a relatively progressive posture.[8]

It didn't. Not only were Republicans immovable, but key elements of the Progressive convention were in no mood for another crusade to Armageddon. William Allen White later recalled that the delegations from New York, New Jersey, Connecticut, and Delaware this time were controlled largely by big businessmen. The platform submitted to the delegates mostly emphasized preparedness, to the extent that, the *Independent* noted, "The Republican platform and the Progressive platform are practically identical." Since the *New Republic* assessed the Republican declaration as "a stupidly, defiantly, and cynically reactionary document," the similarity did nothing to preserve the Progressive party's magic. Worst of all, the Progressives slowly discovered that their standard-bearer had shifted back from Crusader to Republican.[9]

While Progressives negotiating with Republicans in Chicago held out for a joint nomination of Roosevelt, back in Oyster Bay the Rough Rider had thrown in the towel. He resisted urgings, including some from William Randolph Hearst, that he come to Chicago, and over the long-distance telephone, he now suggested as compromise choices several conservative Republicans who shared his foreign policy views. And when—after the Republicans had ignored his suggestions and named Hughes, a Supreme Court justice and former reform governor of New York—the Progressives renominated Roosevelt, he declined with thanks.[10]

7. E. W. Rankin to William Allen White (May 24, 1916), in Meyer J. Nathan, "The Presidential Election of 1916 in the Middle West," unpublished dissertation, Princeton University, 1966. See also John A. Gable, *The Bull Moose Years* (Port Washington, N.Y.: Kennikat Press, 1978), p. 239.
8. *Collier's* (June 3, 1916).
9. William Allen White, *Autobiography* (New York: Macmillan, 1946), p. 521; *Independent* (June 19, 1916); *New Republic* (June 17, 1916).
10. *Los Angeles Examiner* (June 6, 1916); White, ibid., pp. 521–25.

"Litle by little," the *Nation* observed, the Progressive delegates "discovered that they were being toyed with, deceived, cheated, and at last left in a helpless and humiliating position." Without making a nomination, leaving it in the hands of the party's National Committee, the convention adjourned in a mood described by one observer as "intensely anti-Roosevelt." Westerners, in particular, seemed devastated: Edward Costigan, back in Colorado, called the convention "a rare example of political unpreparedness and incredibly poor leadership." Walter Lippmann, with the bitterness of the betrayed believer, declared savagely that the Progressives had deserved what they got from Roosevelt: "They clung to him as a woman without occupation or external interests will cling to her husband. . . . They adored him as no one in a democracy deserved to be adored."[11]

But the *New Republic* editor went on to suggest that the story had not been completed at the end of the convention: "The aggressively nationalistic and military tone, the Bismarckian creed that the party had taken from its leader began to disappear, and the old cries for social justice and popular rule were heard again." The men around Woodrow Wilson had been listening carefully for those cries and immediately began recruiting for their own chorus.[12]

The Democrats moved swiftly to send the Progressives a message with their choice of a chairman of the Democratic National Committee. Although the two Chicago conventions were meeting, House wrote Wilson that they must look beyond well-known party figures: "I am not nearly so afraid of losing the rank and file as I am of not getting the necessary votes from outside to win." Three days later he had a name: Vance McCormick, a Pennsylvania newspaper publisher who had borne both the Democratic and Progressive nominations in his losing campaign for governor in 1914. It was necessary, House told Wilson, to "get an undoubted progressive in order that we may strengthen our appeal for the votes of the progressive party. McCormick lives up to this in all particulars for Roosevelt himself campaigned for McCormick when the latter ran for governor of Pennsylvania." McCormick's Progressive connections even cancelled out other drawbacks, such as his lack of acquaintance with the national party and his coming from

11. *Nation* (June 15, 1916); Fred Greenbaum, *Fighting Progressive: A Biography of Edward F. Costigan* (Washington: Public Affairs Press, 1971), pp. 80–83; Henry L. Stoddard, *As I Knew Them: Presidents and Politics from Grant to Coolidge* (New York: Harper Bros., 1927, 2 vols.), p. 448; Walter Lippman, "At the Chicago Convention," *New Republic* (June 17, 1916).
12. Ibid.

a state that Wilson had no possibility of winning. His selection, noted one journal, was "a bid for the vote that was orphaned at Chicago."[13]

Other Democrats also put out feelers during June. A week after Hughes's nomination, Norman Hapgood, who for three years had been editing *Harper's Weekly* as a Wilson journal, wrote Wilson that "My conferences with Bull Moose leaders this last week have been encouraging. We shall have many of them." Certainly there appeared to be little Progressive enthusiasm for Hughes. At the meeting of the party National Committee, called in late June to tender him its endorsement, a motion to nominate former congressman Victor Murdock of Kansas instead was beaten only 31 to 15. The *New Republic* suggested afterward that many committee members had voted for Hughes against the wishes of their state organizations.[14]

Moreover, as early as June, the attitudes of the two sides toward reform seemed clear. Wilson, with his record of progressive achievement, and with additional bills on their way through Congress, faced Hughes, whose Republican party had shown itself in convention to be firmly controlled by old-line conservatives. The Democratic party seemed to have successfully preempted the reform position, as it sought to do in 1914. "I think we can show Hughes up as a thorough conservative who obtained the name of progressive because of his refusal to let the bosses dictate to him," House wrote Wilson confidently. Frank P. Walsh, the radical Kansas City lawyer whom Wilson had named chairman of the Industrial Commission, exulted, "It is going to be a battle between big business and the people; also 'the empire against democracy.' If Wilson would only go the whole limit on the people's side, I believe we would win a tremendous popular victory."[15]

Yet, there was only a slow trickle of Bull Moosers to Wilson. Although by the end of the campaign, Democrats could point to a substantial number of old Progressives supporting Wilson (including eleven of nineteen members of the 1912 Progressive platform committee), many of those were late conversions; in the early summer revelation came slowly. It took lengthy cultivation before Francis Heney, 1914 Progressive candidate for the Senate from California, endorsed

13. Edward M. House to Woodrow Wilson (June 9, 1916; June 16, 1916), House Papers; *Nation* (June 22, 1916).

14. Norman Hapgood to Woodrow Wilson (June 18, 1916), Wilson Papers, Library of Congress; *Independent* (July 10, 1916); *New York Times* (July 6, 7, 1916); *New Republic* (July 15, 1916).

15. Edward M. House to Woodrow Wilson (June 10, 1916), House Papers; Frank P. Walsh to Basil Manly (June 26, 1916), Walsh Papers, New York Public Library.

198 · *The Wilson Coalition*

Wilson in a public exchange of letters in early July. The Woodrow Wilson Independent League, organized in summer, carried few Bull Moosers on its masthead, listing instead mostly longtime personal friends and supporters of the president.[16]

McCormick could only continue his efforts, insist gamely that there would be "sufficient Progressive support to make the re-election of President Wilson certain," and take hope from the perception of the *New Republic* that "although the majority of [former Progressives] rallied to Hughes, the Wilson minority is increasing rather than diminishing." Those in that minority, however, were beginning to wonder where everybody else was. "I cannot for the life of me," wrote William Kent to Amos Pinchot, "see why any Progressive should accept the bunk and husks that are being handed out by the Hughes' aggregation, unless, like Jim Garfield and Gifford [Pinchot], they blindly follow the mahdi; or unless they have greasy motives such as distinguish the Hon. Perkins."[17]

There was, however, at least one other category of Progressives reluctant to pledge fealty to Woodrow Wilson. A number of Bull Moosers spent a long hot summer wrestling with their consciences and their feelings about the Democratic party, hoping desperately for Hughes to take a forthright position that would end their suffering. It never came, but many of them fell into line behind him (and Roosevelt) anyway. The decisions made by two prominent Progressives illustrate once again the difficulties the Democrats had in persuading midwestern insurgents to take Democratic progressivism seriously, a difficulty that only limited the size of Wilson's victory but has somehow tainted his party's progressive image among historians.[18]

William Allen White could hardly be accused of greasy motives, although his attitude toward Roosevelt did lack a certain cold objectivity. ("Roosevelt bit me," he later recalled, "and I went mad.") But his main difficulty with Wilson was a large blind spot concerning Democrats. He had flatly predicted that the Democratic Senate would never confirm Brandeis; when it did, he sourly attributed it to cultivation of Jewish voters.[19]

16. *Denver Post* (November 1, 1916); Francis J. Heney to Woodrow Wilson (July 2, 1916); Woodrow Wilson to Francis J. Heney (July 4, 1916), Wilson Papers, Library of Congress.

17. *New Republic* (July 10, 1916); William Kent to Amos Pinchot (July 26, 1916), Kent Papers, Yale University.

18. See Harold Ickes, "Who Killed the Progressive Party?" *American Historical Review* (January 1941): 306–37, for one account of Progressive distaste at the choice.

19. *Emporia Gazette* (May 25, 1916), quoted in *The Public*, (June 2, 1916); Meyer J. Nathan, "The Presidential Election of 1916 in the Middle West," p. 34 n.

At the Progressive convention, White was "shocked" at the names suggested by Roosevelt for a joint ticket. Two weeks after Chicago, he told a friend "I am weak and weary, sick and sore. I am without star or compass politically and am up in the air and a mile west." Yet he firmly resisted Norman Hapgood's feelers: "I respect and admire too many of the [splendid] things the President has done to oppose him with any vigor. [But] I can't canvass myself into a position where my naturally low opinion of the Democratic party will permit me to support it—even indirectly by standing for the President." White grew increasingly unhappy with the Hughes campaign, and publicly endorsed the Adamson Act while Hughes vociferously opposed it. Yet, in October, he refused Hapgood's request that he meet with Bainbridge Colby, a Bull Mooser actively supporting Wilson. In November, White unhappily cast his ballot for Hughes, while his wife voted for Wilson.[20]

No Progressive was the object of a more intense recruiting drive than Raymond Robins of Illinois, 1914 Senate candidate and chairman of the 1916 Progressive convention. Hapgood had contacted Robins immediately following the conventions and was encouraged by his attitude, although Robins wanted to wait for Hughes's acceptance speech. Robins's decision, Hapgood told Wilson, "may mean several hundred thousand votes. It could well turn Illinois and several other states." The administration devised a plan to lure Robins with the Democratic nomination for governor of Illinois, which collapsed when Illinois Democrats, including the incumbent governor, objected. But despite all efforts, Robins in early August declared for Hughes, a development Wilson pronounced "indeed disappointing."[21]

Robins's statement endorsing Hughes, which explained that the Republicans had to be the true Progressive party because the Democrats were held down by their southern and immigrant constituencies, illustrated serious problems faced by Wilson in his quest for support from Bull Moosers, problems not to be overcome by the Democrats' progressive record. "The hostility toward the Democratic party was so strong among Progressives," points out a recent student of Robins's ca-

20. William Allen White to Rodney Elward (June 24, 1916), in Walter Johnson, ed., *Selected Letters of William Allen White* (New York: Henry Holt and Co., 1947), p. 169; William Allen White to Norman Hapgood (July 29, 1916), quoted in Nathan, ibid., pp. 206, 175; William Allen White to Norman Hapgood (October 10, 1916), in Johnson, pp. 171, 174.
21. Norman Hapgood to Woodrow Wilson (June 18, 1916; June 28, 1916), Wilson Papers, Library of Congress; Alan R. Havig, "The Raymond Robins Case for Progressive Republicanism," *Illinois State Historical Society Journal* 66 (Winter 1971): 406–408; Woodrow Wilson to Norman Hapgood (August 5, 1916), Wilson Papers, Library of Congress.

reer, "that many of them denied credit to Wilson for the reforms that had been enacted in his administration."[22]

This attitude, impervious to argument or example, was not confined to Bull Moosers; Senator Joseph Bristow of Kansas spoke for many insurgent Republicans in calling Wilson "the most dangerous reactionary of any man who has been in the White House for half a century." For both of these groups, anti-Democratic feeling seems to have mingled with anger at having leadership of the Progressive movement taken from them. In 1916, *Collier's*, while praising individual Democratic accomplishments, still seemed to consider real progressivism to be that practiced in the Roosevelt administration. The Progressive platform had "embodied a demand for legislation for the uplift of human beings," the magazine explained stiffly in July. "The Progressive voter is likely to go to that party which has the best record in the furtherance of such legislation. Obviously that party is the Republican."[23]

Collier's was able to reach this conclusion, at a time when the Democratic Congress was passing a bill to restrict child labor, by comparing the Democratic South with selected northern states such as Wisconsin and California. Sectional opposition to Wilson and the Democrats, as voiced by Robins and *Collier's*, was a popular theme among northern, and particularly midwestern, Republicans. Herbert Margulies points out that insurgents were particularly fond of sectional attacks, as a cheap way of affirming their Republicanism. Wilson's appointments, and southern control of Congress, left him vulnerable to this kind of attack, and Democrats sought to ease the situation in June. "I am hoping," wrote House, "that you will choose Northern men for almost every office that is to be filled between now and November." The issue, however, would continue to hurt.[24]

Privately and publicly, Democrats focused on the Bull Moose vote. When a group of Progressives met in Indianapolis in early August and expressed distrust of both parties, Wilson wrote McCormick inquiring about the effect "upon our plans in this matter of associating some of the Progressives with us. It certainly does not bar us, but will it bar them, do you think?" In a magazine article, Hapgood argued that the major question of the election was, "Are you Liberal or Tory? . . . The

22. *The Public* (August 11, 1916); Havig, ibid., pp. 411, 414.
23. Joseph Bristow to Arthur Capper (February 5, 1915), in A. Bower Sagesser, *Joseph L. Bristow* (Lawrence: University of Kansas Press, 1971), p. 129; *Collier's* (July 22, 1916).
24. Herbert Margulies, *Senator Lenroot of Wisconsin: A Political Biography, 1900–1929* (Columbia: University of Missouri Press, 1977), p. 167; Edward M. House to Woodrow Wilson (June 23, 1916), House Papers.

greater part of the Bull Moose platform of 1912 has already been carried out by the Wilson Administration."[25]

The passage in July of the Child Labor Law brought Wilson the support of Judge Ben Lindsey of Colorado, a prominent Progressive, and the Wilsonians sought to exploit the issue. Robert Woolley, who handled publicity for the National Committee, urged Wilson to hold a public signing of the bill on a different day from the signing of his new preparedness legislation: "This would enable us to double the amount of immediate publicity; furthermore, the pictures taken could be used to appeal to separate groups, whereas one picture might prove of doubtful value." The sensibilities of peace-minded Progressives had to be guarded.[26]

But many of Wilson's targets were still waiting to hear from Hughes. Even though they may have been discomfited at the manner of Hughes's nomination, many of them considered the New York jurist a reasonably good Progressive choice. They waited eagerly for the promulgation of a sincere but safe Republican progressivism that would permit them to flock to his side. Although they listened closely, they did not hear it in Hughes's acceptance speech in early August. But they still hoped that it would sound during his campaign tour of the West later that month.

By the time Hughes reached California, it was clear that they could stop listening. As Hughes extolled the protective tariff, attacked Democratic patronage policies, and criticized the administration for hostility toward business, his listeners had difficulty believing that here was the candidate of the Progressive party. "He talked tariff like Mark Hanna. He talked of industrial affairs like McKinley," recalled a stunned William Allen White after the vote. "His speeches might have been made by Chester Arthur, but hardly by Benjamin Harrison." Democrats watched the result gleefully. "Information from Pacific Coast advises me," a California Democrat oratorically wired McCormick, "that Progressives disappointed with Hughes for feeding them only husks of stale

25. Woodrow Wilson to Vance McCormick (August 4, 1916), McCormick Papers, Yale University; Norman Hapgood, "Tory or Liberal," *Independent* (August 7, 1916).

26. Ben B. Lindsey to Woodrow Wilson (August 9, 1916), Wilson Papers, Child Labor File, Library of Congress; Robert Woolley to Woodrow Wilson (August 23, 1916), Woolley Papers, Library of Congress. Woolley's skills and insights were a considerate asset to the Wilson campaign; see Michael E. McGerr, *The Decline of Popular Politics: The American North, 1865–1928* (New York and Oxford: Oxford University Press, 1986), pp. 163–68.

Republican doctrine from which special privilege and monopoly had eaten the corn and fattened since the Civil War."[27]

Less floridly, others had noticed something odd about the Hughes campaign. The *Nation*, which had exulted in June that "with Mr. Hughes as the Republican nominee, the country will look forward to a Presidential campaign almost unexampled for the high intellectual tone which the two candidates will give to it," admitted by early September that Hughes was causing "pained disappointment to his friends and admirers." The *New Republic* avowed stoutly that "we believe that Mr. Hughes is not doing himself justice in this campaign; that he has a fresher and more penetrating mind than his speeches reveal."[28]

Helpfully, Democrats hastened to explain the nature of the Republican candidate's difficulty. The *World*, reporting the Woodrow Wilson Independents' League's essay contest on the theme, "Why have Hughes's speeches been so disappointing," offered its own entry: Hughes was seeking to hold together a coalition so broad that he could take no "definite, unequivocal" position on anything. Hughes, the *Courier-Journal* explained encouragingly, was doing the best he could under the circumstances; his supporters "cannot possibly agree among themselves upon a program of constructive action."[29]

In their responses, Democrats were pointing out something that many Bull Moosers preferred not to see — the virtual impossibility of running a Progressive campaign on the Republican ticket. As Wilsonians never tired of explaining, Hughes was obliged to retain the support of — and would be obliged to govern with — some very conservative people, the eastern Republicans who had kept control of the party after the Progressives departed. His method for holding these supporters while also appealing to the Progressives involved a constant attack on Wilson's policies and actions, leaving his own positions vague. Progressives complained of this as though it were simple ineptitude and miscalculation, refusing to see that Hughes had little realistic alternative.[30]

Hughes's quandary, and the reaction to it, was clearly illustrated in his campaign's legendary fiasco, his trip to California. That it was a dis-

27. William Allen White, "Who Killed Cock Robin?" *Collier's* (December 16, 1916); Gavin McNab to Vance McCormick (August 17, 1916), McCormick Papers, Yale University.

28. *Nation* (June 15, 1916; September 7, 1916); *New Republic* (August 19, 1916).

29. *New York World* (September 20, 1916); *Louisville Courier-Journal* (October 5, 1916).

30. See *New York World* (October 20, 1916), for a typical Democratic editorial detailing the conservatives who would control Congress after a Republican victory.

aster seemed clear from the outset; shortly after his arrival a California Wilsonian jubilantly wired East that "Hughes would have been better off not coming." The candidate had been quickly taken in hand by California conservatives and insulated from Governor Hiram Johnson and the Progressives. The famous climax of this situation occurred when Hughes and Johnson occupied the same Long Beach hotel, but Hughes, not realizing it, made no effort to make contact. According to legend, enough Johnsonians remembered the snub to provide Wilson's California margin and give him the presidency.[31]

This image, that Hughes could have become president with two calls to room service, is compelling, but it understates the complexity of his problems both in California and in the nation. Long before Long Beach, observers from several perspectives had realized that Hughes would have difficulties. The *New Republic* had warned that since the reunification of the GOP was only "superficial and external," anything Hughes did in California would hurt him with someone. Before Hughes even departed on his tour, Joseph Tumulty had confidently written that any candidate running on Hughes's issues would have a difficult time in the West. The Republican candidate's problems with Progressives, in August and November, derived less from what he did not say to Hiram Johnson than from what he did say to the voters, those statements in which William Allen White unwillingly heard echoes of McKinley and Hanna.[32]

By the end of the summer, the political lineup was clearly what the Progressives had feared and the Democrats had planned: the Democrats in the progressive position against Republicans in the conservative role. This image became even more vivid in early September with a railroad crisis and the response of the two candidates to it.

When, in late August, the Railroad Brotherhoods refused arbitration and threatened a nationwide rail strike to gain the eight-hour workday, one Democrat outside the administration did not see what the problem was. "There is much to be said against any plan that would bind [the workers] to *accept in advance* any finding that a board might make," wrote William Jennings Bryan. "The question of hours is not a matter for arbitration. Congress can fix the length of a working day." Woodrow Wilson and the Democratic Congress agreed, swiftly passing

31. Gavin McNab to William G. McAdoo (August 20, 1916), Thomas J. Walsh Papers, Library of Congress.
32. *New Republic* (August 26, 1916); Joseph P. Tumulty to Raymond T. Baker (August 4, 1916), in Joseph P. Tumulty, *Woodrow Wilson As I Knew Him* (Garden City: Garden City Publishing Co., 1925), p. 195.

the Adamson Act, enforcing an eight-hour workday on the railroads and derailing the strike. Numerous Republicans in the House and La Follette in the Senate voted for the bill as well.[33]

Some, however, found Bryan's reasoning less than persuasive. Hughes seized upon the issue to revive his campaign and now concentrated his speechmaking on the issue. Beginning almost immediately, he launched attacks focused not on the bill itself but on the process of its passage, which he charged was a capitulation to union blackmail. Republican candidates for lesser offices took up the cry.

Originally, the Democrats had rejoiced at the problem's resolution, feeling that it depicted Wilson as an effective problem solver. "The settlement of the strike has been most propitious to the Democratic party," Virginia Senator Claude Swanson wrote to McAdoo. "The republicans have been very much embarrassed by it, and I think we will gain considerably." Shortly, however, problems appeared. "President Wilson's campaign for re-election," recalled Robert Woolley, "took a financial tailspin the day the Adamson Act eight-hour bill was passed."[34]

A week after Swanson's optimistic assessment, Vance McCormick took a different view, complaining to Colonel House that business was now furiously working for Hughes. By September 24, McAdoo warned Wilson that the issue was hurting with businessmen and could be a problem in New York.[35]

Whether the issue ultimately helped or hurt Wilson, the Adamson Act sharply polarized the electorate in general and the Progressive Party in particular. Eastern and business-minded Progressives fell in line behind Hughes. Beveridge and Robins attacked the bill on the stump; Collier's complained that its passage "upset the theory of deliberative legislation"; former Progressive chairman (and J. P. Morgan partner) George W. Perkins protested the pressure used to "force through Congress the so-called eight-hour law."[36] But several advanced Progressives, who had been postponing a choice, broke with Hughes on the

33. William Jennings Bryan to Francis G. Newlands (August 27, 1916), Bryan Papers, Library of Congress.
34. Claude Swanson to William G. McAdoo (September 3, 1916), McAdoo Papers; Robert Woolley, "Politics Is Hell," unpublished manuscript, Chapter 23, Woolley Papers.
35. Vance McCormick to Edward M. House (September 11, 1916), House Papers; William G. McAdoo to Woodrow Wilson (September 24, 1916), McAdoo Papers.
36. Nathan, "The Presidential Election of 1916 in the Middle West," p. 169; Collier's (September 23, 1916); George W. Perkins to Joseph P. Tumulty (September 26, 1916), Perkins Papers, Columbia University.

issue. Victor Murdock of Kansas, former party leader in the House, endorsed the act; the *New Republic* praised Wilson's actions and criticized Hughes's focusing his campaign on it. Eventually, both would endorse Wilson. William Allen White, in perhaps his most uncomfortable posture in an uncomfortable year, endorsed the act while supporting Hughes. La Follette, making no presidential endorsement, strongly supported the Adamson Act in *La Follette's Magazine*.[37]

Equally important, the Democratic embrace of the eight-hour workday bill intensified the already strong attachment of organized labor to Wilson's candidacy and the party's identification with the AFL and the Railroad Brotherhoods. Early in the campaign, Wilson had accepted, "with a great deal of pleasure," an invitation to speak at the dedication of the new AFL offices in Washington, and in late August Gompers wrote happily, "In my experience with the United States Congress of two score years I have not seen anything like the fine spirit toward labor, the rights and welfare of all the people pervading all the branches of the Wilson Administration." By contrast, he pointed out, Hughes had not been particularly friendly either on the Supreme Court or as governor of New York. The Democratic effort to capitalize on the contrast was exemplified by a pamphlet aimed at labor, "If There Had Been No Woodrow Wilson," pointing out that that hypothetical situation would have meant "No Justice Brandeis, No Commission on Industrial Relations, No Federal Child Labor Law, No Labor Section of the Clayton Act" and many other absences.[38]

But if the Adamson Act endeared Wilson even further to labor's leaders, the accompanying business alienation made it seem that he would need all of its affection and that it would have to be demonstrated more forcefully than labor had shown its fondness in the past. "This intensified opposition must . . . be reckoned with," observed Vance McCormick, "and while . . . we should have a united labor vote yet experience has shown that the support of the labor leaders and union organization has not always proved effective, as in the case of Bryan." Democratic doubts about their ally were reaffirmed by the results of Maine's September voting, when the Republicans swept the cities and the state,

37. *The Public* (September 29, 1916); *New Republic* (September 16, 1916); *New York World* (September 27, 1916).
38. Woodrow Wilson to Samuel Gompers (June 1, 1916); Samuel Gompers to Robert Woolley (August 25, 1916); Samuel Gompers to Thomas H. Nichols (August 19, 1916), Gompers Papers, AFL-CIO Headquarters, Washington, D.C.; "If There Had Been No Woodrow Wilson," pamphlet, in Thomas J. Walsh Papers, Library of Congress.

ousting even the three-term prolabor Congressman Daniel McGilli-cuddy. One Wilsonian plaintively summed up the reaction of many, asking Colonel House, "what became of the labor vote?"[39]

The party leaders did not know, but they redoubled their efforts to find it. McAdoo declared "the supreme importance of concentrating our heaviest batteries upon labor"; McCormick noted that the federation's leaders had better realize that they were "making their last stand," and that failure would end forever their claim to political influence. The same thought had apparently occurred to the labor leaders as well. Their memories of 1908, of bold political leadership that turned out to lack followers, were at least as painful and far more embarrassing than McCormick's, but it now seemed that they had to risk it again. As the campaign progressed, the AFL dropped all pretense of nonpartisanship, and functioned almost as an arm of the Democratic effort.[40]

Like Wilson's other arms, it seemed stronger in the West than the East. Whereas eastern campaigners reported very mixed signals, those pounding the prairies found strong enthusiasm. Bryan and Josephus Daniels, who had been stunned by labor's disappearance eight years earlier, sent back word from the plains that this time it might work. "It really seems," Daniels wrote cautiously, "that the railroad men and the working men are with us as never before."[41]

The labor issues took particular hold in two states that would later figure prominently in the Wilson column. In Ohio, where Democrats had long been closely tied to the state federation, the state candidates focused their campaigns tightly on the eight-hour workday and child labor issues. California Democrats rarely reassured headquarters with tales of Johnson's disaffection with Hughes — they tended, in fact, to warn that the governor's active campaigning for the national ticket was likely to cost them the state. But they frequently noted that the labor issues, intensified by Hughes's real blunder on his visit — crossing a picket line in San Francisco — were helping Wilson considerably. "The Labor Unionists here, as I presume elsewhere," a California Democrat

39. Vance McCormick to Edward M. House (September 11, 1916); Thomas W. Gregory to Edward M. House (September 16, 1916), House Papers; *New York Times* (September 13, 1916).

40. William G. McAdoo to Vance McCormick (September 19, 1916); Vance McCormick to William G. McAdoo (September 23, 1916), McAdoo Papers; Marc Karson, *American Labor Unions and Politics, 1900–1918* (Carbondale: 1958) Southern Illinois University Press, pp. 81–87.

41. William Jennings Bryan to Thomas J. Walsh (July 23, 1916), Walsh Papers, Library of Congress; Jonathan Daniels to Addie Daniels (October 4, 1916), Daniels Family Papers, Library of Congress.

told Senator Thomas Walsh of Montana, western chairman of the campaign, "are practically unanimous for the President."[42]

As the shape of the campaign emerged, Walsh and his Chicago office became increasingly important in it. With the assistance of Senator Henry Hollis of New Hampshire, Walsh set up a system of direct communication and support similar to Congressman James Lloyd's earlier Chicago-based operation of the Democratic Congressional Campaign Committee. Even if the national leaders still kept the traditional emphasis on New York's electoral votes, western Democrats had a place to go with their concerns — and their increasingly optimistic reports.

High-level Democrats enjoyed their mail considerably less, however, when it dealt not with Progressives and labor but with the party's traditional supporters. German voters, who in response to Republican pietistic righteousness had long provided the core of the minority Democratic parties of the Midwest, and the proverbially Democratic urban Irish both showed signs of voting not on the Adamson Act but on what they considered an unduly pro-British foreign policy.

Although Theodore Roosevelt attacked Wilson as too weak in his approach to Germany and its submarine warfare, German and Irish voters rejected the president's series of stiff notes to Germany and what they considered his closeness to Britain. Campaign correspondence dealing with the war warned of German and Irish defections at least as often as it cited the benefits of Wilson's peace position. It would profit the party little to gain the *New Republic* and lose its own core.[43]

Throughout 1915, the administration had heard reports that all was not quiet along the midwestern front. Maurice Connolly warned from Iowa that the local German press had unleashed "a fierce tirade against the Administration" in the closing days of the 1914 campaign, and Joseph Davies sent word from Wisconsin that "it is difficult for you to conceive down there the degree or extent to which the German population go in their criticism of the Administration and of the President." As the election came closer, warnings were heard from Kansas, Nebraska, the Dakotas, Missouri, Minnesota, and Indiana as well, along with worries about the urban Germans of New York and New Jersey, where the administration had other ethnic problems. The normal anti-British feeling of Irish voters had been intensified by that year's Easter

42. *Cleveland Plain Dealer* (October 7, 1916); William Kettner to Scott Ferris (September 25, 1916); Justus S. Wardell to Thomas J. Walsh (October 9, 1916) Walsh Papers, Library of Congress.

43. For a report of German disaffection as early as the 1914 election, see Maurice Connolly to Edward M. House (November 7, 1914), House Papers.

revolt and the British response; James K. McGuire of New York warned that there was "absolutely no doubt whatever" of an Irish bolt in the close states.[44]

Wilson, of course, was hardly the president to adapt his foreign policy to such pressures; he had already seen Secretary of State Bryan leave the cabinet over the issue. Instead, the administration would counterattack. Wilson should run on Americanism, House advised him in September 1915: "It might be well to even go so far as to state that you did not desire the support of any citizen who felt allegiance to any other country than this." After the outburst of German-American enthusiasm for Hughes's nomination, McAdoo suggested to Frank Cobb, editor of the *World*, an editorial on the subject, and House boasted to the candidate, "No matter what Hughes may say or do, before November it will be firmly fixed in the minds of the voters that a vote for Hughes will be a vote for the Kaiser." By September, the *World* was hitting the issue daily, with cartoons showing a goose-stepping Hughes, and the country's other Democratic papers joined the chorus.[45]

Unsurprisingly, this approach did not seem to mollify German Democrats. The German press in many areas was almost unanimously against the president, and some early indications were hardly encouraging. In the Nebraska presidential primary, Wilson was actually beaten in some German precincts by one Richard Ross, a "fun-loving livery stable worker." In September, Wilson's choice for senator in his home state of New Jersey lost the nomination to incumbent James Martine, with most of Martine's plurality coming from a 4 to 1 victory in heavily German and Irish Hudson County. It was in response to a telegram from Jeremiah O'Leary of the American Truth Society, boasting of the New Jersey result and warning Wilson about November, that the president issued the famous "I would be mortified to have you or anyone like you vote for me" statement that House had suggested more than a year before.[46]

Meanwhile, the Republicans sought actively to capitalize on the

44. Maurice Connolly to Edward M. House (November 7, 1914); Joseph E. Davies to Edward M. House (August 15, 1915), House Papers; James K. McGuire to William G. McAdoo McAdoo Papers.

45. Edward M. House to Woodrow Wilson (September 29, 1916); William G. McAdoo to Frank Cobb (June 13, 1916); Edward M. House to Woodrow Wilson (June 15, 1916), House Papers; *New York World* (September 20, 1916).

46. Burton W. Folson, "Tinkerers, Tipplers and Traitors: Ethnicity and Democratic Reform in Nebraska during the Progressive Era," *Pacific Historical Review* 50 (February 1981): 63–64; *New York World* (September 28, 29, 1916); Lewis L. Gould, *Reform and Regulation: American Politics, 1900–1916* (New York: John Wiley and Sons, 1916), p. 176.

issue. Hughes met with German groups, and kept his criticism of Wilson's foreign policy bitter but unspecific, stressing the need to protect American rights against British surface ships as well as German U-boats. When Hughes spoke in Milwaukee, the *New York Times* called his hotel "the center of attraction for many who called one another, 'Herr.'" Republican Fiorello La Guardia, in what would be his first successful campaign for Congress from Manhattan, enjoyed heavy support from the *New York Staats-Zeitung*, normally a strong Democratic paper, as well as stump support from its publishers and other angry ethnic voters. In the Midwest, Democrats seemed particularly alarmed by meetings the Republicans were holding with German clergymen, especially from the rural districts.[47]

Democrats did find one tactic that appeared to be effective among German voters, that of stressing the speeches — and presumed postelection influence — of Hughes's most bellicose backer, Theodore Roosevelt. As Roosevelt thundered his charges that Wilson was being despicably weak with Germany, the demands for his presence shifted; the Republicans of St. Louis headed off a campaign appearance by the Rough Rider, while the Democratic state chairman of Kansas asked Walsh to send him more Roosevelt speeches. "If you have any Germans in your county," North Dakota Republican State Chairman William Lemke drily advised his county chairmen, "do not mail them any of Roosevelt's speeches, as they have no use for them."[48]

But although the Roosevelt issue, the pressure from the Americanism strategy, and temporarily better relations with Germany helped ease the bitterness among German voters, these factors could not make it go away. In mid-October, a *New York World* poll of three leading German societies of New York found that 88 percent of those who had voted for Wilson in 1912 would not vote for him again.[49]

In New York, New Jersey, and Illinois, another element complicated the administration's appeal to German and Irish Democrats. Wilson's relations with the urban Democratic machines, the political vehicle of these groups, had hardly improved since 1914, when the infighting had hurt the party in all three states. Although administration hostility had

47. *New York Times* (September 21, 1916); Arthur Mann, *La Guardia, A Fighter against His Times* (Philadelphia: Lippincott, 1959), pp. 68–71; O. A. La Budde to Thomas J. Walsh (October 13, 1916); H. H. Lehman to Thomas J. Walsh (November 4, 1916), Walsh Papers, Library of Congress.

48. *Cleveland Plain Dealer* (October 17, 1916); Herbert Lardner to Thomas J. Walsh (October 11, 1916), Walsh Papers, Library of Congress; Nathan, "The Presidential Election of 1916 in the Middle West," pp. 77–78.

49. *New York World* (October 18, 1916).

eased somewhat, any steps toward the machines would bring complaints from local Wilsonians, warning of treachery. Between their own distaste and the fear of alienating vital independent Progressives, the Wilsonians continued to deal gingerly with the machines.

Even though the administration had largely abandoned its hopes of midwifing a new progressive, anti-Tammany Democratic party, House noted three months before the election that only one member of the Wilson high command, Daniel Roper, was on speaking terms with the regular New York organization. Roper tried to explain why: "The factor unfavorable to us is the feeling among the organization that they have not been properly consulted and considered by the national administration." Slowly, the threads were gathered together. Wilson reluctantly named a loyal Tammanyite the New York postmaster, after an attempt to compromise on Tammany progressive Robert Wagner had failed. The organization agreed to nominate Samuel Seabury, the administration's choice, for governor, and the two sides seem to have reached an un-Wilsonian deal: Tammany would support Wilson in 1916 if the administration would stay out of the New York City elections the next year. By late October, House, the *World*, and the *Times* were all reporting that Tammany was working hard for the ticket.[50]

Roger Sullivan of Chicago, one Wilsonian campaign figure tried to persuade House in April, was "a much misunderstood man." Others felt that they understood him perfectly, and despite his protests of loyalty, his relations with the administration remained strained. Sullivan pledged that he would strongly back Wilson, although his organization had been "entirely ignored by the National Administration," and he resented its efforts to attract Raymond Robins with the Democratic nomination for governor of Illinois. (Sullivan did little for state party harmony himself with his own unsuccessful attempt to dump the incumbent Democratic governor in the primary.) But, by October, another rough armistice had been hammered out. "I am convinced [Sullivan] is in the fight with an earnest desire to see you carry the state of Illinois," Senator Walsh, who as western chairman was based in Chi-

50. House Diary (August 27, 1916); Daniel C. Roper to Edward M. House (August 5, 1916), House Papers; Nancy Joan Weiss, *Charles Francis Murphy, 1858–1924* (Northampton: Smith College Press, 1968), pp. 66–71; *New York World* (October 21, 1916); *New York Times* (October 15, 1916); Edward M. House to Woodrow Wilson (October 23, 1916), Wilson Papers, Library of Congress; Robert F. Wesser, *A Response to Progressivism: The Democratic Party and New York Politics, 1902–1918* (New York and London: New York University Press, 1986), pp. 182–85.

cago, wrote Wilson. "For your information I may say that both Senator Hollis and I have modified very materially the opinion we had of him on coming here."[51]

But the progressives, who habitually ascribed all evil to the bosses, also frequently ascribed too much power to them. Much of Tammany's own German and Irish infrastructure was said to be supporting Hughes, and a spokesman for Tammany boss Charles Francis Murphy, while asserting, "The order has gone forth that New York City must roll up its customary Democratic majority," admitted that the party hoped for, at most, 40 percent of the German vote. Despite Sullivan's efforts, the German wards of Chicago also continued to produce signs of rebellion.[52]

One other group, just beginning to take a role in the urban Democratic machines, had been alienated for reasons having nothing to do with foreign policy. Because of Wilson's policies, blacks were irretrievably lost to his candidacy. The Democrats made little effort to regain black support in 1916, and a September petition to Wilson from the St. Louis Colored Democratic Club, complaining that although every president since Cleveland had expanded black appointments Wilson had cut them back sharply, seems to have gone unanswered.[53]

But at least one traditionally Republican ethnic group had been highly pleased by the first three years of the New Freedom. "I believe the whole business and intelligent part of the community to be thoroughly aroused against Wilson," wrote William Howard Taft in October 1916, "except maybe the Jews and the college professors." Little study has been made on college professors as a voting bloc, but one historian of Jewish political behavior has concluded that "Jewish enthusiasm for Wilson transcended parochial interests." In his first campaign, the scholarly Wilson had dented Jewish Republicanism, recently bolstered by distrust of Bryan and adoration of Theodore Roosevelt, and won both votes and crucial campaign funds. And unlike black voters, Jews had been carefully cultivated by this administration. A list of Jewish appointments, prepared for campaign purposes, could count a number of prestigious positions, topped, of course, by Louis Brandeis's

51. Robert M. Woolley to Edward M. House (April 18, 1916), House Papers; Roger C. Sullivan to Thomas J. Walsh (July 30, 1916); Thomas J. Walsh to Woodrow Wilson (October 9, 1916), Walsh Papers, Library of Congress; *The Public* (September 22, 1916).

52. *New York Times* (October 15, 1916); *Cleveland Plain Dealer* (October 19, 1916); *New York World* (October 29, 1916); Wesser, *A Response to Progressivism*, pp. 185–86.

53. George B. Vaston *et al.*, St. Louis Colored Democratic Club to Woodrow Wilson (September 23, 1916); Wilson Papers, Library of Congress.

seat on the Supreme Court. Wilson also pleased Jewish voters with vetoes of a literacy test for immigrants and restatement of opposition to
czarist anti-Semitism, as well as his domestic reform measures.[54]

The campaign commanders expected this warmth to be particularly
helpful in New York City, where Jews cast 13 percent of the vote in
1916. Hugh C. Wallace, overseeing the party's ethnic operations,
hoped for 75 percent of the New York Jewish vote, up from Wilson's
estimated 40 percent in 1912. New York Democrats counted on this
expected support from Jews, along with gains among labor and Socialists (in New York, largely Jewish as well) to balance the anticipated
losses among other groups.[55]

Ethnic politics, it would seem, played an even more important role
than usual in 1916. And, at least among two of the nation's—and the
Democratic party's—largest ethnic groups, ethnic voting on the war
issue was expected to hurt Wilson badly. On the other hand, the war
issue—or, as the Democrats preferred to call it, the peace issue—was
expected to help Wilson with many voters, especially women. The
Democrats did indeed campaign on the issue, and whatever effect the
slogan "He Kept Us Out of War" had on the outcome, it has vividly
marked the election for historians.

Yet 1916 was not solely the election that occurred during World
War I. It was a referendum on four years of far-reaching progressive
legislation and on the progressive Democratic party that had evolved
since 1896. As the campaign progressed, both sides appeared to talk
less about foreign issues and more about what they considered either
the substantial achievements or the disastrous excesses of the New
Freedom, particularly on labor and the tariff. Whereas the war was
clearly a significant issue, it was hardly rhetorically dominant. And unless the politicians and voters were saying and hearing one thing and
thinking another, it is hard to see how the war could be said to have
saved Wilson or relegated 1916 to the status of a deviating election outside the partisan realignment process.

The staunch conservatism propounded on Hughes's western tour, on
which he praised the American businessman and the protective tariff,

54. William Howard Taft to George Wickersham (October 15, 1916), in Arthur Link,
Wilson: Campaigns for Progressivism and Peace (Princeton: Princeton University Press,
1965), p. 140; Lawrence H. Fuchs, *The Political Behavior of American Jews* (Glencoe: Free
Press, 1956), p. 60; List of Jewish Appointments in Wilson Papers, Jews File, Library
of Congress.

55. Fuchs, ibid., p. 59; Hugh C. Wallace to Edward M. House (August 31, 1916), Wilson Papers, Library of Congress.

turned out to be the model of his campaign utterances. Hughes and other Republicans leaped upon the passage of the Adamson Act, and by mid-September the candidate had decided to focus on the tariff and the railroad eight-hour workday law for the rest of his campaign. Hughes denounced the latter as "government by holdup," and Frederick M. Davenport, a 1912 Progressive explaining to the readers of *Collier's* "Why the Country Needs Hughes," called it a "plain, sinister, and ominous surrender." But as October passed, and the odds favoring Hughes dropped, even the Adamson Act began to appear less often in GOP rhetoric, as Republicans realized that the issue was hurting them. ("If it had not been for the eight-hour day," complained one member of the Hughes executive committee, "the election would have been a walkover for the Republicans.") As election day approached, Republicans went even further back to basics, to what had worked before.[56]

"And so it comes about that Judge Hughes and his supporters have been drifting steadily toward the tariff issue," taunted the *Cleveland Plain Dealer*, calling it a confession of the failure of the foreign policy and labor issues. For whatever reason, the huge outburst of Republican newspaper advertising that closed the campaign focused heavily on the topic that had served the party since Reconstruction. Full page ads warned, "Back to the Breadline if Wilson's Tariff Is Not Repealed," and featured pictures of Hughes and all previous Republican presidents, above text indicating that the group was united on the tariff. On November 4, the *New York Times* carried two and a half pages of Republican protective tariff ads, and that night Hughes closed his campaign with an oration in Madison Square Garden on the subject.[57]

"The best was kept to the last," mocked the *Times*. "On Monday our ancient friend, the Tariff Scare, decrepit, tottering, his white beard sweeping to the ground . . . was supported on to the stage by the Republicans and exhibited to the compassion of spectators. . . . Hearing the antique formulas, you strain your eyes to see if the Bloody Shirt isn't flapping again in the winds of Republican eloquence, your ears to listening till the solemn chant of the Party that freed the slave, saved the Union, rolls from ghostly lips."[58]

To campaign observers, domestic issues seemed to grow more predominant the further west they looked, almost precinct by precinct, just

56. *New York Times* (September 16, 1916); Charles Evans Hughes, "Shall Force or Reason Rule?" *Independent* (October 9, 1916); Frederick M. Davenport, "Why the Country Needs Hughes," *Collier's* (October 21, 1916); *New York Times* (October 18, 1916).
57. *Cleveland Plain Dealer* (October 6, 1916); *New York Times* (November 4, 6, 1916).
58. *New York Times* (November 2, 1916).

as Wilson's prospects steadily rose in the same direction. "The entire section is prosperous," the Republican national committeeman from Nebraska complained about the Middle West. "The people have plenty of money, and advocacy of preparedness and criticism of President Wilson's vacillating foreign policy, important issues in other parts of the country, seem to have little effect there." West of the Mississippi, and outside of the ethnically diverse great cities, the oratory and lead editorials were much less likely to deal with foreign affairs. "Coming directly from the far west to New York City," marveled Arthur Sears Henning, *Chicago Tribune* political correspondent, "I was struck immediately by the fact that I read next to nothing about Wilson having 'kept us out of the war.' The great conflict abroad is much more real to the people of the Atlantic seaboard than to the prairie states."[59]

Gradually, the despatches from the West are reaching historians. Meyer J. Nathan, in a vivid and insightful study of the election of 1916 in the Middle West, argues for the importance of domestic progressivism in the region and notes a strong class consciousness in the campaign. Robert Wilkins notes the extent to which North Dakota Democrats stressed economic issues, and in the most recent study of the election, Samuel D. Lovell maintains that Wilson's progressivism, not peace, was the crucial factor.[60]

Nothing illustrates the campaign's significance as the culmination of twenty years of Democratic progressivism more strikingly than the figure and role of William Jennings Bryan. Despite his split with Wilson over the war, which caused him to resign as secretary of state, Bryan made over 500 speeches throughout the West and Midwest for the president. "If I might be able to compare my work in different campaigns," Bryan wrote Wilson with his own guileless self-fascination, "I believe I am making a more convincing speech in your behalf than I have ever been able to make in support of my own candidacy." Bryan's perception was as accurate as it must have been painful; he himself could not have carried the states Wilson would, but nobody else could so effectively have reached the midwestern farmer or as persuasively have stumped Ohio, warning that Republican victory meant reactionary resurgence in state and nation. Bryan "did his duty like a man in the battle just ended," conceded a postelection editorial in the *Baltimore*

---

59. *New York Times* (July 27, 1916); *Chicago Tribune* (November 2, 1916).

60. Nathan, "The Presidential Election of 1916 in the Middle West"; Robert P. Wilkins, "Referendum on War? The General Election of 1916 in North Dakota," *North Dakota History* 36 (Fall 1969): 296–336; Samuel D. Lovell, *The Election of 1916* (Carbondale: Southern Illinois University Press, 1980), pp. 173–75.

Sun, which had failed to find anything as positive to say when the Commoner was himself a candidate. "And he did it in a section where his voice still counts."[61]

But Bryan could not claim credit for the one shift that more than anything else secured the West for Wilson. The administration's hunt for Bull Moose achieved its greatest results west of the plains, where large parts of the third party apparatus went over to Wilson, following a pattern set in 1914. In Colorado, Progressive leader Ed Costigan and his ally, Judge Ben Lindsey, endorsed Wilson and the Democratic candidate for governor. Former Wyoming governor Joseph Carey, a member of the Progressive party's National Executive Committee, and the secretary of the Montana party endorsed Wilson. In California, 1914 Progressive Senate candidate Francis Heney led a number of Moose into the Democratic camp, and the chairman of the Idaho Democratic party boasted, "We have with us a number of their strongest leaders." Many of the Washington state party leaders and past candidates endorsed Wilson, and Utah Progressives and Democrats joined on a single fusion ticket from electors to constable. In New Mexico, Republican Senator Albert Fall appealed to Roosevelt to intervene against such a fusion — New Mexico Progressives ultimately swallowed Hughes, but endorsed the state Democratic ticket — and by October was imploring the Rough Rider to come to New Mexico to hold the state. "If New Mexico is doubtful," commiserated the *New York Times* gloatingly, "what good man can believe in anything?"[62]

By then, the sharpening of the lines was driving some of the last of the Progressive reluctants off the fence. In mid-October, John M. Parker, who had been named the party's candidate for vice-president and had refused to withdraw when Roosevelt did, abandoned his campaign for his headless ticket and came out for Wilson. A few days later, the patriarchal social reformer, Washington Gladden, who had begun his political life by voting for Lincoln and had never voted Democratic,

61. Boyce House, "Bryan the Orator," *Illinois State Historical Society Journal* 53 (Autumn 1960): 279; William Jennings Bryan to Woodrow Wilson (October 8, 1916), Wilson Papers, Library of Congress; *Cleveland Plain Dealer* (October 24, 1916); *Baltimore Sun* (November 9, 1916).

62. Greenbaum, *Fighting Progressive*, pp. 80–83; *Denver Post* (November 1, 1916); *Salt Lake Tribune* (November 3, 1916); W. R. Hamilton to Thomas J. Walsh (October 10, 1916); Walsh Papers, Library of Congress; *New York Times* (August 7, 1916); John Edgarton to Thomas J. Walsh, (August 24, 1916); Andrieus A. Jones to Thomas J. Walsh (November 6, 1916), Walsh Papers, Library of Congress; Albert Fall to Theodore Roosevelt (August 3, 1916; October 1, 1916); Fall Papers, Huntington Library, San Marino, California; *New York Times* (October 6, 1916).

endorsed the president. President Garfield's sons, longtime prominent devotees of Theodore Roosevelt, split: James, Jr. followed his idol; Harry supported Wilson. In the October 21 *New Republic*, swallowing hard and citing "a reason which . . . a few years ago would have seemed to me incredible," Herbert Croly endorsed Wilson and the Democrats as the more reformist alternative. And in late October, Victor Murdock announced that he would vote for Wilson, a decision that the *Nation* called "particularly impressive at this time." The *New York Times* offered its own interpretation of the timing: Murdock had waited as late as he could for a reason to support Hughes.[63]

The nation's best-known Republican Progressive did not endorse Wilson. Yet, Robert La Follette came as close to violating his lifelong policy of grudging silence about Democratic progressivism as he ever would. He publicly backed neither candidate but praised the Underwood Tariff and the Adamson Act in his own reelection campaign. Democrats carried out their role in the unique relationship solicitously. As before, large numbers of them crossed over to vote for him in the Wisconsin Republican primary. Afterward, the Democratic candidate running against La Follette urged Wilson not to endorse him against the incumbent, and Bryan, campaigning in Wisconsin, made no mention of the Senate race. Although La Follette remained silent, the Madison *State Journal*, edited by a close ally, endorsed Wilson in late October. "Enemies have unkindly remarked that La Follette was sitting on the fence," noted the *Nation*. "But the fence would seem to be located fifty yards inside Woodrow Wilson's lot."[64]

The Wilsonians had largely achieved what they had set out to do: make the election a clear-cut contest between right and left. The defections of Irish and German Democrats complicated the division, but the administration's successful recruitment of prominent Progressives (and Socialists), the apparent enthusiasm of labor, and Hughes's intensifying reversion to Gilded Age Republicanism structured the voter's choice exactly as the Democrats had hoped and planned. "During the campaign," mused the *New Republic* afterward, "the Republican leaders allowed President Wilson to attach in the popular mind Democracy with

63. *The Public* (October 20, 27, 1916); *New Republic* (October 21, 1916); *Nation* (October 26, 1916); *New York Times* (October 24, 1916).

64. *New York Times* (September 9, 1916); Nathan, "The Presidential Campaign of 1916 in the Middle West," p. 119; *New York World* (October 31, 1916); Richard L. Jones to John Sharp Williams (November 16, 1916), Williams Papers, Library of Congress; *Nation* (October 12, 1916).

progressivism and Republicanism with conservatism." Not since 1896 had the choices been so sharp; not until 1936 would they be again.[65]

Conservatives as well as progressives saw the contest in such terms. "The businessmen are thoroughly aroused here," reported William E. Dodd from Chicago; "they are alarmed somewhat as they were in October, 1896, and they are pouring money into the close states in great quantities." Mrs. J. Borden Harriman counted fewer than a half-dozen Wilson supporters in the wealth-stricken resort of Newport, and in Denver a Democrat found that "in the clubs and the business world there is very strong sentiment against us." But despite the resulting financial imbalance—Democrats financed their campaign only by going deeply into debt and yet could give their state committees only half what the Republican National Committee allotted—House claimed to be calm. "It is true we have organized wealth against us, and in such an aggregate as never before," he told his diary in early November. "On the other hand, we are pitting organized labor against it, and the fight is not an unfair one."[66]

The alliance with the unions, with roots stretching from the first Bryan campaign to the Adamson Act, not only helped define the choice—and the party—but it was also expected to compensate for the party's other weaknesses. (Wyoming, estimated one western Democrat, was the kind of state Wilson could win: it had 2500 railroad workers and no Germans.) Possibly because of this need, Democratic rhetoric became ever more Bryanite, ever more strident in its appeals to class consciousness. By early November, the *World* warned that "all the forces of greed in the United States, all the forces of private interest, all the forces of plutocracy" were for Hughes, and Wilson offered his own definition of the choice: "The Republican Party offers the people masters. We offer them comrades and friends."[67]

Even the *Baltimore Sun*, most conservative of the major Democratic papers and three times a bolter from Bryan, sounded a different tone, as though this election was the kind that might cause voters to recon-

65. *New Republic* (November 18, 1916).

66. William E. Dodd to Edward M. House (October 12, 1916), House Papers; Mrs. J. Borden Harriman, *From Pinafores to Politics* (New York: Henry Holt and Co., 1923), p. 203; Huston Thompson to Cary Grayson (July 1916), Wilson Papers, Library of Congress; *Hearings before a Subcommittee of the Committee on Privileges and Elections, United States Senate*, 2 vols. (Washington: 1921), I:536–42; Louise Overacker, *Money in Elections* (New York: Macmillan, 1932), p. 73; House Diary (November 2, 1916), House Papers.

67. Fred Dubois to Thomas J. Walsh (October 1, 1916), Walsh Papers, Library of Congress; *New York World* (November 1, 1916).

sider partisan alliances. "The great division is not upon the handling of the controversy with Germany, or the conduct of relations with Mexico, although these matters are playing important parts," assessed its political correspondent; "the great division is upon the ancient issue of whether the spirit and tone of the government should favor the great body of the people of the 'select' classes."[68] An election on that issue — or, in less partisan phrasing, on the clear and acknowledged identities of the two major parties — could be a realigning election.

Although it might later have seemed ironic, many of the stunned observers of the 1916 results did think they had seen not a deviation but a fundamental shift in American politics. Not only had the Democrats won their first victory in a two-party contest since Grover Cleveland, but Wilson had run powerfully in areas where the terms *Democrat* and *winning* were not commonly used together. Not only did he carry three states (California, Ohio, and New Hampshire) never before Democratic in a two-party election, but he also brought 200 new counties into the party column for the first time, including 10 in genetically Republican Pennsylvania. The long wait for, and narrow decision in, California had minimized Wilson's national popular plurality of half a million votes.

"McCormick says that the vote in the electoral college made the election of 1916 a closer thing than it really was," Ray Stannard Baker later noted while researching his biography of Wilson. "He suggested a study of the New England vote, saying that a change of 25,000 votes in New England would have brought the states into the Wilson column." Similar small switches would have brought Wilson the electoral votes of another half-dozen states. If the Democrats narrowly avoided defeat, they also narrowly missed an electoral landslide.[69]

But even without the landslide, many observers still felt they had witnessed something remarkable. Wilson's reelection, breathed the *New Republic*, was "one of the most extraordinary achievements in the political annals of the United States." They were startled and impressed not only by what Wilson had won — virtually the entire West, Ohio, and New Hampshire in addition to the faithful South — but also by what he had lost, all of the traditional swing states where Democrats since Samuel Tilden had sought the formula for national victory. In this sense, the election of 1916 marked the final end of the Gilded Age, of the Grover Cleveland New York-and-Indiana campaign strategies. The

68. *Baltimore Sun* (October 15, 1916).
69. Memo of conversation with Vance McCormick (September 12, 1930), Ray Stannard Baker Papers.

tradition's demise was utterly unexpected: all the lists of possible and probable states swapped among Democrats before the election had paid tribute to it, and even after the national leaders had decided that New York was probably lost, they continued to send money to the state, aware that to do otherwise would be seen as conceding the entire election. "If anyone had said two days ago that a Democratic Presidential candidate could lose New York, New Jersey, Connecticut, Illinois, Indiana and Wisconsin and still be elected," gloated the *Baltimore Sun*, "he would have been accounted a first-class idiot."[70]

The result was a victory not only for Wilson and the Democrats but also for the West as a region; the *Denver Post* jubilantly headlined "The Rise of a New Political Empire." But to many such as Bryan, the regional nature of the victory underlined rather than detracted from its status as a progressive triumph. "In the alignment between the West and the South," wrote Daniel Roper to Wilson, "we have united the two real Democratic sections of the country and eliminated the plutocracy of wealth." No more, he continued happily, would progressive Democrats have to go hat in hand to New York for its approval. The party, and progressivism, had been liberated.[71]

But, to a number of other observers, the meaning of Wilson's victory went even deeper than sectionalism. "The alignment of states on the physical map of the country is only an accident," maintained the *Nation*. "The change is one of soul, not of region. This we see when we note how shrunken majorities and low estate of the Republican party in New England compare to the astonishing returns from the Western States. It is deep answering to deep. The verdict is in both sections against the standpat policies of the Republicans, and the sit-tight campaign of Mr. Hughes." A month later, the journal added, "it is plain that there are numbers of men who before 1912 expected to live and die Republicans, but who are now balancing in their minds their future party allegiances."[72]

Few would deny that the war issue, pitting the vaguely antiwar position of Wilson against the muddled stance of Hughes, had played a role in the campaign. To the extent that it did, Republicans could console themselves with the idea that the result was ephemeral, that the next time there was an election and no war the electorate would revert to

70. *New Republic* (November 11, 1916); Robert Woolley, "Politics Is Hell," Chapter 23, Woolley Papers; *Baltimore Sun* (November 9, 1916).

71. *Denver Post* (November 9, 11, 1916); Daniel C. Roper to Woodrow Wilson (November 10, 1916), House Papers.

72. *Nation* (November 9, 1916; December 14, 1916).

its normal Republican nature. But to many, Wilson's appeal to the voters seemed not a brief wartime flirtation but a meaningful relationship based upon the reformist nature of the Democratic party and the conservative image that Hughes had obligingly borne. Wilson's victory had less to do with developments in Europe in 1916 than with developments in the Democratic party in the preceding twenty years and in the Wilson administration in the preceding four, both underlined by a campaign in which the two sides ended up in the precise position the Wilsonians had planned. A look at the states that made up Wilson's majority clearly demonstrates the crucial role played by Democratic progressivism and the credibility of the party's reform identity.

"While the East has been thinking in terms of the European war," explained Colorado Progressive leader Ed Costigan after the election, "the Progressives of the West have considered domestic peace and justice of greater importance, and have voted accordingly." Costigan's home state was the leading Wilson state outside the South, giving him 60.7 percent of its vote; the Rocky Mountain region provided four of the president's top states outside the Confederacy (see Table 7.1) and seven of his top nine, generally with percentages high enough to be accounted landslides. Moreover, the result in the Rockies was a party victory; Democrats won all six governorships contested in the region and all six Senate seats, a gain of three, which partially balanced eastern losses and allowed the party to keep control of the upper house. These striking regional returns, which have received little historical notice, were achieved by the persistent recitation of the Wilson reform record and by attracting to the Democratic standard members of three major Mountain voting groups: Bull Moosers, Socialists, and Mormons.[73]

When Mountain Bull Moosers looked for alternatives following the collapse of their own party, they saw a regional Democratic party that had been progressive not since Wilson but since Bryan, a Democratic party without the immigrant taint that eastern Progressives found so disturbing. This attractiveness had already led, in 1914, to Progressive party endorsement of Democratic candidates in Utah, Idaho, and Wyoming and to Progressive gubernatorial candidate Costigan's endorsement of a Democratic congressman in Colorado. In 1916, it led to support of Wilson by Progressive leaders in all those states as well as Montana, and sharp Democratic increases in the counties most strongly for Roosevelt in 1912. In only four states in the country — Idaho, Utah,

73. *New York Times* (November 11, 1916). For a more detailed account of the election in the mountain states, see David Sarasohn, "The Election of 1916: Realigning the Rockies," *Western Historical Quarterly* II (July 1980): 285–305.

Table 7.1 States (outside the Confederacy) with Highest Wilson Percentages

	%		%
Colorado	60.7	Wyoming	54.6
Utah	58.8	Nevada	53.4
Arizona	57.2	Maryland	52.8
Montana	56.9	Idaho	52.0
Nebraska	55.3		

Montana, and Wyoming—did the Democrats actually increase their percentage of the two-party vote over 1912. Clearly, something had created what the *Independent* later called "the conviction on the part of Western Progressives, who are more radical and warm-hearted than their Eastern brothers, that Mr. Wilson was more their kind of a progressive than Mr. Hughes, and the belief that the Democratic party under Mr. Wilson is the party of progress."[74]

Wilson was equally persuasive with the region's numerous Socialists. Four Mountain states had given Eugene Debs more than 10 percent of their vote in 1912, and three were among his top four states. But, as elsewhere, the Socialist vote crumbled in 1916, and counties where Debs had run especially well now showed a sharp surge for Wilson. (See Table 7.2). Meyer Nathan found a similar sharp shift in the Midwest, and Wilson also gained notably among New York Socialists.[75]

In several Mountain states, however, neither of these gains would have been enough without Wilson's other achievement, getting the Saints to come marching into his column. The Mormons had been solidly Republican since 1900, when church leaders, still fearful of federal persecution, had made a deal with McKinley manager Mark Hanna. They had even remained faithful to the luckless Taft, bringing him Utah and nearly Idaho in 1912 (see Table 7.3). But the Wilson adminis-

74. *Nation* (August 6, 1916); Henry J. Peterson, "Wyoming: A Cattle Kingdom," in Thomas C. Donnelly, ed., *Rocky Mountain Politics* (Albuquerque: University of New Mexico Press, 1940), pp. 132–36; Jan Shipps, "Utah Comes of Age Politically: A Study of the State's Politics in the Early Years of the Twentieth Century," *Utah Historical Quarterly* 35 (Spring 1967):108–109; Greenbaum, *Fighting Progressive*, p. 67; Louis H. Bean, *How to Predict Elections* (New York: Alfred A. Knopf, 1948), p. 84; *Independent* (November 20, 1916).

75. Nathan, "The Presidential Election of 1916 in the Middle West," pp. 266–67.

Table 7.2 Vote of Counties Most Strongly for Debs in 1912 and 1916

		Democrat	Republican	Progressive	Socialist
Arizona (2 counties)	1912	38.8	9.8	27.2	24.2
	1916	63.1	26.9		10.1*
Idaho (1 county)	1912	25.4	17.1	30.0	26.8
	1916	52.0	36.8		11.3*
Montana (2 counties)	1912	37.9	19.0	15.6	27.6
	1916	60.0	31.7		8.4
Nevada (5 counties)	1912	37.3	19.2	24.7	24.2
	1916	50.8	34.0		14.5

*Arizona and Idaho Socialist figures include Prohibition vote.

Table 7.3 Vote of Mormon Counties in 1912 and 1916

	% Mormon		Democrat	Republican	Progressive
Arizona (*Graham County*)	71.5	1912	51.4	9.8	23.1
		1916	70.8	22.0	
Idaho (Mormon counties*)	85.0	1912	30.4	47.9	13.0
		1916	55.0	41.5	
Nevada (*Clark County*)	80.3	1912	42.8	13.1	31.5
		1916	60.2	28.5	
Wyoming (*Big Horn County*)	78.0	1912	30.8	35.4	26.5
		1916	53.9	44.7	
Utah	91.8	1912	32.7	37.6	21.6
		1916	58.8	37.8	

*Seven counties in 1912; subdivided into twelve by 1916.
Source: Statistics from U.S. Bureau of the Census, *Religious Bodies, 1916* (Washington, D.C.: Government Printing Office, 1919).

tration managed to persuade Mormons that they could be as safe under a Democratic administration as under the Republicans (one non-Mormon Democrat complained to McAdoo by 1914 that the Utah federal offices were "practically thoroughly Mormonized"), and the church actively proclaimed its neutrality. The result was not only a sweeping landslide in Utah — Democrats won the governorship, a Senate seat, both House seats, and practically the entire state legislature — but also crucial help in Idaho and Wyoming. The church's Republican alliance and political influence relaxed notably; even when, in 1932 and 1936, it again endorsed GOP candidates for the White House, Utah voters failed to follow its advice.[76]

In the Rockies, the election of 1916 reshaped more than Mormon perspectives. Throughout the 1920s, Democratic voting remained high in the region, which became the party's strongest source of governorships and Senate seats outside the South (see Table 7.4). The steady new supply of Democrats from the Rockies helped save the Senate Democrats of the 1920s from their role in the first decade of the century, that of a hopelessly outnumbered Confederate alumni society. And with the return of Democratic prosperity in 1932, the Mountain men were the only nonsoutherners in the Senate with any seniority; they chaired the Foreign Relations, Judiciary, and Public Lands Committees and held three of the top six places on the Appropriations Committee.[77] Such a legacy could hardly stem from Wilson's pledge to stay out of World War I, which at least by 1922 must have lost much of its force. And, even in 1916, there is reason to suspect, from editorials and campaign speeches, that the cannons' roar sounded more faintly in the West.

The same observation seemed to apply in California, even further from the front. But a separate legend has grown up about Wilson's hairsbreadth victory there, suggesting that Hughes's snub of Johnson in Long Beach alienated the progressive governor, causing his followers to give the state and the election to Wilson in a crisp rebuke to bad manners. But, as George Mowry pointed out long ago, California Progressives were less affronted by Hughes's manners than his politics. "The result in California turned, really as the result in the entire west

76. Arthur Wallace Dunn, *From Harrison to Harding*, 2 vols. (New York: Putnam's, 1922), II:340; C. P. Overfield to William G. McAdoo (September 10, 1914), McAdoo Papers; *Deseret Evening News* (October 16, 1916); J. C. Thompson, Jr., of the *Cheyenne Tribune*, quoted in *Literary Digest* (November 18, 1916).

77. *Congressional Directory*, 72nd Congress (Washington: Government Printing Office, 1933).

Table 7.4   Senate Seats and Governorships Held by
Each Party, by Region

Following the Election of		1920	1922	1924	1926	1928	1930
Senate:							
Mountain (8)	D	7	8	8	9	8	9
	R	9	8	8	7	8	7
North (23)	D	4	7	6	8	5	9
	R	42	39	40	38	41	37
Border (6)	D	4	6	4	8	4	7
	R	8	6	8	4	8	5
Governorships:							
Mountain	D	1	5	6	4	3	6
	R	7	3	2	4	5	2
North	D	1	8	4	4	2	6
	R	22	15	19	19	21	17
Border	D	2	2	3	3	2	2
	R	4	4	3	3	4	4

did, upon the real progressivism of the progressives," Secretary of the Interior Franklin K. Lane, a Californian, wrote after the election. "It was not pique because Johnson was not recognized . . . Johnson could not deliver California. Johnson made very strong speeches for Hughes."[78]

California labor, strongly behind Johnson in his own campaigns, spurned his advice on the presidential vote. Michael Rogin has pointed out the importance of labor in Wilson's carrying the state, noting that Wilson ran better in California cities than any Democrat since Bryan. Wilson carried strongly unionized San Francisco by more than 15,000 votes, four times his statewide majority, and a recent study finds that labor voting for Wilson was heavy. Fifty years later, Jack Weinberger of the Hotel and Restaurant Employees and Bartenders Union remem-

78. George Mowry, *The California Progressives* (Berkeley: University of California Press, 1951), p. 274; Franklin K. Lane to Frank I. Cobb (November 11, 1916), in Anne Wintermute Lane, ed., *The Letters of Franklin K. Lane*, 2 vols. (Boston: Houghton Mifflin Co., 1922) II:227.

bered the incident motivating Bay Area unionists as vividly as contemporaries reported it: on Hughes's California trip, before he ever got to Long Beach, the Republican candidate had crossed a San Francisco picket line to address a conservative GOP gathering. This attitude, compared with Wilson's record—and the steady progressive stance of the California Democratic party, from Lane's own campaign for governor (as a "Roosevelt Democrat") in 1902 to James Phelan's surprise election to the Senate in 1914—crystallized the choice and brought both unionists and Bull Moosers to Wilson's standard. The new coalition not only carried the state for Wilson, but it also reelected four Democratic congressmen.[79]

Labor, and a deeply rooted Democratic progressive position, were also decisive in Wilson's landslide victory in Ohio, a state that gave him twice as many electoral votes as California but has not received half as much attention. "What put Ohio in the Democratic column?" asked the *St. Louis Republic* after the votes were counted. "The influence of a man who, being dead, yet speaketh—Tom Johnson." Johnson had never managed to rise from the Cleveland mayoralty to higher office himself, but his influence on the party had fostered the reformist state administrations of Judson Harmon and James Cox. In 1916, Cox regained the governorship; Johnson's old ally, Atlee Pomerene, was reelected to the Senate; and Johnson's successor as mayor, Newton Baker, was Wilson's Secretary of War. "The electorate of this state," one Ohio Democrat proudly wrote Bryan after the election, "has become fairly imbued with the spirit of real progressivism." The editors of the Taft family's *Cincinnati Times-Star* expressed it differently. "There is a large radical element in Ohio," they explained sourly to the *Literary Digest*, "which went largely for Wilson."[80]

Democrats had been fairly confident of Ohio, but few had expected anything like the size of the triumph: Wilson by 90,000, victory for Pomerene and Cox, and the gain of four seats in the House. Labor was crucial, with large margins in Toledo, Columbus, and Johnson's Cleveland overbalancing sharp losses among Cincinnati's Germans. But Wil-

79. Michael Rogin, "Progressivism and the California Electorate," *Journal of American History* 55 (September 1968): 308–309; Gladwin Hill, *Dancing Bear, An Inside Look at California Politics* (Cleveland: World, 1968), p. 64; Thomas R. Clark, "The Voting Behavior of the San Francisco Working Class," *California History* 66 (September 1987): 204–205; Robert E. Hennings, *James D. Phelan and the Wilson Progressives of California* (New York and London: Garland, 1985), pp. 128–45.

80. *St. Louis Republic* (November 9, 1916); M. L. Beard to William Jennings Bryan (November 18, 1916), Bryan Papers, Library of Congress; *Literary Digest* (November 18, 1916).

son also gained among Ohio's Bull Moosers; Hoyt Warner points out that although most party leaders returned to the GOP, the Democrats "gained more ballots from the collapse of the Progressive party than they had lost in its formation." The final tallies not only gave the Democrats a much pleasanter 1916, but they also seemed to promise more in the future: "We are making Ohio," boasted one inhabitant, "a thoroughly reliable Democratic state."[81]

Although historians have been unimpressed, contemporaries were perhaps most awed by Wilson's performance in a region that he lost — New England. "New England's rock-ribbed Republicanism almost cracked under the strain of the trend toward Wilson," breathlessly reported Hearst's International News Service. "Republican pluralities of earlier years dwindled till they almost disappeared." Since 1896, the region's Democratic party — never robust — had shown only the faintest signs of life; in the four presidential elections from 1896 to 1908, the six states had provided twenty-four Republican avalanches, and even in 1912 Wilson had won less than 38 percent of the region's vote. But four years later, he won better than 46 percent to Hughes's 51 percent, carried New Hampshire, and helped elect Rhode Island's first Democratic senator since 1859. Wilson even carried one county in Vermont.[82]

Perhaps the most striking aspect of the showing is that it was achieved with virtually no effort by the Wilson high command. The national leaders had written off the region, and in late October the *New York World* mourned "the heavy dullness of the campaign in Massachusetts." Local Democratic leaders found their pleas for help met with a disbelieving deafness, no matter how strongly they phrased them. "If it could be shown to you or President's advisors," wired Boston port collector Edmund Billings, "that there is a real chance to carry this state if President came to Boston for one speech would there be chance of having him Friday night?" There was not, but Wilson still came within four percentage points of Hughes in the state. John F. Fitzgerald, the Democratic candidate against Senator Henry Cabot Lodge, was considered a political has-been who got the nomination only because no one else wanted it; the strength of his showing, on Wilson's coattails, revitalized his career. By 1930, even Wilson's Democratic National Committee chairman, Vance McCormick, realized that an opportunity

81. Hoyt P. Warner, *Progressivism in Ohio, 1897–1917* (Columbus: Ohio State University Press, 1964), pp. 480–81; Arthur P. Black to John Sharp Williams (November 9, 1916), Williams Papers, Library of Congress.

82. *Los Angeles Examiner* (November 10, 1916); Erwin L. Levine, *Theodore Francis Green: The Rhode Island Years 1906–1936* (Providence: Brown University Press, 1963), p. 76.

had been missed. "We made the mistake of our lives in not putting on a strong campaign in New England, especially in Massachusetts," he told Ray Stannard Baker. "We thought it hopeless, but I think a vigorous campaign would have carried two or three of the states."[83]

Wilson, it seemed, restored to the party a respectability it had lacked since the emergence of Bryan and made it possible again to be at once a Democrat and a Yankee. But here as well, the process had been a cumulative one, surfacing earlier in the election of Democratic governors in Massachusetts, Connecticut, and Maine in 1910. With minimal Republican insurgency in the region, George Mowry points out, "the rebel spirit was funnelled off into the Democratic opposition." The Wilsonian synthesis of rebellion and respectability benefited not only Wilson but subsequent Democrats: two years later, David Walsh was elected the first Democratic Senator from Massachusetts.[84]

It is impossible, of course, to know exactly how much of Wilson's strength in 1916 came from progressivism and how much from the war issue. But the war did play a demonstrably negative role in his showing, costing him the votes of many thousands of ethnic Democrats and probably several states. Arthur Link has maintained that, ultimately, German and Irish defections were unimportant, but this can be true only in the sense that Wilson won despite them. The disaffection of ethnic Democrats sharply limited the size and nature of his victory.[85]

Admittedly, Wilson did not suffer the kind of sweeping German and Irish apostasy that Democratic leaders had feared during the campaign. Nor were the losses universal; in some areas, such as St. Louis and Baltimore, German Democrats maintained their usual levels. (The *Baltimore Sun*, which had warned daily about the Prussian threat for two months, offered "sincere . . . regret for its misapprehensions.") But through much of the country, alienated ethnic Democrats, especially Germans, repudiated Wilson in numbers large enough to affect outcomes. "In the great majority of cases," reports Meyer Nathan on the Middle West, "Wilson either lost support among German Americans

83. *New York World* (October 29, 1916); Edmund Billings to Edward M. House (October 30, 1916), House Papers; John Henry Cutler, *"Honey Fitz"* (Indianapolis: Bobbs-Merrill, 1962), p. 212; Michael E. Hennessey, *Four Decades of Massachusetts Politics* (Norwood: Norwood Press, 1935), p. 243; Memo of conversation with Vance McCormick (September 12, 1930), Ray Stannard Baker Papers, Library of Congress. See also William F. Murray to Edward M. House (October 12, 1916), House Papers.

84. George Mowry, *The Era of Theodore Roosevelt* (New York: Harper and Row, 1958), p. 79.

85. Link, *Campaigns for Progressivism and Peace*, p. 161.

or did not gain support among them as substantially as he did among other voters.[86]

Looking at 110 midwestern counties with sizable German populations, Nathan found that in 44 of them Wilson ran worse in 1916 than he did in the three-sided contest of 1912, and in fifty-three he ran worse than Bryan had run in 1908 — at the same time that, in other counties, he was running ahead of all previous Democratic standards. These were counties that had been, in many cases, the backbones of Democratic strength in their area, counties where defeat or even narrow victory would be normally fatal to Democratic hopes statewide.[87]

Perhaps the most vivid example of Wilson's German defeats, and their costs, is provided by Wisconsin. The Democrats made a strong effort for the state, where they had elected a senator two years before and could count upon a strong appeal to labor, insurgent Republicans, and Milwaukee Socialists as well as the benign neutrality of La Follette. But, throughout the campaign, the warnings of rural German anger grew, and by election day the leaders knew the state was lost. Table 7.5, showing the voting record of the five most heavily German counties in the state, indicates why: traditionally an oasis of solid Democratic majorities in a Republican state, in 1916, German areas suddenly voted more Republican than the state as a whole.[88]

Democrats could count similar defections, with similar effects, in other states. Next door in Minnesota, which Wilson lost by one-tenth of 1 percentage point, the morning-after telegram from the state's Wilson volunteer chairman read simply, "Country German communities disappointing." He might have been thinking of Brown County, which had gone for Bryan in 1908 but now gave Wilson 31.6 percent, or Stearns, which had three times given the Commoner landslides (61.6, 61.3, and 56.8 percent) but now cast 54.4 percent of its votes for Hughes. Clifton Phillips notes German bolting from Wilson in Indiana, which he lost by less than 1 percent of the vote, and where one Democrat reported German ministers circulating anti-Wilson handbills. The *New York World* suggested that German defections in the Fort Wayne area had hurt Wilson seriously, and the returns illustrate the point: Fort Wayne's county, Allen, one of the most German in the

86. *Baltimore Sun* (November 9, 1916); Nathan, "The Presidential Election of 1916 in the Middle West," pp. 259–60.

87. Nathan, ibid., pp. 259–60.

88. Report on Wisconsin (November 4, 1916), McAdoo Papers; Richard L. Jones to John Sharp Williams (November 16, 1916), Williams Papers, Library of Congress.

Table 7.5 German Voting in Wisconsin, 1908–1916

	Statewide		Five Most German Counties	
	Republican	Democrat	Republican	Democrat
1908 (P)	54.5	36.7	44.6	52.4
1910 (G)	59.4	40.6	39.4	60.6
1912 (P)	32.7	41.1	30.9	55.0
1914 (G)	54.1	45.9	44.0	56.0
1916 (P)	49.4	42.8	52.5	43.6

P = Presidential vote, based on total vote, data from Edgar E. Robinson, *Presidential Elections, 1896–1932* (Stanford: Stanford University Press, 1933).
G = Gubernatorial vote, based on two-party vote alone, data from *World Almanac*.
Counties: Dodge, Green Lake, Jefferson, Marathon, Ozaukee.

state, had voted three times for Bryan, by increasing margins each time; now it went for Hughes, with a sharply increased Socialist vote. Oregon's Democratic chairman complained that "the deep-seated antagonism of the German population, especially the German Catholic population," had lost the state, and the International News Service suggested the same about South Dakota.[89]

The tide did not stop at the borders of states Wilson won. In North Dakota, where Republican chairman William Lemke had pushed the issue hard, the Republican showing in the seven most German counties rose from 27.3 percent in 1912 to 61.8 percent in 1916; in two heavily German towns, Wilson won 2 and 9 percent. The exception to Wilson's sweep of Ohio was what the *Cleveland Plain Dealer* called "a surprising majority" for Hughes in Cincinnati's Hamilton County, where Wilson trailed the state ticket throughout the German wards.[90]

89. Z. H. Austin to Thomas J. Walsh (November 8, 1916), Walsh Papers, Library of Congress; Clifton Phillips, *Indiana in Transition* (Indianapolis: Indiana Historical Bureau and Indiana Historical Society, 1968), p. 125; H. H. Lehman to Thomas J. Walsh (November 4, 1916), Walsh Papers, Library of Congress, *New York World* (November 10, 1916); Samuel White to Thomas J. Walsh (November 15, 1916); Walsh Papers, Library of Congress; *Los Angeles Examiner* (November 9, 1916).

90. Edward C. Blackorby, *Prairie Rebel, the Public Life of William Lemke* (Lincoln: University of Nebraska Press, 1963), pp. 48–54; Robert P. Wilkins, "Referendum on War? The General Election of 1916 in North Dakota," p. 329; *Cleveland Plain Dealer* (November 8, 1916).

The defection of the urban Irish from the party of their fathers is more difficult to demonstrate. William O'Leary has argued that the Irish rebellion was insignificant, because Wilson carried the Irish wards and in fact ran better there than other Democratic presidential candidates had. But this is asking the wrong question. Democrats normally won (and needed, for any prospect of city or state victory) large majorities among the Irish, and for Wilson to run better in their wards than the aggressively pietistic Bryan or the hapless Parker would hardly be an indication of enthusiasm of very much use to him. In Chicago's 30th ward, the most Irish of the five Chicago wards O'Leary cites, Wilson did indeed win, with 58.5 percent of the vote. But the Democratic candidates for senator in 1914 and 1918 won 64 percent and 65.4 percent, respectively, and in elections for city clerk—a position in which the organization took a particular interest—the 30th ward went Democratic by 74.2 percent in 1913 and 77.5 percent in 1917.[91]

Wilson's difficulties appeared most vividly, and worse than had been expected, in New York City. With the treaty with Tammany, Democratic leaders had hoped for an old-time Democratic majority in the city, with the *New York World* estimating a margin of 97,000. Instead, Wilson carried the city by less than 40,000, despite huge majorities in the Jewish districts. One source of his problems was evident: in the assembly districts with the highest Irish and German populations, the Democratic percentages dropped off notably from the assembly elections of the year before.[92]

The immediate reaction of many Wilsonians, who in the manner of reformers tended to vest their opposition with limitless reach and powers, was that Tammany had knifed the president. Certainly, given the history of Wilson-Murphy diplomatic relations over the past four years, numerous Tammany tigers felt a coolness toward the Princetonian. But the machine defended itself persuasively. "The President got the top vote here in this city, as against a lesser vote for our own candidates, and he got a big vote," one New York leader wrote McAdoo. "Tammany could not control the Germans of its own party, whom Frank Cobb [editor of the *World*] called every day agents of the Kaiser if they dared vote for any other save Wilson." Tammanyites also cited Wilson's similar difficulties across the river, in Frank Hague's heavily Irish and German Hudson County. "The fact is," the *Chicago Tribune*

91. William M. Leary, Jr., "Woodrow Wilson, Irish-Americans, and the Election of 1916," *Journal of American History* 54 (June 1967): 57–72.
92. *New York World* (November 5, 1916); Wesser, *A Response to Progressivism*, p. 189.

232 · The Wilson Coalition

had explained just before the election, "neither [Buffalo Democratic boss] Connors nor Murphy could engage to deliver their organizations to Wilson without breeding revolt among their normally faithful adherents."[93]

Two years before, the Tammany-allied Democratic governor of New York had plaintively written an administration official of the need for "cooperation between your friends and my friends" if the Democrats were going to carry the state. Between the war and the ongoing party battles, such alliance was impossible in 1914 and 1916, and Democratic division and defeat in New York and the other eastern states was the result. But in 1918, a less favorable Democratic year nationally, candidates emerged who were acceptable both to the ethnic organization Democrats and to those for whom Wilson had made the party respectable, and the results were notable: Al Smith was elected governor of New York, David Walsh senator from Massachusetts, and James Cox reelected governor of Ohio. A year later, Edward Edwards added the governorship of New Jersey.[94]

But disaffection among many ethnic Democratic voters had made such victories impossible for Wilson in 1916. From the Irish West Side of New York City to the rural German counties of the Midwest, the war stripped him of Democratic votes—by the *New Republic's* estimate, half a million. It might also have hurt him among eastern Progressives, who had strong cultural and emotional ties with England and the Allies and thought they heard in Hughes's statements a stronger commitment to that side. "I would have been for Wilson for 1916," claimed Bull Mooser Harold Ickes (much) subsequently, "if I hadn't been persuaded that his re-election would mean that England and France and all they had meant to our civilization might go to the dogs for all that we might do." Rather than Wilson being reelected because "he kept us out of war," it seems more likely that the war nearly evicted him from the White House.[95]

It also gave a deceptively rural complexion to Wilson's coalition, and obscured one of his more notable achievements. It has become an article of faith that the Democrats' appeal to urban voters was largely created by Al Smith in 1928, an impression greatly stimulated by an article

93. Joseph Johnson to William G. McAdoo (November 13, 1916), McAdoo Papers; *New York Times* (November 9, 1916); *Chicago Tribune* (November 4, 1916).

94. Martin Glynn to Joseph P. Tumulty (May 18, 1914), Tumulty Papers; Wesser, *A Response to Progressivism*, pp. 225–27.

95. *New Republic* (November 11, 1916); Harold Ickes, *Autobiography of a Curmudgeon* (New York: Reynal and Hitchcock, 1937), p. 184.

comparing Democratic votes in 1928 and 1920. But outside the Northeast, where Wilson had his greatest urban war losses, his urban record
was hardly embarrassing. Wilson carried Baltimore, Cleveland,
Minneapolis–St. Paul, Kansas City, Denver, and Seattle – all of which
Smith would lose twelve years later; he ran better than Smith in San
Francisco, which both won, and Detroit, which both lost; and he
ran only slightly worse than Smith in Cook County, Illinois. Despite
the look of the election map, there was an urban component in the Wilson coalition.[96]

On the day after the election – or more accurately, three days after
the election, when the winner was finally definite – Wilson found himself not only reelected over a single Republican opponent but at the
head of an implausibly united Democratic party, which had established
its identity as the nation's reform party and shown convincing strength
in previously unpromising territory. The party's future looked bright.
The long years of minority status seemed over.

It did not, of course, work out that way. The Democrats lost control
of Congress in 1918 and were turned out of the White House two years
later in as utter a repudiation as an incumbent party has ever suffered.
Two more Republican landslides followed, in 1924 and 1928, and only
the Great Depression returned the party to national power.

Unsurprisingly, historians have looked at the Republican 1920s and
concluded that 1916 was a "deviating" election, that the Democratic
victories of the Progressive Era were aberrations. Political historians
who concur on little else are in perfect accord that "the voting shift
of the Progressive years were in fact transitory in nature," that "the
success of the Democrats in 1912 and 1916 should not be taken as a
sign of fundamental change in voter preference." The traditional view,
David Burner sums up, is that the Democrats of the Progressive Era
enjoyed "success disproportionate to their basic political resources," a
success that provided only a brief interruption to the Republican "System of '96" that lasted until Franklin Roosevelt.[97]

96. Carl N. Degler, "American Political Parties and the Rise of the City: An Interpretation," *Journal of American History* 51 (June 1964): Wilson did, however, run much worse
than Smith would in New York, Boston, Philadelphia, and St. Louis.

97. Howard W. Allen and Jerome Clubb, "Progressive Reform and the Political System," *Pacific Northwest Quarterly* 65 (July 1974): 143–44; Degler, ibid, p. 50; Jerome
Clubb, William H. Flanigan, and Nancy H. Zingale, *Partisan Realignment* (Beverly Hills
and London: Sage, 1980), p. 175; James L. Sundquist, *Dynamics of the Party System* (Washington: Brookings Institution, 1973), p. 165; David Burner, *The Politics of Provincialism:
The Democratic Party in Transition, 1918–1932* (New York: Alfred A. Knopf, 1968), p. 33.

This perception of the evanescence of Democratic strength has vividly colored ideas of just what was there in the first place, what progressive politics was like before 1916. "The Progressive Era came and went without any such [politically realigning] upheaval. The distribution of party strength when the era closed did not differ radically from the pattern established in the 1890s," says James Sundquist. "It seems clear that realignment was averted because (1) the major parties responded to the demands for reform, and (2) they responded at about the same time and to the same degree, so that no sharp distinctions could be drawn between them."[98]

To say that the two major parties were indistinguishably progressive during the first two decades of the century is to deny nearly the entire political history of the period, not only the campaign oratory but congressional behavior and the party struggles within many states. It is also to misunderstand the role and importance of parties; however logical and direct the tie between a pervasive national reform mood and subsequent progressive legislation may seem, the route between the two ran, as it usually does, through the party system.

There is reason to think that voters, in 1916 and 1896 and in many of the elections in between, voted Democratic in order to take that route. National parties may be largely alliances of ethnic and geographic components, but such groups have political and economic interests as well, and the outsiders' coalition that was the Democratic party came to exemplify those interests and attract other voters who decided they shared them.

Unfortunately, this does not explain the fact that has led Sundquist and others to question the depth and force of Democratic Progressivism: Republican preeminence in national politics did resume during the 1920s. But the politics of that decade were not the politics of the McKinley-Roosevelt years, reclaiming their rightful place after a brief deviation. Instead, politics during the 1920s and afterward would bear the imprint of 1916 and the events that led up to it.

The loudest of the lingering notes of 1916, and the one that historians have heard most clearly, was the persistence of the ethnic strains that nearly cost Wilson his reelection. In each of the three succeeding presidential years, Democrats found that ethnocultural issues shattered their coalition and their hopes of victory, costing them not only the White House but congressional position. Bitterness over the war and its settlement shredded the party's vote in 1920, converting the ethnic

98. Sundquist, ibid., p. 155.

unhappiness of 1916 to a vivid anger that drove the Democrats from some of their strongest traditional redoubts. Four years later, the social issues of Prohibition and the revived Ku Klux Klan destroyed the Democrats' chances before their convention had even ended, and Robert La Follette's antiwar record drew votes for his independent candidacy from German Democrats. Al Smith's Catholicism may not have been the decisive factor in 1928, but it did cost the Democratic candidate substantial support. These strains led to the common image of the Democratic party in the decade, that of a hopeless minority clinging to the southeast corner of election maps.

But, as David Burner points out, the party was far more than that and demonstrated it in every midterm election from 1918 to 1930. In 1922, the Democrats charged back from annihilation to within a dozen votes of controlling the House, and in the 1926 elections the party came within two votes of a Senate majority. Moreover, the party's victories largely followed the patterns set during the Wilson years: persistent strength in the Rockies, and gains in areas of Wilson strength in 1916. In 1922, Democrats held their Senate seats in the mountain states and Rhode Island and elected their first senator ever from Washington, which Wilson had won with heavy Bull Moose support. The party elected governors in Kansas, Nebraska, New Hampshire, and Ohio, where Victor Donahey's three successive victories exemplified a pattern of Democratic triumphs in big industrial states also seen in New York, New Jersey, and Massachusetts during the decade. The party's strength in the larger states was aided, in part, by the persistence in the Democratic party (after a deviating vote in 1920) of a group for whom Wilson had greatly increased the party's attraction: Jewish voters.[99]

To see the 1920s as a simple return of the century's first decade, when virtually all Democrats in the Senate drawled and a northern Democratic governor was so rare that he was automatically considered presidential timber, is to ignore everything but actual control of Congress. The Democrats were a minority party in both periods but they were two very different kinds of minority party.

The significance of 1916 and Democratic progressivism appeared even more strongly in 1932, when for the first time in sixteen years reform and economic issues predominated over ethnocultural ones. Allan Lichtman has discovered "a consistently strong relationship between Woodrow Wilson's 1916 percentages and later Democratic percentages," especially those of Franklin D. Roosevelt. And the cast of the

99. Burner, *The Politics of Provincialism*, passim.

1932 convention demonstrated that Democratic progressivism was not a passing aberration but the source of the party's Depression-era leadership. The major contenders were Roosevelt, who became a national figure as Wilson's assistant secretary of the navy; John Nance Garner, a House whip under Champ Clark; Newton Baker, Tom Johnson's successor as mayor of Cleveland and Wilson's secretary of war; and Al Smith, who built his career on the reform legislation passed by the New York state legislature from 1911 to 1914.[100]

Exemplifying the attitudes of most historians of the period, Sundquist titles his chapter on the Progressive Era "Realignment Averted." Looking at the following decade, it does appear that 1916 lacked the first qualification for a realigning election, V. O. Key's requirement that "new and durable electoral groups are formed." But the election did boast a number of other components proposed by Key, Gerald Pomper, and Walter Dean Burnham. The election was preceded by a time of unease, reflected by the rise of third parties, as stressed by Pomper, and reflected a "short-lived but intense disruption of traditional voting behavior," in the words of Walter Dean Burnham. As a result of the persistent effort and planning of the Wilsonians—and the nature of the Republican party—the campaign also was marked by "a considerable increase in ideological polarizations" and "abnormally heavy voter participation for the time": 1916 was the only election between 1900 and 1924 with an increase in voter turnout. Wilson's reelection, it would seem, had all the characteristics of a realigning election except the realignment.[101]

The reason it lacked the last part was that, like Hoover's landslide in 1928 and Johnson's in 1964, it was rapidly followed by developments that radically altered the political landscape. The impact of World War I and related social strains broke down the emerging Democratic coalition but did not reduce the party to its pre-1910 weakness. Instead of "Realignment Averted," a better epitaph for the period might be, "Realignment Unexpectedly Postponed."

The election of 1916 was not only a culmination of political events since 1896; it was also almost a recapitulation of them. Not only was it progressivism's last, and arguably least ambiguous, triumph, but it

100. Allan J. Lichtman, "Critical Election Theory and the Reality of American Presidential Politics, 1916–1940," *American Historical Review* 81 (April 1976), p. 330.

101. V. O. Key, Jr., "A Theory of Critical Elections," *Journal of Politics* 17 (February 1955): 3–4; Gerald Pomper, "Classification of Presidential Elections," *Journal of Politics* 2a (August 1967): 561–62; Walter Dean Burnham, *Critical Elections and the Mainsprings of American Politics* (New York: Norton, 1970), pp. 6–8, 84.

was also an election shaped by the factors that had marked party politics throughout the Progressive Era. As much as the elections of 1896 and 1936, it exemplified its time.

Like the entire period, the campaign was marked by the unexpected emergence of clear and contrasting party identities. During the Roosevelt and Taft administrations, there had been considerable talk of the blurring of parties, since there were progressives in both — an attitude that became less visible after it became clear that progressive Republicans could not control their party, while progressive Democrats dominated theirs and used it to produce reform legislation. Yet, progressive Republicans, including the Bull Moose species, took new hope from the nomination of Hughes, with his pre-1910 reform reputation. Only after the nature of Hughes's Republican responsibilities became clear, when it was no longer possible (despite the Progressives' best efforts) to view the contest as one between two reformers, did many of them shift toward Wilson. By the end of the campaign, there could be little question about which party occupied the progressive and which the conservative position.

The lines were fixed by essentially the same issues that Democrats had stressed throughout the era, issues reflected not only in partisan rhetoric, but also in legislative behavior. Since the shine had gone off silver as an issue, Bryan and the Democrats had talked about the tariff and the trusts, the rights of labor, and the income tax. In 1916, Wilson and his party campaigned on the Adamson Act and the Child Labor bill and warned about returning government to control by business. The new, more steeply graduated version of the income tax, passed by Congress during the campaign, proved an effective appeal to the *New Republic* editors and other advanced Progressives. Hughes and the Republicans concentrated their fire on the Democratic tariff and the administration's labor policies, which they depicted as part of its unreasonable hostility toward businessmen. The Democratic issues, as well as the Democratic politicians, had dominated the era.

As a result, the election produced the first crystallized image of the alliance that had been evolving throughout the period and would mark politics in the future: a close tie between the Democrats and organized labor, an alliance seeking to offset corporate Republicanism. Earlier attempts at such alliance had proven abortive, and even in 1916 the connection was not as close or effective as it would later become. But Wilson and his party that year inspired a unity and enthusiasm among labor's leaders and a resentment and opposition among the leaders of business which was more commonly ascribed only to the next Democratic president.

In more ways than that, the election of 1916 pointed toward the future. The Wilson coalition was not a passing phenomenon built upon the deft exploitation of the war issue. To the old Democratic alliance of the South and the urban machines, years of party policy and planning had added western progressives, renegade Bull Moosers, organized labor, Jewish voters, and liberal intellectuals in a proto-New Deal coalition. Although social strains already apparent in 1916 postponed the coalition's next national electoral victory, its emergence reshaped the Democratic party's attitudes and electorate and made it a force during the 1920s. And at the beginning of the next decade, when economic and reform issues again overrode social themes, the deferred realignment would finally take place.

Bibliographical Essay

S ources and study on the Democratic Party in the Progressive Era are dominated by a massive triple trove of Wilsoniana. This consists of the papers of Woodrow Wilson, in the Library of Congress and to a lesser degree in the New Jersey State Library and the Princeton University Library; *The Papers of Woodrow Wilson*, edited by Arthur S. Link (Princeton: Princeton University Press, 1966–); and Arthur S. Link's five-volume biography of Wilson, also from Princeton University Press: *The Road to the White House* (1946), *The New Freedom* (1956), *The Struggle for Neutrality* (1960), *Confusion and Crises* (1964), and *Campaigns for Progressivism and Peace* (1965). All are indispensable and inexhaustibly rich, although the view they provide of the Democratic party is necessarily through a single lens.

No other manuscript source, of course, approaches Wilson's in extent. William Jennings Bryan's papers, in the Library of Congress and the library of Occidental College in Los Angeles, are important but incomplete. The papers of Josephus Daniels in the Library of Congress are a very rewarding collection dealing with the Democratic affairs and stretching over the entire Progressive Era; along with the papers of Louis Post, also in the Library of Congress, they provide considerable insight into Bryan. The importance of Democratic newspaper publishers in the life of the party can be seen in the papers of Joseph Pulitzer and the *New York World* at Columbia University and the Library of Congress, and in the papers of Henry Watterson in the Library of Congress.

Manuscript collections depicting Democratic behavior in Congress during this period include those of Henry D. Flood, Francis Burton Harrison, Henry Rainey, and John Sharp Williams at the Library of Congress; W. Bourke Cockran at the New York Public Library; William B. Wilson at the Historical Society of Pennsylvania; Claude Kitchin at the University of North Carolina; and William Kent and especially Francis G. Newlands at Yale University. The papers of Thomas J. Walsh at the Library of Congress deserve special mention because they are also important for the campaign of 1916. Also particularly useful for that campaign are the papers of Robert Woolley at the Library of Congress, which include an unpublished autobiography covering much of his lengthy career in Democratic politics, and those of Byron Newton at Yale University. Important collections by figures close to Wilson include the papers of William G. McAdoo, Joseph P. Tumulty, and Ray Stannard Baker at the Library of Congress; those of Edward M. House at Yale University; and the papers of Frank P. Walsh at New York Public Library.

A view of the party from a figure outside it but close to it is provided by the Samuel Gompers papers at AFL-CIO headquarters in Washington, D. C., and the American Federation of Labor Letterbooks, consulted in microfilm at the Library of Congress. Other collections used include the George W. Perkins papers at Columbia University, the Baldwin Family papers at Yale University and the papers of Albert B. Fall and Simon Bolivar Buckner, an unreconstructible Gold Democrat, at the Huntington Library in San Marino, California.

William Jennings Bryan left behind two published works: the unfinished *The Memoirs of William Jennings Bryan* (Chicago: John C. Winston, 1925), published under a joint byline with his wife Mary Baird Bryan, and *A Tale of Two Conventions* (New York: Funk and Wagnalls, 1912), his advocacy journalism report on the Democratic and Republican conventions of that year. Again, a richer view is provided by his close friend Josephus Daniels in *Editor in Politics* and *The Wilson Era, Years of Peace, 1910–1917* (Chapel Hill: University of North Carolina Press, 1941–1944). A different look at the Wilson Era is offered by Daniels' son, Jonathan, in *The End of Innocence* (Philadelphia: J.B. Lippincott, 1954).

Champ Clark wrote a two-volume autobiography, *My Quarter-Century of American Politics* (New York: Harper, 1920), which does little to improve his historical image but contains some interesting details. The same description would fit Oscar W. Underwood's *Drifting Sands of Party Politics* (New York: Century, 1926).

The more substantive political memoirs of the period came from less central party figures or from those just beginning their careers. The most useful are James M. Cox, *Journey Through My Years* (New York: Simon and Schuster, 1946); James M. Curley, *I'd Do It Again* (Englewood Cliffs: Prentice-Hall, 1957); James W. Gerard, *My First Eighty-Three Years in America* (New York: Doubleday, 1951); Carter H. Harrison, *Stormy Years* (Indianapolis: Bobbs-Merrill, 1935); Cordell Hull, *Memoirs* (London: Hodder and Stoughton, 1948, 2 vols.); Edward Keating, *The Gentleman from Colorado* (Denver: Sage Books, 1964); Arthur Mullen, *Western Democrat* (New York: Wilfred Funk, 1940); and

Harold Syrett, ed., *The Gentleman and the Tiger, the Autobiography of George B. McClellan Jr.* (Philadelphia: J.B. Lippincott, 1956).

Also dredged from the memory of Democrats of the period are Henry F. Ashurst, *A Many-Colored Toga*, ed. George F. Sparks (Tucson: University of Arizona Press, 1962); Clarence C. Dill, *Where Water Falls* (Spokane: C.C. Dill, 1970); Mrs. J. Borden Harriman, *From Pinafores to Politics* (New York: Henry Holt and Company, 1923); Richard Pettigrew, *Imperial Washington* (Chicago: Charles Kerr and Co., 1922); Ellen Maury Slayden, *Washington Wife: Journal of Ellen Maury Slayden, 1897–1919* (New York: Harper's, 1962); and Sewell Thomas, ed., *Silhouettes of Charles S. Thomas* (Caldwell: The Caxton Printers, 1959).

The group close to Wilson produced a substantial number of useful memoirs. The most widely consulted and most frequently challenged, is Charles Seymour, *Intimate Memoirs of Colonel House* (Boston: Houghton, Mifflin, 1926–1928, 4 vols.), which may rather inflate the colonel's role in human history. Also important are James J. Kerney, *The Political Education of Woodrow Wilson* (New York: Century, 1926); William G. McAdoo, *Crowded Years* (Cambridge: Riverside Press, 1931); Henry Morgenthau, *All in a Lifetime* (Garden City: Doubleday, Page and Co., 1922); and Joseph P. Tumulty, *Woodrow Wilson as I Knew Him* (Garden City: Garden City Publishing Co., 1925). Bringing up the rear is the chatty account by Wilson's vice president, Thomas R. Marshall, *Recollections* (Indianapolis: Bobbs-Merrill, 1925).

An important collection of letters bearing on the party in the period is Melvin I. Urofsky and Daniel W. Levy, *Letters of Louis D. Brandeis* (Albany: State University of New York Press, 1971–1975, 4 vols.). Elting E. Morison, ed., *The Letters of Theodore Roosevelt* (Cambridge: Harvard University Press, 1951–1954, 8 vols.) is essential on the politics of the Progressive Era, and also useful are Henry Cabot Lodge, ed., *Selections from the Correspondence of Theodore Roosevelt and Henry Cabot Lodge* (New York: Charles Scribner's Sons, 1925, 2 vols.), Lawrence F. Abbott, ed., *The Letters of Archie Butt* (Garden City: Doubleday, 1924); and Archibald Butt, *Taft and Roosevelt* (Doubleday, Doran and Co., 1930, 2 vols.), especially for the Taft period.

An interesting collection of Democratic correspondence is Anne Wintermute Lane, ed., *The Letters of Franklin K. Lane* (Boston: Houghton Mifflin, 1922). Also worth consulting are the collected papers of two North Carolinians: A.L. Brooks and H.T. Lefler, eds., *The Papers of Walter Clark* (Chapel Hill: University of North Carolina Press, 1950, 2 vols.) and J. Fred Rippy, ed., *F. M. Simmons, Statesman of the New South, Memoirs and Addresses* (Durham: Duke University Press,

1936). A very different view of the Washington of the time can be found in Worthington Chauncey Ford, ed., *The Letters of Henry Adams, 1892–1918* (Boston: Houghton Mifflin, 1938).

In reminiscence, as often in oratory, Progressive Era Democrats were generally less articulate than insurgent Republicans and political journalists. Some of the best insights into the figures of the period came from a shining example of both, William Allen White, in *Autobiography* (New York: Macmillan, 1946); *Masks in a Pageant* (New York: Macmillan, 1928); and Walter Johnson, ed., *Selected Letters of William Allen White* (New York: Henry Holt and Company, 1947).

Memoirs by others who blurred the line between journalism and public activity include George Creel, *Rebel at Large* (New York: Putnam's, 1947) and Norman Hapgood, *The Changing Years* (New York: Farrar and Rinehart, 1930). Among relevant reminiscences by unwavering political journalists are Willis J. Abbot, *Watching the World Go By* (Boston: Little, Brown and Co., 1933); Oscar King Davis, *Released for Publication* (Boston: E. P. Dutton, 1925); Arthur Wallace Dunn, *Gridiron Nights* (New York: Frederick A. Stokes, 1915) and *From Harrison to Harding* (New York: E. P. Dutton, 1925, 2 vols.); Michael E. Hennessey, *Four Decades of Massachusetts Politics* (Norwood: Norwood Press, 1935); Lincoln Steffens, *Autobiography* (New York: Harcourt Brace, 1931, 2 vols.); and Charles Willis Thompson, *Presidents I've Known and Two Near-Presidents* (Indianapolis: Bobbs-Merrill, 1929); and Oswald Garrison Villard, *Fighting Years* (New York: Harcourt, Brace, 1939).

Democrats are viewed through insurgent Republican eyes in Colin B. Goodykoontz, ed., *Papers of Edward Costigan Relating to the Progressive Movement of Colorado* (Boulder: University of Colorado Press, 1941); Robert M. La Follette, *La Follette's Autobiography* (Madison: La Follette Company, 1913); Fiorello La Guardia, *The Making of an Insurgent* (New York: Lippincott, 1948); George Norris, *Fighting Liberal* (New York: Macmillan, 1945); and Amos Pinchot, *History of the Progressive Party, 1912–1916*, ed. H. M. Hooker (New York: New York University Press, 1958).

Memoirs by prominent social progressive activists include Harold Ickes, *Autobiography of a Curmudgeon* (New York: Reynal and Hitchcock, 1973), and "Who Killed the Progressive Party?" *American Historical Review* 46 (January 1941): 306–37; Frances Perkins, *The Roosevelt I Knew* (New York: Viking, 1946); and Donald Richberg, *My Hero* (New York: Putnam's, 1954). Samuel Gompers, *Seventy Years of Life and Labor* (New

York: E. P. Dutton, 1925, 2 vols.); W. E. B. Du Bois, *Dusk at Dawn* (New York: Harcourt, Brace, 1940); and Simon Wolf, *Presidents I Have Known from 1860–1918* (Washington: Press of Byron S. Adams, 1918) provide views of Progressive Era politics from activists outside middle-class reform circles. Also worth reading are the memoirs of a pair of Indiana organization Republicans, Will Hays, *Memoirs* (Garden City: Doubleday, 1955) and James E. Watson, *As I Knew Them* (Indianapolis: Bobbs-Merrill, 1936), and from another view, Owen Wister, *Roosevelt, the Story of a Friendship* (New York: Macmillan, 1930).

First-person accounts of Progressive Era politics not contained between book covers can be found at the Oral History Research Office at Columbia University: *Reminiscences* of Henry Breckenridge, John W. Davis, Roy S. Durstine, John T. Hetterick, and William Prendergast.

The best place to trace the behavior of Democrats in Congress is, of course, the *Congressional Record* and, the biographical and organizational material in the various editions of the *Congressional Directory*. The permanent gap between Democratic and Republican financial resources can be seen in two congressional reports: *Hearings before a Subcommittee of the Committee on Privileges and Elections, United States Senate* (Washington: 1921, 2 vols.) and *Testimony Before a Subcommittee of the Committee on Privileges and Elections, United States Senate* (Washington: 1912, 2 vols.).

The best place to trace the course of the party in general is its newspapers, on which I have relied heavily. The one most influential and most extensively used was the *New York World*; also important were the reports of the *Louisville Courier-Journal* and the *Los Angeles Examiner*, which retailed the national political views of William Randolph Hearst. The *Baltimore Sun*, *Boston Post*, *Cleveland Plain Dealer*, Denver *Rocky Mountain News*, and *St. Louis Republic* provided useful coverage of Democrats in their regions and in the nation; and the *New York Times* was the firmest voice of Grover Cleveland Democrats. Newspapers consulted on particular developments included the *Chicago Tribune*, the *Denver Post*, the *Los Angeles Times*, the *New York Tribune*, and the Salt Lake City *Deseret Evening News*.

Particularly important for the study of Progressive Era politics were magazines, the national media of the time, home of many of the muckrakers. *Collier's* was perhaps the most influential, and the same middle-class uplift path was followed by *The American Magazine*, the *Outlook* and *World's Work*. More narrowly political were the *Independent*, the *Nation*, *The Public*, and later the *New Republic*. A Democratic view was offered briefly by the *National Monthly* and more extensively by William Jennings Bryan's *Commoner*. Following their own particular agendas were *Hearst's Magazine* and the *American Federationist*.

The Democrats of the Progressive Era are bracketed by two detailed studies of the party just before and afterward: J. Rogers Hollingsworth, *The Whirligig of Politics: Democracy from Cleveland to Bryan* (Chicago: University of Chicago Press, 1963) and David Burner, *The Politics of Provincialism: The Democratic Party in Transition, 1918–1932* (New York: Alfred A. Knopf, 1967), which is particularly provocative.

A valuable new synthesis on Progressive Era politics, showing some evidence of a new attitude toward the Democrats, is Lewis L. Gould, *Reform and Regulation: American Politics, 1900–1916* (New York: John Wiley, 1916). For the latter part of the period, the standard work is still Arthur S. Link, *Woodrow Wilson and the Progressive Era, 1910–1917* (New York: Harper, 1954). In studies of the earlier period, Democrats are glimpsed through the lines of George Mowry, *The Era of Theodore Roosevelt, 1900–1912* (New York: Harper, 1958) and Horace Samuel Merrill and Marion Galbraith Merrill, *The Republican Command, 1897–1913* (Lexington: University Press of Kentucky, 1971) like Rosencrantz and Guildenstern.

Significant recent reconsiderations of American politics during the late nineteenth and early twentieth centuries include Michael E. McGerr, *The Decline of Popular Politics: The American North, 1865–1928* (New York: Oxford University Press, 1986), which stresses the decline in popular participation, and Richard L. McCormick, *The Party Period and Public Policy* (New York: Oxford University Press, 1986), a collection of essays that includes "The Discovery that Business Corrupts Politics: A Reappraisal of the Origins of Progressivism," *American Historical Review* 86 (April 1981): 247–74. One particularly exciting new work on the period is John Milton Cooper, Jr., *The Warrior and the Priest* (Cambridge: Belknap Press of Harvard University Press, 1983), a study of Roosevelt and Wilson with a keen insight into the role of party identity in the career of each.

Reconsideration of the significance of William Jennings Bryan received a powerful boost from Lawrence W. Levine, *Defender of the Faith: William Jennings Bryan, the Last Decade, 1915–1925* (New York: Columbia University Press, 1965). Paolo Coletta's three-volume biography, *William Jennings Bryan* (Lincoln: University of Nebraska Press, 1964–1969), is thorough and important, but sometimes takes Bryan too much at face value. A more hard-eyed assessment is provided in Louis W. Koenig, *Bryan* (New York: Putnam's, 1971). Interesting article insights on Bryan are offered in Boyce House, "Bryan the Orator," *Illinois State Historical Society Journal* 53 (Autumn 1960): 266–82; William H. Smith, "William Jennings Bryan and Racism," *Journal of Negro History* 54 (April 1969): 127–49; and importantly, Larry G. Osnes, "Charles W. Bryan: His Brother's Keeper," *Nebraska History* 48, (Spring 1967): 45–67.

A vital part of recent literature reconsidering the Democrats in the Progressive Era deals with their roles on the state level. A groundbreaking synthesis on the question is John D. Buenker, *Urban Liberalism and Progressive Reform* (New York: Scribner's, 1973), and I have also referred to three of his numerous articles: "Edward F. Dunne: The Urban New Stock Democrat as Progressive," *Mid-America* 50 (January 1968): 3–21; "Urban Liberalism and the Federal Income Tax Amendment," *Pennsylvania History*, 26 (April 1969): 192–215; and "Urban, New-Stock Liberalism and Progressive Reform in New Jersey," *New Jersey History* 87 (Summer 1969): 79–104.

On Democratic politics in the most important state of the period, a tone was set by J. Joseph Huthmacher in "Charles Evans Hughes and Charles Francis Murphy: The Metamorphosis of Urban Progressivism," *New York History* 46 (January 1965): 25–40, and in the early chapters of *Robert F. Wagner and the Rise of Urban Liberalism* (New York: Atheneum, 1968). Similar points were made in Nancy Joan Weiss, *Charles Francis Murphy, 1858–1924* (Northampton: Smith College, 1968) and now most thoroughly and impressively in Robert F. Wesser, *A Response to Progressivism: The Democratic Party and New York Politics, 1902–1918* (New York: New York University Press, 1986). Other views of Murphy are seen in Lately Thomas, *The Mayor Who Mastered New York* (New York: William Morrow, 1969) and Herbert Mitgang, *The Man Who Rode the Tiger* (Philadelphia: J. B. Lippincott, 1963); and readers can find a traditional look at Tammany in Howard Zink, *City Bosses in the United States* (Durham: Duke University Press, 1930). Also useful on the Democratic role in New York is Irwin Yellowitz, *Labor and the Progressive Movement in New York State, 1897–1916* (Ithaca: Cornell University Press, 1965). Views of the state Republican party during the period are provided by Robert F. Wesser, *Charles Evans Hughes: Politics and Reform in New York, 1905–1910* (Ithaca: Cornell University Press, 1967), and Richard L. McCormick, *From Realignment to Reform: Political Change in New York State, 1893–1910* (Ithaca: Cornell University Press, 1979). Also worth consulting is David M. Ellis, James A. Frost, Harold C. Syrett and Harry J. Carman, *A History of New York State* (Ithaca: Cornell University Press, 1967).

On Massachusetts, the tone has been set by Richard Abrams, *Conservatism in a Progressive Era* (Cambridge: Harvard University Press, 1964). Biographical studies of prominent Massachusetts Democrats in the period include Leslie G. Ainsley, *Boston Mahatma* (Boston: William M. Predible, 1949), about ward boss Martin Lomasney; John Henry Cutler, *"Honey Fitz"* (Indianapolis: Bobbs-Merrill, 1962), about John F. Fitzgerald; Dorothy G. Wayman, *David I. Walsh, Citizen Patriot* (Milwaukee: Bruce Publishers, 1952); and Richard B. Sherman, "Foss of Massachusetts: Demagogue or Progressive?" *Mid-America* 43 (April 1969): 75–94. Also touching the subject is Richard B. Sherman, "Charles Sumner Bird and the Progressive Party in Massachusetts," *New England Quarterly* 33 (March 1960): 325–40.

Works relating to Democratic reformism elsewhere in New England include Frederic M. Heath, "Labor and the Progressive Movement in Connecticut," *Labor History* 12 (Winter 1971):52–67; Frederick H. Jackson, *Simeon Eben Baldwin* (New York: Kings Crown Press, 1955); and Erwin L. Levine, *Theodore Francis Green: The Rhode Island Years, 1906–1936* (Providence: Brown University Press, 1963).

The model state of Democratic progressivism was Ohio, and the standard work is Hoyt L. Warner, *Progressivism in Ohio, 1897–1917* (Columbus: Ohio State University Press, 1964). Warner's book has now been supplemented by James E. Cebula, *James M. Cox, Journalist and Politician* (New York: Garland, 1985) and, on a particular reform, Patrick D. Reagan, "The Ideology of Social Harmony and Efficiency: Workmen's Compensation in Ohio, 1904–1919," *Ohio History* 90 (Autumn 1981):317–31.

Two revealing works on progressive politics next door in Indiana are Clifton J. Phillips, *Indiana in Transition, 1880–1920* (Indianapolis: Indiana Historical Bureau and Indiana Historical Society, 1968), and Philip R. Vandermeer, *The Hoosier Politician* (Urbana: University of Illinois Press, 1985).

Depictions of other Democratic reform activities on the state level include Keith L. Bryant, *Alfalfa Bill Murray* (Norman: University of Oklahoma Press, 1968); Frank A. Day and Theodore M. Knappen, *Life of John Albert Johnson* (Chicago: Forbes and Co., 1910); Louis G. Geiger, *Joseph W. Folk of Missouri* (Columbia: University of Missouri Press, 1953); Winifred G. Helmes, *John A. Johnson, the People's Governor* (Minneapolis: University of Minnesota Press, 1949); and Charles N. Glaab, "The Failure of North Dakota Progressivism," *Mid-America* 39 (July 1957): 180–91.

No reconsideration of the Democratic party would have been possible without a rethinking of the attitudes of southern Democrats. Following Arthur S. Link, "The Progressive Movement in the South, 1870–1914," *North Carolina Historical Review* 23 (October 1946): 483–94, early reevaluations included Anne Firor Scott, "A Progressive Wind from the South," *Journal of Southern History* 29 (February 1963):53–70, and Dewey Grantham, *The Democratic South* (New York: W. W. Norton, 1965). Jack T. Kirby, *Darkness at the Dawning: Race and Reform in the Progressive South* (Philadelphia: Lippincott, 1972) stresses the interrelation of the two themes; and Dewey Grantham, *Southern Progressivism: The Reconciliation of Progress and Tradition* (Knoxville: University of Tennessee Press, 1983) presents a magisterial survey of reform in the region. It also spurred an insightful review essay, David P. Thelen, "Where Did Progressivism Go? A Search amid the South," *Georgia Historical Quarterly* 68 (Spring 1984):60–70. Still important, of course, are George B. Tindall, *The Emergence of the New South, 1914–1945* (Baton Rouge: Louisiana State University Press, 1967) and C. Vann Woodward, *The Origins of the New South, 1877–1914* (Baton Rouge: Louisiana State University Press, 1951).

Useful in tracking reform through a few specific southern areas are Lewis L. Gould, *Progressives and Prohibitionists: Texas Democrats in the Wilson Era* (Austin: University of Texas Press, 1973); James B. Crooks, *Politics and Progress: The Rise of Urban Progressivism in Baltimore* (Baton Rouge: Louisiana State University Press, 1968); Albert Kirwan, *Revolt of the Rednecks: Mississippi Politics 1876–1925* (Lexington: University of Kentucky Press, 1951); Allen W. Moger, *Virginia: Bourbonism to Byrd, 1870–1925* (Charlottesville: University Press of Virginia, 1968); and Worth Robert Miller, "Building a Progressive Coalition in Texas: The Populist-Reform Democrat Rapprochement, 1900–1907," *Journal of Southern History* 52 (May 1986):163–82. For a look at one southerner who exemplified much of the region's political shifts during the time, see C. Vann Woodward, *Tom Watson: Agrarian Rebel* (New York: Macmillan, 1938).

For much of the period, the Democratic presence on the national level was confined to Congress. Book-length looks at the congressional Democrats of the period are found in three unpublished dissertations: Edward R. Silbert, "Support for Reform among Congressional Democrats, 1897–1913" (University of Florida, 1966); Thomas W. Patton, "An Urban Congressional Delegation in an Age of Reform: The New York County Democratic Delegation to the House of Representatives,

1901–1917" (New York University, 1978); and especially Claude M. Barfield, "Congressional Democrats in the Taft Administration" (Northwestern University, 1969).

Evans C. Johnson, *Oscar W. Underwood: A Political Biography* (Baton Rouge: Louisiana State University Press, 1980) provides both an illuminating look at Democrats in Congress through the period and a model for needed studies of other Democratic leaders of the time. (Also worth examining on Underwood is James S. Fleming, "Re-establishing Leadership in the House of Representatives: the Case of Oscar W. Underwood," *Mid-America* 54 (October 1972):235–50, and Arthur Link, "The Underwood Presidential Movement of 1912," *Journal of Southern History* 11 (May 1945):230–45. W. L. Webb, *Champ Clark* (New York: Neale Publishing Co., 1912), a campaign biography, is still the only book on the four-time speaker. John W. Kern, Bryan's 1908 running mate and Wilson's first-term Senate majority leader, has had no study since Claude Bowers' adoring *The Life of John Worth Kern* (Indianapolis: Hollinbeck Press, 1918), except for Virginia Haughton, "John W. Kern, Senate Majority Leader and Labor Legislation, 1913–1917," *Mid-America* 57 (July 1975):184–94. Thomas S. Martin, Senate Democratic leader before and after Kern, is examined only in Wythe W. Holt, Jr., "The Senator from Virginia and the Democratic Floor Leadership: Thomas S. Martin and Conservatism in the Progressive Era," *Virginia Magazine of History and Biography* 83 (January 1975):3–21.

Useful, if sometimes dated, studies of prominent Democrats in Congress at the time include Sam Hanna Acheson, *Joe Bailey: The Last Democrat* (New York: Macmillan, 1932); Alex S. Arnett, *Claude Kitchin and the Wilson War Policies* (Boston: Little, Brown and Co., 1937); Stanley Coben, *A. Mitchell Palmer, Politician* (Princeton: Princeton University Press, 1963); Henry C. Ferrell, Jr., *Claude Swanson of Virginia* (Lexington: University Press of Kentucky, 1985), which is particularly well done; Wayne C. Flynt, *Duncan Upshaw Fletcher: Dixie's Reluctant Progressive* (Tallahassee: Florida State University Press, 1971); William Henry Harbaugh, *Lawyer's Lawyer: The Life of John W. Davis* (New York: Oxford University Press, 1973); Robert E. Hennings, *James D. Phelan and the Wilson Progressives of California* (New York: Garland, 1985), and his unpublished dissertation of the same name (University of California, Berkeley, 1961); George C. Osborn, *John Sharp Williams, Planter-Statesman of the Deep South* (Gloucester: Peter Smith, 1964); Francis B. Simkins, *Pitchfork Ben Tillman: South Carolinian* (Baton Rouge: Louisiana State University Press, 1944); Robert A. Waller, *Rainey of Illinois*

(Urbana: University of Illinois Press, 1977); Marvin Block, "Henry T. Rainey of Illinois," *Illinois State Historical Quarterly* 65 (Summer 1972): 142–57; Nicholas C. Burckel, "A. O. Stanley and Progressive Reform, 1902–1919," *The Register of the Kentucky Historical Society* 79 (Spring 1981):136–81; William D. Jenkins, "Robert Bulkley, Progressive Profile," *Ohio History* 88 (Winter 1979); and Robert Earl Smith, "Colorado's Progressive Senators and Representatives," *Colorado Magazine* 45 (Winter 1968):27–41. Also available are James William Madden, *Charles Allen Culberson* (Austin: Gammel's Book Store, 1929); Lee Meriwether, *Jim Reed, "Senatorial Immortal"* (Webster Groves: International Mark Twain Society, 1948); and Josephine O'Keane, *Thomas J. Walsh* (Francistown: Marshall Jones Co., 1955).

Studies of earlier and later Democratic congressional figures whose careers reached into the Progressive Era include C. Dwight Dorough, *Mr. Sam* (New York: Random House, 1962); Elmer Ellis, *Henry Moore Teller* (Caldwell: Caxton Press, 1941); Fred L. Israel, *Nevada's Key Pittman* (Lincoln: University of Nebraska Press, 1963); Marquis James, *Mr. Garner of Texas* (Indianapolis: Bobbs-Merrill, 1939); John R. Lambert, *Arthur Pue Gorman* (Baton Rouge: Louisiana State University Press, 1953); James McGurrin, *Bourke Cockran* (New York: Charles Scribner's Sons, 1948); Rixey Smith and Norman Beasley, *Carter Glass* (New York: Longmans, Green and Co., 1939); and Bascom Timmons, *Garner of Texas* (New York: Harper and Bros., 1948).

Several contemporary journalists also provided portraits of congressional leaders of the period. See George Rothwell Brown, *Leadership in Congress* (Indianapolis: Bobbs-Merrill, 1922); Charles Willis Thompson, *Party Leaders of the Time* (New York: Dillingham, 1906); and Edward G. Lowry, *Washington Close-ups* (Boston: Houghton Mifflin, 1921).

Analyses of how Democrats operated in and changed Congress during the Progressive Era can be found in De Alva S. Alexander, *History and Procedure of the House of Representatives* (Boston: Houghton Mifflin, 1916); Chang-wei Chiu, *The Speaker of the House of Representatives since 1896* (New York: Columbia University Press, 1928); Charles O. Jones, *The Minority Party in Congress* (Boston: Little, Brown and Co., 1970) and "Joseph G. Cannon and Howard W. Smith: An Essay on the Limits of Leadership in the House of Representatives," *Journal of Politics* 30 (August 1968):617–46; Nelson W. Polsby, Miriam Gallaher, and Barry Spencer Rundquist, "The Growth of the Seniority System in the U.S. House of Representatives," *American Political Science Review* 63

(September 1969)787–807; and Wilder H. Haines, "The Congressional Caucus of Today," *American Political Science Review* 9 (November 1915):696–706.

General surveys of partisan congressional voting patterns are offered in Howard W. Allen, "Geography and Politics: Voting on Reform Issues in the United States Senate, 1911–1916," *Journal of Southern History* 27 (May 1961):216–28, and in a considerably reexamined form in Howard W. Allen and Jerome Clubb, "Progressive Reform and the Political System," *Pacific Northwest Quarterly* 65 (July 1974). Accounts of Democratic behavior on particular issues include John D. Baker, "The Character of the Congressional Revolution of 1910," *Journal of American History* 60 (December 1973):679–691; and Claude M. Barfield, " 'Our Share of the Booty': The Democratic Party, Cannonism and the Payne-Aldrich Tariff Act," *Journal of American History* 57 (September 1970):308–23. A useful look at the operation of a single Congress in the period, and at some of the players, can be found in Seward Livermore, *Politics Is Adjourned: Woodrow Wilson and the War Congress: 1916–1918* (Middletown: Wesleyan University Press, 1966).

On the issues that concerned Progressive Era Democrats, contemporary surveys of the tariff from a reform perspective are studied in Franklin Pierce, *The Tariff and the Trusts* (New York: Macmillan, 1907); Ida Tarbell, *The Tariff History of the United States* (New York: Macmillan, 1911); and Frank W. Taussig, *The Tariff History of the United States* (New York: Putnam's, 1910, 5th edition).

The role of the labor issue is covered in Marc Karson, *American Labor Unions and Politics, 1900–1918* (Carbondale: Southern Illinois University Press, 1958); Grace Heilman Stimson, *Rise of the Labor Movement in Los Angeles* (Berkeley: University of California Press, 1955); Eugene Tobin, *Organize or Perish* (Westport: Greenwood Press, 1986); R. F. Hoxie, "President Gompers and the Labor Vote," *Journal of Political Economy* 16, no. 10 (December 1908):693–700; and Janice A. Petterchak, "Conflict of Ideals: Samuel Gompers v. Uncle Joe Cannon," *Journal of Illinois State Historical Society* 74 (September 1981): 31–40.

Insurgents in Congress have been widely examined. General studies begin with Thomas Dreier, *Heroes of Insurgency* (Boston: Human Life Publishing Co., 1910) and now include Kenneth W. Hechler, *Insurgency* (New York: Columbia University Press, 1940) and the more measured J. Lawrence Holt, *Congressional Insurgents and the Party System* (Cambridge: Harvard University Press, 1967). They also figure prominently in Russel B. Nye, *Midwestern Progressive Politics, 1870–1958* (East Lansing: Michigan State University Press, 1959).

The insurgents have also attracted a wealth of biographers. Robert M. La Follette has been profiled in Belle Case La Follette and Fola La Follette, *Robert M. La Follette* (New York: Macmillan, 1953, 2 vols.); Robert S. Maxwell, *La Follette and the Rise of the Progressives in Wisconsin* (Madison: State Historical Society of Wisconsin, 1955); and David P. Thelen, *Robert La Follette and the Insurgent Spirit* (Boston: Little, Brown and Co., 1976). Equally extended treatment has been given to George W. Norris, in Albert Lief, *Democracy's Norris* (New York: Stackpole Press, 1939); Richard Lowitt, *George W. Norris* (Syracuse: Syracuse University Press, 1963–1978, 3 vols.); and Richard L. Neuberger and Stephen B. Kahn, *Integrity: The Life of George W. Norris* (New York: Vanguard Press, 1937).

Other studies of insurgents in Congress include Howard W. Allen, *Poindexter of Washington: A Study in Progressive Politics* (Carbondale: Southern Illinois University Press, 1981), which also includes some useful material on congressional voting; Edward C. Blackorby, *Prairie Rebel: The Public Life of William Lemke* (Lincoln: University of Nebraska Press, 1963); John Braeman, *Albert J. Beveridge* (Chicago: University of Chicago Press, 1971); John Ely Briggs, *William Peters Hepburn* (Iowa City: State Historical Association of Iowa, 1919); Fred Greenbaum, *Fighting Progressive: A Political Biography of Edward P. Costigan* (Washington: Public Affairs Press, 1971); Arthur Mann, *La Guardia: A Fighter against His Times* (Philadelphia: Lippincott, 1959); Herbert Margulies, *Senator Lenroot of Wisconsin: A Political Biography, 1900–1929* (Springfield: University of Missouri Press, 1977); Marion C. McKenna, *Borah* (Ann Arbor: University of Michigan Press, 1961); Thomas Richard Ross, *Jonathan Prentiss Dolliver* (Iowa City: State Historical Society of Iowa, 1958); A. Bower Sagesser, *Joseph L. Bristow* (Lawrence: University of Kansas Press, 1968); and Roger E. Wyman, "Insurgency in Minnesota: The Defeat of James A. Tawney in 1910," *Minnesota History* 40 (Fall 1967):317–24.

Especially worth reading is the biography of one insurgent out of Congress: Walter Johnson, *William Allen White's America* (New York: Henry Holt and Company, 1947). A recent view of the social activist progressives, fairly dismissive of the movement's political side, can be found in Robert M. Crunden, *Ministers of Reform* (New York: Basic Books, 1982). The outlook of a prominent figure in that group is outlined in Alan R. Havig, "The Raymond Robins Case for Progressive Republicanism," *Illinois State Historical Society Journal* 64 (Winter 1971): 401–18.

Insurgents on the state level are examined in Robert Sherman La Forte, *Leaders of Reform: Progressive Republicans in Kansas, 1900–1916*

(Lawrence: University of Kansas, 1974); Herbert Margulies, *Decline of the Progressive Movement in Wisconsin* (Madison: Historical Society of Wisconsin, 1968); George Mowry, *The California Progressives* (Berkeley: University of California Press, 1951); Spencer C. Olin, Jr., *California's Prodigal Sons* (Berkeley: University of California Press, 1968); William T. Kerr, Jr., "The Progressives of Washington, 1910–1912," *Pacific Northwest Quarterly* 55 (January 1964):16–27; and Robert W. Larson, "The Profile of a New Mexico Progressive," *New Mexico Historical Review* 45 (July 1970): 233–44.

Theodore Roosevelt, of course, was the dominant political figure of at least the first half of the Progressive Era. The most insightful portraits of him are John Morton Blum, *The Republican Roosevelt* (Cambridge: Harvard University Press, 1954); and William Henry Harbaugh, *Power and Responsibility: The Life of Theodore Roosevelt* (New York: Farrar, Straus, and Cudahy, 1961). Also worth reading is William Manners, *TR and Will* (New York: Harcourt, Brace, 1969). Dated but with some good material is George Mowry, *Theodore Roosevelt and the Progressive Movement* (Madison: University of Wisconsin Press, 1946), which has been in some ways superseded by John A. Gable, *The Bull Moose Years* (Port Washington: Kennikat Press, 1978).

Several biographies of conservative Republicans also provide a viewpoint on the Democrats of the period. See William Rea Gwinn, *Uncle Joe Cannon, Archfoe of Insurgency* (New York: Bookman Associates, 1957); Henry F. Holthusen, *James W. Wadsworth, Jr.* (New York: Putnam's, 1926); William T. Hutchinson, *Lowden of Illinois* (Chicago: University of Chicago Press, 1957, 2 vols.); Oscar Lambert, *Stephen Benton Elkins* (Pittsburgh: University of Pittsburgh Press, 1955); Francis G. Russell, *The Shadow of Blooming Grove* (New York: McGraw-Hill, 1968), on Warren Harding; Karl Schriftgiesser, *The Gentleman from Massachusetts* (Boston: Little, Brown and Co., 1945), on Henry Cabot Lodge; Nathanial W. Stephenson, *Nelson W. Aldrich* (New York: Scribner's, 1930); and Leon Burr Richardson, *William E. Chandler, Republican* (New York: Dodd, Mead and Co., 1940).

One important recent biography of a figure close to Wilson is John J. Broesamle, *William Gibbs McAdoo: A Passion for Change, 1863–1917* (Port Washington: Kennikat Press, 1973). Also useful for depictions of the inner operations of the Wilson administration are John Morton Blum, *Joe Tumulty and the Wilson Era* (Boston: Little, Brown and Co., 1951); C. H. Cramer, *Newton D. Baker* (New York: World Publishing, 1961); Frank Freidel, *Franklin D. Roosevelt: The Apprenticeship* (Boston: Little, Brown and Co., 1952); Keith Olson, *Biography of a Progressive:*

Franklin K. Lane (Westport: Greenwood Press, 1979); Gregory Ross, *Walter Hines Page* (Lexington: University Press of Kentucky, 1971); and Adrian Anderson, "President Wilson's Politician: Albert Sidney Burleson of Texas," *Southwestern Historical Quarterly* 77 (January 1974): 339–54.

The Democratic press lords who wielded such influence in the party have all attracted several biographers. W. A. Swanberg, *Pulitzer* (New York: Charles Scribner's Sons, 1967) is the best work now available on the ruler of the *New York World*, and also useful are Don C. Seitz, *Joseph Pulitzer: His Life and Letters* (New York: Simon and Schuster, 1924); and W. R. Reynolds, "Joseph Pulitzer" (unpublished dissertation, Columbia University, 1950). Swanberg's *Citizen Hearst* (New York: Charles Scribner's Sons, 1961) has also replaced John K. Winkler, *William Randolph Hearst: An American Phenomenon* (New York: Simon and Schuster, 1928), but a good political biography of Hearst would be welcome. Joseph Frazier Wall, *Henry Watterson* (New York: Oxford University Press, 1956) is thorough, while Isaac Marcosson, *"Marse Henry"* (New York: Dodd, Mead and Co., 1951) is chatty.

Casting light on other important Democratic journals and journalists are Gerald W. Johnson, *An Honorable Titan* (New York: Harper and Bros., 1946), about Adolph Ochs of the *New York Times*; Gerald W. Johnson, Frank R. Kent, H. L. Mencken, and Hamilton Owens, *The Sunpapers of Baltimore* (New York: Alfred A. Knopf, 1937); Willis F. Johnson, *George Harvey, "A Passionate Patriot"* (Cambridge: Riverside Press, 1929); Robert L. Perkins, *The First Hundred Years* (Garden City: Doubleday and Co., 1959), on the *Rocky Mountain News*; Archer H. Shaw, *The Plain Dealer* (New York: Alfred A. Knopf, 1942); and Oswald Garrison Villard, *Some Newspapers and Newspapermen* (New York: Alfred A. Knopf, 1926). Also useful on the journalism of the period is Louis Lyons, *Newspaper Story: One Hundred Years of the Boston Globe* (Cambridge: Belknap Press of Harvard University Press, 1971); Frank Luther Mott, *American Journalism* (New York: Macmillan, rev. ed., 1950); and James E. Pollard, *The Presidents and the Press* (New York: Macmillan, 1947).

Early ties between Democrats and black voters are surveyed in Lawrence Grossman, *The Democratic Party and the Negro, 1865–1892* (Urbana: University of Illinois Press, 1976); their sad dead end during the Progressive Era is traced in Kathleen Long Wohlgemuth, "Woodrow Wilson's Appointment Policy and the Negro," *Journal of Southern History* 24 (November 1958):457–71. Reactions of national black leaders are depicted in Francis L. Broderick, *W. E. B. Du Bois* (Stanford: Stanford University Press, 1959); Louis R. Harlan's impressive *Booker T. Washington: The Wizard of Tuskegee* (New York: Oxford University Press, 1983); and Elliott M. Rudwick, *W. E. B. Du Bois* (Philadelphia: University of Pennsylvania Press, 1960). Patterns in one state can be followed in David A. Gerber, *Black Ohio and the Color Line, 1860–1915* (Urbana: University of Illinois Press, 1976).

Political tendencies of other ethnic groups during the period are discussed in Lawrence H. Fuchs, *The Political Behavior of American Jews* (Glencoe: Free Press, 1956); William Shannon, *The American Irish* (London: Macmillan, 1966, rev. ed.); and Carl Wittke, *German-Americans and the World War* (Columbus: Ohio State Archaeological and Historical Society, 1936). Specific examinations of ethnic voting in the 1916 election, with which I partly disagree, are Thomas J. Kerr IV, "German-Americans and Neutrality in the 1916 Election," *Mid-America* 43 (April 1961):95–103; and William M. Leary, Jr., "Woodrow Wilson, Irish-Americans, and the Election of 1916," *Journal of American History* 56 (June 1967):57–72. A conclusion closer to my own can be found in Burton W. Folsom, "Tinkerers, Tipplers and Traitors: Ethnicity and Democratic Reform in Nebraska during the Progressive Era," *Pacific Historical Review* 50 (February 1981):52–76.

On that election, Samuel D. Lovell, *The Presidential Election of 1916* (Carbondale: Southern Illinois University Press, 1980); and Meyer Nathan's insightful "The Election of 1916 in the Middle West" (unpublished dissertation, Princeton University, 1966) both tend to support my argument on the importance of domestic reform issues. The same point in a more local context is made by Robert P. Wilkins, "Referendum on War? The General Election of 1916 in North Dakota," *North Dakota History* 36 (Fall 1969):296–336.

My study of the election of 1916 looks particularly closely at the Rocky Mountain region. Useful on contemporary politics there was Thomas C. Donnelly, ed., *Rocky Mountain Politics* (Albuquerque: University of New Mexico Press, 1940); Percy Stanley Fritz, *Colorado: The Centennial State* (New York: Prentice Hall, 1941); Wallace Turner, *The Mormon Establishment* (Boston: Houghton Mifflin, 1966); Richard Vetterli, *Mormonism, Americanism and Politics* (Salt Lake City: Ensign, 1961); Frank H. Jones and Garth H. Jones, "Utah Presidential Elections, 1896–1952," *Utah Historical Quarterly* 34 (October 1956):289–307; Kenneth W. Owens, "Politics and Structure in Western Territorial Politics," *Western Historical Quarterly* 1 (October 1970):373–92; Jan Shipps, "Utah Comes of Age Politically," *Utah Historical Quarterly* 35 (Spring 1967):97–111; Merle W. Wells, "Fred T. Dubois and the Idaho

Progressives, 1900–1914," *Idaho Yesterdays* 4 (Summer 1960):24–31; and Ralph L. McBride, "Conservatism in the Mountain West," (unpublished dissertation, Brigham Young University, 1976). Important works on the election of 1916 in California are Gladwin Hill, *Dancing Bear: An Inside Look at California Politics* (Cleveland: World Publishing, 1968); Thomas R. Clark, "The Voting Behavior of the San Francisco Working Class, 1912–1916," *California History* 66 (September 1987); and Michael Rogin, "Progressivism and the California Electorate," *Journal of American History* 55 (September 1987):297–314.

My thinking about the election of 1916, particularly in the Rockies, was somewhat shaped by critical election theories. The basic works I consulted included Walter Dean Burnham, *Critical Elections and the Mainspring of American Politics* (New York: W. W. Norton, 1966); Jerome M. Clubb, William H. Flanigan, and Nancy H. Zingale, *Partisan Realignment* (Beverly Hills: Sage, 1980); V. O. Key, Jr., "A Theory of Critical Elections," *Journal of Politics* 17 (February 1955):3–10; Allan J. Lichtman, "Critical Election Theory and the Reality of American Presidential Politics, 1916–1940," *American Historical Review* 81 (April 1976):317–51; and Gerald Pomper, "Classification of Presidential Elections," *Journal of Politics* 29 (August 1976). Basic sources used in election calculations were Paul T. David, *Party Strength in the United States* (Charlottesville: University Press of Virginia, 1972); Cortez A. M. Ewing, *Congressional Elections, 1896–1944* (Norman: University of Oklahoma Press, 1947); Kirk H. Porter and Donald Bruce Johnson, eds., *National Party Platforms 1840–1960* (Urbana: University of Illinois Press, 1961); and Edgar Eugene Robinson, *The Presidential Vote 1896–1932* (Stanford: Stanford University Press, 1934). Vital in a slightly different way is Louise Overacker, *Money in Elections* (New York: Macmillan, 1932).

Provocative secondary discussions of party power over time include Louis H. Bean, *How to Predict Elections* (New York: Alfred A. Knopf, 1948); Wilfred Binkley, *American Political Parties: Their Natural History* (New York: Alfred A. Knopf, 1943); Kevin P. Phillips, *The Emerging Republican Majority* (New York: Arlington House, 1969); James Sundquist, *Dynamics of the Party System* (Washington: Brookings Institute, 1973); Carl Degler, "American Political Parties and the Rise of the City: An Interpretation," *Journal of American History* 51 (June 1964): 41–54; and Samuel P. Hays, "The Social Analysis of American Political History," *Political Science Quarterly* 80 (September 1965):373–94.

On the political theory of progressivism, the place to begin is with the books themselves: Herbert Croly, *The Promise of American Life*, ed.

Arthur M. Schlesinger, Jr. (Cambridge: Belknap Press of Harvard University, 1965) and *Progressive Democracy* (New York: Macmillan, 1914); Walter Weyl, *The New Democracy* (New York: Macmillan, 1912); and Walter Lippmann, *A Preface to Politics* (New York: M. Kennerly, 1913) and *Drift and Mastery* (New York: M. Kennerly, 1914).

Influential modern assessments of the thought and influence of progressivism are Charles Forcey, *The Crossroads of Liberalism* (New York: Oxford University Press, 1961); Christopher Lasch, *The New Radicalism in America, 1889–1963* (New York: Alfred A. Knopf, 1965); David Noble, *The Paradox of Progressive Thought* (Minneapolis: University of Minnesota Press, 1958); and Richard Crockett, "American Liberalism and the Atlantic World, 1916–1917," *Journal of American Studies* 2 (April 1977):123–43. A more caustic contemporary view of them is found in John Chamberlain, *Farewell to Reform* (Chicago: Quadrangle Press, 1965), and a highly critical assessment of Croly's thinking in Douglas Walter Jaenicke, "Herbert Croly, Progressive Ideology, and the FTC Act," *Political Science Quarterly* 93 (Fall 1978):471–94. Ronald Steel, *Walter Lippmann and the American Century* (Boston: Atlantic Monthly Press, 1980) is a remarkable American biography.

I have argued in this book that Louis D. Brandeis offered a Democratic alternative to the thinking of Croly, Weyl, and Lippmann; and his outlook is most extensively spelled out in *Other People's Money, and How the Bankers Use It*, ed. Richard M. Abrams (New York: Harper Torchbooks, 1967). The standard biography of Brandeis is still Alpheus T. Mason, *Brandeis: A Free Man's Life* (New York: Viking, 1946), but there have been several more recent interpretive monographs, including Melvin I. Urofsky, *A Mind of One Piece: Brandeis and American Reform* (New York: Charles Scribner's Sons, 1971); and recently and impressively, Allon Gal, *Brandeis of Boston* (Cambridge: Harvard University Press, 1980). Also important is the highly critical section on Brandeis' thought in Thomas K. McCraw, *Prophets of Regulation* (Cambridge: Harvard University Press, 1984). Aging but still notable assessments of the entire period are Eric Goldman, *Rendezvous with Destiny* (New York: Alfred A. Knopf, 1952); and Richard Hofstadter, *The Age of Reform* (New York: Harper's, 1955). Progressivism era revisionism largely began with Gabriel Kolko, *Railroads and Regulation, 1877–1916* (Princeton: Princeton University Press, 1965) and *The Triumph of Conservatism* (New York, Free Press of Glencoe, 1963); James Weinstein, *The Corporate Ideal in the Liberal World* (Boston: Beacon Press, 1968); and the particularly impressive and influential work by Robert Wiebe, *Businessmen and Reform: A Study of the Progressive Movement* (Cambridge: Harvard University Press, 1962).

Finally, virtually everyone working on the period has relaxed into the consolations of Mark Sullivan, *Our Times* (New York: Charles Scribner's Sons, 1926–1933, 6 vols.).

Index